Juvenile
Delinquency
in
Perspective

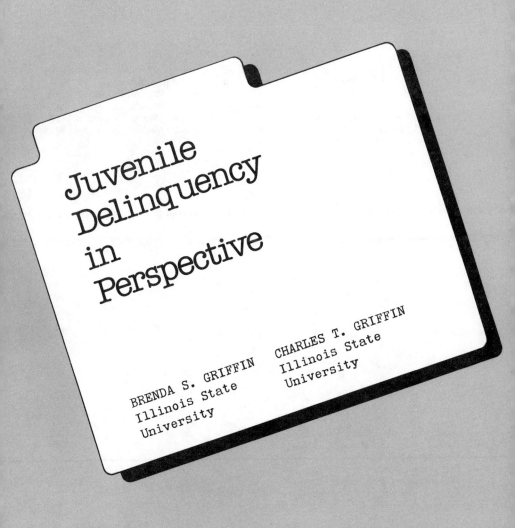

Juvenile Delinquency in Perspective

BRENDA S. GRIFFIN
Illinois State
University

CHARLES T. GRIFFIN
Illinois State
University

Harper & Row, Publishers
New York, Hagerstown, San Francisco, London

Photo Credits:
Culver, p. 7; Druskis, EPA, p. 27; Johnson, Woodfin Camp, p. 47; Anderson, Woodfin Camp, p. 79 left; Gatewood, Magnum, p. 79 right; U.S. Postal Service, p. 95; IBM, p. 121; Culver, p. 139; Borea, EPA, p. 167; Sacks, EPA, p. 185; Anderson, Woodfin Camp, p. 219; Strickler, Monkmeyer, p. 246; Bernheim, Woodfin Camp, p. 247; Stanton, Magnum, p. 275; Heron, Monkmeyer, p. 297; Berndt, Stock, Boston, p. 323; Southwick, Stock, Boston, p. 343; Michel Cosson, p. 365; Michel Cosson, p. 381; Erwitt, Magnum, p. 407.

Sponsoring Editor: Dale Tharp
Project Editor: David Nickol
Designer: Michel Craig
Production Supervisor: Stefania J. Taflinska
Photo Researcher: Myra Schachne
Compositor: Maryland Linotype Composition Co., Inc.
Printer and binder: The Maple Press Company
Art Studio: Vantage Art, Inc.

JUVENILE DELINQUENCY IN PERSPECTIVE

Library of Congress Cataloging in Publication Data

Griffin, Brenda S
  Juvenile delinquency in perspective.

  Bibliography: p.
  Includes index.
  1. Juvenile delinquency. 2. Juvenile justice,
Administration of. 3. Juvenile delinquency—Prevention.
I. Griffin, Charles T., joint author. II. Title.
HV9069.G84 364.36 77-13315
ISBN 0-06-042512-1

To our son, Michael,
and
his friends Max and Durk

CONTENTS

PREFACE

The juvenile delinquency problem involves millions of America's youth. It has been estimated that 95 percent of all our youths have engaged in juvenile delinquent behavior at one time or another. Of course, many youths are never processed through the juvenile justice system, but this does not diminish the importance or impact of the problem. Many approaches have been developed to study the delinquency problem, but it still remains a complex and difficult area.

Our approach is threefold. History, theory, and research are emphasized as essential ingredients for an adequate assessment of the delinquency problem. We develop a classification scheme for theory and critically assess current theory in the light of delinquency research. The emphasis on theory and research does not mean that institutional efforts for control, treatment, rehabilitation, and prevention are ignored. The text, however, reflects our belief that the development of an adequate theoretical base to understand juvenile delinquency is the primary goal to which professionals in the area should be devoting their efforts. A theory that is well grounded in research should be one of the most practical tools available to the practitioner.

This book is designed primarily as a text for undergraduates in sociology, but it should be a valuable tool for students in social work, criminal justice programs, corrections programs, psychology, law, and other areas where the graduate will work with children. In addition, we believe that professional groups working directly with delinquent youths will find the book useful, stimulating, and challenging. We attempted to bring together, integrate, and make available in a text some of the excellent and often specialized work that has appeared in recent years in the discipline called juvenile delinquency.

This text is designed to provide a broad picture of the field of delinquency as it has developed and as it is, and its hopes for what it can become. This has not always been an easy task. An adequate assessment of the field requires an unemotional and unsentimental critical detachment. Where children are involved, ideological commitment and sentimentality are attractive pitfalls. However, they cannot contribute to an understanding of the problem or provide a basis for the development of effective policy. We hope the book will contribute to a better understanding of the field of juvenile delinquency based on history and a critical assessment of current knowledge. If we stimulate an interest in juvenile delinquency or encourage a critical assessment of current theory or future verificational and evaluative research, we have done our work well.

Part One provides a descriptive account of the nature of juvenile delinquency. The history of the field is presented first to illustrate the separation of delinquency from criminology. Delinquency is defined, and the characteristics of delinquents are introduced. One chapter is devoted to an evaluation of the extent and nature of juvenile delinquency as seen through the official statistics of governmental agencies. Misconceptions about juvenile delinquency are discussed in relation to current knowledge. Other chapters introduce group factors in delinquency and classification schemes used in the field.

Part Two is devoted primarily to an assessment of theories of juvenile delinquency. One chapter introduces and defines the concepts of theory and causation. While we consider this chapter to be important for an evaluation of current theory, some professors may choose to omit Chapter 6. Omission of this chapter should present few problems in terms of continuity for most courses in juvenile delinquency. Early theories about child crime set the stage for discussion of more recent theoretical approaches to juvenile delinquency as they develop separately from criminology. Constitutional, psychological, and psychiatric theories are presented, but the primary emphasis is on sociological theory. An assessment of theory in the light of current thought and research is attempted in each case. Interdisciplinary and contributing factors are presented in separate chapters.

Part Three follows the juvenile from initial police contact through the juvenile court to possible placement in a correctional facility, release, and reception back into the community. The available diversionary tactics at each stage of the delinquent's career are examined. Arrest and police disposition, detention, youth services, the juvenile court, probation, and correction are some of the topics discussed. Our primary concern in each chapter is to describe the organization and present both theoretical and research factors which might allow us to assess the impact of the organization on both the youth and the society.

Part Four discusses prevention and treatment strategies and social policy issues. Theory development, verificational, and evaluative research are emphasized as high-priority areas which demand the attention of policy makers. In addition, a program of resource mobilization for community-based control, prevention, and treatment of juvenile delinquency is cited as one way to approach the problem of juvenile delinquency.

Throughout this book, we have tried to provide answers to three questions: Where have we been? Where are we now? Where are we going? We have attempted to combine a knowledge of the history of the field with current theory, research, and practice. Knowledge in each of these vital areas contributes to an assessment of developmental trends. We recognize that juvenile delinquency has been characterized by a relatively close relationship between theoretical development and changes in the social policies associated with control, prevention, and treatment. Theory and research are emphasized in this text in the belief that nothing is more practical for the practitioner than a well-grounded understanding of the phenomena. If juvenile delinquency can be better understood, the development of effective organizations for control, prevention, and treatment may become a reality.

As with all social enterprises, we have not produced this text in isolation. Howard S. Bergman, Anne Rankin Mahoney, Ronald A. Klocke, and Leonard Savitz provided helpful comments on an early draft of the manuscript. David Bordua, Stanley Grupp, and Ray Schmitt deserve special thanks for their encouragement. Stanley Grupp provided access to materials from his personal files which were unavailable to us from other sources. Bob Walsh and Bill Tolone are thanked primarily because they were able to tolerate, in good humor, two prospective authors in adjoining offices. Despite efforts to expand their research operation, we have found them to be good neighbors. Delois Green typed rough draft copy, while Pat McCarney typed the manuscript in final form. Pat McCarney was especially helpful; her attention to detail and willingness to work with us through the inevitable last-minute rush will not be soon forgotten. At this point in many texts, the author gratefully acknowledges the many contributions of his wife; as joint and equal authors, we acknowledge the aide of our "housewife." Her loyalty and devotion to duty while ignoring the clutter in our study deserves a special note of gratitude.

B. S. G.
C. T. G.

Juvenile
Delinquency
in
Perspective

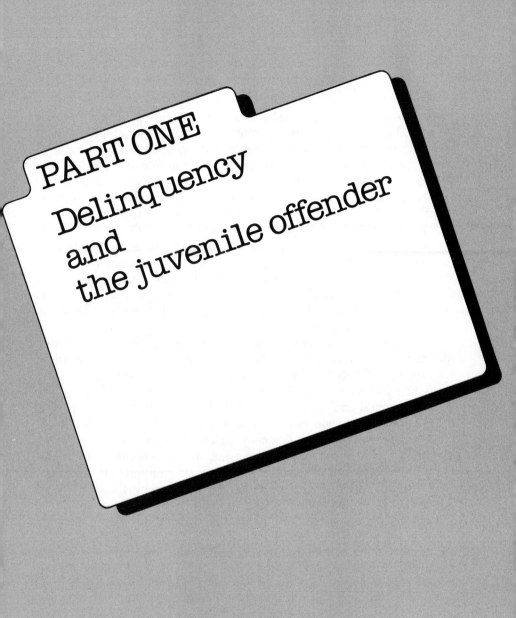

PART ONE
Delinquency and the juvenile offender

Juvenile delinquency is an elusive concept. Although it is commonly perceived as a legal term which refers to youthful violations of law, it is much more inclusive. Juvenile delinquency is used to describe a large range of commissions or omissions by both children and adults. Juvenile delinquency may be used to distinguish violations of the criminal statutes by juveniles, but it also refers to behavior that is considered inappropriate only for youths. Robbery, rape, and assault may be considered delinquent acts when committed by minors. Curfew violations, truancy, and running away are also delinquent. Juvenile delinquency may also be a result of the omissions of adults. When parents neglect the care and supervision of their children, the children may be found dependent and brought to the court and treated as delinquent youths. Definitions of juvenile delinquency are so broad that nearly all youth are subject to treatment as juvenile delinquents.

Legal statutes governing juvenile delinquency have broadened the state's control over youth. Before the twentieth century, children who violated the criminal law were brought to justice as adults. Dependency and minor misbehavior was believed to be a private matter between a child and his parents. Children whose parents were unable or unwilling to provide care and supervision were treated by private child-saving organizations. Concern for the treatment of law-violating children brought about many reforms in criminal correction institutions, but with each reform the state's authority over children was increased.

Juvenile delinquents are not merely young criminals. Part One of this text will examine the process by which a new conception of juvenile offenders arose and how this conception shapes societal reaction to misbehaving youth in modern society. Chapter 1 discusses the historical development of modern ideas regarding the proper methods for dealing with troublesome youths. The philosophy upon which modern treatment is based does not represent an abrupt change in thought about the nature of youth. Rather it can be seen that the development of the modern treatment perspective was a logical extension of earlier ideas.

Chapter 2 presents a discussion of the nature of juvenile delinquency. Various definitions of, and the criteria for, delinquent status are examined. It is clear that juvenile delinquency is not uniformly defined by various jurisdictions. A broad definition which encompasses all juvenile delinquency statutes in the United States is presented for clarification of the area. Definitions of the individual delinquent are discussed to suggest the problems encountered when studying juvenile delinquency as a social problem.

Collective delinquency is the topic of Chapter 3. A large proportion of delinquent acts are committed by groups of youths. Youths are group oriented; therefore, it is not surprising that delinquency often involves group participation. Group structure and norms are discussed to emphasize the conformist nature of many delinquent activities.

Chapter 4 uses statistics to suggest the extent of juvenile delinquency in American society. Statistical sources are discussed to indicate the problems encountered when trying to quantify juvenile delinquency. Several factors appear to obscure general knowledge about the extent of delinquency in contemporary society. Each of these is examined.

Chapter 5 deals with classification schemes used to enable the study of juvenile delinquency. In a society where a broad range of behavior is subsumed under the category juvenile delinquency and all youths are potential delinquents, there must be some technique for managing the proliferation of data on juveniles. A number of classification schemes have been proposed. Several of these are examined for their utility in describing and explaining juvenile delinquency. Although none of the schemes has been accepted as the proper one, there is little argument that a comprehensive typology is needed.

CHAPTER 1

From child crime to juvenile delinquency

The concept of juvenile delinquency is new, but the youthful behavior to which it refers is centuries old. The term was not coined to describe a new type of behavior but rather signaled important developments in the approach to treatment of juvenile offenders. The ideas and rationale behind the separation of children and adults for punishment of prohibited behavior or rehabilitation evolved over many centuries. Early codes of law provided prohibitions and prescribed punishment for child offenders, and although these early codes bear little outward resemblance to the juvenile delinquency codes of the twentieth century, some of their basic underlying principles are still being reflected in modern statutes.

It has often been remarked that historical accounts of child crime do not indicate the content or scope of modern juvenile delinquency. It is true that history may not determine what should be contained in present codes or correctional practice, but they do place the field of juvenile delinquency in perspective, indicating where the field has been, where it is, and, through examination of trends, where it is going.

EARLY CONCEPTIONS OF CHILD CRIME

Criminal codes applying specifically to children have been documented to a period as early as the twenty-second century B.C. with the Code of Hammurabi. The code regulated a wide range of activities, such as property rights, business transactions, and personal relationships. Special provisions for the protection of children were included.

For example, the receipt of certain property from a child without parental consent was a capital offense.[1] Family relationships were also regulated, and severe punishments were provided for disloyalty and rebellion. Although the code provided many items for the care, protection, and conduct of children, special provisions for children committing public offenses such as theft and assault were not specified.[2] It is not certain whether children were punished by the family or were subject to punishment under adult law.

The Mosaic Code similarly regulated family relationships, providing severe penalties, even capital punishment, for striking or cursing parents. In practice, however, it is doubtful that such severe punishment was often applied. The punishments provided for such violations were eased considerably by the provisions of the Talmud, which established procedural and substantive requirements for conviction.[3] For a first offense, both parents were required to make formal complaint, and the child was warned and flogged by a local tribunal. Subsequent offenses required the supportive statements of eyewitnesses for conviction. A systematic attempt was made in later rabbinic law to delineate youthful responsibility with a division of youths into three classifications: (1) infant (to age 6), (2) prepubescent (age 7 to puberty), and (3) adolescent (puberty to age 20). Apparently, the penalties for criminal acts increased with maturity and the assignment of responsibility.[4]

Roman Law

Roman law had a significant influence on the Anglo-American common law in fixing the responsibility of youth. As early as the fifth century B.C., the Twelve Tables specified more lenient punishments for children by virtue of their immaturity. Absolute immunity was granted, however, only to infants incapable of speech. By the sixth century A.D., under Justinian law, the terminus of infancy was recognized as age 7. Until this age, it was assumed that a child lacked understanding and therefore was incapable of committing any crime. This rule of absolute immunity became a part of the English common law and remains an important principle in a majority of Anglo-American jurisdictions.[5]

Children beyond the age of 7 were eligible for mitigated treatment until the attainment of puberty. Between infancy and puberty, responsibility was judged on the basis of (1) chronological age and physical development, (2) nature of the offense, and (3) mental capacity of the youthful offender. Conditional and limited liability, like absolute immunity of infants, became a part of the common law upon which later Anglo-American statute law was based.

The contributions of the Romans were not limited to precedents for the common law structure. It was in Rome that the first institution specifically for the treatment of wayward children was opened. The

Hospice of San Michele was established in 1704 by Pope Clement XI "for the correction and instruction of profligate youth, that they who when idle were injurious, may when taught become useful to the state."[6]

Designed along monastic lines and run by a religious order, the institution received those under age 20 convicted of criminal offenses and incorrigibles who could not be handled by parents.[7] Young offenders worked together by day in chains and under strict orders of silence in the great central hall. At night they were returned to their separate tiny cubicles for rest and meditation. Incorrigibles were at all times separated from the less corrupt criminal offenders.

The Hospice of San Michele has had important consequences for juvenile corrections in America. Its design, with group work areas and cells for rest periods, has served as a model for a large number of correctional institutions for both adults and children. Its separation of inmates into offenders and incorrigibles was a precursor of modern systems which distinguish between offenders and children in need of parental supervision. The fact that the institution is still standing and being used as a detention center only adds to its importance.[8]

English Common Law

Fragmentary evidence suggests that very early English law was based on group responsibility. The laws of King Ine (688–725) provided punishment for commission or knowledge of commission of theft: "If any one steal, so that his wife and his children know it not, let him pay LX shillings as 'wite' [punishment]. But if he steal with the knowledge of all his household, let them all go into slavery."[9] Under the laws of King Aethelstan (924–939) capital punishment requirements for youthful offenders was eased: "No younger person should be slain than XV years, except he should make resistance or flee, and would not surrender himself. . . . And the king has also ordained, that no one should be slain for less property than XII penceworth, unless he will flee or defend himself."[10]

After the Norman Conquest, children under 7 remained criminally liable, but pardons were granted as a matter of course upon conviction. Pardons and judgments were dispensed with in 1456, but a trial and finding of guilt were required before dismissal was possible for lack of discretion. Sometime before the seventeenth century, however, dismissals were permitted on proof of infancy (below age 7) without trial or verdict.[11]

CONDITIONAL RESPONSIBILITY

Recognizing the need for conditional or qualified immunity for youth beyond infancy, some early judges often provided lighter sentences for children. However, they were not always in agreement about who might be eligible for lenient treatment. Decisions were made for each individual case on the basis of (1) maturity, (2) severity of punishment for the offense, (3) understanding of the difference between right and wrong, and (4) evidence of criminal intent. Although there was concern about standardizing the upper limit for conditional responsibility by chronological age, such a plan was not feasible until the appearance of parish registration of baptism during the reign of Henry VIII (1509–1547).[12]

Adoption of the Roman rules in the seventeenth century led to a variety of interpretations regarding the upper age limit, but by 1800 the upper age limit for conditional immunity was generally considered to be 14. Blackstone summarized the law on the responsibility of youth in these words:

> Under seven years of age indeed an infant cannot be guilty of a felony; for then a felonious discretion is almost an impossibility in nature; but at eight years old he may be guilty of a felony. Also, under fourteen, though an infant be prima facie adjudged doli incapax, yet it appears to the court and jury that he was doli capax and could discern between good and evil, he may be convicted and suffer death. . . . But, in all such cases, the evidence of that malice which is to supply age ought to be strong and clear beyond all doubt and contradiction.[13]

Proof of malice and understanding of the offense became an important element in the conviction of youthful offenders. Both common law and practice assumed that children were guilty and that the jury's responsibility in such cases was limited to a determination of whether a child understood his offense.[14] Children infrequently suffered capital or corporal punishment under this system, however. The evidence suggests that the severity of the law was mitigated by refusal to prosecute or reduction of charges.[15] Children brought to trial were sometimes acquitted for "lack of knowledge" by juries reluctant to impose severe penalties on children. Even those children sentenced to death were, for the most part, not executed but were granted king's pardon or commutation.[16] Transportation to Australia or south Wales was substituted for the death penalty in some cases.

SEPARATE FACILITIES

Along with the tendency toward less severe penalties for child offenders was a growing interest in separating children from adult offenders. As early as 1552, the citizens of London petitioned the king for a place to house the poor and teach children industrious habits. Scattered individual efforts to reform potential delinquents were in evidence, but the first organized attempt in this direction was initiated by the Philanthropic Society of London in 1788.[17] Although the project began with a single child, by its second year it assumed an organized form based on an agricultural family system. It distributed the children into families of 12 in each cottage with resident house parents. A general superintendent coordinated and supervised the activities of each house. In 1806 the society was incorporated by Parliament, and the institution reorganized. The apparent success of private institutions for young criminals so impressed a parliamentary committee in 1835 that it recommended making reformatories an integral part of the prison system in England. As a result of the committee's report, a government reformatory was established on the Isle of Wight in 1838.[18]

THE AMERICAN EXPERIENCE

During the early years of English settlement in the American wilderness, the colonists developed a "rude, untechnical popular law"[19] suitable to conditions in the New World. As conditions improved and the study of law became more practicable, the settlements gradually came to adopt the English common law. When conditions merited it, however, the settlers ignored or modified portions of the common law. In broad principles, nevertheless, the laws in colonial America, with an emphasis on corporal and capital punishment, paralleled those of the rest of the Western world.

Child Crime in the Colonies

Children in colonial America were subject to the common law and the laws of God. The statutes were not uniform from colony to colony, but they generally called for the religious and vocational training of children to assure that they knew enough to support themselves honestly and not become public charges. In the early years only the Puritans provided specific public punishments for children accused of infractions.[20] Disobedience and other misdemeanors resulted in corporal punishment such as whipping. Theft by children resulted in the assessment of triple damages (or fines) against their parents or whipping. Capital punishment was, for the most part, reserved for individuals above age 16. Children were also, like adults, subject to imprisonment at hard labor in the house of correction.[21] Mindful of adult influence on children, the General Court (Massachusetts) in 1672 added a law making it an offense to lure children away from work or studies. This was probably the first law ever against contributing to the delinquency of a minor. While the Puritans did not specifically define juvenile delinquency, their records indicate that they did have a relatively coherent set of ideas regarding youthful misconduct.

The first laws of colonial New York and Pennsylvania, the Duke's Laws, also stressed the need for vocational training for children but contained no statutes prescribing punishment for children who disobeyed the law. The Quakers did not disregard the misconduct of children. On the contrary, their public meetings often dealt with minor offenses of youth. The family also provided suitable punishment for wayward children. The misbehavior of children was not a matter of law but rather a family or a community affair.

Colonial Virginia provided few laws and restrictions on the behavior of children. The first code in Virginia, the Articles, Lawes and Orders, Divine, Politique, and Martiall of 1610, did not even mention children. When the settlers felt the population dangerously low, the Virginia Company made arrangements with the Common Council of London to have 100 vagrant youth from the streets of London sent to Virginia in 1618. After the arrival of these children, the General Assembly met to replace the articles with a code closer to the common law. Early statutes provided for the religious instruction of children (1636) and advocated apprenticeship and training of youth (1646) but did not contain specific provisions for the treatment of youthful offenders.

Although the criminal codes made little mention of children in colonial times, special consideration for misbehaving youth was being developed in the application of contract law. During the settlement period, children were frequently bound out or apprenticed to individuals who could teach them a trade. The apprenticeship agreement, or contract, between an apprentice and his master typically required the apprentice to obey his master and protect his property and set forth restrictions on the apprentice's behavior. Young males were frequently offered apprenticeships but females were generally indentured servants. On occasion, the masters asked the courts to discipline children who violated their contracts. The courts meted out punishment on the merits of the individual case. Certainly the colonists recognized the special status of children in requiring religious and vocational training and had some experience with juvenile offenders through the courts. But juvenile delinquency was yet to be defined, and specialized treatment and reform of the juvenile offender was not yet entertained in early America.[22]

Penal Reform

The penal system in colonial America closely paralleled that of the rest of the Western world. Although the criminal code was somewhat milder in America than in England, the primary emphasis was on capital and corporal punishment. The influence of European ideas on crime and punishment was felt in America. During the eighteenth century, a new direction in attitudes on justice was initiated through the writings of scholars.

THE RATIONAL APPROACH

Voltaire, Montesquieu, and Beccaria advocated the reform of criminal law along rational lines. Voltaire pointed out the abuses of law; Montesquieu argued that punishments were too harsh to fit the crime; and Beccaria suggested a direction for reform.[23] The philosophy that the severity of punishment would deter crime had provided the basis for the strict criminal codes of the period. Beccaria argued for a more rational approach to the relationship between crime and punishment. In his essay *On Crime and Punishments*, he asserted that punishment should be no more severe than required to deter the would-be criminal. Beccaria stressed the importance of clear, unambiguous laws and certain, immediate punishment in proportion to the crime committed, as determined by the laws.[24] Although Beccaria's essay did not result in immediate reform, when supported by an exposé of English prisons by John Howard, sheriff of Bedford, it did have a profound influence on reformers later in the century.

In America the writings of Howard, Beccaria, Montesquieu, and Bentham influenced a number of Quakers in Pennsylvania. A small group of interested and influential Philadelphians founded the Philadelphia Society for Assisting Distressed Prisoners in 1776. Undeterred by the organization's collapse during British occupation, the reformers founded the Philadelphia Society for Alleviating the Miseries of Public Prisoners in 1787 to establish a penal system for the reform of criminals. The society worked for and achieved reform of the criminal code. New provisions required imprisonment for most criminal offenses.

The Philadelphia reformers also sought to establish a penitentiary system based on the cellular confinement plan in which prisoners would be classified by age, sex, and nature of offense.

A movement along similar lines but based on a modified group confinement plan—solitary confinement by night, congregate work by day—was taking place in Auburn, New York, at the same time. Thus, by the 1830s there were two rival penal systems in the United States— the Pennsylvania system and the Auburn system. Neither fulfilled its founder's expectations. The penitentiaries did not prevent crime or reform criminals. The reformers shifted their emphasis from reform of hardened criminals to prevention of crime by reformation of youthful offenders.

THE HOUSES OF REFUGE

By the early nineteenth century, intellectuals in New York City began to realize that American cities were coming to have the same kinds of problems that plagued the cities of the Old World. Crime and poverty were increasingly evident. The problem of wayward and criminal children captured the attention of Edward Livingston, the mayor of New York City, who attempted to found a society to help young ex-convicts in 1803. His project was dropped for lack of interest. Even when the Common Council of New York City designated the Almshouse as "an asylum for lost children" in 1809, the conditions experienced by vagrants and youthful criminals were unchanged.

A number of respected citizens and groups in New York and abroad continued to call for reform in the treatment of juveniles, and advice and information was freely exchanged.[25] Informal gatherings set the stage for a formal organization to deal with the problems of the lower classes in New York City. In December 1817 the Society for the Prevention of Pauperism was formed. A committee was appointed to draw up a constitution, study the causes of pauperism, and suggest remedies. The committee report listed "juvenile delinquency" as one of the major causes of pauperism and recommended that children be confined in buildings separate from prisons for adult criminals. This 1818 report probably contained the first public reference to the term *juvenile delinquency.*

By 1823, the various efforts to establish a separate institution for wayward children and juvenile delinquents had coalesced into a movement. A public meeting was called by the Society for the Prevention of Pauperism to discuss the problem of juvenile delinquency. The society's report, supported by evidence from the district attorney and the keeper of the Bridewell jail, recommended that a house of refuge for boys involved in petty crimes or vagrancy, and a separate department for girls, be established. The U.S. Arsenal, publicly owned and standing unused, was selected as an appropriate site. The society began to solicit state financial aid. New York chartered the House of Refuge in 1824, placing it under state supervision, but public funds were not secured for its operation until 1829. The New York House of Refuge began operations under its charter in 1825 with funds provided by the Society for the Prevention of Pauperism. The charter defined juvenile delinquents as those youths convicted of criminal offenses or found in vagrancy. Children were confined for the period of their minority or until they were judged reformed by refuge managers. The managers, influenced by fashionable theories of child development, believed that the child's behavior would change through vigilant instruction. Misbehaving children should be punished, and the public had the responsibility where natural parents or guardians refused to do so.[26]

Parents were not explicitly bound by law to relinquish their child to the House of Refuge. Parents occasionally volunteered to place the child in the institution, but more often they saw commitment as interference in family matters. Confronted by such opposition, refuge officials undertook a program to strengthen the institution's authority. The authority of the refuge managers to retain children was finally established in a Pennsylvania court decision. The *Ex Parte Crouse* decision (1838) defined the state's right to intervene in behalf of children's interests as *parens patriae*.

Classification The House of Refuge classified entering children on the basis of their "moral conduct" into four categories: (1) best behaved and most orderly, not using indecent language and not quarrelsome; (2) next best, but not free from all vices; (3) more immoral in conduct; and (4) vicious, bad, and wicked.[27] Each Sunday the children were reclassified. Punishment for unacceptable behavior varied from reclassification and loss of privileges to whipping.

Daily Routine The labor of children in the House of Refuge was frequently contracted out or the children were apprenticed or indentured. The managers of the House of Refuge sometimes entered into contracts with local businessmen to provide the children's labor for a fee. Usually this amounted to a set price per piece of finished work. This type of labor was welcomed by the staff; it kept idle, mischievous hands at work and out of trouble. Less frequently children were released to the care of responsible individuals in the community. Indentures were arranged to provide children training in practical occupations. In return for training, the child was required to work a specified period of time after the end of the training period. The evidence suggests that a number of children laboring under indenture were exploited, but a complaint about responsibilities or treatment could result in return to the institution.

A typical day in the House of Refuge began at sunrise with a highly disciplined and regimented routine. The inmates were given 15 minutes to dress and straighten their cells, after which the children washed and assembled for inspection. Morning prayers and a 1½-hour school session preceded breakfast. A work session filled the rest of the morning until the noon meal. The afternoon work session lasted until 5:00 and the evening meal. Another 1½-hour school session and evening prayers preceded a return to the cells and the rule of silence.[28]

Although managers of the New York House of Refuge claimed great success, the system was not without problems. Some critics disapproved of harsh disciplinary treatment and health hazards. Escapes were frequent, and the average period of confinement was lengthy. The fact that the magazine of the old arsenal still contained gun powder worried others. Security was tightened and sanitary conditions improved when a new building was erected using inmate labor in 1826.[29] The institution for the most part enjoyed considerable acclaim, and similar institutions were soon founded for juveniles in Boston and Philadelphia. By 1860 there were 20 such institutions for juvenile delinquents in the United States. Although the statutes establishing these institutions did not change the fundamental principles or application of the common law, they did recognize the need for differential treatment for children. Their role in providing a definition of juvenile delinquency and establishing the state's parental responsibility over children was considerable.

CHILD-SAVING SOCIETIES

Several organizations disagreed with the house-of-refuge and reform-school concept. Philanthropists in the child-saving movement believed that the family, not the institution, was the best reform school.[30] Representative of this movement was the Children's Aid Society, based in New York. Headed by Charles Loring Brace, the society sought to "save the homeless, vagrant and semi-criminal children of the city by drawing them into places of instruction and shelter, and then by transferring them to carefully-selected homes in the rural districts."[31] To this end the society established several institutions; most notable were (1) day industrial and night schools, (2) lodging houses, and (3) placing out.

The day industrial and night schools was the initial project of the Children's Aid Society. The organization at first tried to concentrate its energy on some of the worst "fever nests" of the city by offering workshops for boys, where they could earn money and learn a trade. The workshops failed because they could not compete with established factories.[32] Industrial schools were introduced in 1853 for children too poor or ragged to attend public schools or forced to work on the street to earn a living. The schools provided a meal, shoes, or clothing, where indicated, and vocational training.[33] Although the schools claimed a degree of success, they fell short of the organization's expectations.

The society recognized that many homeless children were capable of earning a living by selling newspapers, boot blacking, or other honest trades. For these children, the greatest need was a place to stay at night. Cheap but clean and wholesome surroundings could be found at any of the Children's Aid Society's lodging houses (several houses were provided throughout the city). Any boy who had no home or parents was permitted to enter. No lodging houses were established for girls. A small fee was charged to promote industriousness, and a bank was established to encourage thrift. Residents were required to abstain from vice and embrace cleanliness. Night school and placing-out services were available to those who requested them.

Of all the services offered by the Children's Aid Society, placing out was considered the most important. Fresh air, sunshine, hard work, and family atmosphere were believed to be the key ingredients for building upright citizens. By placing vagrant children in rural homes in the West, they would be saved from the vice inherent among the poor in the city. Homeless and neglected children, boys and girls, were recruited by district visitors who went from house to house to ascertain living conditions for the society. When a sufficient number were obtained and screened, a special agent accompanied the children on the trip west by railroad. In various towns along the way, children were given to families as the agents saw fit. No apprenticeship or binding-out agreement was involved, so the child and his new family were free to end their relationship if it was not satisfactory.[34] By 1884 the Children's Aid Society had placed out over 60,000 vagrant children and youthful petty offenders.[35]

The society's placing-out system enjoyed considerable public support. However, critics representing asylum interests and states hit with an influx of placed children complained loudly. As a result of the growing controversy, Michigan passed the first law regulating interstate placement of children in 1887.[36] With the passage of similar laws in other western states and the closing of the frontier, placing out was greatly diminished by 1900.

Self-government Experiments   A somewhat different child-saving response involved juvenile self-government experiments. Probably the most prominent among these projects was the George Junior Republic for boys, founded by William R. George. As a supporter of the Fresh Air movement, George offered poor urban children a two-week summer camp stay in a rural setting. After a few years of experience with the camp, he came to believe that the arrangement conditioned the children to a life of dependency instead of promoting growth. George began to require that everything be paid for by camp labor and established self-government, retaining only veto power for himself, to promote self-reliance. The youths established their own legislature and judiciary, passed laws, and provided trial and punishment for violators. The experiment met with such success that the George Junior Republic was incorporated in 1895 and opened year-round to both dependent and delinquent youths.[37]

Although this was not the first attempt at self-government for dependent and delinquent youths,[38] the George Junior Republic experiment was instrumental in promoting change in existing juvenile institutions. The adoption of self-government as a method for reform spread into existing juvenile institutions, and this promising innovation was viewed as an important device for mitigating the harsh treatment prevalent in juvenile institutions. In many instances, however, reform school self-government degenerated into another tool of administrative control.

Reform and Training Schools.   The reform schools evolved from earlier, privately financed experiments with the houses of refuge. Strictly speaking, houses of refuge were privately managed municipal institutions located in, and used to shelter delinquency-prone youths of, a particular city. Reform schools, on the other hand, were state-supported institutions that received delinquent youth from all over the state.[39] Like the houses of refuge, reform and training schools aimed at delinquency prevention by identifying delinquency-prone and mis-behaving children and redirecting their behavior through discipline, vocational training, and stress on the values of hard work.

The first reform school was established in Massachusetts in 1847. The reformers promoting the institution envisioned the limitation of its use to very young minor offenders. However, enabling legislation set the upper age limit at 16. A program of reform was developed to handle the most hardened juvenile offenders. By the 1850s, these insti-tutions had earned a reputation for strict, and even harsh, discipline. As a result, only the hardened cases were sent there. As the juvenile institutions became more and more like miniature prisons, relying heavily on the contract system for financial support, they increasingly came under attack. Reformers proposed several alternatives to the existing system; among these were the cottage plan for reform schools, industrial training, reformatories for older juveniles and young adults, and more extensive use of probation.

Philanthropists of the child-saving movement and penal reform leaders examined the ever-growing rates of youthful misconduct and concluded that existing institutions were ineffective. Some of the critics were convinced that more stringent measures were needed to instill self-discipline in the hardened young offender. Others were quick to point out the need for a more wholesome environment in which to promote the child's self-development. The controversy between the supporters of correctional institutions and the child-saving reformers appeared irreconcilable.

Glowing reports of success in European facilities, however, brought hope for a compromise.

Continental Models   Two institutions in Europe were gaining ac-claim for their approaches and success in treating wayward boys. Rauhe Haus, in Germany, provided an informal family atmosphere for its charges. The children were separated into residential units, each con-taining 12 boys. Each of the "families" was under the supervision of a staff member. The program of each unit combined agricultural labor with religious training and formal instruction.[40]

The facility at Mettray, in France, combined the most promising features of Rauhe Haus and the houses of refuge. Family units were larger; each unit numbered 40 inmates. Both institutions, however, stressed the importance of farm labor and fresh air.

The Cottage Plan in the United States The success of juvenile institutions established on the "family" plan in Europe reaffirmed the child savers' conviction that the family, not the institution, was the best reform school. Based on the experiment at Mettray, the cottage plan provided an acceptable compromise between family and institution for the reformation of youth. First introduced in the United States at the Massachusetts State Reform School for Girls at Lancaster in 1855 and the Ohio State Reform Farm in 1857, the cottage plan divided children into groups of 40 or fewer.[41] Each "family," or cottage, had its own house and an autonomous schedule. The ideal cottage plan encouraged individuality and responsibility by allowing each family member to participate in family management. Each house was managed by a set of surrogate parents who answered only to the central head of the total institution.

Where possible, the schools were placed in a rural setting to provide farm training for inmates. Besides the fresh air and sunshine such a setting provided, other benefits were evident. With the children producing their own food and many other essentials, the cost to the state was kept at a minimum. Furthermore, the trend away from the contract system effectively skirted criticism directed at the more traditional institutions.

Industrial Schools The popularity of scientific ideas regarding juvenile delinquency which were in vogue in the 1880s was evidenced by the increased scope, precision, and systematization of inmate records and other innovations introduced by this time. However, the continued use of the contract system remained under heavy attack. Opponents of the system charged that it encouraged retention of boys, valuable to contractors, who were entitled to early release. Public attention to the problems of the contract system resulted in its decline, and reform school officials sought new ways to occupy the time of inmates. Resources were not always available to abandon the large congregate institutions and build new facilities based on the cottage plan. Furthermore, as some critics pointed out, the agricultural program offered in the cottage schools did not prepare students for a successful return to their urban environment. An acceptable alternative was secured in 1885 when New York State approved the establishment of an industrial training program at the Western House of Refuge. The new industrial programs required expensive machinery and skilled supervisory workers, and as a result the number of reform schools on the less expensive agricultural cottage plan increased.[42]

The industrial schools can be considered to have been somewhat successful, since reform schools began to call themselves industrial schools and, when that name became suspect, training schools. These institutions nevertheless remained under criticism for their harsh custodial treatment of children. As a result, the private child-saving organizations assumed greater responsibility for delinquency-prone youths. Placing the children in the hands of private organizations did not solve the problems of wayward youths for long. Rivalries between religious and philanthropic groups running the institutions soon required state intervention.

Development of the Juvenile Court

In the late nineteenth century, the increasingly violent and exploitative nature of reform schools were once again under attack. Several legal decisions questioned the state's right to interfere in family matters.[43] Although philanthropic groups in the East had earlier led the battle to reform delinquents without incarceration, it was Illinois that was to formally designate the first juvenile court.

JUVENILE CORRECTIONS IN CHICAGO

During the final decade of the nineteenth century, a vacuum of state care for delinquent and dependent children had developed in Illinois. Although Chicago had established a progressive municipal reform school before the Civil War, the old prison-type structure was destroyed by fire in 1856. The structure that replaced this institution was run on the confidential system. Lockups were eliminated, and inmates were given institutional positions and granted weekend passes. By 1862 preadmission screening by the reform school commissioner was authorized, and first-time offenders were frequently released.[44]

The combined effect of the *O'Connell* decision (1870) and the great Chicago fire, however, were soon to signal the collapse of the juvenile system (1871). The *O'Connell* court case restricted the state's authority over children. No longer could children be sentenced to the reform school for nonstatutory and minor offenses. Offenders between ages 10 and 16 were to be treated as adults. If sent to the juvenile reform school, the offender was to receive a determinant sentence.[45] The decision effectively stripped the institution of its special programs for delinquency-prone children. When the building was destroyed in the great Chicago fire only a year later, there was little inclination to rebuild.

In the absence of state reform schools Illinois authorized the establishment of private industrial schools (1879), but like the earlier Chicago Reform School, their legality soon came under question. By 1893 the jails contained hundreds of children, and the Chicago Board of Education was given the responsibility for supervising youths under 17 in the city prison. Under the supervision of the Board of Education, the John Worthy manual training school and separate juvenile dormitories were provided within the city prison by 1897.[46] Accommodations for children within the institutions were so deteriorated that the police often simply released petty offenders. Serious cases were referred to the Cook County grand jury for indictment, but only about a quarter of the cases were brought to trial. Even where trial and sentence were secured, "pardon" could be easily obtained.[47] The system was a failure. Child crime was on the increase in Chicago.

The absence of proper juvenile facilities coupled with the publication of scandals involving police treatment of children resulted in indignant outrage among child-saving groups in Chicago. At the annual meeting of the Illinois Conference of Charities (1898) a coordinated plan of action for the development of a separate children's court was implemented.[48] As a result of vigorous lobbying on the part of the Chicago Bar Association, the Chicago Women's Club, and child-saving groups, the Illinois legislature unanimously passed "an act to regulate the treatment and control of dependent, neglected and delinquent children" on the final day of the 1899 session. More generally known as the Juvenile Court Act, this legislation was hailed as a significant advance in the treatment of children.

THE JUVENILE COURT ACT

The Juvenile Court Act of 1899 was an attempt to fill the vacuum in child welfare legislation in Illinois.[49] As such it had more far-reaching goals than the mere establishment of a separate jurisdiction for juvenile cases. The act contained three related sections which defined delinquents, established procedure, and regulated institutions for juveniles within the state. Although few of its provisions were untried in one jurisdiction or another, the law was innovative as the first comprehensive system for the protection of delinquent and dependent children.

A Definition of Delinquency   The first section of the act contained a brief legal description of juvenile delinquency. A delinquent child was identified as any child under the age of 16 who violates a state law or any village or city ordinance. Also covered under the law were neglected and dependent children. A separate juvenile court with a separate docket and record and a specially assigned judge provided by the statute would have original jurisdiction over these children, and special noncriminal procedures were to be used in dealing with them.

Court Procedure   Under the act, children were brought to court through petitions brought by "reputable" persons who had knowledge of a neglected, dependent, or delinquent child. Instead of the usual arrest and arraignment used in criminal cases, the court would issue a summons for appearance. Cases coming before the court were to be heard in a special separate courtroom under a summary (informal) proceeding and by a jury of six if requested.

Disposition alternatives defined by the law provided the court broad powers to deal with both delinquent and dependent children. The law was clear regarding the separation of juvenile from adult

---

TABLE 1.1 CALENDAR OF REFORM IN JUVENILE JUSTICE

First institution for the treatment of juvenile offenders, Hospice
   of San Michele   1704
Juvenile delinquency defined   1818
First house of refuge in United States   1825
State reform and industrial schools   1847
First official use of probation (Massachusetts)   1869
Agent of Board of Charity to investigate cases and attend hearings   1869
First use of separate trials for juveniles (Massachusetts)   1870
Separate dockets and records (Massachusetts)   1877
First probation system applicable to juveniles   1880
Segregation of children under 16 awaiting trial (Rhode Island)   1898
First Juvenile Court Act (Illinois)   1899
Children's Bureau established   1912

---

offenders. In all cases, children were to be separated from adults when both were confined in the same institution, and placement of children under 12 in jails or police stations was prohibited. The act provided for the appointment of probation officers as regular court personnel to investigate cases, provide background information for judicial disposition, and supervise adjudicated youths in the community.[50] Thus probation became a realistic alternative to incarceration.

Regulatory Functions   The act also regulated the use of private institutions and child-placing agencies operating in Illinois. Institutions were placed under the supervision of the Illinois Board of State Commissioners of Public Charities, and judges of courts having jurisdiction over children were prohibited from sending them to uncertified institutions. Child-placing agencies were required to provide guarantees; prohibited from placing children who were diseased, feeble-minded, or of poor character; and required to accept the return of children who became public charges. Families accepting children from noncomplying placement agencies were to be fined.

SIGNIFICANCE OF THE FIRST JUVENILE COURT ACT

The procedural and regulatory provisions of the Juvenile Court Act were not revolutionary. Table 1.1 provides a calendar of some of the major events that led to the juvenile court philosophy. Michigan passed the first law regulating interstate placement of children in 1887.[51] The differential treatment, of juveniles in the criminal justice system had long been a target of reformers. The separation of juveniles from adult offenders was provided as early as 1825 in New York City with the House of Refuge and later with state reform and industrial schools in Massachusetts in 1847. The use of a specially appointed official to hear minor charges against children between ages 6 and 17 was instituted in Chicago in 1861; then came alternative dispositions for juveniles, including probation (Massachusetts, 1870), placement in foster homes, and institutionalization. Separate trials for juveniles were provided in Massachusetts (1870) with separate dockets and records (1877). Rhode Island instituted the segregation of children under 16 awaiting trial in 1898.[52]

The Juvenile Court Act was a comprehensive child welfare law that incorporated earlier significant reforms in the treatment of children. The Illinois law, however, went beyond these reforms and created a new institution, the juvenile court, which extended the flexible rules and procedures of equity jurisdiction to delinquent children.

The juvenile court concept embodied in the Illinois Juvenile Court Act of 1899 spread across the country with unusual speed. Within 12 years, 22 states had adopted juvenile court measures. By 1925, there was provision for juvenile courts in all but two states,[53] and even these states fell in line by 1945. Juvenile court statutes were already in effect in Alaska and Hawaii on their entry into the Union. With the adoption of the various juvenile court statutes, the modern conception of juvenile delinquency was firmly established in American society. Juvenile offenders were no longer perceived as miniature criminals. They were now viewed as a distinctly different type of offender with special problems deserving differential treatment and understanding.

THE EVOLUTION OF CHILD CRIME IN PERSPECTIVE

There has long been a concern with the problem of youthful misbehavior. Early criminal codes stressed the dependent nature of children to their parents and demanded strict obedience. Although the special circumstance of child crime was not formally recognized in early law, there are indications that juveniles were often dealt with more leniently than their adult counterparts. Children were allowed even greater understanding and consideration once the concept of responsibility was incorporated into the law.

Juvenile delinquency was recognized as a distinctly different phenomenon and a target for special concern in the application of English common law. However, it was only after the beginnings of reform in the adult correctional system that significant advances were made. The child-saving movement culminated in the United States with the establishment of the juvenile court. The new court system provided by the statutes established a pattern of handling and treatment that began to take into account the special problems of troublesome and neglected youths. No longer were these youths defined as child criminals. Instead they were given attention as a special type of individual needing understanding and protection.

NOTES

[1] Frederick J. Ludwig, *Youth and the Law: Handbook on Laws Affecting Youth* (Mineola, N.Y.: Foundation Press, 1955), p. 12.

[2] Ruth Shonle Cavan, *Juvenile Delinquency* (Philadelphia: Lippincott, 1962), p. 4.

22 FROM CHILD CRIME TO JUVENILE DELINQUENCY

[3] Ludwig, *op. cit.*, pp. 12–13.

[4] *Ibid.*

[5] *Ibid.*, pp. 14–15.

[6] Cited in Cavan, *op. cit.*, p. 5.

[7] Harry Elmer Barnes and Negley K. Teeters, *New Horizons in Criminology*, 3d ed. (Englewood Cliffs, N.J.: Prentice-Hall, 1959), pp. 333–334.

[8] *Ibid.*, p. 334.

[9] Wiley B. Sanders, *Juvenile Offenders for a Thousand Years* (Chapel Hill: University of North Carolina Press, 1970), p. 3.

[10] *Ibid.*

[11] Ludwig, *op. cit.*, p. 16.

[12] Before this time, no official records were available to determine the exact age of a youth. Without documentation, verification of the child's eligibility for leniency rested on a cursory examination of his or her physical development.

[13] William Blackstone, *Commentaries on the Laws of England*, vol. 4 (Oxford: Clarendon Press, 1776), p. 23.

[14] Robert M. Mennell, "Origins of the Juvenile Court: Changing Perspectives on the Legal Rights of Juvenile Delinquents," *Crime and Delinquency* 18 (January 1972): 70.

[15] Anthony M. Platt, *The Child Savers: The Invention of Delinquency* (Chicago: University of Chicago Press, 1969, p. 186.

[16] Sanders, *op. cit.*, pp. 144–145.

[17] E. C. Wines, *The State of Prisons and Child-saving Institutions in the Civilized World* (Montclair, N.J.: Patterson Smith, 1968), pp. 75–76.

[18] *Ibid.*

[19] Paul Samuel Reinich, *English Common Law in the Early American Colonies*, University of Wisconsin *Bulletin*, no. 31 (Madison, 1899).

[20] Joseph M. Hawes, *Children in Urban Society: Juvenile Delinquency in Nineteenth Century America* (New York: Oxford University Press, 1971), p. 12.

[21] Sanders, *op. cit.*, p. 20.

[22] *Hawes, op. cit.*, p. 20.

[23] Marcello Maestro, *Voltaire and Beccaria as Reformers of Criminal Law* (New York: Columbia University Press, 1942), p. 50.

[24] Cesare Beccaria, *An Essay on Crimes and Punishment* (Philadelphia: Philip H. Nicklin, 1819).

[25] Robert S. Pickett, *House of Refuge: Origins of Juvenile Reform in New York State* (Syracuse, N.Y.: Syracuse University Press, 1969), p. 31.

[26] Hawes, *op. cit.*, pp. 46–47.

[27] *Ibid.*, p. 48.

[28] *Ibid.*, p. 49.

[29] *Ibid.*, pp. 43–44.

[30] Robert M. Mennel, *Thorns and Thistles: Juvenile Delinquents in the United States, 1825–1940* (Hanover, N.H.: University Press of New England, 1973), p. 13.

[31] Wines, *op. cit.*, p. 127.

[32] Hawes, *op. cit.*, p. 94.

[33] Wines, *op. cit.*, p. 129.

[34] Mennel, *op. cit.*, p. 35.

[35] Hawes, *op. cit.*, p. 102.

[36] *Ibid.*, p. 107.

[37] Mennel, *op. cit.*, pp. 116–120.

[38] Wells and Curtis had initiated such an experiment in the early days of the Boston House of Reformation and the New York House of Refuge.

[39] Hawes, *op. cit.*, p. 86.

[40] *Ibid.*, p. 79.

[41] Mennel, *op. cit.*, p. 52.

[42] *Ibid.*, pp. 104–109.

[43] *The People* v. *Turner*, 55 Illinois 280 (1870); *State* v. *Ray*, 63 New Hampshire 405 (1886); *Ex Parte Bicknell*, 51 Pacific Reporter 692 (California, 1897).

[44] Mennel, *op. cit.*, p. 127.

[45] Platt, *op. cit.*, p. 104.

[46] *Ibid.*, p. 127.

[47] Hawes, *op. cit.*, p. 162.

[48] The Chicago Women's Club had been concerned with the creation of a juvenile court as early as 1891 and convinced Judge Richard Tuthill to hold separate court for children on Saturday mornings.

[49] The act establishing the juvenile court in Chicago is found in the Illinois Session Laws of 1899, pp. 132–137; it can also be found in Grace Abbott, *The Child and the State* (Chicago: University of Chicago Press, 1938).

[50] J. Lawrence Schultz, "Cycle of Juvenile Court History," *Crime and Delinquency* 19 (October 1973): 458.

[51] Hawes, *op. cit.*, p. 107.

[52] President's Commission on Law Enforcement and Administration of Justice, *Task Force Report: Juvenile Delinquency and Youth Crime* (Washington, D.C.: Government Printing Office, 1967), p. 3.

[53] *Ibid.*

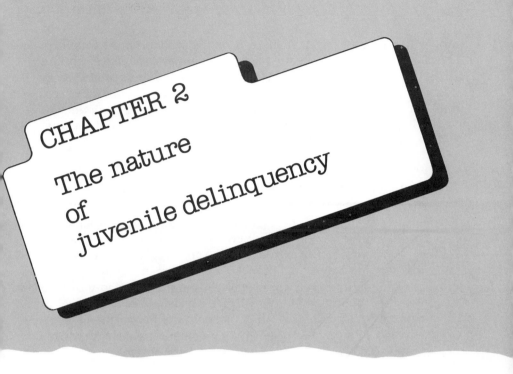

CHAPTER 2
The nature of juvenile delinquency

Reports in the mass media have led the general public to believe that juvenile delinquency is an urgent social problem of such proportions that it is unprecedented in history. Authorities point out the evidence to support this claim. Current statistics reveal that approximately one in every nine youths will be referred to juvenile court in connection with a delinquent act before his or her eighteenth birthday.[1] Moreover, self-report studies suggest that as many as 90 to 95 percent of all juveniles have committed at least one act for which they could have been brought before the juvenile court.[2] In reviewing the prevalence of crime and delinquency in American society, some social commentators suggest that the decline and decay of the society is at hand.

The crisis of juvenile misbehavior is not unique to modern American society. Nearly every generation has been concerned with the "unprecedented" proportions of the problem of youthful misconduct. An Egyptian priest 6000 years ago wrote: "Our earth is degenerate in these latter days. There are signs that the world is coming to an end because children no longer obey their parents."[3] Writing some 3600 years later, Socrates lamented over children who have "bad manners" and "contempt for authority" and who show "disrespect for elders."[4] In more recent times, an English report of 1818 stated, "Juvenile delinquency has of later years increased to an unprecedented extent, and is still rapidly and progressively increasing; . . . the crimes committed by the youthful offender are often of the worst description. . . ."[5]

After over 6000 years of serious concern and discussion of the problem, it is surprising that there is no single uniform definition of juvenile delinquency. There are many conceptions and misconceptions about what constitutes juvenile delinquency and how delinquency ought to be defined. Popular definitions are often contradictory and thus do little to aid our understanding of juvenile delinquency. Scholarly research likewise often fails to provide a clear and comprehensive definition of the problem.

POPULAR CONCEPTIONS
AND DEVIANCE DEFINITIONS

The term *juvenile delinquency* is heard and used so frequently that it is often assumed that everyone means the same thing when using it. Yet definitions of juvenile delinquency differ widely in meaning and content. People generally agree that juvenile delinquency is misbehavior by children, but there is much less agreement on the specifics of what constitutes misbehavior or who falls into the category of children. Because popular definitions of juvenile delinquency (as well as other types of human behavior) are based on social norms, these definitions may vary with the observer's group memberships and individually held personal values.

Norms, Values, and Social Control

Social relationships and behavior are regulated for the protection and convenience of social groups through social norms. These standardized ways of acting, or expectations governing limits of variation in behavior, provide order and make social life predictable. Some social norms prescribing acceptable and proscribing unacceptable juvenile behavior are widespread; others are not. Prescribed dating practices, for example, require that the dating partners not be closely related to each other. The prescribed minimum age limits for dating, however, vary from one area to another. Some social norms are subject to rapid change in a manner similar to fads and fashions, but most norms appear to be more enduring. For example, acceptable clothing styles change from season to season, but public consensus has long held that clothing of some type must be worn in all public places. Many norms have public support, and sanctions are prescribed by law to enforce compliance.

Definitions of what is unacceptable juvenile behavior may vary with social group membership, regional location, age, and changes in political power. Among homogeneous peoples, most norms and values are perceived in a somewhat similar manner; however, in a more complex society such as the United States the diverse experiences of heterogeneous peoples lead to varied conceptions of right and wrong modes of behavior.

Along with variations in the definitions of right and wrong behavior according to group membership, there is variation according to personally held values and norms of conduct. Each individual has

experiences or sequences of experiences different from those of other individuals. Through the process of learning, societal values are embraced to a greater or lesser extent according to life experiences. An individual whose life experiences have resulted in a greater value being placed on privacy than material comfort, for example, will tend to place more severe sanctions on invasion of privacy than on petty property offenses. What is regarded as acceptable youthful mischief to one individual may seem quite intolerable to another, who defines it as delinquent behavior. In the popular sense, delinquency is deviant behavior by youth which is contrary to the interests of the group and the individuals involved. With the diversity of group norms and personal values within a complex society such as the United States, it is no wonder that popular definitions of juvenile delinquency are so vague and varied.

Institutional Definitions

The problem of defining juvenile delinquency is not restricted to lay individuals. Institutions dealing with delinquent or deviant youth encounter the same types of problems experienced by the general public. Individuals within the institution define delinquency on the basis of deviation from norms which promote the interests of the institution. Since the interests of various institutions are different, it is not surprising that their definitions do not always coincide with, or even complement, each other. The interests and goals of a particular institution may change over time, resulting in different responses to similar juvenile behaviors. Furthermore, the policies used to implement programs in the interest of institutional goals are tempered by the group memberships and personal values of individuals in decision-making positions within the organization.

EDUCATION

School administrators view delinquency as deviation from norms which effects the functioning of the school. Norms for effective functioning of the system may vary, moreover, with the values and goals of administrators and school personnel and with the structure and type of learning facility, as well as any number of other factors. In the traditional classroom setting, order and discipline have a high priority, whereas the open classroom emphasizes creative learning in a less structured setting. Activity that might be considered a vital part of the learning experience in the open classroom may be considered disruptive in the traditional classroom.

RELIGION

Religious leaders often consider delinquency a special class of sin; however, doctrines vary from one religion to another and frequently within one religion from one locality to another. Dancing, wearing makeup, and other frivolous activity is considered sinful by some religious groups but is acceptable behavior for youth by the standards of others.

FAMILY

Parental definitions of delinquency also vary. As individuals, parents display greater or lesser degrees of tolerance for youthful misbehavior. While one mother may petition the court as a result of her child's disobedience, another may view the behavior as reflecting growing independence and maturity. There might also be a lack of uniform tolerance depending on whether their own children or others are involved in the misconduct.

LAW ENFORCEMENT AGENCIES

To the legal system that deals with juveniles, juvenile delinquency is illegal conduct by minors which results in apprehension by the police and entry into the legal system. Definitions of this sort are tempered by the norms of the policing agency, by the values of the enforcement officials, and by the size of case loads of the policing institutions. This "action law" definition of delinquency indicates that it is not statutorily prohibited behaviors that determine what delinquency is but the priorities established by the justice system.[6]

Problems in Standardization

Popular deviance conceptions of delinquency are difficult to apply to a clear delineation of juvenile delinquency. They fail in that they

examine delinquency in terms of deviant conduct but do not differentiate between delinquency and other types of deviant behavior.
Furthermore, there is no general agreement on what constitutes deviant
conduct or juvenile delinquency aside from statute laws which provide
definitions of law-violating behavior.

THE LEGAL CHARACTER OF JUVENILE DELINQUENCY

Juvenile delinquency is a legal concept and is, therefore, what
the law says it is.[7] By 1945 each state, the District of Columbia, Puerto
Rico, and the federal government had passed laws that defined delinquency.[8] The result was 53 separate definitions of juvenile delinquency.
Although each jurisdiction provided an enumeration of acts to be
defined as delinquent and specific applications, these delinquency-
defining statutes varied in content and scope from one jurisdiction to
another.

Content of Delinquency Statutes

The juvenile court acts that legally define juvenile delinquency
specify two types of behavior that fall under the heading of delinquency. Every statutory definition of delinquency includes violations
of laws and ordinances by children. Under this category are the traditional offenses, such as burglary, assault, traffic violations, and others,
applied to juveniles. A second category—status offenses—are acts prohibited to children but not to adults and has been included in all jurisdictions except that of the federal government.[9] Under this second
category of offenses, children are liable for the following acts in various
jurisdictions:

- habitual truancy
- association with thieves or with vicious or immoral persons
- incorrigibility
- being beyond parental control
- growing up in idleness or crime
- conduct that injures or endangers one's self or others
- absence from home without consent
- immoral or indecent acts
- use of vile, obscene, or vulgar language in public
- knowing visitation of a house of ill repute
- use or visitation of a policy shop or gaming place
- train jumping or entry without authority
- patronizing a saloon or dram house where liquor is sold
- curfew violations
- patronizing a public poolroom or bucket shop
- occupation of a place or being in a situation that is dangerous to one's self or others
- immoral conduct around a school or other public place
- cigarette smoking or use of tobacco
- being found in a place where an adult may be punished for allowing children

· disorderly conduct
· begging
· use of intoxicating liquor
· indecent proposals
· loitering, sleeping in alleys, or vagrancy
· running away from state or charitable institutions
· attempting to marry without consent, in violation of the law
· being given to sexual irregularities[10]

This listing of status offenses indicates the inclusiveness of juvenile delinquency statutes. Practically any juvenile could qualify as a delinquent under a broad interpretation of these offenses. What child has not engaged in "disorderly conduct," smoked a cigarette, or had a beer during his minority? State lottery tickets are sold in grocery stores in some areas. Other offenses, such as incorrigibility, being beyond the control of parents or guardians, and being given to sexual irregularities, are subject to broad and vague interpretation by those concerned with juvenile behavior. Children are charged and adjudicated under these statutes at the discretion of parents, school officials, neighbors, and policing agencies.

Offenses listed as specific to juveniles are frequently dated. Of the juvenile-specific offenses listed above as being named in juvenile court statutes, at least three contain language virtually unknown to today's youth. (A policy shop is an establishment dealing with the numbers game or a lottery; a dram house serves liquor by the drink; and a bucket shop is an establishment that sells beer in large quantities to be carried out in buckets.) Other statutes are concerned with train jumping and other relatively outmoded juvenile activities. Few state juvenile court statutes specifically describe violations involving automobiles. The juvenile court statutes were generally written in the early 1900s and few have been fully updated to meet the requirements of the changing times.

A number of statutes defining delinquency overlap with criminal codes. Provisions against violations of laws and ordinances are the most obvious, but other examples can also be cited. In a number of jurisdictions, visitation to houses of prostitution, immoral conduct, engaging in illegal occupations, and other such offenses are also prohibited to adults under criminal law or local ordinances.[11] In such cases the juvenile is subject to double prohibition. Although provisions for status offenses may be construed as overly broad or vague, sometimes dated, and often overlapping, each state averages eight or ten prohibitions of this nature. Indiana lists the greatest number of acts of this type—17—while Maine lists only one.

There has been an attempt in a number of states to provide special treatment for status offenders. Twenty-five states have adopted new quasi-delinquent classifications to deal with these offenders.[12] Terms such as "child in need of supervision" (CHINS), "deprived child," "incorrigible child," "minor in need of supervision" (MINS), and "person in need of supervision" (PINS) are used to avoid the stigmatizing delinquency label. Where the distinction is made between youthful violators of the criminal code and status offenders, pressures are exerted to divert the quasi-delinquents out of the official juvenile justice system.

Other states classify status offenders as delinquents. Little or no distinction is made between the child who engages in criminal behavior and the status offender. Both are subject to the same sanctions. Levin and Sarri listed 26 states in this category (Alabama, Arkansas, Connecticut, Delaware, Idaho, Indiana, Iowa, Kentucky, Louisiana, Maine, Michigan, Minnesota, Mississippi, Missouri, Montana, New Hampshire, New Jersey, New Mexico, Nevada, Oregon, Pennsylvania, South Carolina, Texas, Utah, Virginia, and West Virginia).[13] Since this list was compiled, only Pennsylvania has passed new legislation which provides special treatment for quasi-delinquents.[14]

There appears to be a national trend toward distinguishing between criminal and status offenders. A number of experts have even begun to suggest that status offenses be removed from the delinquency statutes altogether. While this has not been accomplished in any of the 50 states up to this time, there is a growing tendency to reduce the number of status offenses for which juveniles are held liable.

Statutes defining delinquency and the powers of the juvenile court generally include provisions for nondelinquent children in need of state protection. Provisions for neglected or dependent children often place them under the supervision of the juvenile or family court. Although they are not classified as delinquent, these youth sometimes find themselves in probation offices and state institutions for children. The appearance of these nondelinquent children in agencies of the juvenile justice system serves to add even more confusion to the definition of the term *juvenile delinquent*.

Scope of Delinquency Statutes

Delinquency statutes not only define the acts that constitute delinquency but also restrict who may be included under the statutes. The most significant of these specifications are age, offense, and sex.

AGE

The common law rule and the most prevalent statutory rule is that children under the age of 7 are not capable of committing a crime. The child between 7 and 14 is also presumed incapable of committing a crime unless the state can prove, in criminal proceedings, that the child is sufficiently mature to entertain criminal intent. In juvenile court, however, these assumptions about the child's responsibility are not present.[15] While several states have penal codes that specify a lower age limit under which a child cannot be convicted of a crime, these statutes do not preclude a finding of delinquency for children below the age limits for precisely the same acts. A few juvenile court acts do provide a lower age limit for the finding of delinquency, but the majority of juvenile court laws have no age floor.

The upper age limit for juvenile delinquency varies from 15 to 21 years in the different states, with a terminal age for juvenile court control after jurisdiction has been established, generally at age 21. The most common upper age limit is 18 years. The upper age limits are not to be taken as hard and fast rules, however. In many statutes it is not clear whether the age of original court jurisdiction relates to the age of the offender at the time of the commission of the offense or the age at the time of the initiation of court proceedings. Case law has most frequently held that age at the time of court proceedings is determinative.[16] Therefore an offense committed by a youth near the maximum age limit may be prosecuted criminally where action is deferred until the alleged offender has passed the age of juvenile court jurisdiction; conversely, proceedings may be hurried up so the individual can come under the jurisdiction of the juvenile court.

OFFENSE

Upper age limits for juvenile court jurisdiction are also complicated by the nature or seriousness of the offense. Although violations of laws and ordinances are covered by juvenile court statutes, a number of jurisdictions give exclusive or concurrent control over certain serious offenses, such as murder, to the criminal court. Furthermore, states may lower the upper age limit for delinquency findings in broad categories of offenses; in New Mexico, for example, a juvenile of age 14 or over who is charged with a felony may have jurisdiction transferred to criminal court at the discretion of the court. Some states have provided laws governing older adolescents and special categories and intermediate courts for such individuals.[17] The general trend in recent years has been to raise the upper age limit of juvenile court jurisdiction to provide broader inclusion. The ratification of the Twenty-sixth Amendment, giving 18-year-olds the right to vote, however, signals a reversal of the trend. A number of states have enacted legislation granting full adult rights and responsibilities at a lower age—generally 18 or 19. One result of this legislation is the loss of juvenile court jurisdiction and protection for older youths.

SEX

Upper age limits for juvenile court jurisdiction may also vary with the sex of the offender. Several states provide different upper age limits for males and females. In the recent past, eight states have made this distinction, but these practices (as well as general age limits for juvenile court jurisdiction) have been brought into question by the Twenty-sixth Amendment and accompanying state statutes.

Legal Definitions of Juvenile Delinquency

It is clear from a comparison of juvenile court statutes that a uniform legal definition of juvenile delinquency does not exist. Juvenile delinquency is what the law says it is in 53 separate jurisdictions in the United States. Delinquency encompasses all those acts for which an individual of minority age may be adjudicated.

Although the lack of uniform definition and differential enforcement have frequently been lamented, little has been done to provide a single official, uniform definition of juvenile delinquency throughout the United States. A movement in this direction, however, was initiated by the National Probation and Parole Association's publication of the Standard Juvenile Court Act. Endorsed by the National Conference on Juvenile Delinquency in 1946 as a model for all states, the Standard Juvenile Court Act gave jurisdiction to juvenile courts in only two items other than violations of laws or ordinances: (1) deserting one's home or being disobedient or beyond the control of one's parents or guardians and (2) truancy.

Since the time of the first Standard Juvenile Court Act, standards have gradually evolved to guide legislators in improving laws concerning juveniles. These standards are formulated and under constant revision by three cooperating national agencies: the National Council on Crime and Delinquency, the United States Children's Bureau, and the National Council of Juvenile Court Judges.[18] It should be noted that these guidelines do not carry the force of law but are only suggestions for improving the juvenile court system.

There have been no major movements on the part of state jurisdictions to conform to a uniform national definition or code of juvenile delinquency which would specify delinquent offenses and standardized age limits. Until such standardization is achieved, students of juvenile delinquency will have to depend on jurisdictional definitions or specified interpretations of juvenile delinquency.

THE JUVENILE DELINQUENT

Even if a clear and uniform definition of juvenile delinquency were established, the question of who a juvenile delinquent is would not automatically be answered. A number of definitions of the juvenile delinquent have been given which reflect the needs of the definers. Three major definitions have gained prominence; these are based on (1) commission of a delinquent act, (2) arrest, and (3) adjudication. Each of these major types of definition has advantages and disadvantages for practical application.

Juvenile Offenders

Definitions based on the commission of delinquent acts describe the juvenile delinquent as any individual of minority age who commits a delinquent act. This definition would encompass a large proportion of American youth, since self-report studies reveal that from 90 to 95 percent of all youths fall into this category. The application of this definition would allow researchers to make a more realistic assessment of the types and amounts of law-violating behavior engaged in by juveniles. A knowledge and understanding of all delinquencies would provide a background for the intelligent development of social policies dealing with juvenile misbehavior without the intrusion of differential enforcement and judicial procedures.

Several practical problems, unfortunately, are involved with the application of the juvenile-offender definition. First, the lack of uniformity in juvenile delinquency statutes would result in 53 separate jurisdictional definitions of the juvenile delinquent. In this situation, location rather than behavior may be the determining factor in delinquency. Second, there are no official or uniform statistics that report all violations committed by juveniles. Though rough estimates can be made on the number of reported violations of laws and ordinances each year, there is no conclusive method of determining whether these were committed by juveniles or adults unless an arrest is made. Third, self-report studies, which have been undertaken to estimate the prevalence of delinquent behavior, have not been used on a wide enough scale for generalization to the entire juvenile population. Even the self-report method has been brought into question by a number of individuals. It is sometimes claimed that self-reports may result in over-reporting or underreporting of law-violating behavior. The problem of validity is found in all scientific research; however, at the present time self-report techniques have no superior when it comes to identifying *all* offenses committed and *all* offenders.

Arrested Juveniles

Another definition of the juvenile delinquent involves all minors who have been arrested by law enforcement agencies. Approximately 20 percent of the juvenile population would be classified as juvenile delinquents under this definition.[19] Several assumptions are generally made when the criterion of arrest is the determining factor. Initially, it must be assumed that arrest is an indication of the seriousness and frequency with which offenses are committed by a juvenile and that differential enforcement is based upon these factors rather than other, alternative elements. Research studies do not support this assumption.[20] While seriousness of offense may be an important criterion in the initial confrontation with a youth, other factors, such as demeanor, may also have great significance. The use of the arrest criterion also implies that all juveniles who are arrested actually committed the alleged offenses, and this is a strange assumption indeed, particularly since about one-half of all juveniles arrested are not even referred to juvenile court.[21] The use of arrest statistics to determine the extent of delinquency and even what constitutes delinquency is subject to distortion. Artificial changes in arrest statistics may reflect modifications in policing policies, professionalization of police forces, improved reporting procedures, or a number of other factors rather than a change in delinquent behavior.

Several advantages may be attributed to the use of arrest as the determining factor in the definition of the juvenile delinquent. Arrest statistics are readily available for analysis and comparison of juvenile offenders from differing jurisdictions. In the absence of reliable, general data on all juvenile offenders, arrest statistics provide a valuable tool for policy-making agencies when the limitations of the data are understood and taken into consideration. The use of the arrest criterion has the further advantages of standardization and clarity of definition. The concrete arrest situation which defines the delinquent indicates the limits of public tolerance and provides the first clear example of societal reaction against the offending youth.

Adjudicated Juveniles

A third type of definition involves adjudication by a juvenile court. According to this legal definition, only those juveniles adjudicated delinquent by a juvenile court are included. Only about 5 percent of the juvenile population fell into this category in 1971.[22] Although this definition provides a uniform category of offenders and has an accompanying body of representative statistics,[23] it has essentially the same problems as those definitions based on the arrest criterion. Delinquency statutes are vague and enforcement policies lack uniformity, but the procedures followed by juvenile courts reflect the same lack of clarity and uniformity. Nevertheless, in a strict legal sense, the juvenile delinquent is a youth so adjudicated by a juvenile court.

Regardless of the fact that *juvenile delinquency* and *juvenile delinquent* are legal terms, their legal definitions are subject to criticism and severe limitations. The limitations of the legal definition must be taken into consideration in research and policy applications, and it should be remembered that the behavioral differences between the self-reported offender and the juvenile delinquent can be small if not insignificant.

A Comment on Definitions

The significance of a definition lies not so much in its content as in its application. Each of the major definitions of the juvenile offender has valuable but limited application. In an ideal situation, complete knowledge of offenders and offenses must be maintained and broken down into smaller categories, such as unofficial offenders, arrested offenders, and adjudicated delinquents, to better understand the offender and provide knowledge for more intelligent social policy. A realistic view of current information systems and methodology, however, indicates that such specification is unlikely in the immediate future. Although a distinction may be made between the offender and the "juvenile delinquent" who has been adjudicated by a juvenile court, making such a distinction does not yield answers to the questions of what causes delinquent behavior or how it can be prevented or decreased. To answer questions such as these, all channels of investigation on juvenile offenders must be left open to gather knowledge regardless of whether they are based on offenses, arrest, or adjudication. It is not profitable to hold steadfastly to a rigid definition of the juvenile delinquent if doing so means the loss of potentially valuable information. The codification of information on the juvenile offender does require, however, specifying concepts in any research or writing as well as linking these specifications to earlier research and theory.

DELINQUENT AND CRIMINAL STATUS

Delinquent and criminal status are generally regarded as basically similar. While they share the distinction of expressing the position of individuals in relation to the law-making structure of a society, there are important quantitative and qualitative differences between the two terms. The most apparent difference is their application to different age groups. It is generally assumed that the term *juvenile delinquency* is used as a convenience to indicate an extension of the concept of criminality to individuals of a younger age group. The delinquency concept, however, is also set apart from the criminal concept in regard to the behavior involved, responsibility, adjudication, and treatment of offenders.

According to criminal law, a crime is an action or omission which is defined and codified in law. Delinquency includes this type of behavior but adds a category of less well-defined behavior prohibited to juveniles, such as truancy and incorrigibility. Serious offenses, as defined by criminal codes, committed by juveniles may result in the extension of majority to the juvenile to enable criminal trial. Offenses prohibited only to juveniles may not be handled in this manner. The extension of majority status to juveniles in the case of criminal-type offenses is based on the concepts of responsibility and intent. If the child is aware of his or her act and its consequences, knows the difference between "right" and wrong," and willfully committed the offense in the absence of mitigating circumstances, he or she may be considered responsible and capable of criminal intent. A finding of delinquency, however, does not require responsibility or criminal intent on the part of the juvenile offender.

Court procedures and outcomes provide an additional distinction between criminal and delinquent behavior. The formal public trial and a variety of rights afforded the adult offender are not extended to juveniles in juvenile court hearings. Furthermore, the findings resulting from adjudication (official court application of the delinquency label to an individual) differ qualitatively in criminal and delinquency proceedings. Whereas criminal proceedings determine innocence or guilt of the accused in alleged criminal behavior, juvenile proceedings are not based on a finding of guilt in regard to an offense. A delinquency finding expresses the court's belief that the child is in need of the court's protection and guidance. The offense studied in the court proceeding is not the problem at issue but may be considered a symptom of the disorder which requires the attention of various agencies in the community.

Treatment of offenders also varies with criminal or delinquent status. Criminal statutes provide established minimum and maximum sentences for criminal offenses; sentencing is left to the discretion of the judge in juvenile proceedings even when a criminal-type offense is involved. An adult may be sentenced to life imprisonment and a juvenile sent to a foster home for the same statutorily defined offense— murder. Conversely, the juvenile may be placed under the supervision of the court for the term of his minority for actions that are not prohibited to adults or if prohibited result in a small fine or short sentence.

Although there are basic similarities between the concepts of criminality and juvenile delinquency, important differences in the substantive definition of behavior and outcomes for the offender make a careful distinction between these concepts vital to the study of juvenile delinquency.

SOCIAL CONTEXT OF DELINQUENT STATUS

Although definitions of delinquent behavior and juvenile delinquents establish parameters for the study of delinquency, they do not indicate the meaning of delinquency status in the social context of state, community, and interpersonal relations. Each of these social perspectives has separate but interrelated and reinforcing implications for the individual delinquent in its reactions to his behavior.

The State

The relationship between the state and the delinquent has traditionally been viewed as a passive response to active behavior through detection, law enforcement, and adjudication.[24] State agencies, however, may play an important role in legitimizing the juvenile offender's delinquent status. Some studies suggest that individuals are selectively chosen by state agencies for official attention,[25] initiating processes that may result in further delinquent behavior.[26] Moreover, state agencies may complicate the juvenile delinquent's reentry into the conventional social world. Many police departments continue supervision of the activities of released delinquents to prevent further delinquencies and maintain a ready pool of suspects for the solution of reported offenses.[27]

The most important role of the state, however, is in its effect on the reactions of other social units. Individuals respond to others informally and in an unorganized way unless those persons are defined as falling into specified categories.[28] The official label of juvenile delinquent has the effect of placing the juvenile in such a category by a type of degradation ritual that has been described by Erickson. The juvenile offender is successfully removed from his normal social position to a distinct deviant role through the processes of confrontation, judgment, and placement. There are no formalized methods of reversing these processes.[29]

There has been a great deal of discussion in recent years centering on the state's responsibility in creating juvenile delinquents. One school of thought suggests that the official label places the minor offender in a deviant category from which there is little likelihood of escape, thereby producing the conditions for more serious delinquent or criminal behavior. The opponents of this approach point out that the label is applied only after the fact of delinquent behavior. In this perspective, the state does not promote delinquent behavior; instead, it provides official recognition of a condition that already exists. Whether or not the state "causes" delinquent behavior, its recognition of a misbehaving youth does affect other's reactions to him.

The Community

Public opinion is divided on what *ought* to be considered crime or delinquency, but there is a general consensus on what crime and delinquency *are*. Crime and juvenile delinquency are what the law says they are. Criminals and juvenile delinquents are individuals who have been caught violating the law. The perceived difference between criminals and delinquents has for the most part centered on the age of the offender. Juvenile delinquents are just young criminals in the public mind. Perceptions of this nature are buttressed by mass media accounts of juveniles who are involved in violent crimes such as murder, rape, and armed robbery.

Although statutes regarding disclosure and publicity of information on delinquent offenders vary from one jurisdiction to another, the question of publicity is primarily decided by the individual juvenile court judge. (It should be noted that the official stand of the National Council on Crime and Delinquency released in the *Guides for Juvenile Court Judges on News Media Relations* favors anonymity for delinquents appearing in juvenile courts.[30]) Children are often shielded from public disclosure of identifying information, but more general and offense-specific information is frequently made available to the public in regard to serious offenses in response to public interest. While a headline such as "GIRL SHOOTS BROTHER" arouses public interest and concern, it is unlikely that a headline proclaiming "BOY DIS-OBEYS MOM" would spark enthusiastic interest in the reader. Lesser offenses do not invite major publicity, and as a result it is generally assumed that only serious offenders or habitual minor offenders are selected for official attention. These assumptions are not borne out by arrest and court statistics (see Chapter 3). Juvenile offenders are most frequently apprehended and "arrested or referred to court for petty larceny, fighting, disorderly conduct, liquor-related offenses, and conduct not in violation of the criminal law. . . ."[31]

Because violation of criminal statutes as well as offenses peculiar to juveniles, such as truancy, running away, and disobedience, may be tried in juvenile court, the delinquency label is often believed to be synonymous with "young criminal." Thus, if the police and the courts apprehend and label juveniles as juvenile delinquents, the community is likely to regard them as young criminals and treat them accordingly.

Reactions to the delinquent in the community may be expressed on both the institutional and individual levels. On an institutional level juveniles who have arrest records may have difficulty finding employment, entering military service, or reentering educational institutions whether or not they have been referred to court and found delinquent. Restrictions in these areas deter the reintegration of the individual into society and may hamper efforts at rehabilitation. Even more demoralizing and detrimental to the juvenile offender may be the informal, individual-level responses by others. Informal controls on the future behavior of offenders may involve gossip, criticism, suspicion, disapproval, and avoidance as well as other methods. Children may be warned to keep away from the offender, segregating him from "normal" society. In order to find companionship, the offender may find it practical to gravitate toward other offenders or deviant elements in the society, reinforcing his deviant or law-violating behavior. The closed nature of the juvenile justice process may prevent or restrict the operation of some of these community processes. An employer or potential employer may not know of an arrest. Even neighbors may be unaware of a youth's problems with the law.

The Individual Delinquent

The consequences of the juvenile delinquency label once it is applied can be severe for the juvenile offender. Aside from the apparent frustration in securing reintegration into the normal society, the juvenile is confronted with additional problems involving his self-concept and his relationships with others. Depending upon the reactions of others, the juvenile's response to the delinquency label may vary from cautious reassessment or reinforcement of his or her behavior to denial and moral indignation.

In the traditional view, it is believed that sometime during the processes of apprehension, arrest, and adjudication, the juvenile offender will gain insight into the gravity and consequences of his or her actions and in doing so will be deterred from further delinquent behavior. If the juvenile does not appear to be reformed, he or she may be taken out of the environment that promoted the behavior and placed in an environment "suitable" for reform. The child, according to this perspective, is not to be considered a young criminal but a misguided youth. In enlightened communities, this approach could be effective; where delinquency and the delinquent are viewed in this light, cautious reassessment and change in behavior may be the response of the individual delinquent.

The labeling approach to delinquent behavior suggests that the juvenile offender may develop a delinquent self-concept when he or she is labeled a juvenile delinquent and treated accordingly.[32] When societal reactions preclude the juvenile's reentry into normal society, his or her only viable alternative is to play the delinquent role or to withdraw. These are not always considered undesirable consequences by the juvenile. For example, members of delinquent subcultures often enjoy considerable prestige from peers because of their records.[33] Withdrawal, on the other hand, may lead to less delinquency but does not change the delinquent label. Moreover, withdrawal may involve a drawing away from "normal" society and gravitation toward a delinquent subculture where the individual's record and label are appreciated.

A third view of the individual delinquent's reaction involves the denial of delinquency. Sykes and Matza suggest that juvenile offenders may try to neutralize their actions by suggesting that the behavior was justifiable and no criminal intent was involved.[34] Although the offenders have been labeled, they deny the suitability and justification of its application to them. Individual delinquents who respond in this manner do not develop a delinquent self-concept and may or may not engage in further delinquent behavior. A further reaction to the delinquent label is moral indignation. The delinquent feels that the label is not justified because "everybody does it" and "others get away with it." Differential enforcement of the law is viewed as the great divider between delinquents and nondelinquents. In this situation, the system is regarded as the offender, and juveniles are the victims who are no worse than the offenders who got away.

Although each of these types of response appears logical and individual cases can be cited to support them, the responses of individual delinquents are varied and unique in each case. One element is common to all of these responses; namely, each is based on societal reaction to delinquency in general and to the individual delinquent. Perhaps if societal reactions were more uniform the individual delinquent's response would be more predictable. It is unlikely that uniformity will be achieved, however, because the content of both societal reaction and individual response are based on varied group interests, norms, and personal values.

THE NATURE OF DELINQUENCY IN PERSPECTIVE

Although the concept of juvenile delinquency as separate and distinct from criminality is relatively new (the first juvenile court act defining delinquent behavior was enacted in 1899), juvenile delinquency has been studied extensively. Data has been gathered in regard to offenses, characteristics of offenders, and causes of juvenile delinquency, but many problems remain even in the basic delineation of the area.

The definition of juvenile delinquency is neither uniform nor clear. Aside from the numerous popular conceptions and deviance definitions, 53 separate jurisdictions provide varying legal definitions of *juvenile delinquency* and *juvenile delinquent* in the United States. Although *juvenile delinquency* and *juvenile delinquent* are legal terms, legal definitions have not been completely satisfactory. Legal definitions, the philosophy behind the juvenile court system, and the outcomes of the juvenile justice system have variously been upheld and assailed. Theoretical writings, research studies, and social policy statements have frequently failed to clearly specify definitions or have departed from legal definitions for the convenience provided by other definitions or because the legal definition did not represent a true picture of the offender or his offense. The lack of standardization in the definition of delinquent behavior resulting from these practices has far-reaching consequences not only for theory and research but also for social policy and societal reaction to the individual juvenile offender.

In using research for building and verifying theories of delinquent behavior, problems are encountered similar to those found in other scientific studies. Specification and generalization fallacies can present special difficulties even for the seasoned researcher in vaguely defined areas. When juvenile delinquents are variously defined as officially detected offenders, arrested offenders, or adjudicated offenders, the definition represents only a portion of the overall category of juvenile delinquent. The term *juvenile delinquency* itself is often used in a generic sense to refer to a wide variety of different acts. We must question, for example, whether knowledge of why children steal automobiles tells us about the generic juvenile delinquency or whether this knowledge of automobile theft by juveniles would contribute to an understanding of other juvenile offenses such as incorrigibility. Until clear, general definitions of *delinquency* and *juvenile delinquent* are agreed upon, it will be necessary to continue to study all varieties and conceptions of delinquency to reach a full understanding of the problem. Standardization and careful attention to clear and precise statements of interim definitions and conceptions, however, is vital to the codification and application of research findings.

Ideally, social policy is guided by careful study and verified knowledge of an issue. The fragmentary information gathered on juvenile delinquency (its causes, the characteristics of offenders, and the meanings of delinquent status) has not been of a nature to generate many informed social programs to cope with the problem. The failure to distinguish between, and to catalogue, various types of delinquent offenses has resulted in an overly broad application of established methods of prevention and rehabilitation. Methods for effective rehabilitation of offenders may vary with the offense or with any number of other factors.

Societal reaction, for the most part, reflects official social policy. Current policy often deals with delinquency as a special type of, or an extension of, criminality with treatment tempered according to the age of the offender. These policy orientations frequently result in the public treatment of delinquents as young criminals. Little has been accomplished in regard to the development of enlightened and coherent social policy in the areas of appropriate legislation and policing practices even though suggestions for improvement based on scientific research have been provided. Changes and improvements in these areas have been piecemeal, reflecting the fragmentary nature of research studies and the resistance to change by organizations and institutions involved in this problem area. Until codification and adequate theories of causation can be created, future action programs and accompanying societal reaction will not change appreciably.

NOTES

[1] President's Commission on Law Enforcement and Administration of Justice, *The Challenge of Crime in a Free Society* (Washington, D.C.: Government Printing Office, 1967), pp. 55–89.

[2] *Ibid.*

[3] Edward H. Stullken, "Misconceptions About Juvenile Delinquency," *Journal of Criminal Law, Criminology and Police Science* 46 (1966): 833.

[4] *Ibid.*

[5] Ruth Shonle Cavan, *Juvenile Delinquency* (Philadelphia: Lippincott, 1962), p. 5.

[6] John P. Reed and Fuad Baali, *Faces of Delinquency* (Englewood Cliffs, N.J.: Prentice-Hall, 1972), p. 2.

[7] Sol Rubin, "The Legal Character of Juvenile Delinquency," *Annals of the American Academy of Political and Social Science* 261 (January 1949): 2.

[8] Martin R. Haskell and Lewis Yablonsky, *Crime and Delinquency* (Skokie, Ill.: Rand McNally, 1971), p. 227.

[9] Thorsten Sellin and Marvin E. Wolfgang, *The Measurement of Delinquency* (New York: Wiley, 1964), pp. 71–86.

[10] Condensed and rephrased from Frederick B. Sussman, *Law of Juvenile Delinquency* (Dobbs Ferry, N.Y.: Oceana, 1959), p. 21.

[11] These are offenses listed by Sussman as applied specifically to juveniles under various jurisdictional statutes.

[12] Daniel Katkin, Drew Hyman, and John Kramer, *Juvenile Delinquency and the Juvenile Justice System* (North Scituate, Mass.: Duxbury Press, 1976), p. 17.

[13] Mark M. Levin and Rosemary C. Sarri, *Juvenile Delinquency: A Comparative Analysis of Legal Codes in the United States* (Ann Arbor, Mich.: National Assessment of Juvenile Corrections, 1974).

[14] Katkin, Hyman, and Kramer, *op. cit.*

[15] Rubin, *op. cit.*, p. 6.

[16] Paul W. Tappan, *Comparative Survey of Juvenile Delinquency, Part I: North America* (New York: United Nations, 1958).

[17] Cavan, *op. cit.*, p. 17.

[18] *Ibid.*, p. 267.

[19] President's Commission, *op. cit.*

[20] See Irving Piliavin and Scott Briar, "Police Encounters with Juveniles," *American Journal of Sociology* 70 (September 1964): 206–214 for an analysis of police disposition decisions; also see Nathan Goldman, *The Differential Selection of Juvenile Offenders for Court Appearances* (New York: National Council on Crime and Delinquency, 1963).

[21] Federal Bureau of Investigation, *Uniform Crime Reports, 1971* (Washington, D.C.: Government Printing Office, 1972), table 18, p. 112.

[22] Department of Health, Education, and Welfare, Children's Bureau, *Juvenile Court Statistics, 1970* (Washington, D.C.: Government Printing Office, 1971), p. 4.

[23] *Ibid.*, p. 1–5.

[24] Stanton Wheeler and Leonard S. Cottrell, Jr., *Juvenile Delinquency: Its Prevention and Control* (New York: Russell Sage Foundation, 1966), p. 22.

[25] See Piliavin and Briar, *op. cit.*; also see Goldman, *op. cit.*

[26] A discussion of labeling and its consequences is contained in Edwin M. Schur, *Labeling Deviant Behavior* (New York: Harper & Row, 1971).

[27] Kai T. Erickson, "Notes on the Sociology of Deviance," *Social Problems* 10 (spring 1962): 313.

[28] Wheeler and Cottrell, *op. cit.*, pp. 22–23.

[29] Erickson, *op. cit.*, p. 310.

[30] National Council on Crime and Delinquency, *Guides for Juvenile Court Judges on News Media Relations* (New York: 1957).

[31] President's Commission, *op. cit.*

[32] Wheeler and Cottrell, *op. cit.*, p. 22.

[33] Frederick M. Thrasher, *The Gang* (Chicago: University of Chicago Press, 1927), p. 62.

[34] Gresham M. Sykes and David Matza, "Techniques of Neutralization: A Theory of Delinquency," *American Sociological Review* 22 (1957): 664–670.

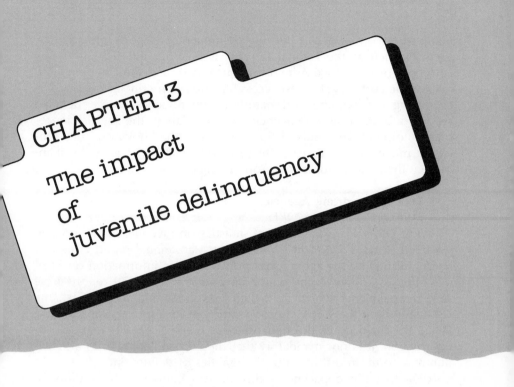

CHAPTER 3
The impact of juvenile delinquency

Juvenile delinquency is a pervasive problem in American society. It touches the lives of all the people—rich or poor, powerful or powerless, self-assured or unsure. For each delinquent adjudicated there is, in the background, a family crisis, a distressed victim, concerned friends, and an army of workers recruited to handle the problems of crime and delinquency. Most juveniles commit acts for which they could be adjudicated, but only a small proportion are formally processed through the entire sequence of steps to adjudication. Thus official statistics represent only the tip of the iceberg in estimating numbers of offenders and costs to the society. Some costs cannot be measured.

The scope and impact of delinquency has not yet been fully quantified. Special methods are needed just to ascertain who is delinquent and how many juvenile offenders there are. Widely scattered reports on crime and delinquency must be used to provide a rough estimate of the nature and extent of the delinquency problem until better methods are perfected for more precise measurement.

JUVENILE DELINQUENCY STATISTICS
Statistics on delinquency are often neither readily available nor highly reliable. Official statistical reports produced by governmental agencies provide much of the data used to estimate the extent and nature of juvenile delinquency. Because they provide the most comprehensive information available on juvenile offenders, they influence

many of our ideas about juvenile delinquency. Reports provided by agencies such as the Federal Bureau of Investigation (FBI), the Law Enforcement Assistance Administration (LEAA), and the Children's Bureau, while currently the best accessible, are often criticized for underestimating the volume and nature of delinquency. More detailed reports published by state agencies and scholars in the social sciences seem to discourage generalization. Taken together, however, they provide a much more balanced and complete picture of juvenile delinquency than can be obtained from a single source.

Federal Reporting Agencies
UNIFORM CRIME REPORTS

The FBI is a major source of statistics on juvenile delinquency in the United States. *Uniform Crime Reports,* an annual report compiled and published by the agency, has provided basic information on juvenile offenses known to the police since 1930.[1] These FBI reports have several weaknesses which limit their usefulness and scope. First, the FBI depends on the voluntary cooperation of local police departments. While the majority of the departments comply with FBI requests for information, it is not mandatory that they do so. Voluntary participation may result in distortion of the realities of delinquency. It is quite possible that the departments that do not cooperate have different case loads from those departments that voluntarily supply case data. The FBI sends out report forms to be filled out by the personnel of local police departments. There are no representatives who call on the police to check the accuracy and completeness of their reports. Although the bureau provides a list of definitions needed to complete the standardized forms, these are subject to differential interpretation. The definitions are sufficiently broad and overlapping that different police departments may classify the same offense under two different categories.[2]

The FBI classification system was primarily developed to measure crime; therefore it does not include many of the minor offenses for which juveniles may be taken into custody and adjudicated. The FBI provides data on curfew and loitering law violations (5 percent of all juvenile arrests in 1975) and runaways (6 percent of all juvenile arrests in 1975). However, most of the exclusively juvenile offenses (those for which an adult could not be prosecuted) are lumped into a category labeled "all other offenses except traffic." Twelve percent of the individuals under 18 arrested in 1975 were placed in this category. The curfew and loitering, runaway, and "all other" categories accounted for about 23 percent of all juvenile arrests in 1975.[3] Furthermore, the *Uniform Crime Reports* do not include traffic violations (except arrests for driving under the influence), which make up a large proportion of all juvenile delinquent offenses. The *Juvenile Court Statistics* for

1972 estimated that more than one-third of all juvenile court cases involved traffic offenses.

Probably the greatest limitation of the FBI data is its scope. The criterion for inclusion in the *Reports* is arrest. We know, however, that a large proportion of the youthful offenders detected by police are informally handled. Those youngsters not arrested or taken into custody will not be included in the data set. The extent of delinquency in the United States is greatly underestimated by the *Reports*. Various studies suggest that relative age, sex, race, social class, and seriousness of the offense may determine whether arrest will occur.[4] These findings indicate that the use of arrest statistics alone may provide a distorted picture of the average offender.

Although the *Uniform Crime Reports* apparently give an incomplete accounting of offenders and offenses, they remain very useful. Used in conjunction with other sources, they provide a basic source of information.

JUVENILE COURT STATISTICS

The yearly *Juvenile Court Statistics* report the number and disposition of juvenile court cases. Like the *Uniform Crime Reports*, these data are compiled from voluntary reports from the local agencies. The information received is not highly standardized. Not all juvenile courts provide information on the same population. The courts' jurisdictions are established by state law; therefore the ages of children and the types of offenses represented vary from one jurisdiction to another. The reliance on juvenile courts in handling misbehaving youths may also vary considerably from one jurisdiction to another. In some areas, such as large urban centers, social service agencies may be plentiful and receive many referrals for juvenile misconduct. In other areas, where fewer community services are available, the juvenile court is used to a far greater extent. Of course, community opinion and parental attitudes may also be important factors in determining whether a child will ever come before a juvenile court. Because local conditions for jurisdiction and handling vary so greatly, the *Juvenile Court Statistics* are not highly comparable. The statistics may, in fact, be misleading when used to compare one city with another. Although they provide some vital information to indicate how often the juvenile courts are used to handle offenders, they cannot be used alone to illustrate the extent and nature of juvenile delinquency.

The *Juvenile Court Statistics* have been the responsibility of a wide variety of governmental agencies in recent years and are difficult to locate and obtain. Since June 1975 they have been compiled by the LEAA. In previous years the statistics were produced in the Department of Health, Education, and Welfare (HEW) by the Office of Youth Development, Office of Juvenile Delinquency and Youth Development, and the Children's Bureau. The shuffling of responsibility from one department or agency to another has been accompanied by changes in data collection and reporting procedures. Between 1957 and 1970, the data were drawn, with the aid of the Census Bureau, from a representative sample of juvenile courts.[5] Since 1970, however, all juvenile courts volunteering information have been used to calculate the national statistics.[6] The data base may not be standard from year to year. In 1973 Alaska, Arizona, Arkansas, Minnesota, and New Mexico failed to provide information. It cannot be assumed that these same states will fail to report in the future.

In 1973 1,143,700 nontraffic cases were handled in juvenile courts. An estimated 986,000 children (some were referred more than once during the year) were involved. This figure represents 3 percent of the children between the ages of 10 and 17 in the United States population. There was an increase of 3 percent in the number of juvenile court cases from 1972 to 1973. However, the population between ages 10 and 17 increased only about 1 percent. In most years the increase in delinquency cases exceeds the increase in the child population. Between 1960 and 1972 the number of delinquency cases increased 124 percent, while the child population increased 32 percent. Urban courts exhibited only a slight increase in the number of cases (0.3 percent), while the suburban courts and rural courts experienced higher increases in the number of cases handled—5 percent and 15 percent, respectively.[7]

When the *Juvenile Court Statistics* and the *Uniform Crime Reports* are compared, some similarities are evident. Both sets of data suggest rapid increases in delinquency during World War II, decreases after the war, and steady increases since 1949 (with the exception of decreases in 1961 and 1972) in the number of juvenile court cases. In 1973 the *Uniform Crime Reports* and *Juvenile Court Statistics* reported increases of 5 and 3 percent, respectively.

SOURCEBOOK OF CRIMINAL JUSTICE STATISTICS

The *Sourcebook of Criminal Justice Statistics* is a recent publication, having first appeared in 1973 under the auspices of the LEAA of the Department of Justice. While primarily oriented to adult criminal justice systems, this yearly publication also brings together a considerable amount of valuable information about juvenile delinquency.[8] Statistics are compiled from a variety of governmental and private agencies and brought together in a single volume. The statistics are primarily nationwide in scope, but LEAA also draws upon state and local sources of information. Of course, the data in the *Sourcebook* cannot be more complete or more accurate than the sources of the original data. In most cases, tables and statistics are reported without alteration from their original source. The data in the *Sourcebook*, therefore, has many of the same limitations of the official statistics found in the *Uniform Crime Reports* and the *Juvenile Court Statistics*, from which some of the data are drawn.

The *Sourcebook of Criminal Justice Statistics* represents a significant attempt to increase the comparability of juvenile and criminal justice statistics. But because the data-gathering responsibilities remain divided among a wide variety of agencies, the goal of obtaining comparability in statistics about the juvenile justice system remains unmet. Some agencies do not maintain a publishing schedule, and their data is several years old when released. In addition, some agencies report their statistics using the fiscal year, which ends on June 30, while others use a year that ends on December 31 as the base for reporting statistics. These factors limit the ability of students of delinquency to compare the statistics from different agencies. The goal of comparability will probably never be met until the responsibility for gathering and reporting statistical data is given to a single agency, such as LEAA. The *Sourcebook* and the National Criminal Justice Information and Statistical Service, however, are significant steps in this direction.

State and Local Reporting Agencies

Many state and local agencies compile and report information that is essential to an understanding of juvenile delinquency. The local statistics reflect a wide variety of reporting procedures and purposes, and they may not be comparable from state to state or between cities within the same state. The state of Illinois, through its Juvenile Division of the Department of Corrections, for example, issues semiannual reports or statistical summaries dealing with such subjects as the population and length of stay in youth correctional centers and forestry camps, type of offenses leading to commitment, sex of offenders, race of offenders, and marital and income status of parents.[9]

The various states do not have a standard report organization. Therefore when the need for data from various areas of the country arises, considerable time and energy must be expended to ferret out the relevant source agencies. Release of information is subject to local or state policies. Often there appears to be no formal channel of authorization for release of information on juveniles. Many local jurisdictions apply standards of secrecy and confidentiality to all juvenile records.

Scientific Studies

Much of the detailed information available on juvenile offenders and offenses comes from studies of individual localities. Researchers from educational institutions frequently study the behavior of youth. Surveys to determine the extent of delinquency, the types of acts committed, and the backgrounds of offenders are not unusual. Some researchers go out into the community to engage in participant observation. They have ridden in police cars to observe law enforcement in action, lived among delinquent gangs, and served as caseworkers. Case studies have also been used to gather information on how juvenile delinquents perceive themselves, their acts, and the juvenile justice system. A wide range of valuable information has been gathered using these various techniques.

These studies have for the most part reflected the interests of the individuals designing them. The types of information gained have not been standard from one study to another. Therefore the studies often lack comparability. The limitations of financial resources and time generally result in highly localized studies, and generalizations may not apply to other areas. When used in conjunction with federal, state, and local official data, however, scientific studies may help fill in the gaps and provide a more accurate picture of juvenile delinquency.

The Role of Juvenile Statistics

In the absence of data to describe the extent and nature of juvenile misbehavior, there is little to guide a society in dealing with the problem. An understanding of what is happening enables individuals and governments to cope with the situation. Unreliable or inadequate statistics provide a shaky base for policy decisions; however, a shaky base is better than no foundation at all. Our understanding of, and ability to deal with, delinquency problems would be greatly facilitated if a uniform worldwide, or even nationwide, procedure for the collection of delinquency statistics were in use. However, no such system has been developed.

There is little consensus on who qualifies as a juvenile. In the United States, seriousness of offense, sex of offender, and relative age are generally taken into consideration when the applicability of juvenile jurisdiction is questioned. The criteria are not standard from state to state or from country to country.[10] The National Council on Crime and Delinquency, the Children's Bureau, and the federal courts advocate the use of the age criterion alone, setting an upper age limit of 18. Certainly the use of a single uniform age criterion would simplify the handling of juveniles and the collection of data on juvenile offenders. On the other hand, setting arbitrary upper and lower age limits for juvenile consideration might prevent the court from handling each juvenile in an individual manner. Maturation occurs at an uneven rate, and an inflexibly set age limit may result in the rejection of immature but older youths for special consideration.

THE EXTENT OF JUVENILE DELINQUENCY

The answer to the question of who a juvenile delinquent is can be answered by a definition. The juvenile delinquent is generally perceived as a youth who has been adjudicated by a juvenile court. This definition does not, however, give a very clear picture of the delinquency problem in the United States. The numbers of youths adjudicated delinquent is only a small proportion of the number of juvenile offenders. A comprehensive view of delinquency requires that we look at all offenders and their offenses no matter how they were handled.

Hidden Delinquency

A major problem associated with official statistics is that not all juveniles who commit delinquent acts are included in the reports. Some serious delinquent acts are not detected. Others are detected but not reported to the police. Friends and neighbors may informally "take care of" the problem caused by the child. For example, the parents may agree to repair damage to property or to provide doctor's care for an injured party. Schools often do not report many delinquent acts that occur in or near the school but rather handle them informally. Some store owners and operators who catch young shoplifters do not report the youths but informally handle the situation by retrieving their merchandise and informing the parents. A trend toward increased reporting as opposed to informal handling of shoplifters has been noted in recent years, however.

Juvenile misbehavior is common in the United States. A great deal of the disapproved behavior is hidden; it does not come to the attention of official agencies. Of course, many of the offenses engaged in by juveniles are minor, but there is reason to believe that serious violations of law are also included within the hidden category. Hidden delinquency also encompasses juvenile misbehavior that is known to the police but is not recorded or officially handled.

Although there are no concise figures to indicate the full extent of delinquency in the United States, estimates suggest that delinquency is more prevalent than indicated by official statistics. Self-report studies reveal that 90 percent of all juveniles have committed acts for which

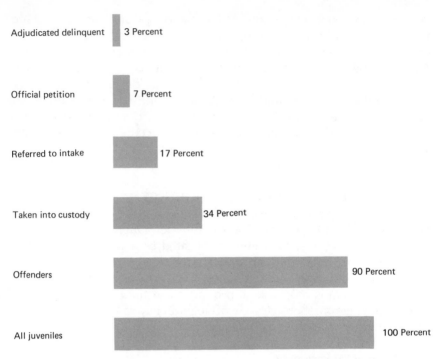

Figure 3.1 Determination of Delinquent Status: Percentage of Juveniles in the Procedural Process

they could have been adjudicated during their minority,[11] even though only 3 percent of the nation's juveniles are actually adjudicated delinquent.[12] It is apparent that many juvenile offenders are not processed through all of the stages of the juvenile justice system. Official sources estimate that only about half of the juveniles taken into police custody are referred to juvenile court.[13] Of those juveniles referred to court, about half are handled by petition.[14] The proportion of youths represented in each of these categories is shown in Figure 3.1.

Reported and Recorded Delinquency

Official reports are made when children are taken into custody. The *Uniform Crime Reports* for 1975 indicated that 2,078,459 arrests, or 26 percent of all arrests, involved juveniles.[15] The number of juveniles arrested is probably a somewhat lower figure, however, because a juvenile might be taken into custody more than once in a given year. A further distortion in the figures for known delinquency involves unofficial police contacts on the streets. Young vandals, for example, may be asked to clean up their mess and be given a warning without any official report being made. Police took youths into custody for a wide range of behaviors, as shown in Table 3.1.

The arrest statistics underestimate the number of offenses committed by juveniles. Of the offenses reported to police in 1975, less than 25 percent resulted in the arrest of a suspect.[16] While there is no way to determine what proportion of the unsolved crimes were committed by juveniles, we can be relatively certain that a substantial number did involve juveniles. Serious crimes as well as petty offenses remained unsolved. Nearly 3,000 murders or nonnegligent manslaughter cases; 246,000 cases of robbery; 622,000 cases of auto theft; 108,000 cases of aggravated assault; and many other cases went unsolved.[17]

TABLE 3.1 TOTAL ARRESTS BY AGE, 1975

	AGES			
OFFENSES	UNDER 15	UNDER 18	18 AND OVER	GRAND TOTAL, ALL AGES
CRIME INDEX OFFENSES				
Criminal homicide:				
murder and nonnegligent manslaughter	184	1,573	14,912	16,485
negligent manslaughter	80	368	2,673	3,041
Forcible rape	867	3,863	18,100	21,963
Robbery	12,515	44,470	85,318	129,788
Aggravated assault	10,600	35,512	166,705	202,217
Burglary—breaking and entering	90,189	236,192	212,963	449,155
Larceny—theft	192,495	432,019	526,919	958,938
Motor vehicle theft	17,290	65,564	54,660	120,224
VIOLENT CRIME[a]	24,166	85,418	285,035	370,453
percentage[b]	6.5	23.1	76.9	100.0
PROPERTY CRIME[c]	299,974	733,775	794,542	1,528,317
percentage	19.6	40.8	52.0	100.0
Subtotal for Crime Index offenses	324,220	819,561	1,082,250	1,901,811
OTHER OFFENSES				
Other assaults	26,280	69,965	282,683	352,648
Arson	4,904	7,727	6,862	14,589
Forgery and counterfeiting	1,215	7,320	50,483	57,803
Fraud	851	4,665	141,588	146,253
Embezzlement	157	679	8,623	9,302
Stolen property: buying, receiving, possessing	9,445	32,891	68,012	100,903
Vandalism	66,663	115,046	60,819	175,865
Weapons: carrying, possessing	5,127	21,365	109,568	130,933
Prostitution and commercialized vice	177	2,362	47,867	50,229
Sex offenses (except forcible rapes and prostitution)	3,928	10,876	39,961	50,837

TABLE 3.1 CONTINUED

	AGES		
OFFENSES	UNDER 15	UNDER 18	18 AND OVER	GRAND TOTAL, ALL AGES
Narcotic drug laws	16,229	122,857	385,332	508,189
Gambling	263	1,763	47,706	49,469
Offenses against family and children	2,884	6,271	47,061	53,332
Driving under the influence	289	17,020	891,660	908,680
Liquor laws	9,429	105,813	161,244	267,057
Drunkenness	4,243	41,457	1,134,664	1,176,121
Disorderly conduct	34,989	120,278	512,283	632,561
Vagrancy	1,296	5,323	53,954	59,277
All other offenses (except traffic)	95,020	256,568	781,186	1,037,754
Suspicion	2,365	7,718	21,380	29,098
Curfew and loitering law violations	29,974	112,117	——	112,117
Runaways	76,258	118,817	——	188,817
Subtotal for other offenses	391,986	1,258,898	4,852,934	6,111,834
TOTAL FOR ALL OFFENSES	716,206	2,078,459	5,935,186	8,013,645
PERCENTAGE	8.9	25.9	74.1	100.0

[a] Violent crime is murder, forcible rape, robbery, and aggravated assault.
[b] Percentages do not add up to total due to rounding off.
[c] Property crime is burglary, larceny, and auto theft.
Source: Federal Bureau of Investigation, *Uniform Crime Reports, 1975* (Washington, D.C.: Government Printing Office, 1976), pp. 188–189.

A large number of juveniles who acquire a delinquency arrest record are never referred to juvenile court. The various alternative dispositions and the frequency of their use is shown in Table 3.2. Slightly more than 50 percent of the juveniles taken into custody by police are referred to juvenile court for handling. About 40 percent of the cases are disposed of by the local police department.

Adjudicated Delinquency

Most juvenile offenders are screened out of the juvenile justice system before they ever reach a juvenile court hearing. Of the 90 percent of all juveniles who report delinquent activity in a self-report study, only about 17 percent will reach the juvenile court. Nonetheless, the number of juveniles who are being handled has reached alarming proportions. In 1973, there were 1,143,700 juvenile cases handled by the juvenile court, and an estimated 986,000 children made appearances

TABLE 3.2 DISPOSITION OF JUVENILE
OFFENDERS TAKEN INTO POLICE CUSTODY, 1975

DISPOSITION	TOTAL	PERCENTAGE
Handled within department and released	697,061	41.6
Referred to juvenile court jurisdiction	883,736	52.7
Referred to welfare agency	24,293	1.4
Referred to other police agency	31,663	1.9
Referred to criminal or adult court	38,958	2.3
Total all agencies	1,675,711[a]	100.0[b]

[a] Includes all offenses except traffic and dependency cases.
[b] Percentages do not add up to total due to rounding off.
Source: Derived from Federal Bureau of Investigation, *Uniform Crime Reports,
1975* (Washington, D.C.: Government Printing Office, 1976), p. 177.

(the same child may have made more than one appearance during the year).[18] Despite the popularity of practices to divert juveniles out of the juvenile justice system to prevent labeling, the number and rate of referrals to the juvenile court are increasing. Figure 3.2 illustrates this trend. Since the proportion of police cases referred to juvenile court remains approximately the same, the figures would suggest that delinquency is increasing faster than the youthful population.[19]

Many of the cases coming before the juvenile courts are handled unofficially, without petition, by officers of the court. In 1973, 54 percent of the youths referred to juvenile courts for offenses other than traffic or dependency were disposed of nonjudicially.[20] The remaining 46 percent (522,000) were adjudicated.

THE COST OF DELINQUENCY

One way that juvenile delinquency affects the United States is that it costs everybody money. A presidential commission in 1967 estimated that crime cost the public $815 million in loss of earnings, $3.932 billion in loss of property, and $2.036 billion in public and personal losses from other crimes. Illegal goods and services cost an additional $8.075 billion. The American taxpayer also footed the bill for a $4.212 billion annual program of law enforcement, judicial review, and corrections. Private costs for burglar alarms, security systems, insurance, and attorneys' fees reached $1.910 billion.[21] Figure 3.3 gives a graphic representation of the economic costs of crime.

Not all of these costs are directly related to juvenile delinquency, of course. The report giving these figures examined the costs of all crime, not just crime engaged in by juveniles. These costs cannot be separated. In over 75 percent of the offenses, no suspect is arrested; therefore the age of the offender is unknown. Indirectly most of these costs may be attributed to juvenile delinquency, however. While most

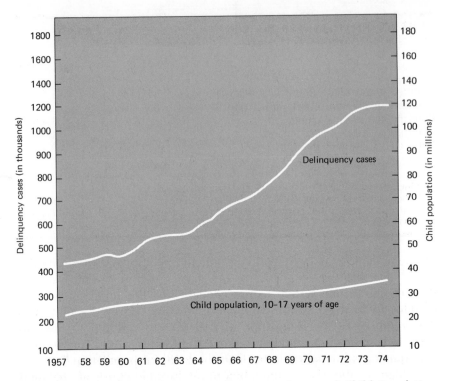

Figure 3.2 Trend in Juvenile Court Delinquency Cases and Child Population 10–17 Years of Age, 1957–1973

Source: Department of Health, Education, and Welfare, Office of Youth Development, *Juvenile Court Statistics, 1973* (Washington, D.C.: Government Printing Office, 1974, p. 9.

juvenile delinquents do not become criminals, most criminals began their careers as juvenile delinquents.

Because delinquency may be very financially costly to a society, we might expect that vast resources would be mobilized to rehabilitate juvenile offenders and prevent their return to delinquency. In 1971, however, less money was spent on the rehabilitation of youth than was spent on mechanical security devices and insurance to recover crime-related losses. Nearly half of the $456,474,000 spent on juvenile correctional institutions and detention facilities during that year was used to maintain security and retain custodial personnel.[22]

Other efforts to reduce crime and delinquency have been instituted to supplement the traditional system. The Omnibus Crime Control and Safe Streets Act (1968) specified a coordinated and intergovernmental approach to efforts to reduce crime and delinquency while improving the whole justice system. The primary responsibility for carrying out the provisions of the bill was vested in the state and local

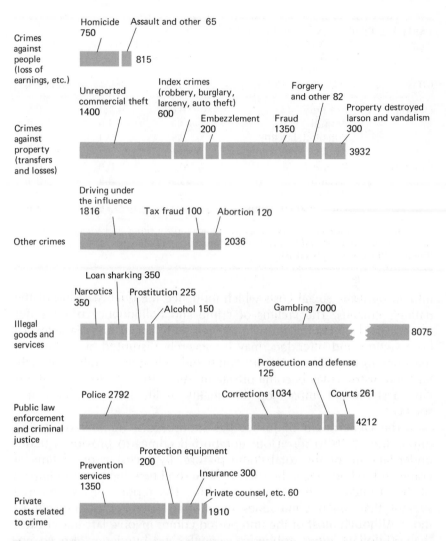

Figure 3.3 Economic Impact of Crime (in estimated millions of dollars)

Source: President's Commission on Law Enforcement and Administration of Justice, *The Challenge of Crime in a Free Society* (Washington, D.C.: Government Printing Office, 1967), p. 33.

governments. The governments formed State Planning Agencies to handle and coordinate the improvement of the justice system and administer federal grant funds provided through the Law Enforcement Assistance Administration. Appropriations for the Safe Streets Act have gradually increased so that it represented almost $12 billion, or almost 6 percent of all criminal justice expenditure, in 1972.

The economic cost of crime and justice does not fully describe the impact of crime and delinquency on a society. It does not take

TABLE 3.3 PERCENTAGE OF PERSONS
AGE 16 AND OVER VICTIMIZED BY PERSONAL CRIMES BY SEX, 1971

CITY	TYPE OF PERSONAL CRIME	TOTAL	MALE	FEMALE
Dayton	Robbery	0.8	1.1	0.5
	Assault	3.1	4.6	1.8
	Personal larceny	0.4	0.4	0.4
	All personal crimes	4.2	5.9	2.7
San Jose	Robbery	0.7	0.9	0.4
	Assault	3.2	4.5	2.1
	Personal larceny	0.3	0.4	0.2
	All personal crimes	4.1	5.8	2.6

Source: Law Enforcement Assistance Administration, *Crimes and Victims: A Report on the Dayton-San Jose Pilot Survey of Victimization* (Washington, D.C.: Government Printing Office, 1974), pp. 80–81.

into account the social costs which influence the quality of life of the nation's citizens. The victims of crime and delinquency often suffer physical and psychological pain as well as financial loss. Families, of both victims and offenders, may be severely disrupted as a result of reactions to the offense. Where crime and delinquency rates are high, fear and distrust may become prevalent. All of these factors and others have a significant impact on the quality of life for individuals in a society.

The Department of Justice has sponsored a number of studies during the 1970s to ferret out unreported crimes to provide a better understanding of the total crime picture. By focusing on victims of crime and delinquency, the surveys have shed new light on the impact of the problem for the American public. The reports of the research suggest that much crime goes unreported—perhaps 50 percent or more. Although most of the unreported crimes involve larcenies of less than 50 dollars, rapes, robberies, assaults, and burglaries also go unreported.

Preliminary surveys of Dayton and San Jose conducted in 1971 suggested that more than 4 percent of the population over age 16 were victimized by personal crimes during a one-year period (see Table 3.3). Furthermore, two out of very five households experienced some form of property crime (burglary, larceny, or auto theft) in a single year.[23] Victims sometimes observed the offenders in their crimes. Those reporting lone offenders judged that they were juveniles in one-third of all cases. More than half of the offender groups, however, were reported to be juveniles. Less than 10 percent of the observed offenses were carried out by females acting alone.[24]

Similar findings were reported in a survey of 13 cities (Boston, Buffalo, Cincinnati, Houston, Miami, Milwaukee, Minneapolis, New

Orleans, Oakland, Pittsburgh, San Diego, San Francisco, and Washington, D.C.).[25] The report of this survey suggests that some individuals are more likely than others to become victims of crime. Males are more often victims than females. Members of families earning less than $10,000 annually are more likely to become victims of assault. Moreover, middle- and upper-income families are most likely to be victims of theft, although some evidence suggests that personal larceny, in which the victim comes face to face with the aggressor, occurs more frequently to low-income individuals. Other research on the five largest cities tends to confirm these findings.[26]

Crime and delinquency directly touches the lives of a substantial percentage of the population each year. There are few among us who do not personally know a victim of crime. Our own experience, however, cannot adequately convey the losses suffered by the members of the American public in terms of time, money, physical suffering, and mental anguish.

CHARACTERISTICS OF THE JUVENILE OFFENDER

Although most juveniles admit to behavior that might result in adjudication as a delinquent, some youths are more likely than others to be officially labeled delinquent. Some authorities claim that these differences represent the seriousness of the delinquencies committed; others suggest that the differences are a result of bias in the handling of offenders through the juvenile justice system. Perhaps by examining the background characteristics of offenders we may be able to come to a better understanding of the nature of juvenile delinquency and the juvenile delinquent.

Age

Arrests of juveniles are not equally distributed among the different age groups. Arrests of children under age 10 are relatively infrequent— only about 4 percent of all juvenile arrests. Of course, juvenile offenses by children of this age are more likely to be handled informally and thus not to be reported in the official statistics. Arrests and official handling begin to increase as slightly older youths are considered. During 1975 arrests of 11- and 12-year-olds accounted for nearly 8 percent, while arrests of 13- and 14-year-olds accounted for 23 percent, of the total number of juvenile arrests in the United States. Older youths (ages 15 through 17) accounted for most of the arrests. The age distribution for juvenile arrests in 1975 is shown in Table 3.4.

Older juveniles spend a greater proportion of their time with peers away from the supervision of parents than do the younger juveniles. They have greater access to speedy and efficient means of transportation and relatively greater personal freedom than ever before. The pressures to succeed, to acquire material symbols of success, are firmly impressed upon older youths, and it is not surprising that they

TABLE 3.4 JUVENILE ARRESTS BY AGE, 1975

AGE	NUMBER OF ARRESTS	PERCENTAGE OF ALL JUVENILE ARRESTS
10 and under	79,160	3.8
11–12	159,210	7.7
13–14	477,836	23.0
15	409,297	19.7
16	478,886	23.0
17	474,070	22.8
Total under age 18	2,078,459	100.0

Source: Federal Bureau of Investigation, *Uniform Crime Reports, 1975* (Washington, D.C.: Government Printing Office, 1976), p. 188.

account for a major share of arrests for property theft in the United States.

Sex

Juvenile delinquency has traditionally been a predominantly male enterprise. Females are increasingly being included in the official statistics, however. In the past, the ratio of males to females arrested or referred to juvenile court has been relatively constant at four-to-one. However, between 1965 and 1973, the rates of referral for females increased much more rapidly than for males. Delinquency cases involving females more than doubled, while male cases increased only 52 percent.[27] By 1973, the ratio of males to females had narrowed to three-to-one.

Arrests of females are also increasing. Approximately 22 percent of all juvenile arrests in 1975 involved females. And the gap between male and female arrests is narrowing. The character of female delinquency is also changing. Formerly, overt aggressive or hostile offenses were believed to be male acts, and arrest statistics confirmed the contention. Females were more likely to engage in nonaggressive, private offenses. In recent years, females have increasingly engaged in activities that involve hostile behavior toward others. Table 3.5 suggests that females no longer victimize only themselves. Larceny-theft is the second most frequent offense for which juvenile girls are arrested. On the other hand, running away and "all other" offenses (which may involve promiscuity, incorrigibility, or other vague juvenile offenses) still contribute significantly to the female arrest rates.

It is not known whether the rise in female arrests reflects an increase in female delinquency or merely a greater willingness to handle females officially. Both may be contributing factors. Public opinion is increasingly willing to grant equality of the sexes in American society. It should not come as a surprise that equality is reflected

TABLE 3.5 ARRESTS OF PERSONS
UNDER 18 BY SEX AND TYPE OF OFFENSE, 1975

		MALE		FEMALE	
OFFENSE CHARGED	TOTAL ARRESTS UNDER 18	NUM-BER	PER-CENTAGE	NUM-BER	PER-CENTAGE
Criminal homicide	1,373	1,235	90	138	10
Robbery	40,796	37,763	93	3,033	07
Aggravated assault	30,858	25,966	84	4,892	16
Burglary	201,569	191,202	95	10,367	05
Larceny-theft	378,713	269,415	71	109,298	29
Vandalism	100,942	93,325	92	7,617	08
Disorderly conduct	101,060	84,159	83	16,901	17
Curfew and loitering	99,100	79,500	80	19,600	20
Runaways	158,460	67,894	43	90,566	57
All other, except traffic	225,222	178,923	79	46,299	21

Source: Derived from Federal Bureau of Investigation, *Uniform Crime Reports,
1975* (Washington, D.C.: Government Printing Office, 1976), p. 187.

in the commission of delinquent acts and the willingness to arrest
female offenders. Females are still more likely to be informally handled
by police and juvenile courts, but this differential treatment probably
accounts for only part of the difference in delinquency between males
and females.

Despite the increases in female delinquency, males still account
for the major share of juvenile offenses reported in the official statistics. This fact probably reflects the willingness of parents and other
adults to allow boys a great deal more freedom to move about un-
supervised in the community. The higher runaway rate for females
suggests that they are more likely to perceive family life as being
restrictive. As supervision of females becomes less strict, their delinquency rate may rise much higher.

Race and Nationality

The FBI's *Uniform Crime Reports* compare arrest data for several
racial and national groups ("negro," "white," Indian, Chinese, Japanese, and an "all other" category).[28] Anthropologists, sociologists, and
other social scientists suggest that the categories used may be artificial
distinctions and therefore of little value. As long as the public makes
these distinctions, however, they must be examined.

Blacks accounted for 22 percent of the arrests for persons under
the age of 18 during 1975; whites accounted for 76 percent; and the
other groups together accounted for 2 percent.[29] Since blacks make

up only about 12 percent of the United States population, the arrest rate for blacks appears disproportionately high. Furthermore, black youths appear to be disproportionately represented among those arrested for both violent and property crimes (see Table 3.6). These statistics should not be used to justify a belief in the violent nature of blacks, however. There is no evidence that delinquency or criminality is part of the biological heritage of any racial group either now or in the past.

Discrimination has contributed to the existence of a disproportionate number of blacks in the lower classes in American society. Despite the fact that the median income for the black family has been increasing, it is still considerably less than the median income for a comparable white family. In addition, the unemployment levels for black youths in the central cities have been near depression levels for years, leaving many youngsters with nothing to do but hang out on the streets during the summer months. Black youths are more likely to come from low-income families than white youths, and members of the lower-income categories tend to be overrepresented in the arrest statistics regardless of whether they are black or white.

The belief that members of minority groups commit more crimes often leads to increased attention and vigilance in their neighborhoods. The result is likely to be more arrests. The number of arrests may reflect not the greater frequency of crime but the intensified attention resulting from citizen attitudes and police policy. There may not be more crime even though the official arrest statistics show a greater number of arrests. If suburban police were as vigilant as urban police, the arrest rates in the suburbs might be as high as or higher than those in the inner cities. The police might, for example, set up roadblocks after a college or professional football game to locate drunken drivers.

The disproportionately high arrest rate for blacks is not explained by racial background. When income and migration are considered, the differences between black and white arrest rates are less striking. The best available evidence suggests that delinquency rates for blacks do not differ greatly from those of whites living under similar conditions.

Before immigration to the United States was restricted in 1924, and for a while after restriction, the delinquency problem was attributed to the children of foreign-born parents who had made their way to America. The Statue of Liberty read "give me your tired, your poor, your huddled masses, yearning to breathe free," but many Americans felt that they got thieves, delinquents, criminals, and radicals who were too free with the money and property of the "good" native American. Millions of people migrated from southern and eastern Europe to America from about 1880 to 1910. Some sought economic opportunity and the better life. They often settled in the developing large

TABLE 3.6 PERCENTAGE DISTRIBUTION OF ARRESTS OF PERSONS UNDER 18 by Race, 1975

OFFENSE CHARGED	WHITE	BLACK	INDIAN	CHINESE	JAPANESE	ALL OTHERS
VIOLENT CRIME[a]	45.7	52.4	0.6	0.1	0.1	1.1
PROPERTY CRIME[b]	71.3	26.6	0.7	0.1	0.1	1.1
Stolen property: buying, selling, possessing	70.1	28.5	0.4	0.1	0.1	0.8
Vandalism	86.0	12.8	0.5	—	—	0.6
Weapons: carrying, possessing, etc.	67.1	31.0	0.6	0.1	0.1	1.1
Liquor laws	95.1	2.5	1.7	—	0.1	0.6
Drunkenness	90.2	6.5	2.6	—	—	0.6
Disorderly conduct	77.2	21.6	0.7	—	—	0.5
Curfew and loitering	72.4	25.6	1.1	—	0.1	0.7
Runaways	87.8	10.1	1.2	—	0.1	0.9
All other offenses, except traffic	76.5	21.4	0.7	—	0.1	1.2

[a] Crime Index offenses, including murder, forcible rape, robbery, and aggravated assault.
[b] Crime Index offenses, including burglary, larceny, and auto theft.
Source: Federal Bureau of Investigation, *Uniform Crime Reports, 1975* (Washington, D.C.: Government Printing Office, 1976), p. 193.

cities; of course, many of the nationality groups were culturally different from the northern and western Europeans who had settled in the United States prior to this period. These differences, coupled with a belief in their tendencies to inherit criminality, contributed to calls for migration restriction. Quotas were set up in 1924 that discriminated against southern and eastern Europeans. There did not seem to be large numbers of the tired, the poor, and the huddled masses in the more industrialized northern sections of Europe, and immigration dropped off. A need still existed, however, for cheap labor in northern factories, and Southern rural blacks moved to the northern industrial cities to replace the immigrants.

The relationship between nationality and juvenile delinquency has never been fully documented. Statistics are often not collected on nationality even though some information can be obtained from state or municipal statistics. It has been necessary to separately study the delinquency of groups such as Japanese, Jews, and Puerto Ricans. Scattered evidence suggests that delinquency rates decline as each group obtains more education and middle-class occupational and social status. Many of the nationality groups, however, had cultural differences but not the added racial differences that compound the problem for blacks. It is interesting to note that poor Southern whites, or "hillbillies," have also faced many of the problems encountered by ethnic and racial groups upon moving to the central cities.

Social Class

Juvenile delinquency is found among individuals from all income, educational, and status levels. It is not clear whether the upper or lower classes produce more delinquency, but juveniles from the lower classes more frequently come in official contact with the juvenile justice system. Official statistics may overstate the proportions of all delinquency that can be attributed to the lower classes because of the undetected or hidden nature of middle- and upper-class delinquency. Differential detection may also help account for some of the reported difference in rates of delinquency.

A great deal of research has focused on the social status of juvenile offenders. Some researchers have used an ecological approach; others have used the individual case study method. Those using the ecological method locate poverty pockets within a city and compare the official crime rates there with the rates found in more stable, affluent areas. A number of studies taking this approach have suggested that delinquency is more prevalent in lower-class neighborhoods.[30] Other ecological studies suggest that social class is less important than instability in producing juvenile delinquency.[31]

Studies using the individual case as the unit of analysis have reported similar findings. Reiss and Rhodes, for example, report that more frequent and more serious delinquent behavior is found among lower-class youths.[32] For the most part, studies that seek to establish a relationship between social class and delinquency have relied heavily on official statistics. Critics have pointed out the possibility of bias in arrest and court statistics. Carter's study of juvenile dispositions in the San Francisco-Oakland area appears to confirm suspicions of differential handling. He found that individuals in upper-income areas were more likely to handle juvenile offenders informally, without police assistance. Furthermore, the rate of police referral to juvenile court was 10 percent lower for upper-income youths than for lower-income offenders.[33] A number of criminologists have used self-report studies to eliminate the biases of official statistics—with mixed results. These efforts have been met with skepticism and hostility by defenders of official statistics.[34] The question as to whether official statistics or self-reports provide a more adequate picture of juvenile delinquency remains unresolved.

MIDDLE-CLASS DELINQUENCY

Middle-class youths have been involved in a wide variety of delinquent activities. Drug use, sexual promiscuity, vandalism, and offenses involving automobiles are the most frequently reported activities.[35] There are some indications that middle-class delinquency is at least as frequent as lower-class delinquency.[36] Middle-class delinquencies, however, appear to be of a different type. Chilton reported that "children from low income areas are overrepresented for offenses involving permanent gain, personal injury to others, or what the police believe to be the threat of injury to property or people. Children from high income areas are more likely to come into court for property offenses that do not lead to personal gain, or for the violation of rules intended to control the driving, drinking, and late hours of teenagers."[37] Despite this trend, some very serious delinquent offenses are committed by middle-class youths.[38]

In spite of the prevalence of middle-class delinquency, official statistics continue to reveal that middle-class juveniles are less likely to be reported, arrested, referred to juvenile court, or placed in correctional institutions.[39] Middle-class parents and other interested adults prefer settling juvenile problems informally, without the aid of law enforcement officials. When middle-class juveniles are stopped by police, their demeanor and dress is likely to result in favorable disposition. In the relatively few cases where they are arrested and referred to court, placement in a juvenile correctional institution is infrequent. Juvenile judges are reluctant to remove a child from his home if it is unbroken and provides an environment conducive to reform.

UPPER-CLASS DELINQUENCY

There is little known about delinquency among the upper classes in American society, possibly because most criminologists are middle-class and encounter difficulties in gaining entrance to study the rich.

The upper classes are better able to protect their youth because of their secure social position. Violation of upper-class norms tends to be disapproved, and boarding schools, parents, relatives, and other people and institutions share a part of the burden of handling any delinquencies. Some youths who continue to cause their parents problems may be put into the hands of a psychiatrist, but they are rarely handled by the police.

LOWER-CLASS DELINQUENCY

As Thio points out, there has been more research done on the lower class than on any other social class, and there is therefore more information available on them.[40] A number of studies suggest that there is a relationship between lower-class membership and delinquency. Lower-class juveniles are more likely to commit the offenses that are of greatest concern to the average citizen. Theft, assault, and other serious crimes have resulted in high rates of arrest for lower-class youths. Some studies suggest that the difference between the types of delinquencies committed by lower-class and middle-class boys reflects the values supported by their respective cultures. Fannin and Clinard report that there appears to be a difference between the middle- and lower-class boys in their conception of themselves as males. The lower-class boys believe that they are "tougher, more powerful, fierce, fearless, and dangerous" than middle-class delinquent boys. Middle-class boys describe themselves as "more loyal, clever, smart, smooth and bad." These differences in attitude toward themselves are apparently reflected in delinquent behavior, with the lower-class boys involved in more physical violence, toughness, and callousness toward females.[41] Of course, lower-class juveniles may also engage in activities popular among middle-class youths. Truancy, the use of drugs and alcohol, and other social-based delinquencies are found in the lower-class culture.

Studies of lower-class delinquency have suggested that lower-class youths are more deeply involved in their delinquencies. Gang studies, which focus primarily on lower-class youths, provide a view that lower-class youths are more organized in their crimes than other classes.[42] Gang members are presented as tough individuals whose lives revolve around the activities of the gang. Little attention is generally given to other social groups within which the juvenile spends a good portion of his time.

There have been suggestions that lower-class juveniles are more likely to appear in juvenile courts or have delinquency records than middle-class youngsters who engage in similar activities. A great deal of discretion is given to public officials throughout the juvenile justice system. Since the majority of these authorities come from middle-class backgrounds, the official statistics may reflect middle-class values in the decision-making process. Judged by these standards, many lower-class youths may not measure up. The result is likely to be official handling.

Place of Residence

The spatial patterning of juvenile delinquency has long been an area of study for sociologists. The earliest comprehensive studies to discover where delinquents live was conducted by Clifford Shaw during the 1920s.[43] Using official court and police statistics, Shaw and his associates mapped the concentration of delinquency in Chicago. They found that the highest delinquency rates were concentrated near the center of the city and that the rates decreased progressively out from the center, reaching a low near the outer boundaries of the city.[44] Studies of 20 other American cities confirmed this spatial patterning.[45] Some studies have challenged the ability of spatial location to predict delinquency rates. Critics of the ecological school claim that housing conditions, education, social class, race, and other factors may be more important.

The FBI's *Uniform Crime Reports* collect data from all types of geographic areas in the United States. These reports give a breakdown of arrests of juveniles for urban, suburban, and rural areas. Some of these data are shown in Table 3.7. It appears from the arrest statistics that the nature of delinquency does not greatly differ from one type of geographic location to another. The percentages of arrests for each of the types of offense are about the same in all three areas. Property crime, for example, accounts for 36 percent of all juvenile arrests in cities, 33 percent in suburbs, and 31 percent in rural areas. Curfew violations account for a greater percentage of arrests in urban areas than in rural areas. This may be explained by the fact that curfews are more likely to be imposed in urban areas. Rural youths are also more likely to be arrested for running away and violating liquor laws.

URBAN DELINQUENCY

Juvenile delinquency is most highly visible in the cities. Great concentrations of people limit the privacy of the individual and increase the possibility that activities will be monitored or detected by others. There is a greater likelihood that a single individual's behavior might be injurious or perceived as potentially injurious to others. The availability of cartable resources is greater in the cities than in rural areas. It is not unreasonable to expect that more property crimes will be committed where property is more available. Large concentrations of people result in a greater number of impersonal relationships and perhaps a greater number of crimes against persons. The FBI's arrest statistics do indicate that greater numbers of crimes and delinquencies are committed in cities. However, the nature of these crimes does not differ significantly from those committed in the suburbs and rural areas.

TABLE 3.7 NUMBER AND PERCENTAGES OF ARRESTS
BY GEOGRAPHIC AREA AND TYPE OF OFFENSE, 1975

	GEOGRAPHIC AREA					
TYPE OF CRIME	CITY	PER-CENT-AGE	SUB-URBAN	PER-CENT-AGE	RURAL	PER-CENT-AGE
VIOLENT CRIME[a]	74,505	4	20,715	3	2,517	2
PROPERTY CRIME[b]	619,489	36	251,110	33	33,940	31
Stolen property: buying, receiving, possessing	27,971	2	13,005	2	1,176	1
Vandalism	95,669	5	51,495	7	6,076	6
Weapons: carrying, possessing, etc.	18,990	1	7,033	1	546	1
Liquor laws	85,911	5	48,662	6	9,711	9
Drunkenness	34,020	2	14,241	2	3,690	3
Disorderly conduct	105,485	6	49,214	7	3,350	3
Curfew and loitering	105,175	6	33,317	4	2,278	2
Runaways	136,907	8	75,839	10	17,783	16
All other offenses, except traffic	216,776	12	92,083	12	13,244	12
Other categories	219,314	13	97,333	13	14,021	13
Total	1,740,212	100	754,047	100	108,332	100[c]

[a] Crime Index offenses, including murder, forcible rape, robbery, and aggravated assault.
[b] Crime Index offenses, including burglary, larceny, and auto theft.
[c] Percentages do not add up to total due to rounding off.
Source: Federal Bureau of Investigation, *Uniform Crime Reports, 1975* (Washington, D.C.: Government Printing Office, 1976), tables 42, 48, and 53.

RURAL DELINQUENCY

The city has traditionally been seen as the source of crime and delinquency, vice, disease, prostitution, and all that was considered bad. The land, the farm, or rural small-town America was viewed as the best place for raising children. If the child could only grow up on a few acres then he could be taught the value of work, family stability, land, and money. Rural life was believed to contribute to the formation of settled, stable individuals with a belief in, and acceptance of, the controls necessary for ordered and settled community life. These beliefs have become deeply embedded in our culture.[46] Thoreau extolled the virtues of rural life in *Walden*; Mark Twain and many other writers continued the tradition. More modern writers, such as B. F. Skinner in *Walden Two*, have continued the opposition to the American city and the glorification of rural or small-town life. The desire for this type of life is still strong, and many people want a few acres and independence or escape from the pressures of big-city life. The problem is that these beliefs have allowed Americans to retreat from the task of facing the problems of cities and building adequate patterns of urban life.

The small towns in America often have ugly, deteriorated areas with some of the poorest housing in the nation. Small-town and rural poverty and the monotony and close association between the haves and have-nots have led some youths to leave rural areas for the opportunity of the city. The automobile has permitted many rural and small-town youths to escape the confines of their existence for the greater availability of recreational and other facilities in the larger towns and cities. The youths are often less willing to settle in rural areas as they get older and leave home.

Evidence suggests that delinquency rates have been lower in rural areas in both America and Europe.[47] Rural areas, however, have been changing, giving the urban areas greater and greater influence and control. Towns have grown larger, and fewer and fewer people have remained on the farm, even though many people have sought a few acres and a house on the edge of a town or in a suburban tract. Mass communications helped lead to the reduction in the differences between urban and rural areas as well as to the standardization of American culture. One piece of evidence that suggests standardization is the fact that the nature of crime and delinquency is nearly the same from one area to another (see Table 3.7).

These changes have led to a reduction in the differences between urban and rural areas in terms of delinquency rates. Rural and suburban delinquency appears to be growing faster than urban delinquency. The delinquency rates rise from the rural hinterland to a city of 50,000 or more and then tend to level off.[48] The rates of delinquency are lower in agricultural counties but higher in industrial and mining counties in the United States.

SUBURBAN DELINQUENCY

The arrest rate in suburban areas is increasing faster than in urban areas but not as fast as in rural areas. The suburbs, which are frequently considered havens for the middle class seeking an escape from big-city problems, are not free of delinquency. Offenses resulting in the highest rates of arrest for persons under 18 include larceny-theft and other property crimes, but assault and violent crimes are relatively common. Vandalism, sex offenses, drug violations, liquor violations, disorderly conduct, suspicion, running away from home, and curfew violations are also common offenses.

Youngsters from suburban areas are more likely than central city youths to be released to parents, given a lecture, and then released and handled informally by both the police and courts when their delinquent acts are detected. Even though the arrest rates are lower for suburban youth in comparison to city youth, the delinquency rate may not be markedly different if undetected delinquency or informal handling is considered.

The Individual Delinquent

The individual delinquent is a youth who has been adjudicated delinquent by a juvenile court. The average delinquent or record offender, according to official statistics, is a male between the ages of 15 and 17. He is most likely to live in an urban area and come from a lower-class, minority-group background.

It is not certain what causes delinquency or what motivates the delinquent offender. A number of theories have been set forth; however, none has been accepted as the final and exclusive perspective from which delinquency must be approached. Several of the recognized approaches are discussed in later chapters.

Although statistics are couched in terms of individual cases, it is believed that individual delinquency (acts committed by a single youth, without aid or companionship) is relatively rare. Estimates suggest that only approximately 15 percent of all delinquent acts are the work of a single youth. The isolated delinquent is limited in the number and types of delinquency he can carry out; much delinquency requires coordinated effort by several individuals for successful completion.

There has been little research conducted on truly individual delinquency. Therefore it is impossible to do little more than speculate on its nature. We might suggest that individual delinquency may be found in all social classes; however, research is needed even on this very simple question.

JUVENILE DELINQUENCY IN OTHER COUNTRIES

Juvenile delinquency is not a uniquely American phenomenon. Available data suggest that juvenile delinquency is a source of concern in many nations. Studies conducted under the auspices of the United Nations reveal that most European countries have correctional institutions for youths.[49] In Asia and the Far East, special legal provisions for juveniles are in evidence even where juvenile justice systems have not been fully developed or implemented.[50] Countries of the Middle East and Near East recognize the special problem of youth in the general criminal codes.[51] United Nations reports also cite special delinquency prevention programs in selected African nations and the Soviet Union.[52] It is clear that juvenile delinquency is a worldwide phenomenon.

Not only is delinquency present worldwide, but recent reports indicate that it is increasing.[53] There is some suggestion that delinquency is "more widespread, more organized and more serious in form in the United States than any place else."[54] However, the available cross-cultural literature is not at present comprehensive enough to support more than conjecture on this point. Evidence to support such a conclusion may involve more than the data-gathering operations used in recent cross-cultural research.

Problems of Cross-cultural Comparisons

Comparison of delinquency cross-culturally involves a number of difficulties. It is not possible directly to compare juvenile delinquency rates because of differing concepts of juvenile delinquency, different age limits, and the differences in the manner in which juvenile offenders are handled. Cross-cultural studies are confronted with many of the same problems encountered in studies that attempt to generalize across the United States.

Concepts of delinquency vary from one country to another. Many of the problems of American youth are unheard of in other countries. Auto theft is improbable where autos are rare; drug busts are not realistic expectations where drugs are unavailable. Truancy is no cause for alarm where educational institutions have not been established. What constitutes juvenile misbehavior will vary from place to place along with the material aspects of the culture. Agricultural societies will define delinquency in a different manner than will industrial societies.

Different age limits will obscure the results of cross-cultural studies. When the juvenile is legally defined in the law, the upper age limit varies. Many countries have set an upper age limit of 18; however, age limits may vary from as low as 15 to as high as 20 or 21 in some countries. Criteria for identifying youths, furthermore, are not always limited to age. Maturity, tradition, education, and occupational status have also been used as determinants.[55] The concept of youth may vary over the course of time, according to geographic location within a country, and with other special circumstances. In order to achieve adequate comparisons, it is essential that a uniform set of limits be applied cross-culturally. Unfortunately, according to authorities at the United Nations, "it appears unfeasible and inappropriate to establish at the international level a single applicable set of limits to identify the youth."[56]

Methods of handling misbehaving youth have not been standardized cross-culturally. The variation in this aspect of delinquency is very great. In some areas, little official attention is given youthful misconduct. In simple tribal societies children are generally under the supervision of family members, and any disapproved behavior is handled within the family unit. In other areas, highly formalized and complex systems have been developed to handle all aspects of juvenile misbehavior, from definition to release of adjudicated and confined youth.

It appears that the major barriers to cross-cultural comparison of juvenile delinquency lie in the wide variations in culture from country to country. The evidence suggests that the spread of modernization, affluence, and industrialization will continue to lessen cultural differences and make comparison a realistic goal.[57] Until that time, however, it is not valid to assume that juvenile misbehavior is a uniquely urban phenomenon. The fact that rural areas are less likely to formally institute agencies for special treatment of youths does not make their misbehavior less damaging to a society. Until universal comparison becomes a reality, we will have to be content with descriptive analyses of single societies or comparisons of similar cultures.

THE IMPACT OF DELINQUENCY IN PERSPECTIVE

Statistics are readily available on aspects of juvenile delinquency from official governmental agencies such as the FBI and LEAA. These statistics often reflect official handling, but there are many delinquent activities that go unreported and undetected. In addition, many detected delinquent acts are handled unofficially and informally by police, parents, shopkeepers, teachers, and other adults. Thus despite the impressive statistical reports from governmental agencies, the full extent of delinquency is not known. Certainly, the official reports do not tell the full story and may grossly underestimate the extent and nature of the problem.

Our analysis of delinquency and ideas about delinquency is often influenced by reports from agencies that are limited in terms of source of data and other factors. On the other hand, if interest centers on reported and officially handled delinquency cases, the official statistics shed considerable light on juvenile delinquency. In this way official statistics provide an indispensable tool for the analysis of juvenile delinquency.

Juvenile delinquency has a tremendous impact on American society. Financial losses run into the billions of dollars. Social and psychological costs cannot be measured, but there is reason to believe that delinquency is equally burdensome in these areas. Unfortunately, efforts to deal with delinquency have focused on mechanical detection systems, judicial and policing agencies, and insurance to recover losses rather than on the correction and rehabilitation of youths.

Delinquency statistics give us some indication of who is likely to be arrested or adjudicated delinquent; however, they have not been systematically used to lessen the problem of delinquency in American society.

NOTES
[1] Gilbert Geis, "Statistics Concerning Race and Crime," Crime and Delinquency 11 (April 1965): 142–150.

[2] Law Enforcement Assistance Administration, Sourcebook of Criminal Justice Statistics, 1974 (Washington, D.C.: Government Printing Office, 1975).

[3] Federal Bureau of Investigation, Uniform Crime Reports, 1975 (Washington, D.C.: Governing Printing Office, 1976).

[4] Chapter 12 provides a discussion of the influences of these factors on arrest.

[5] Department of Health, Education, and Welfare, Office of Youth Development, *Juvenile Court Statistics, 1968* (Washington, D.C.: Government Printing Office, 1970).

[6] Department of Health, Education, and Welfare, Office of Youth Development, *Juvenile Court Statistics, 1973* (Washington, D.C.: Government Printing Office, 1974).

[7] *Ibid.*

[8] *Sourcebook of Criminal Justice Statistics, 1974, op. cit.*

[9] Illinois Department of Corrections, Juvenile Division, *Semi-annual Statistical Summary, 1974,* prepared by Garland A. Kingery, Judie Egelhoff, and Rick Nehoff (Springfield, 1974).

[10] Stephen Schafer and Richard D. Knudten, *Juvenile Delinquency* (New York: Random House, 1970), p. 20.

[11] President's Commission on Law Enforcement and Administration of Justice, *The Challenge of Crime in a Free Society* (Washington, D.C.: Government Printing Office, 1967), p. 55.

[12] *Juvenile Court Statistics, 1973, op. cit.,* p. 1.

[13] President's Commission, *op. cit.,* p. 55, and *Uniform Crime Reports, 1975, op. cit.,* p. 119.

[14] President's Commission on Law Enforcement and Administration of Justice, *Task Force Report: Juvenile Delinquency and Youth Crime* (Washington, D.C.: Government Printing Office, 1967), p. 14.

[15] *Uniform Crime Reports, 1975, op. cit.,* pp. 188–189.

[16] *Ibid.*

[17] *Ibid.*

[18] *Juvenile Court Statistics, 1973, op. cit.*

[19] *Ibid.*

[20] *Ibid.*

[21] President's Commission, *The Challenge of Crime in a Free Society, op. cit.,* p. 33.

[22] Law Enforcement Assistance Administration, *Children in Custody: A Report on the Juvenile Detention and Correctional Facility Census of 1971* (Washington, D.C.: Government Printing Office, 1974), p. 54.

[23] Law Enforcement Assistance Administration, *Crimes and Victims: A Report on the Dayton-San Jose Pilot Survey of Victimization* (Washington, D.C.: Government Printing Office, 1974), p. 22.

[24] *Ibid.,* p. 25.

[25] Law Enforcement Assistance Administration, *Criminal Victimization in Thirteen American Cities* (Washington, D.C.: Government Printing Office, 1975).

[26] Law Enforcement Assistance Administration, *Criminal Victimization in Five Major Cities* (Washington, D.C.: Government Printing Office, 1975).

[27] *Juvenile Court Statistics, 1973, op. cit.*

[28] *Uniform Crime Reports, 1975, op. cit.*

[29] *Ibid.,* p. 193.

[30] Clifford Shaw and Henry McKay, *Juvenile Delinquency and Urban Areas* (Chicago: University of Chicago Press, 1942); Karl Schuessler, "Components of Variation in City Crime Rates," *Social Problems* 9 (spring 1962): 314–323; Roland Chilton, "Delinquency Area Research in Baltimore, Detroit and Indianapolis," *American Sociological Review* 29 (February 1964): 71–83; O. Galle, "Population Density and Pathology: What Are the Relations for Man?" *Science* 176 (April 1972): 23–30.

[31] Bernard Lander, *Toward an Understanding of Juvenile Delinquency*

(New York: Columbia University Press, 1954); David Bordua, "Juvenile Delinquency and Anomie: An Attempt at Replication," *Social Problems* 6 (winter 1958): 230–238; Kenneth Polk, "Juvenile Delinquency and Social Areas," *Social Problems* 5 (winter 1957): 214–217.

[32] Albert J. Reiss, Jr., and Albert Lewis Rhodes, "The Distribution of Delinquency in the Social Class Structure," *American Sociological Review* 26 (October 1961): 732.

[33] Robert Carter, *Middle Class Delinquency: An Experiment in Community Control* (Berkeley School of Criminology, University of California Press, 1968).

[34] See Gwynn Nettler, *Explaining Crime* (New York: McGraw-Hill, 1974), pp. 62–97, for a discussion of the perceived weaknesses of self-report studies.

[35] Ralph England, "A Theory of Middle Class Juvenile Delinquency," *Journal of Criminal Law, Criminology and Police Science* 50 (April 1960): 535–540; John P. Clark and Eugene Wenninger, "Social Class and Area as Correlates of Illegal Behavior Among Juveniles," *American Sociological Review* 8 (February 1973): 1–12; Roland J. Chilton, "Middle Class Delinquency and Specific Offense Analysis," in *Middle Class Juvenile Delinquency*, ed. Edmund W. Vaz (New York: Harper & Row, 1967), pp. 91–100; Edmund W. Vaz, *Middle Class Juvenile Delinquency* (New York: Harper & Row, 1967), pp. 131–137; David Loth, *Crime in the Suburbs* (New York: Morrow, 1967).

[36] LaMar T. Emprey and Maynard L. Erickson, "Hidden Delinquency and Social Status," *Social Forces* 44 (June 1966): 546–554; England, *op. cit.*, pp. 535–540; Clark and Wenninger, *op. cit.*, pp. 826–834.

[37] Chilton, *op. cit.*, p. 96.

[38] Fred J. Stanley, "Middle Class Delinquency as a Social Problem," *Sociology and Social Research* 51 (January 1967): 185–198; LaMar T. Emprey and Maynard L. Erickson, *Hidden Delinquency: Evidence on Old Issues* (Provo, Utah: Brigham Young University, 1965).

[39] Chilton, *op. cit.*; Carter, *op. cit.*; William J. Chambliss, "The Saints and the Rough Necks," *Society* 11 (December 1973): 24–31.

[40] Alex Thio, "Class Bias in the Sociology of Deviance," *American Sociologist* 8 (February 1973): 1–12.

[41] See Leon F. Fannin and Marshall B. Clinard, "Differences in the Conception of Self as a Male Among Lower and Middle Class Delinquents," *Social Problems* 13 (fall 1965): 205–214.

[42] Donald R. Cressey, "Organized Crime and Inner-City Youth," *Crime and Delinquency* 16 (April 1970): 129–138; Leon Jansyn, "Solidarity and Delinquency in a Street Corner Group," *American Sociological Review* 31 (October 1966): 600–614; James F. Short, Jr., and Fred L. Strodtbeck, *Group Process and Gang Delinquency* (Chicago: University of Chicago Press, 1974).

[43] Clifford Shaw, Frederick M. Zorbaugh, Henry D. McKay, and Leonard Cottrell, "The Juvenile Delinquent," in *The Illinois Crime Survey*, compiled by Illinois Association of Criminal Justice (Springfield, 1929). Less sophisticated and systematic studies were conducted earlier by Sophonesha P. Breckenridge and Edith Abbott, *The Delinquent Child and the Home* (New York: Random House, 1912).

[44] Clifford R. Shaw and Henry D. McKay, *Juvenile Delinquency and Urban Areas* (Chicago: University of Chicago Press, 1942).

[45] *Ibid.*

[46] Morton White and Lucia White, *The Intellectual versus the City* (Cambridge, Mass.: Harvard University Press, 1962).

[47] Marshall B. Clinard, *Sociology of Deviant Behavior* (New York: Holt, Rinehart and Winston, 1957), pp. 68–76.

⁴⁸ Paul Wiers, *Economic Factors in Michigan Delinquency* (New York: Columbia University Press, 1944), pp. 17–18.

⁴⁹ United Nations, Bureau of Social Affairs, Department of Economic and Social Affairs, *The Prevention of Juvenile Delinquency in Selected European Countries* (New York: Columbia University Press, 1955).

⁵⁰ United Nations, Division of Social Welfare, Department of Social Affairs, *Comparative Survey on Juvenile Delinquency: Asia and the Far East* (New York: Columbia University Press, 1953).

⁵¹ *Ibid.*

⁵² United Nations, International Labor Organization, Third United Nations Congress on the Prevention of Crime and the Treatment of Offenders, *Special Preventive and Treatment Measures for Young Adults* (New York, 1965).

⁵³ See United Nations, International Labor Organization, Third United Nations Congress on the Prevention of Crime and the Treatment of Offenders, *The Role of Vocational Guidance, Training, Employment Opportunity and Work in Youth Adjustment and the Prevention of Juvenile Delinquency* (New York, 1965); also T. C. N. Gibbins and R. H. Ahrenfeldt, *Cultural Factors in Delinquency* (Philadelphia: Lippincott, 1966); Toby Jackson, "Affluence and Adolescent Crime," in President's Commission, *Task Force Report, op. cit.*; Ruth Shonle Cavan and Jordan T. Cavan, *Delinquency and Crime: Cross-cultural Perspectives* (Philadelphia: Lippincott, 1968); in addition, see Toby Jackson, "The Prospects for Reducing Delinquency Rates in Industrial Society," *Federal Probation* 27 (December 1963); E. Jackson Bauer, "The Trend of Juvenile Offenders in the Netherlands and the United States," *Journal of Criminal Law, Criminology and Police Science* 55 (September 1964): pp. 359–369.

⁵⁴ Don C. Gibbons, *op. cit.*, p. 219.

⁵⁵ *Special Preventive and Treatment Measures for Young Adults, op. cit.*

⁵⁶ *Ibid.*, p. 2.

⁵⁷ Cavan and Cavan, *op. cit.*

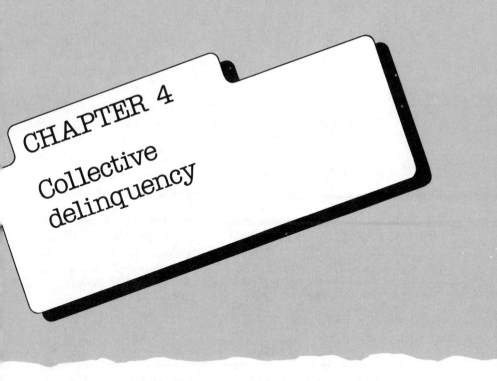

CHAPTER 4
Collective delinquency

The popular conception of the juvenile offender as a lone, asocial individual who carries out his delinquent activities without aid does not represent the norm. Statistics suggest that from 60 to 90 percent of the offenses committed by juveniles can be attributed to groups.[1] Reference to collective delinquency calls up visions of large, violent, and well-organized gangs; however, group delinquency may take a variety of forms. The clique, composed of a small number of youngsters, is the most common pattern. Even where involved youth are members of organized gangs, delinquent activities are most frequently carried out in groups of two or three. Few delinquencies can be successfully carried out by larger groups, since the likelihood of discovery increases with the size of the group.

Older juveniles, who make up the group that accounts for the greatest number of delinquent acts, are particularly susceptible to peer influence. In their study of 102 delinquent boys in New York City, Craig and Budd found that older boys are more likely than younger ones to commit serious offenses, to repeat delinquent behavior, and to have companions in delinquency.[2] Of the delinquent boys under 14 years of age, only 25 percent had companions in their delinquent acts; among the boys aged 14 to 16, however, 48 percent had companions. The type of offense is also correlated with group delinquency. Ninety-one percent of the more serious offenses committed by the juveniles in the study were carried out with companions. Only 28 percent of the minor offenses involved group participation.

Collective delinquency is not an isolated phenomenon. Gangs have been a source of concern in widely scattered areas of the world. They are found not only in Western industrialized nations but are reported in Communist countries, the Far East, and developing countries such as Ghana and Kenya.[3] Collective delinquency has become a problem of major proportions and as such it must be included in the study of juvenile delinquency.

THE INFLUENCE OF PEERS

Every society differentiates between, and confers status on, individuals on the basis of age. From early childhood, nearly all youngsters are members of a peer group which occupies a large proportion of their free time. The peer group is an informal network of individuals of similar age, and generally the same sex who share common interests and experiences. It is usually formed spontaneously in areas where children readily meet and interact. Some peer groups arise in the area of residence—usually the home block—around ties of kinship, family friendship, and neighborhood contacts. Others form around the school, usually in the homeroom or on the playground and among children who participate in organized and supervised activities together. Peers are, then, persons with whom an individual shares common problems and experiences. For a child, it means another child with whom he can associate on terms of equal status. Because its members can readily identify with each other, communication is very effective in the peer group. Its role in the development of the norms and values of the individual members is readily apparent. The juvenile peer group is a major agency for producing conformity. The years of its greatest impact are those of adolescence, between ages 13 and 18.

The criteria for membership in the juvenile peer group not only define the collective but also distinguish outsiders. The juvenile peer group is more than an association of equals; it is also a grouping from which the adult is assigned alien status. Identification with adults emphasizes the child's dependent status, whereas affiliation with peers suggests that the youth is an individual in his own right. To some extent, every adolescent peer group teaches its members some kinds of deviance, since variance from the standards of parents, teachers, and the adult establishment is integral to establishing an independent identity.

JUVENILE COLLECTIVES

A great number of efforts are directed to channeling the energies of youth into socially approved activities. Generally this involves parental approval of associates and provision for adult-supervised activities. However, strict parental control of children is difficult, if not impossible, to accomplish in highly urbanized societies such as the United States. Children and parents spend a large portion of their waking

hours outside the home in schools, at work, or elsewhere. As a result, urban children can organize themselves without the consent, and with only the partial knowledge, of parents.

The great majority of peer groups are self-governing, unaffiliated friendship groups. That is, they are not formally organized and sponsored by adults. They rarely are formed for the express purpose of pursuing delinquent activities. However, the desire of adolescent youths to establish their independence from parental control may lead to activities that are viewed as delinquent by the society at large.

Not all potentially delinquent collectives have high visibility or stability. Although we are generally predisposed to believe that collective delinquency is the exclusive territory of the urban ghetto gang, other juvenile collectives may contribute a substantial number of delinquent acts. Cliques, ad hoc collectives, and confederations share responsibility with the traditional gang for the majority of juvenile offenses.

CLIQUES

Most peer groups are small and loosely organized. They meet to discuss problems, make plans for entertainment, or just "hang around." They often have favorite meeting places and favorite activities to occupy their time. We generally hesitate to call these innocent gatherings gangs. Their major concerns are socially approved activities, and they are therefore not considered harmful. Nevertheless, these collectivities may occasionally engage in delinquent behavior. Their parties may involve underage drinking or pill popping or serve as a launching pad for premarital sexual activities disapproved of by parents. Peers sometimes encourage extraordinary behavior. Street racing and other daring activities promote group solidarity.

Small, loosely organized groups do not have high visibility. When these small groups unite with other groups, however, visibility increases, as does public concern. When the group reaches an optimum size, it is commonly referred to as a gang. There is little agreement on the magic number of members required to make a gang. However, we will suggest the arbitrary figure of ten individuals. In order for a group of this size to constitute an informal friendship group, 45 primary relations must be maintained by the members without significant conflict, which might result in the withdrawal of individual members from the group.

Size is not the only defining characteristic of the gang, however. Structure and organization are also important considerations in distinguishing between the traditional conception of the gang and other juvenile collectives.

AD HOC COLLECTIVES

Large juvenile gangs are often formed by the ad hoc cooperation of smaller cliques. One or more members of a clique frequently have ties with members of another small group. When aid is needed or a larger number of individuals is required for planned activities, the individual may call on his friends from other groups. Once the planned activity is completed, the groups involved may go their separate ways. In this ad hoc collective, norms are not highly elaborated nor roles fully defined.

CONFEDERATIONS

Sometimes cliques make long-term agreements for cooperation. Where the collective consists of a loose alliance of small cliques, group loyalty is vested primarily in the clique. Most activities are carried out within the clique, and a joint effort is initiated only when conditions arise that are specified in the joint pact. Several small cliques, for example, may agree to join forces when one of the groups is challenged by an "alien" group. Norms are elaborated for joint pursuits, and activity-related roles are loosely defined. Alliances are beneficial for the small groups involved. They widen the scope of activity available to each small group and increase their power. Although each group involved has its own leader, a single core leader emerges when collective activities are pursued.

THE TRADITIONAL GANG

The traditional gang is distinguished from other juvenile collectives by its structure and organization. It is not a collection of small groups but rather a single distinguishable unit. While its members may have favorites within the gang, their primary loyalty is to the group as a whole. Gang norms are highly elaborate and cover a wide range of behaviors. In fact, they might be perceived as a subculture, since they cover almost all aspects of the members' lives. Roles are defined for each of the members and are ranked according to their importance for maintaining the group.

Unlike the clique, the gang is not dependent upon individual personalities. The members of a clique interact on an informal basis. Each individual is an integral part of the group and is not readily replaceable; because all members interact on the basis of approximately equal rank, personality is the only distinguishing characteristic of each member. Where a group structure is highly elaborated, as in the traditional gang, distinctions of rank become more important than personality.

Gangs are generally larger than informal cliques. However, size is not an important feature in distinguishing the gang from ad hoc collectives or confederations. Even where gang structures are highly elaborated, their membership rarely exceeds 25 same-sex members, and the size fluctuates over time.[4]

Gang Structure

Traditionally, gangs have been almost exclusively a male prerogative. Few unaffiliated female gangs have been organized. In the most tightly structured gangs, a hierarchical and autocratic structure prevails. The organization of a gang generally calls for a leader, an inner circle, the rank-and-file members, and hangers-on. The gang leader is seldom elected. Nor is the office filled by force; the neighborhood "tough" is rarely given this status. The leader is, on the contrary, generally an individual with an active imagination who can suggest new and interesting things to do. He generally has good relations with functional leaders in the inner circle. The identity of the leader is not always apparent to outsiders. Communication and negotiations with outsiders are often carried out by members or lieutenants in the inner circle and not by the leader.[5]

Closely associated with the leader is a core group of individuals who take on tasks that provide planning, coordination, and unity for the group. In a well-organized conflict gang, the war counselor is a prominent member of the inner circle. It is his job to set dates and locations for confrontations with hostile gangs. He plans strategy, oversees weapon procural, and negotiates with rival gangs. In some gangs, the war counselor may have a "light-up" man or "armorer" who is in charge of the cache of weapons between "rumbles," and he dispatches them prior to conflicts. The inner circle might also include a "vice-president" who serves as a back-up man for the leader, providing advice and acting in the leader's absence.

Other intimates are also members of the leader's clique or close friendship circle. A "goat" is frequently admitted to the circle to provide tension release and protection. He is recruited for his loyalty and slow wit to be sacrificed or used as a decoy in encounters with the police. A clown may also be allowed a place in the circle; his irresponsible behavior is tolerated because of the humor he contributes. On the fringe of the core group is often found the membership committee—a group of individuals who may have had difficulty gaining membership themselves—which sets admission requirements and initiation ceremonies for new members, subject to the approval of the leader or the inner circle.

The rank-and-file members are those who can be counted on to join in gang-organized activities but who do not occupy positions of leadership. They are bound by the gang code established by the inner group. According to the code, it may be acceptable to steal or commit other offenses against outsiders, but to "rat" or "squeal" on each other is a serious violation. Group members are expected to be honest and open in intragroup dealings; concealment of personal matters is generally condemned. Although the code emphasizes a sharing of resources, the constant "moocher" is subject to strong sanctions.[6]

Leaders and the inner circle use several techniques to keep the rank and file under control and accomplish the goals of the gang. The threat of punishment is particularly effective in conflict gangs, whereas ridicule and praise are more commonly used in other types of gangs. Adherence to the gang code and cooperation with members of the inner circle is often perceived as a mechanism for achieving social mobility in the gang.

Fringe members are those individuals who participate intermittently in gang activities. They may be willing to add their numbers to complete an athletic team, attend parties, or join rap sessions, but they may draw the line at criminal or violent activity. As marginal members, they do not generally attain high prestige within the group. However, they are unlikely to break the gang code or give anybody trouble.

Relations between gang members are characterized by a number of conventions, as are relations within more conventional groups. Norms may be highly elaborated with accompanying sanctions for noncompliance. From the perspective of the gang culture, its members' behavior is highly conformist. The gang, like all social groups, tends to develop its own rules by which it seeks to control the members. It tends to negatively evaluate those who violate its rules and views with approval those who are loyal and conforming. While gang members may appear nonconformist in relation to the dominant culture, their behavior is highly regulated and conformist within their subcultural context.

STABILITY

Discussions of the gang structure suggest that gangs are tightly organized and stable. While this may be the case for a small portion of gangs, a fluid unstable quality is characteristic of most gangs. Individual members are constantly joining and leaving, and entire gangs may dissolve. Members of the gang may move out of the area, enter military service, marry, or go to jail. Others may simply outgrow the gang, move up to a higher-prestige adult group, or leave as a result of internal conflicts. Where gangs are not highly structured or conventionalized, the gang may dissolve if its leaders are no longer effective. Conflicts between gangs may also be instrumental in the breakup of a group; if it cannot secure its territory a gang cannot retain its independent standing. The remnants of the gang may merge with another group, or they may combine under a new name.

SUBSIDIARY GROUPS

The relationship between groups is not always one of conflict. Some of the more structured gangs have subsidiaries and auxiliaries. Subsidiary gangs are frequently age-graded. Each subgang has its own leaders and activities but maintains a dependency relationship with the core gang overseeing, controlling, and establishing behavior patterns for the younger groups. As the older members leave the gang, a younger subgroup steps up to form the core. Loose alliances may also characterize the relationships between gangs. Agreements are sometimes made between similar groups whereby they do not fight against one another and join together to defend territory or attack hostile gangs. Brother gangs may also be formed when group members move to other neighborhoods. When old members form new gangs in the area, they frequently keep in touch with the old gang, and they may form protective alliances.

FEMALE AUXILIARIES

Female auxiliaries are not uncommon. Groups of females may align with a male gang for protection and security. Something of an exchange relationship is agreed upon whereby each group provides for some of the needs of the other. The absence of conventional regard for females often characterizes the association between gang members and their auxiliaries. Meetings between a gang member and his "deb" generally occur within a group setting. Although some social visiting in the girl's home is acceptable, the usual arrangement is for the boy to meet the girl at a prearranged place rather than escorting her there.

Girls are often a cause of gang conflict. Gang code forbids forcible violation of the girl friends of other gang members, but girls may submit to sexual relations under threat. Propositioning or assault of a "deb" by a rival gang member may also lead to gang reprisals. In a "fall" (raid) on the rival gang, girls may provide support by concealing weapons, knowing that there is less risk of being searched by police for females than for the males. Girls' auxiliaries are more likely to be found attached to highly organized gangs than to less formal groups. Probably less than one-fifth of all gangs will boast of a girls' auxiliary.

Gang Dynamics

In approaching the study of the gang, it is common to focus on those characteristics that set them apart from conventional social groups and to examine gang behavior as unconventional or non-conformist behavior. A closer examination of gangs, however, indicates that such an assumption is unwarranted. Gang members use many devices that conventional groups use, and they engage in highly conformist behavior.

JARGON

Many gangs or delinquent groups use special terms and symbols. The development of an unconventional language serves to identify members, create prestige, and promote group solidarity. The terms that are used to label their major interests and activities and the gang itself suggest dominant values held by members. Names of gangs often hold special significance. They may identify the "turf," or territory, of the gang. Membership based on clearly defined territorial boundaries is often crucial in maintaining order and structure within urban gangs. Other names suggest attributes of the gang or provide warnings to others. Names such as Warriors, Cobras, and Daggers may indicate a willingness to fight all opponents. Still other titles suggest prestige or high status, for example, Vice Lords and Egyptian Kings.[7]

Special terms for particular activities suggest the concerns of the gang. The wide variety of terms for fighting, courage, sex, and the con indicate fine distinctions often recognized in these areas. Although certain segments of the terminology may be widely shared and used in communication with other gangs, specialized forms of delinquency, such as the drug trade, have their own distinct terminology. Similar specialized jargon is found in the professions, the sports world, the movie industry, and so on. Like the terminology of more conventional special interest groups, the language of gangs tends to evolve or change over time. Gang vocabulary has its fashions and varies according to geographic location. A comparison of vocabulary from one time period to another suggests the futility of compiling a list of terms common to all gangs. In the middle 1950s, for example, the working vocabulary included "sneak" (an attack or raid on another gang), "rumble" (a fight between gangs), "strays" (boys without group affiliation), and "heater" (gun).[8] By 1960 the vocabulary had changed in some areas. An attack or raid on another gang became a "fall," a fight between gangs was "humbugging," unaffiliated boys were "coolies," and a gun became a "piece."[9] Other terms, such as "deb" (a girl), "burn" (shoot), "turf" (territory), and "rep" (standing or status), retained legitimacy over the same time period.

DRESS

Gang identification and solidarity is further emphasized by some characteristic pattern of dress or hair style. Some gangs wear special jackets in the gang colors with the "club" name or symbols inscribed on the back. Others may adopt a special type of shirt or hat which distinguishes members from outsiders. Girls' auxiliaries frequently adopt somewhat similar patterns of dress.

GROUP ACTIVITIES

Only a small proportion of a gang member's time is spent in delinquent activity. Furthermore, the gang member spends relatively little time acting with the gang as a whole. Most of his activities are carried out in small groups of two to five individuals. Small groups lend themselves to spontaneous activity, a minimum of coordination, and maximum participation by each group member. Like members of other juvenile collectives, the gang member occupies his time "hanging around," "shooting the bull," and organizing or participating in informal games. Basketball, bowling, and pool are often favored activities. Very rarely does the gang or clique within the gang focus exclusively on delinquent activity.

When the gang does act as a whole, its attentions are most likely to be focused on social activities. The gang may plan a party, a bowling tournament, or a ball game which calls for the participation of all members. These social activities may have, as a by-product, delinquent behavior. Alcohol, drugs, and premarital sex sometimes becomes a part of the scene. If the gang does plan and organize for specialized delinquent activity, it is generally carried out to protect the group or secure resources (money or reputation) for its maintenance. The fighting gang does not attack another group merely for the excitement and adventure it might provide. Rather, the members respond with violence to perceived intrusions on their territory or to even the score for wrongs done them by members of other gangs. A gang may resort to theft to finance important group activities when its own resources are low.

The majority of so-called gang delinquencies are carried out by small groups within the gang. These splinter groups or cliques within the gang may operate with or without the knowledge or approval of the gang hierarchy. Theft, assault, or a good con may enhance the reputation of the members of the splinter group and provide material rewards as well. The gang may provide a rich breeding ground for the development of delinquent cliques.

IDENTIFYING THE GANG

The divergence of opinion about which peer groups should be included under the term gang reflects the manner in which various concepts have been used in the delinquency literature. Lack of uniformity and the careless use of terms have contributed to confusion in this area. Clarification of terms such as gang, club, subculture, and gang delinquency may provide a framework within which collective delinquency can be better understood.

Gangs

The definition of *gang* is not clear. Popular conceptions of the gang are varied. The mass media generally use the term in the context of highly organized groups that engage in criminal or violent behavior. Inquiries among university students, however, indicate that *gang* may also be applied to peer groups whose behavior is harmless, displaying a spirit of bravado.[10] The same inconsistency of definition is apparent in sociology. The term *gang* has been applied to an assortment of peer groups, from street clubs to violent, delinquent gangs, which differ in degree of group integration, structure, size, and purpose.

One common characteristic appears to be present in all of the diverse conceptions: Gangs are seen as autonomous peer groups. That is, they are networks of similar-aged, same-sex individuals who are unaffiliated with adult-sponsored or adult-supervised organizations and are therefore self-governing.[11] This definition does not impute a particular type of behavior to the group. As indicated earlier, even those gangs that are organized primarily for violence or intergang conflict do not engage solely in violent activities. Much time is spent in social activities within the gang, and a proportionately smaller amount of time is allotted to actual warfare.

Clubs

A club is defined as an organization of individuals for a stated purpose or activity. Youth clubs are usually conceived and operated under adult sponsorship or supervision. Clubs may be organized or sponsored by adults for socially disapproved behavior, such as drag racing or auto theft. But the club is popularly conceived of as an organization to promote socially approved activities. This conception is so pervasive that delinquency-oriented groups generally refer to themselves not as gangs but as clubs—a respectable term which implies that the group does not engage in reprehensible behavior.[12] The distinction between gangs and clubs is not one of the moral validity of group activities but rather autonomy. Gangs are autonomous peer groups, whereas clubs are governed, at least in part, by individuals outside the active membership.

Subcultures

Subcultures are patterns of norms, values, and attitudes which have become accepted as traditional among certain groups. People do not constitute a subculture; a subculture is a pattern of norms and values. A subculture defines what is proper and improper behavior for whom and under what circumstances. A delinquent subculture provides the roles for delinquency, but individuals engage in delinquent activities. The subculture provides the motives, techniques, and rationalizations for activities, but the activities themselves are carried out by individuals.

Although the terms have been used interchangeably, it is important to distinguish between gangs and subcultures. Gangs are networks of individuals, whereas subcultures are networks of conduct rules and attitudes and are not constituted of individuals. In most cases, gangs and subcultures are not coterminous. What happens within any one particular group is not only a function of that group's values and attitudes, but it also depends to a considerable extent upon contiguous groups. The impact of a particular subculture on an individual's behavior is determined by the nature of his relationships with carriers of the subculture. The adolescent may associate entirely with his kinship group, or he may disavow blood ties and choose to associate with others. In either case, his kinship group is an important reference group which shapes his own attitudes and values by providing models which are to be followed or avoided.

The presence of subcultural patterns in a youth's environment does not automatically result in his adherence to those patterns. Each individual has a variety of patterns available. An individual's reference groups may be of many types, including occupation, ethnic identity, age, grade, social class, and sex. These groups and their importance will change over time. In the case of gangs, subcultural orientations may change over time, or they may remain very much the same while the membership changes.

Gang Delinquency

The term *gang delinquency* should not be construed to mean all the activities of a delinquency-oriented gang. Only a small proportion of the interaction between gang members involves the planning, preparation, and carrying out of unlawful activities. Nor is it essential that the entire membership of a particular gang engage in a delinquent activity for it to be defined as gang delinquency. Organized gangs seldom commit delinquencies as a unit. Few delinquencies can be carried out successfully by the simultaneous, common action of large groups because of the increased likelihood of detection and apprehension. Intergang fighting, vandalism, and drug or sex parties provide the rare opportunity for mass participation of the membership. Gang members join in concerted attempts to carry out delinquent activities through a division of labor. Lone individuals or cliques are responsible for one or more tasks deemed essential to the enterprise. In a burglary, for example, one group may engage in diversionary tactics, another provide a lookout, a third carry out the theft, and a fourth provide the equipment and transportation.

It is not sufficient that an individual have recognized membership in a gang for his activities to be considered gang delinquency. To be so considered his behavior must be a function of his membership in the gang. It must provide the techniques, motives, or opportunity for delinquent participation. Certainly we would not assume that a member of the Boy Scouts, acting alone and without encouragement or instruction from the group, goes shoplifting as a result of his group membership. Nor can we assume that all delinquent behavior engaged in by a member of a delinquent gang is a function of gang membership. Some of his delinquent behavior may be as disapproved of and discouraged from within the gang as from without. The gang is not the only group that guides the youth's behavior.

VARIATIONS IN COLLECTIVE DELINQUENCY

Gangs are only one type of law-violating collectivity in which juveniles may become involved. Collective delinquency may also involve a loose collection of individuals who respond collectively to a crisis situation. Joint participation in delinquent or criminal acts does not necessarily signal individual commitment to delinquent values. Individuals who generally lead conventional, law-abiding lives may be drawn into deviant activity given the right occasion.

Movements

The semistructured collectivity may use illegal action as a means of strengthening the existing pattern of law and order or to change the existing social structures. Recent failures of law enforcement authorities to apprehend and prosecute alleged rapists, for example, has led to a new method of enforcement. In several cities, women have banded together to form patrols which search out and punish individuals caught perpetrating sexual assault. Student strikes and occupation of buildings on college campuses in the late 1960s and early 1970s provide ample documentation of illegal activity used as a means of correcting perceived injustices and making changes in the social structure. While illegal activities are sometimes used to attain valued goals, they are not viewed as a repudiation of conventional norms or as an acceptance of a delinquent subculture.

This type of illegal activity was mentioned in the early criminal typologies of Cesare Lombroso and Franz von Liszt. Schafer describes the "convictional" delinquent as an individual who engages in illegal activity "to realize a universalistic or suprauniversalistic ideology that tends to emphasize a concept of justice."[13] Motivation may be a political, social, moral, or religious ideal. The civil rights activist who breaks the law in order to point out the need for equal protection, the governor who bars the schoolhouse door to hamper a desegregation order, members of the underground who injure others to repel the invader, and the father who kidnaps his daughter from a commune of religious zealots all believe in the rightness of their causes. They violated established laws in order to realize their ideal goals.

The consequences for convictional violators are varied. Their lawless acts may be legitimized if the laws are changed as a result of their actions or if they manage to gain power. True convictional delinquents do not discount the possibility of punishment, but they feel obligated to uphold their ideals. Where punishment is applied, the convictional offender may be considered a martyr by like-minded individuals. In such a case, the cause is strengthened, and the punishment itself becomes idealized and approved of.

Convictional offenders often seek out like-minded individuals for concerted action against injustice. Unlike gangs, however, such movements are not wholly autonomous. Furthering the cause and reaching the goal requires a close examination of, and movement within, the "system," or they may bring pressure from without. Autonomy is sought only when it will not interfere with the goal attainment of the group. Groups developed for convictional purposes cut across age, sex, and class boundaries. They only infrequently become the primary social role for most of their members.

Opportunistic Delinquency

Occasionally acts that are taken as indications of gang delinquency involve greater individual action than is generally perceived. Movements and isolated instances of collective delinquency may afford the opportunity for nonmembers to take advantage of volatile and disorganized situations. An offender may use the ideals of a movement as an excuse or cover for his illegal behavior. Where a group is engaged in illegal activities, unattached individuals may take advantage of the confusion to steal, assault, or vandalize. The arrest of such an offender, along with members of the movement or the gang, suggests a bond between the offender and the group where none exists. Organized movements are frequently credited with illegal acts apart from those established in their plan of action despite their leaders' exhortations to hold fast to the plan. Many of these illegal activities repudiated by the organization are no doubt the work of unattached opportunistic delinquents.

Events such as the Watt's riot in 1966 and the Newark riot in 1967 provide an opportunity for the exhibition of lawlessness by ordinarily law-abiding citizens. The initial confrontations with injustice may involve only a small contingent of individuals. As word of the confrontation spreads, however, individuals unconvinced of the effectiveness or fairness of the law enforcement agencies begin to take matters into their own hands by using vigilante tactics. This display of lawlessness by "reputable" members of the community provides an opportunity, an excuse, and a cover for those motivated by less ideal goals.

Unlike gangs, contingents of individuals involved in opportunistic delinquency have few interpersonal bonds. The collective experience may provide their only link with each other. Action is taken by autonomous individuals or cliques and is not expected to recur in the same manner. What appears to be an organized effort—in looting, for example—is merely the simultaneous action of distinct, autonomous units, either individuals or small cliques.

Societal Reaction

Toleration of the various delinquency forms depends upon a number of factors. Toleration is mitigated by a belief in the validity of the goal. Societal values provide broad guidelines for the identification of valued goals and the means that may be legitimately used to reach them. Some goals are more acceptable than others and hence receive greater societal support. Acceptable goals may be in conflict with the law. Where this is the case, both the goal and the law cannot guide the individual's behavior. Here a decision must be made either for actions to reach the goal or for law-abiding behavior.

A strongly held value in democratic society is freedom. During World War II, a band of individuals in France became convinced that freedom could only be secured through resistance to invading armies. Work with the established order was not believed to be sufficient to repel the invaders, and the group therefore went underground. Any means necessary to reach their goal was considered appropriate by the group—robbery, assault, sabotage, and murder. Activities of the group received a great deal of support from public opinion in a society convinced of the inherent wrongness of such acts but equally convinced of the value of freedom. The activities were given legitimacy because the motives of the group were believed to be legitimate. Crimes were committed not for personal gain but for the public good through support of a broadly held value. Few would condemn members of the underground for resistance to foreign invaders; however, the legitimacy of convictional crime and delinquency is not always so apparent.

More frequently, convictional delinquents are opposed by defenders of the status quo. Societal values are often so broad that they are defined in diverse manners by different segments of society. Broad societal values may dictate equality and opportunity for all, but the interpretations of what this means in day-to-day living may conflict sharply. The proliferation of values in a complex society contain those that conflict with one another. Separate segments of society sometimes align priorities in a different manner. Society is composed of many different groups that are separated from each other by age, sex, marital status, and economic and political barriers. A high priority for the teen-age sector may come in conflict with values held by the parental sector. The deviance of individual or group behavior depends in large part upon who makes the evaluation of the behavior.

Another factor that affects toleration is individual motivation. Unlawful behavior used to satisfy selfish ends is generally condemned. Delinquency that has its roots in personal material gain and deprivation of others does not have a favorable audience. A distinction is made in many quarters between "borrowing" an auto for a joy ride and "swiping" a car for resale or salvage, although both acts deprive the owner of his property. Delinquencies that have unselfish motives, while not fully acceptable, may receive less unfavorable responses. Actions taken to further a cause or to help others may be excused by segments of the society. A classic example of this response is the legend of Robin Hood. The hero received support from large numbers of people who believed justice was being served when he robbed from the rich and gave to the poor. Certainly public response would have been less favorable if he had robbed the rich to line his own pockets.

Societal toleration is also mitigated by the circumstances of the offender or the situation. The public has sympathy for individuals who are pushed into crime or delinquency by need, but few people sympathize with the criminal who kills an innocent bystander in the commission of a robbery. However, the home owner who kills an intruder receives far less criticism. So long as the gain realized from a delinquent action does not exceed the perceived need of the offender, the public may express sympathy. Theft of a loaf of bread to feed a hungry family does not outrage law-abiding citizens to the extent that bank robbery to feed the same family would.

Some of the factors that mitigate toleration, then, are intent, or goal, motivation, and circumstance. In some instances these factors are built into the law; in others they are not. Public tolerance is especially important in cases where no provisions are made in the legal code. Pressure to prosecute cases in the judicial system often determines the outcome for the alleged offender. The law is constantly being interpreted and reinterpreted to take into account mitigating factors in individual cases.

COLLECTIVE DELINQUENCY IN PERSPECTIVE

Statistics reveal that a great deal of delinquent behavior is the work of groups rather than lone offenders. The problem is particularly acute in urbanized society, where youngsters have ample opportunity to form peer groups without parental supervision or approval. Although it is generally agreed that gang delinquency is a problem, there is no clear definition of what a gang is.

Juvenile collectives take on several different forms. They may be distinguished by size, organization, and affiliation. The basic juvenile collective is the clique—a small, informal, and unaffiliated peer group. More complex groups, such as the ad hoc collective and the confederation, are larger and have a semblance of structure. None of these groups, however, is more highly visible or considered less desirable than the traditional gang. Its highly elaborated structure and colorful behavior makes it suspect to the society at large. Any of these collectives, from the clique to the gang, may engage in illegal or socially disapproved behavior.

Gangs are not the only juvenile collectives that contribute to the problem of delinquency. There are other collectives which do not exhibit the characteristics that are often associated with the gang that nevertheless engage in law-violating behavior. Movements designed to promote social change often produce convictional offenders. Furthermore, opportunist individuals may use crisis situations to enhance their own personal gains.

NOTES

[1] LaMar Emprey, "Delinquency Theory and Recent Research," *Journal of Research in Crime and Delinquency* 4 (January 1967): 28–42.

[2] Mender M. Craig and Lila A. Budd, "The Juvenile Offender: Recidivism and Companions," *Crime and Delinquency* 13 (1967): 344–351.

[3] James F. Short, Jr., and Fred L. Strodtbeck, *Group Processes and Gang Delinquency* (Chicago: University of Chicago Press, 1965), p. 1.

[4] Frederick M. Thrasher, *The Gang* (Chicago: University of Chicago Press, 1967); James F. Short, Jr., Ray A. Tennyson, and Kenneth I. Howard, "Behavior Dimensions of Gang Delinquency," *American Sociological Review* 28 (June 1963); Leon Jansyn, "Solidarity and Delinquency in a Street Corner Group," *American Sociological Review* 31 (October 1966); Short and Strodtbeck, *op. cit.*

[5] Harry M. Shulman, *Juvenile Delinquency in American Society* (New York: Harper & Row, 1961).

[6] Walter B. Miller, Mildred Geertz, and Henry Cutter, "Aggression in a Boy's Street Corner Group," *Psychiatry* 24 (November 1961): 283–398.

[7] R. Lincoln Keiser, *The Vice Lords* (New York: Holt, Rinehart and Winston, 1969).

[8] Stacy V. Jones, "The Cougars: Life with a Brooklyn Gang," *Harpers Magazine* (November 1954), p. 36.

[9] Harrison E. Salisbury, *The Shook-up Generation* (Greenwich, Conn.: Fawcett Publications, 1958), and *Reaching the Fighting Gang* (New York: Youth Board, 1960).

[10] Edwin H. Sutherland and Donald R. Cressey, *Criminology*, 8th ed. (Philadelphia: Lippincott, 1970), p. 188.

[11] Schulman, *op. cit.*, p. 443.

[12] Ruth S. Cavan and Theodore N. Ferdinand, *Juvenile Delinquency* (Philadelphia: Lippincott, 1975), p. 126.

[13] Stephen Schafer and Richard D. Knudten, *Juvenile Delinquency: An Introduction* (New York: Random House, 1970), p. 165.

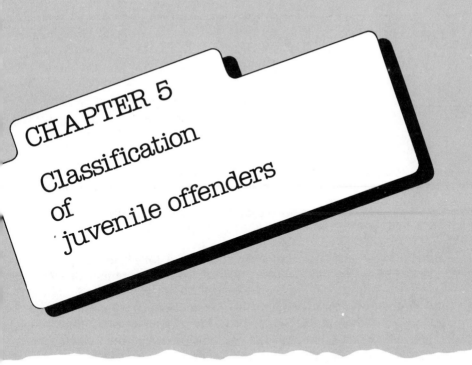

CHAPTER 5
Classification of juvenile offenders

It is obvious from an examination of the data available on juvenile delinquency that not all juvenile offenders are alike. Since 90 to 95 percent of all juveniles are at some time or another actively engaged in delinquent behavior, it is evident that their personal characteristics vary nearly as widely as do those of the entire population of juveniles. Furthermore, the behavior that brings attention to troublesome youths also varies considerably. Juveniles have been adjudicated for offenses that range in seriousness from disobeying parents to homicide. Some youths engage in repeated delinquent acts, while others are involved in delinquent behavior infrequently. Youngsters may engage in delinquent behavior alone or with a group of companions. If companions are involved, they may constitute an informal clique or they may be a part of a larger organized gang. These facts suggest that there is a great deal of variation in delinquency and in the juvenile offender. In view of these variations, it is a mistake to deal with the delinquency problem by assuming that all delinquents are alike.

Common sense suggests that differences in delinquency may be explained by differences in cause. We would expect that there would be a variety of answers to questions such as the following: Why does a juvenile disobey parents? Why does a juvenile rob a store? Why do some delinquents persist in delinquent behavior? Why do some juveniles infrequently engage in misbehavior? Why do some juveniles organize for delinquent activities?

No one answer can adequately answers all of these questions.

Criminologists generally agree that there are many types of juvenile delinquency, each having its own set of causal factors and a distinct configuration of characteristics. Barron's statement is representative of this view:

> Delinquency is a legal category, and probably the only thing that is alike in all delinquencies is that they are violations of the law. Otherwise delinquency has no inherent quality or property applying to all types under all conditions. Since it has no inherent universal property, one cannot expect to find, in the variety of persons who are adjudicated delinquent, any one psychological type, any one character trait, that differentiates delinquents from all other persons. The endless vicissitudes of circumstance, opportunity, and personal history preclude the expectation of any single inclusive formula.[1]

The failure of any single influence to account for all forms of delinquency has resulted in a general recognition that a number of factors in combination may be necessary to provide an adequate solution to the problem of cause. Individuals—not motives, frustrations, or environments—commit delinquent acts.[2] Any number of factors associated with the development of an individual may be influential in producing the tendency to commit delinquent acts.

Because delinquency is so variable, there is a hesitation to lump all juvenile offenders and offenses into a single category. The trend in the social sciences has been to break down broad categories into smaller, more homogeneous classifications. Rather than investigating all delinquencies, the criminologist may limit his scope to one or two more specific kinds of delinquency.

A content analysis of current textbooks on juvenile delinquency reveals that classification and typology building is a highly respected endeavor. A number of texts devote entire sections to offender typologies.[3] Even where typologies are not given the central focus, they are certainly not ignored. Several texts treat classification systematically in one chapter.[4] It is apparent that the use of classification is not diminishing in the area of juvenile delinquency.

PRACTICAL USES OF TYPOLOGIES

Although there appears to be a general consensus that typologies are important for a full understanding of delinquent behavior, there is less agreement on the specific uses of constructed typologies. Claims for the uses of typologies may be very modest, as is the proposal offered by Barnes and Teeters:

> Classifications seem to satisfy a certain interest in orderliness, a desire for neat categories. . . . From the standpoint of convenience, classifications have an advantage. . . . However, about the only value in the practice is that it does enable investigators to make comparisons with those in other disciplines as an aid in their own work whether this be diagnostic, therapeutic, or theoretical.[5]

Other writers believe that classification has a broader range of uses. Gibbons suggests that an adequate typology serves to collate existing knowledge and indicates directions for research,[6] ties existing social and psychological theories together,[7] and provides a basis for planning effective treatment programs.[8] Wood concludes that typologies will provide insights for prevention and the control of offenders and provide a useful base for theory testing.[9] Glueck and Glueck similarly speak of the value of typology in understanding etiology and in designing preventive and therapeutic programs.[10]

Claims for the purposes of classification vary widely. It is not surprising, therefore, that many different approaches are used in building new classification systems. Each system is constructed with specific purposes in mind. A typology that uses categories to distinguish between types of victimization (i.e., offense-specific categories) will yield different results than one based upon individual psychological characteristics. One may be used to build prevention programs, while the other may be used to build rehabilitation programs for those offenders not reached by prevention programs.

There are a number of acceptable typologies currently under

study. Each has been constructed for a specific purpose. If a typology is used for its intended purposes, the scheme may be a useful tool. Each classification scheme, however, has practical limitations, and these should be carefully analyzed before the scheme is placed in use.

A Typology of Typologies

Typologies themselves can be classified by kind. Analysis of the origins and uses of various typologies suggests that two broad types of typologies can be distinguished. These have been identified as the ideal, or *constructed*, typology and the empirical, or *extracted*, typology. Arthur Lewis Wood has clarified the differences between these typological forms. Our discussion is based primarily on Wood's discussion of typologies in deviance and control.[11]

IDEAL TYPOLOGIES

Ideal typologies are based upon theory. They describe a combination of compatible characteristics that are believed to be interrelated. Ideal types are constructed in accordance with specific middle-range theories. The characteristics that are used to define the categories have referents in the empirical world, but concrete examples of the category that meet all criteria may be rare or nonexistent.

The gang typology developed by Cloward and Ohlin provides an excellent example of the ideal typology.[12] Their typology was developed from the integration of anomie and differential association theories. From this theoretical perspective, Cloward and Ohlin propose that varying sociocultural conditions in the immediate environment give rise to different forms of juvenile gangs (see Chapter 10). Where the lack of legitimate opportunity structures prevail, juveniles will seek alternative avenues for success. The individual's interaction with opportunity structures in the community gives rise to the development of alternatives. Each of the types of gangs that results from this ongoing process (criminal, conflict, and retreatist) has its own unique set of values, norms, and patterns of delinquency. The gangs described by Cloward and Ohlin are ideal types. We would not expect to actually find specific concrete examples of gangs that precisely meet all the criteria used to develop the classification scheme.

Ideal typologies draw on theory to provide insight into the causes of specific forms of delinquency. The use of a theoretical base provides a systematic and logical strategy for drawing and arranging variables that may be related to delinquency. The number of variable characteristics that can be used to distinguish one adolescent from another is enormous. The systematic identification and study of all possible factors would be very time-consuming and economically prohibitive. Theory specifies the avenues that are most likely to produce fruitful results.

The design of typologies from theory offers other advantages as well. It forces the theorist to consider strategies for operationalizing theory. The attempt to provide research strategies may lead to greater specification of the theory to include all possible variations within a broad area of behavior. Sources of incompatibility between characteristics within the theory may also be flushed out. Where the theory appears to retain its strength under the critical analysis necessary for the construction of a typology, it may provide policy implications that go beyond common-sense speculation.

Because they are basically conceptual in origin, ideal typologies are limited by the restrictions of logic and theory. They do not pretend to explain all aspects of delinquency and therefore have a limited scope. These limitations, however, do not diminish their value. Ideal typologies are not constructed to describe delinquency in detail but rather to provide a limited number of hypotheses regarding its nature and causes that can be tested.

EMPIRICAL TYPOLOGIES

Empirical typologies are based primarily on objective observations in the real world. Variable characteristics of individuals are compared with behavior modalities. For example, personality and biological and sociocultural traits may be related to behavioral categories (i.e., criminal and noncriminal). An analysis of the frequency with which certain characteristics combine may provide valuable clues about the nature of juvenile delinquency.

The typologies developed by Sheldon and Eleanor Glueck are a prime example of constructed, or empirical, typologies.[13] These researchers collected a wide variety of data on delinquents and nondelinquents. Information on several hundred different personal characteristics was collected and duly recorded for each delinquent and nondelinquent participating in the study. The Gluecks believed that analysis of the data might help to identify the more important variables related to juvenile delinquency. Unfortunately, much of the data collected did not provide clear distinctions between delinquents and nondelinquents. Similar attempts to identify variables associated with delinquency have not proved very fruitful. Wood attributes this failure to a conception of the typology as an end in itself and suggests that the potential value of a typology rests not in the development of classes but rather in its use for constructing hypotheses to explain delinquency.[14]

Empirical typologies have certain advantages over ideal typologies. They may promote serendipitous discovery. In examining a wide variety of factors, relationships that were not intuitively apparent may be discovered. Although such serendipitous discovery is relatively rare, it is an important reason for using this approach to classification. Ideal typologies do not offer this advantage. Reliance on a theoretical base may result in the exclusion of little-apparent but important relationships.

Because they rely on empirical observation, empirical typologies may also be of value in constructing new theories, modifying established ones, or providing evidence for the relative efficiency of competing theories. Observations in the real world are necessary to an understanding of the nature of real social problems, and empirical typologies take this into consideration.

Characteristics of the Model Typology

Classification schemes in juvenile delinquency display considerable variety. Some focus on the type of delinquent behavior involved; others deal with the characteristics of individual offenders. The number of categories used may be as few as two to as many as eight or more. While many originate from theoretical perspectives, others are developed from empirical data. There is no uniform pattern easily distinguished from an examination of examples of current classification schemes.

Whatever the form and focus taken in a classification scheme, several criteria distinguish it as a typology. A "good" typology should be all-inclusive. Each individual case of juvenile delinquency must be accounted for. Therefore there must be a sufficient number of categories for the assignment of all cases. At the same time, the number of categories must be kept to a minimum. A typology that boasts of a profusion of categories cannot prove very useful in generalization and offers little advantage over analyzing delinquency on a case-by-case basis.

Categories should also be mutually exclusive. This criterion involves the clear definition and specification of categories. Definitions that are overly broad or overlapping may result in confusion. Miscellaneous or catchall categories have little meaning or utility for the description and prediction of behavior. Each case of delinquency should fit into one, and only one, category. Where independent observers cannot agree on the placement of a particular case, the typology fails.

In constructing categories within a typology, several considerations are important. The criteria that are used to define a category must have empirical referents. In other words, observable traits must be specified that will allow the objective assignment of cases. All of the variables used to define a category should be mutually compatible. The traits that combine to make up a category must be logically related and not merely a result of random selection. Each of the categories derived, either from a theory or research, should display a systematic arrangement of the variables that constitute the basis for the typology. For example, if a category uses a particular personality trait as a criterion for inclusion, all other categories in the typology should use different personality traits as criteria. Ideally, the criteria used to distinguish types are qualitative and not quantitative. Taken together, the categories of a typology should suggest a broad explanation or description of juvenile delinquency.

No delinquency typology is without error. All classification schemes are more or less arbitrary descriptions of social life and human behavior. However, those typologies that are constructed according to the model rules will not create confusion in an already vague area. They will help bring order to chaos and contribute to a better understanding of juvenile delinquency.

THE VALUE OF CLASSIFICATION SCHEMES

Classification is indispensable to an understanding of juvenile delinquency and the youthful offender. Individuals are unique, and the number of factors associated with their life situations is overwhelming. Some of these factors can logically be eliminated as influences on delinquent behavior. Eye color, shoe size, and a hundred other characteristics are easily and readily removed from the list of possible influences. The number of relevant possibilities remaining, however, is still unmanageable. Only by focusing on a limited number of factors can an in-depth analysis be made. In short, classifying individuals on the basis of psychological, interpersonal, and environmental characteristics provides a crude technique for introducing controls for ease in analysis. When particular traits can be identified in most or all of the juveniles exhibiting similar behavior, causal inferences can be explored.

The comparison of traits with delinquent or nondelinquent status may suggest that delinquent and nondelinquent youths share common characteristics. Indeed, the number of differences between delinquents and nondelinquents may be smaller than the number of differences between different varieties of delinquents. It is not unreasonable to speculate that the youngster who violates curfew laws may have more in common with the nondelinquent than with the juvenile arsonist or armed robber. In view of these wide variations in delinquent behavior, it is probably more useful to study various types of delinquency and delinquents than to attempt to make distinctions between delinquents and nondelinquents. Of course, conclusions generated from the study of narrow types of behavior would apply only to that behavior alone. A comparison of the conclusions based on each subcategory of delinquent behavior may eventually, however, suggest characteristics common to all delinquents and all offenses.

By breaking down delinquent behavior into more narrow types, crucial distinctions may be discovered which are not evident in the study of the broader phenomena. Rather than narrowing the amount of knowledge gained, the study of specific types of behavior offers in-depth coverage. It permits the summary and description of vast amounts of information. In the absence of such a scheme, the delinquency analyst and practitioner is reduced to ad hoc analysis of each individual instance of juvenile delinquency.

Although classification provides a valuable base upon which an understanding of juvenile delinquency can be built, it is not without pitfalls. It must be remembered that typologies are mere approximations of reality and run the risk, when misused or too strictly adhered to, of distorting the nature of delinquency. By focusing on and magnifying presumed differences, more important variables may be overlooked and dismissed as possible causes of juvenile delinquency.

When typologies are taken as infallible truths, they may lead to erroneous conclusions and promote the very behavior they seek to describe. Familiarity with, and belief in, a typology of delinquency may give individuals a rigid, fixed, and negative view of the delinquent's background. If it is believed, for example, that delinquent behavior results from psychological frustration, the researcher or practitioner will tend to look for frustration to explain the behavior. Upon discovery of some frustration-inducing situations or events in the offender's background, support is claimed for the typology.

The construction of typologies always involves a calculated risk. It is impossible to know which variables to control and which to ignore. Attempts to include a large array of variables under a single classification scheme may invalidate the reasons for using a typology in the first place. The failure of criminologists to agree on a single classification scheme for juvenile delinquency underscores the problems involved in typology construction.

Typologies can be helpful tools. They provide a useful and necessary framework for the study of delinquency. However, caution must be used in their construction and application. Typologies that become ends in themselves or promote the behavior they seek to describe can be useless or even harmful.

EARLY CLASSIFICATION SCHEMES

The classification of law violators was popular even before the distinction between adult and juvenile law violators was made. As early as the year 200, the Greek philosopher Claudine Galen distinguished between the choleric, phlegmatic, sanguine, and melancholic criminal types.[15] The earliest classification schemes tended to emphasize a single factor which was believed to cause delinquent or criminal behavior in the individual.

The bases of classification have often followed fads or fashionable beliefs about the causes of misbehavior. When certain evil spirits were believed to cause crime, individuals were classified in terms of the manner in which evil spirits entered their bodies. Some individuals were victims of possession, others were witches, and a few were labeled heretics. As interest shifted to biology as an explanation, physical characteristics became an important criterion for distinguishing between offenders. As the field of criminology began to develop as a systematic scientific discipline, classification schemes began to assume a new importance. The categories used were more precisely defined and the system more comprehensive.

The first recognized "scientific" classification system was probably that proposed by Cesare Lombroso in the nineteenth century. Lombroso believed that biological factors were very important to the development of criminal behavior. Realizing that individual criminals differed in terms of the number and types of offenses, he was convinced that varying types of inherited attitudes were involved. He was able to identify and classify at least four major types: the born criminal, the insane criminal, the criminal by passion, and the occasional criminal.

Lombroso's ideas and his classification scheme represented a major change in perspective on the causes of crime. Prior to his work, free will and moral responsibility were widely accepted as the major factors to account for crime. The new approach shifted the emphasis from the crime to the criminal. For the first time there was an attempt to study the problem through a scientific understanding of the offender.

MODERN TYPOLOGIES

The popularity of classification has not declined. Many modern criminologists continue to develop and elaborate criminal and delinquent offender typologies. The simplest classification scheme may involve only two categories—delinquent and nondelinquent. More complex schemes may involve a dozen or more categories. The basis of classification varies from one typology to another. Some focus on behavior—its type, its frequency, and its target. Others look at characteristics of the offender—personality, constitutional traits, sociability, and life style.

Although there is a general consensus that a valid comprehensive typology is needed, there is little agreement on what form it should take. The inability of the discipline to arrive at a consensus has resulted in a proliferation of classification schemes, each reflecting the interests and theoretical beliefs of its developer. The typological systems currently popular can be examined most fruitfully by organizing them according to their focus. A basic distinction may be made between those schemes that focus on individual delinquents and those that emphasize the group nature of delinquents by describing delinquent groups. Within each of these categories, additional specification distinguishes one scheme from another.

Classification of Individual Offenders

Individuals commit delinquent acts, although certain social, psychological, or environmental factors may predispose an individual to take advantage of a situation that makes delinquency possible. Because delinquency is not equally evident in all individuals and because individuals are not all alike, it is often suggested that individual characteristics may be important to an understanding of delinquent behavior. A number of typologies have been developed from this perspective. Since individuals are unique and the number of variations associated with them is virtually unlimited, it is not surprising that the number and variety of typologies growing out of this perspective is tremendous.

Some of the major approaches to the classification of individuals are based on the type of offense committed, the personal characteristics of the offender, the frequency of delinquent behavior, and the degree of commitment to engage in delinquent behavior. Because the various systems begin with different approaches to analyze the same phenomena, the offender and his offenses, it is not surprising that many of the classification schemes overlap.

CLASSIFICATION BY OFFENSE

Offenders are most frequently classified by the type of offense they committed. Such a classification presumably enables us to group offenders according to what they did and to show the society's limit of tolerance for each particular crime in the differing penalties of the law.[16] Furthermore, it is frequently argued that the individual offender can be classified by the seriousness of his or her offense, and proper rehabilitative procedures can be instituted.

One of the simplest classifications of this nature is Ruth Cavan's early typology, which distinguished between offenses that were injurious to the rights or the safety and lives of other people and offenses that were injurious primarily to the health or personality development of the offender himself.[17] Her classification can also be viewed as a dual classification scheme, since she took into account gang behavior as a separate type of delinquency.[18]

Clinard used three categories to describe the major types of crime. Crimes against persons involved bodily injury to others and included offenses such as rape, assault, and murder. Property crimes involved the illegal transfer or destruction of private property. The third category consisted of crimes that were not physically damaging but constituted offenses against the public order. Prostitution, gambling, drug use, and other vices were subsumed under this third category.[19] He later rejected this scheme, however, for a career classification.

Other classification schemes have been considerably more complex. Eaton and Polk proposed five offense categories:

> 1. *Minor violations.* Included here are offenses such as curfew violations, traffic offenses, and disorderly conduct.
> 2. *Property violations.* This includes the theft of property except for stealing of automobiles.

3. *Major traffic offenses.* Auto theft is included in this section along with other offenses involving the auto, such as driving while under the influence.

4. *Human addiction.* This is a general category which includes drug addiction and sex-related offenses, but not rape.

5. *Bodily harm.* This offense category includes violent activity that may result in harm to other people. Rape, assault, and murder are examples.[20]

Sellin and Wolfgang's classification of delinquent offenses included an element of victimization as a criterion for establishing the differences between various acts. Their classification scheme identified two major classes of delinquency, as follows:

Class 1   (a) *bodily injury*
           (b) *property crime*
           (c) *property damage (vandalism)*
Class 2   (a) *intimidation*
           (b) *property loss*
           (c) *primary victimization (crime against a person)*
           (d) *secondary victimization (offense against a business)*
           (e) *tertiary victimization (curfew violations, disorderly conduct, and other offenses against public order)*
           (f) *mutual victimization (adultery or statutory rape where both participants are victimized)*
           (g) *the absence of victimization (truancy, incorrigibility).*[21]

Probably the most prominent classification scheme based upon offense categories is that used by the FBI in its *Uniform Crime Reports.*[22] Crimes are divided in two categories—Part I and Part II offenses. Part I offenses make up the Crime Index and include homicide, rape, robbery, assault, burglary, larceny-theft, and auto theft. Part II offenses include all other (less serious) offenses. Because the FBI data is the most readily available on crime and delinquency, it has had a significant impact on the study of crime and delinquency.

Schemes for classifying offenders on the basis of specific legal offenses have several drawbacks, particularly when applied to juvenile delinquency. First, the nature of delinquency laws are such that they do not always provide a clear-cut definition of the delinquent act. The legal category of incorrigibility, for example, includes a wide variety of behavior patterns. It is a catchall category that does not distinguish between such things as violent and nonviolent behavior, or single instances of disapproved behavior and serial occurrence. Even where legal categories are somewhat more well defined, as in rape, a wide range of behavior may be included in the single classification.

Another problem with this approach is the fact that individual offenders may commit more than one type of offense. A juvenile may not only be involved in vandalism but he may also engage in theft. In such instances, it is impossible to place the offender in one category or the other. If the offender is placed in both categories, the distinctions between the two are blurred and useless.

FREQUENCY AND COMMITMENT

It has long been assumed that individuals who commit single illegal acts are in some way different from those who make crime their life's work. In the 1800s, Cesare Lombroso made the distinction between the occasional offender and the habitual criminal.[23] This distinction is still considered important today, but the categories have increased in number and complexity. It is assumed that the frequency of delinquent behavior gives a rough indication of the individual's commitment to engage in delinquent behavior.

Early typologies of this nature were concerned with the differences among accidental offenders, situational offenders, occasional offenders, habitual offenders, and professional offenders. Accidental offenders were juveniles who stumbled into delinquency. For example, they may have gone to a party where drugs were unexpectedly offered and taken those drugs to be part of the group. Situational offenders were juveniles who took advantage of questionable situations. They might, for example, keep money found in a lost purse even though identification enabled its return. Occasional offenders planned their delinquent activities but do not reveal a consistent pattern and their delinquencies do not frequently occur. Conformist behavior was more likely to characterize most of their activities. Habitual offenders showed a consistent pattern. Their activities might involve regular drunkenness, drug use, or other consistently delinquent behavior patterns. Professional offenders were those who supported themselves by profits gained from their crimes.

Some of the more recent classification schemes concerned with frequency and individual commitment to delinquency deal with the delinquent role. These typologies attempt to describe how delinquent norms are incorporated into the offender and what his delinquent behavior means to him. Clinard suggested that offenders could be placed on a continuum that ranged from the noncareer type to the pure career type. His criteria were the individual's development of the role, life organization, identification with other criminals, and progression in crime.[24] He then arranged various offenses along the continuum with the criminally insane and exhibitionist near the noncareer end and con men and safecrackers at the career end.

Gibbons's "patterned social roles" typologies were even more complex. He categorized juvenile offenders on the basis of the pattern of illegal role behavior (offense), the social context in which it occurred (individual or group), self-perception, and role-related attitudes. Using these criteria, he distinguished nine delinquent types: (1) predatory gang delinquent, (2) conflict gang delinquent, (3) casual gang delinquent, (4) non-gang member casual delinquent, (5) automobile thief ("joyrider"), (6) drug user (heroin), (7) overly aggressive delinquent, (8) female delinquent, and (9) "behavior problem" delinquent.[25] Gibbons provided a descriptive account of each of these different types. Although some of the types have a gang label, it appears that each is meant to be applied to individuals rather than groups.

Several problems are evident in the typologies developed to describe offender commitment. Those that make a distinction on the basis of offense frequency alone do not take into account the nature of the offense itself. Surely it cannot be logically argued that the habitual drunk and the confirmed counterfeiter can be described, and their offenses explained, by the same factors. Frequency of offense might better provide a distinction between offenders who have committed the same offense. Another problem involves the definition of categories. Too often the labels attached in frequency classifications are so broad as to be useless. There are few guidelines to indicate, for example, whether an individual should be placed in the occasional or situational categories in certain instances.

The career type classification schemes were developed in an attempt to achieve greater specificity. However, the result is often a proliferation of overlapping categories and glaring omissions. The Gibbons typology, for example, contains a separate category for female offenders. There appears to be little reason to believe that all female offenders have similar delinquent careers. Some are runaways or sex offenders, but many others have engaged in assaultive behavior, taken drugs, or committed theft. Such girls may fit more suitably into Gibbons's categories of overly aggressive delinquent, drug user, or behavior problem delinquent.

Studies of the backgrounds and careers of offenders have generally been taken from an adjudicated population. Two sources of contamination are readily apparent. Findings may be distorted through the use of plea bargaining, whereby the offender admits to a lesser offense in order to escape liability for penalties of more serious violations of the law. More important, however, are distortions that result from the differential application of sanctions. Unofficially handled cases and undetected violations are not generally accounted for in the construction of typologies of delinquent careers.

OFFENDERS' PERSONAL TRAITS

Classifications of juvenile delinquents have frequently focused upon personal characteristics of the offender. Some of the earliest classifications of this type focused on physique and inherited constitutional traits. Lombroso's scheme, while not the first of its kind, received considerable attention and was influential in the development of criminology. Other classifications have focused on temperament or personality.

Body Types A number of delinquency analysts have attempted to develop classification schemes based on the assumption that body types are associated with temperament and are thereby predictive of delinquent tendencies. The typologies employed by Kretschmer, Hooten, Spranger, and Sheldon provide examples of this type of classification scheme. Sheldon's scheme identified three body types which were believed to be related to distinct temperamental characteristics.[26] In the physique categories, he distinguished between the endomorphic, mesomorphic, and ectomorphic individuals. The endomorphic body type featured short limbs, small bones, smooth skin, and a soft, round overall shape. This type was associated with a viscerotonic temperament—a relaxed, extroverted character with a desire for comfort and ease. The mesomorphic body was characterized by large bones, a heavy chest and trunk, and a muscular appearance. Persons displaying this physique were believed to be noisy, aggressive, adventurous, and assertive, with the somatonic temperament. The thin, fragile ectomorphic individual was expected to exhibit an introverted, cerebrotonic temperament. This sickly person often displayed an endless array of physical complaints.

Although research by the Gluecks and others have produced supportive evidence for the existence of a relationship between body type and temperament, this approach to delinquency has been severely criticized by those who claim that the relationship of body type to delinquency is not clear. These schemes generally involve so few categories that they cannot be used to make fine distinctions.

Personality Several classification schemes have been developed to distinguish between offender personalities without reference to body type. Emotional, temperamental, and intellectual factors generally serve as a focus. Underlying these typologies is the assumption that personality guides or produces behavior tendencies.

Jenkins and Hewitt developed an empirical typology on the basis of their clinical experiences in a child guidance institute. With a solid background in Freudian theory, they examined 500 juvenile cases and identified three delinquent types.[27]

Type I was the overly inhibited personality. These children tended to display neurotic symptoms including shyness, tics, nail biting, and other indications of fear, anxiety, and tension. Parent-child relationships were reported to exhibit excessive repression or strictness in child rearing. These children were under pressure to be excessively good and developed few emotional outlets. Every "bad" act brought anxiety because of the fear of parental rejection or loss of love.

Type II was the underinhibited personality. This type was considered the opposite of Type I. In this case, the individual had not developed adequate controls over his impulses. The child appeared to be unsocialized and extremely aggressive. Children of this type were believed to come from rejecting parents. These children expressed little or no guilt following the commission of a delinquent act. They often did not get along with other children and had few friends because they tended to be selfish, bossy, and antagonistic.

Type III was the pseudosocial delinquent. Children of this type were normal, but they possessed a "shell" so that they had no inhibitions against premature impulses toward people who were not a part of an in-group. This type of person was considered the loyal soldier in a gang who would take on the rest of the world if possible.

Cavan and Ferdinand's "synthetic typology" took a social psychological perspective. Beginning from Lewin's field theory,[28] they identified six delinquent types:

> 1. *Cultural identifiers* are individuals who exhibit organization ability and have leadership potential. Their ability to sympathize with the underdog makes them prime candidates for gang leadership. They may transform loosely organized cliques into viable organizations with ideological goals.
> 2. *Manipulators* have an uncanny ability to judge the character of those with whom they interact and identify their weaknesses. Ruthless and self-centered, their relations with others are generally quite shallow.
> 3. *Asocial aggressive* individuals tend to use violence to solve all frustrations. Their unpredictable and unreliable nature is not conducive to sociability.
> 4. *Asocial passive* individuals are isolated from others. Their personality is therefore primitive and underdeveloped.
> 5. *Immature conformists* or *cultural conformists* seek the approval of others and readily succumb to group pressures. They do whatever is necessary to maintain friendship and are ineffective when left alone.
> 6. *Neurotic delinquents* are unhappy, inhibited individuals who often play the scapegoat in group situations. Delinquent activities may seek to establish a sense of power or control.[29]

Cavan and Ferdinand suggest that each of these types may be associated with particular kinds of offenses but allow flexibility in assigning particular offenses to specific categories.

Another classification scheme based on personality type was developed by the California Youth Authority.[30] Because this scheme is similar to the Cavan and Ferdinand as well as the Jenkins and Hewitt classification, only the basic elements of this scheme will be presented. The Youth Authority classified delinquents after administering psychological tests and identifying three basic maturity levels illustrating delinquent types. The maturity levels are each divided into subtypes and given descriptive titles, as summarized below:

Maturity Level	Delinquent Subtype
I₂	unsocialized, aggressive
	unsocialized, passive
I₃	conformist, immature
	conformist, cultural
	manipulator
I₄	neurotic, acting out
	neurotic, anxious
	cultural identifier
	situational emotional reaction

Personality classifications have a great number of adherents and are currently popular in the field of juvenile delinquency. They are not without critics, however. The major arguments against classifications of this sort are that they do not distinguish delinquents from non-delinquents and that they are sufficiently vague that they do not permit objective verification.

Classification of Delinquent Collectives

Many delinquencies are social activities. That is, a number of individuals may engage in cooperative, coordinated efforts to achieve delinquent goals. Where this occurs, individualistic typologies may not be perceived as an adequate framework for analysis. A number of classification schemes have been developed to fill this analytical gap in the field. One group of delinquency analysts bases its typologies on the organizational structure of juvenile collectives. Others focus on the classification of gangs by goals and behavior orientation.

ORGANIZATIONAL STRUCTURE

In his classic study of 1313 gangs operating in the Chicago area during the 1920s, Frederick Thrasher identified or described four general types of gangs on the basis of organization. The *diffuse* gang, Thrasher suggested, is the most loosely organized group that can be called a gang. Group solidarity and loyalty is minimal, and the leadership is relatively unstructured. In the *solidified* gang, on the other hand, members have attained a high degree of loyalty and morale as a result of extended conflict with outsiders. His example of the solidified gang suggests that although the leadership is subject to shifts, the leaders are recognized by all members. The *conventionalized* gang resembles a formal organization. It often has a constitution, stated rules, and elected officers. If supervised, like an athletic club, for example, it may become conformist. However, it may also serve as a destructive and demoralizing force in the community. Thrasher's *criminal* gang has the organizational features of the conventionalized gang but also pursues organized delinquent activities.[31] Thrasher believed that the fully developed delinquent gang exhibited each of these types at some time in its history.[32] Play groups which attempt to imitate the gang but without acquiring its organizational characteristics Thrasher called *pseudogangs*.[33]

Yablonski expanded the organizational framework to classify gangs according to their degree of cohesion, norms, and role definitions.[34] Gangs are placed on a continuum from the least structured (the mob) to the most highly structured (social and delinquent gangs). Cavan and Ferdinand make a distinction between the clique and the traditional gang. They identify the clique as a small, loosely organized group and suggest that the traditional gang may be composed of many small cliques.[35] The gang is distinguished by its leadership structure and division of labor.

Schafer and Knudten make the distinction between organized delinquency and collective delinquency. An examination of the features of each suggests that permanence and degree of organization are the determinant criteria for placing groups into one category or the other. They recognize the delinquent gang as an example of an organized delinquent group; the mob is given as an example of a group engaging in collective delinquency.[36]

ORGANIZATIONAL GOALS

The organizational distinction has been used primarily to distinguish between gangs and other juvenile groupings. Many delinquency analysts prefer to focus attention on recognized gangs and distinguish between the organizational goals pursued cooperatively by its members. Some theorists distinguish subcultural differences displayed by various gangs. Gangs organized for different focal activities differ in terms of attitudes and values.

Cloward and Ohlin identify three subcultural forms: criminal, conflict, and retreatist gangs.[37] Each of the gangs is said to arise in response to the absence of legitimate opportunity structures in the community. Stressing the anomie concept, Cloward and Ohlin suggest that the breakdown in the regulation of goals encourages unlimited aspirations and pressures to pursue unorthodox means to reach status or monetary goals. The criminal gang provides an opportunity for lower-class youths to achieve economic success by illegal means. Gang activities often involve theft and the distribution of booty among its members. Because criminal gang membership is a highly desirable goal, the number of vacant positions is limited. Some youths must turn to other activities to achieve status. One alternative is the conflict gang, which confers status and "rep" on its members. Violence is the predominant behavioral mode in these groups. Individuals who are unable to meet the requirements of the criminal or conflict gang may withdraw into the retreatist subculture of drugs.

Walter Miller identified a general lower-class subcultural pattern of delinquency. Noting that some lower-class communities are well integrated and have few criminals within their structures, Miller pointed out that the concerns of the lower class are important elements in the development of delinquency in such areas. Because the lower-class male is concerned with masculinity, toughness, and effectively handling trouble with the police, he often seeks activities that involve high risks and danger. As a result of the orientations of lower-class youths, delinquent acts center around assault, burglary, and other exciting forms of behavior which may be illegal. These activities may involve groups of lower-class youngsters, but they sometimes include full-fledged gangs.[38] It would be surprising if delinquency were not found among individuals who accept the culture described by Miller.

Spergel introduced a subcultural pattern not identified by Cloward and Ohlin called the *theft subculture*.[39] Spergel found it difficult to separate the theft culture from a more general culture of the lower class, but the pattern is integrated into the life of a lower-class child and includes a variety of types of theft. Of course the delinquency pursued in this subcultural type is relatively mild in comparison to subcultural patterns described by Miller or the conflict, retreatist, and criminal cultures described by Cloward and Ohlin.

Schafer and Knudten identify gangs on the basis of sociability and behavioral orientations: social, asocial, and antisocial gangs.[40] The social gang members are oriented to conforming activities, such as chess, stamp collecting, and other harmless hobbies. The asocial gang, on the other hand, engages in nonconformist activity that threatens the community. Theft, destruction, and violence are focal activities. The asocial gang is described as a passive delinquent collective which succumbs to pressures toward delinquency. Drug use, promiscuity, truancy, and participation in the counterculture are favored modes of behavior.

Distinguishing between juvenile gangs on the basis of goals presents some problems. Field workers, carrying on research among gangs or providing social work programs, have found that it is often difficult to place a gang in one category or another. Although gangs may specialize in one pattern, other activities also occupy the group from time to time. A conflict gang whose calculated goal is physical fighting with other gangs, for example, may also engage in retreatist (drug use), criminal (petty theft), and social (bull sessions) activities. Furthermore, some theoretical patterns of gang delinquency do not appear to fit in the empirical arena. Short, Tennyson, and Howard, in a study of Chicago gangs, failed to find any criminally oriented gangs and were able to locate only one drug-oriented retreatist gang in over a year's research time.[41]

Most of these typologies have shown a lower-class bias, the assumption being that only lower-class juveniles engage in gang delinquency.[42] In order to fill the gap left by the subcultural theorists,

Ferdinand attempted to describe gang patterns displayed by middle- and upper-class youths.[43] His typology suggests an "aggressive exploitive" pattern characterized by competition and sexual prowess. This middle-class pattern may or may not involve delinquent activities. Organized gangs, according to Ferdinand, are not common in the middle class. The "mischievous indulgent" pattern characterized by drug and alcohol abuse is more common for upper-class youths. Some theft and sexual adventure may be exhibited. Here again, gang organization appears to be lacking.

Field studies of middle-class juvenile groups generally report little evidence for the existence of middle-class gangs.[44] Vaz's collection of readings on middle-class juvenile delinquency contains only one reading on gang behavior.[45] Gangs are perceived as a lower-class phenomenon. Arrest statistics, however, indicate that middle-class youths are often arrested in small groups. A complete, comprehensive typology of collective juvenile delinquency must take this fact into consideration.

Dual Classifications

A number of classification schemes are designed to take into account both individual and group delinquency. Where this is the case, collective or organized delinquency is generally placed in a category separate from those describing the individual delinquent. In essence, there is a combining of two separate and distinctly different sets of criteria for the development of a single typology. The inconsistent use of classification criteria will inevitably result in confusion and overlapping of categories, thereby reducing the efficiency of the classification scheme.

Certainly, it is important to analyze and describe the integration of the individual offender into social groups that engage in delinquent behavior. However, organizational structures and goals do not commit delinquencies. The individual offender must remain the primary unit of analysis, with special attention given to his or her interaction with others, both delinquent and nondelinquent.

CLASSIFICATION IN PERSPECTIVE

Consensus regarding the necessity of a comprehensive typology of juvenile delinquency has resulted in a proliferation of classification schemes. Some of the schemes have been rather simple twofold classifications; however, most have involved the manipulation of a complex variety of criteria. None of the typologies thus far developed has received wide recognition and approval.

The various typologies have been constructed for very specialized needs and therefore have different emphases. Because classification provides a tool for organizing vast amounts of data, almost any classification scheme is useful for one task or another. The various schemes, however, need to be integrated and codified to build a standard system which will enable the comparison of delinquency research and theoretical work.

NOTES

[1] Milton L. Barron, *The Juvenile in Delinquent Society* (New York: Knopf, 1956), p. 83.

[2] Arthur Lewis Wood, "Ideal and Empirical Typologies for Research in Deviance and Control," in *Faces of Delinquency*, ed. John P. Reed and Fuad Baali (Englewood Cliffs, N.J.: Prentice-Hall, 1972), p. 138.

[3] See, for example, Don C. Gibbons, *Delinquent Behavior*, 2d ed. (Englewood Cliffs, N.J.: Prentice-Hall, 1976); Martin R. Haskell and Lewis Yablonski, *Juvenile Delinquency* (Skokie, Ill.: Rand McNally, 1974); Stephen Schafer and Richard D. Knudten, *Juvenile Delinquency: An Introduction* (New York: Random House, 1970).

[4] See Ruth Shonle Cavan and Theodore N. Ferdinand, *Juvenile Delinquency*, 3d ed. (Philadelphia: Lippincott, 1975); Robert C. Trojanowicz, *Juvenile Delinquency: Concepts and Control* (Englewood Cliffs, N.J.: Prentice-Hall, 1973); Edwin H. Sutherland and Donald R. Cressey, *Criminology*, 8th ed. (Philadelphia: Lippincott, 1970).

[5] Harry Elmer Barnes and Negley K. Teeters, *New Horizons in Criminology*, 3d ed. (Englewood Cliffs, N.J.: Prentice-Hall, 1959), pp. 52–53.

[6] Don C. Gibbons, *Society, Crime and Criminal Careers* (Englewood Cliffs, N.J.: Prentice-Hall, 1973), p. 242.

[7] Don C. Gibbons, *Changing the Lawbreaker* (Englewood Cliffs, N.J.: Prentice-Hall, 1965), pp. 24–39.

[8] *Ibid.*

[9] Arthur Lewis Wood, "Ideal and Empirical Typologies for Research in Deviance and Control," *Sociology and Social Research* 53 (January 1969): 227–241.

[10] Sheldon Glueck and Eleanor Glueck, "Varieties of Delinquent Types," in Reed and Baali, *op. cit.*, p. 143.

[11] Wood, *op. cit.*

[12] Richard C. Cloward and Lloyd E. Ohlin, *Delinquency and Opportunity* (New York: Free Press, 1960).

[13] Sheldon Glueck and Eleanor Glueck, *Unraveling Juvenile Delinquency* (Cambridge, Mass.: Harvard University Press, 1950).

[14] Wood, *op. cit.*

[15] Schafer and Knudten, *op. cit.*, p. 69.

[16] Marshall Clinard, *Sociology of Deviant Behavior* (New York: Holt, Rinehart and Winston, 1963), p. 205.

[17] Ruth Shonle Cavan, *Juvenile Delinquency* (Philadelphia: Lippincott, 1962), pp. 141–162.

[18] *Ibid.*, pp. 164–177.

[19] Clinard, *op. cit.*

[20] Joseph W. Eaton and Kenneth Polk, *Measuring Delinquency* (Pittsburgh: University of Pittsburgh Press, 1961).

[21] Thorsten Sellin and Marvin Wolfgang, *The Measurement of Delinquency* (New York: Wiley, 1964); the scheme is discussed in Trojanowicz, *op. cit.*

[22] Federal Bureau of Investigation, *Uniform Crime Reports, 1973* (Washington, D.C.: Government Printing Office, 1974), pp. 55–56.

[23] Barnes and Teeters, *op. cit.*, pp. 126–127.

[24] Clinard, op. cit., pp. 200–216.

[25] Don C. Gibbons, "Types as Role Careers," Reed and Baali, op. cit., p. 160.

[26] William H. Sheldon, S. S. Stevens, and W. B. Tucker, Varieties of Human Physique (New York: Harper & Row, 1940); William H. Sheldon, Varieties of Temperament (New York: Harper & Row, 1942); William H. Sheldon, Emil M. Hartl, and Eugene McDermott, Varieties of Delinquent Youth (New York: Harper & Row, 1949).

[27] R. L. Jenkins and L. Hewitt, "Types of Personality Structure Encountered in Child Guidance Clinics," American Journal of Orthopsychiatry 14 (1944):84.

[28] Kurt Lewin, Field Theory in Social Science (New York: Harper & Row, 1951).

[29] Cavan and Ferdinand, op. cit., pp. 162–167.

[30] John E. Riggs, William Underwood, and Marguerite Q. Warren, Interpersonal Maturity Level Classification: Juvenile, C.T.P. Research Report, no. 4 (Sacramento: California Youth Authority, 1964), pp. 1–12.

[31] Frederick M. Thrasher, The Gang, abr. ed. (Chicago: University of Chicago Press, 1963), pp. 48–55.

[32] Ibid., p. 47.

[33] Ibid.

[34] Lewis Yablonski, The Violent Gang (Baltimore: Penguin Books, 1966). Also see Haskell and Yablonski, op. cit., pp. 182–184.

[35] Cavan and Ferdinand, op. cit., pp. 116–117.

[36] Schafer and Knudten, op. cit., pp. 128–177. A similar conception is offered by Lewis Yablonski, "The Delinquent Gang as a Near-Group," Social Problems 7 (fall 1959): 108–117.

[37] Richard C. Cloward and Lloyd Ohlin, Delinquency and Opportunity (New York: Free Press, 1960).

[38] Walter B. Miller, "Lower Class Culture as a Generating Milieu of Gang Delinquency," Journal of Social Issues 14 (fall 1958): 5–19.

[39] Irving Spergel, Racketville, Slumtown and Haulberg (Chicago: University of Chicago Press, 1964).

[40] Schafer and Knudten, op. cit., pp. 138–139.

[41] James F. Short, Jr., Ray A. Tennyson, and Kenneth I. Howard, "Behavior Dimensions of Gang Delinquency," American Sociological Review 28 (June 1963): 411–428.

[42] Alex Thio, "Class Bias in the Sociology of Deviance," American Sociologist 8 (February 1973): 1–12.

[43] Theodore N. Ferdinand, Typologies of Delinquency (New York: Random House, 1966).

[44] Howard L. Myerhoff and Barbara G. Myerhoff, "Field Observations of Middle Class 'Gangs'," Social Forces 42 (March 1964): 328–336.

[45] Edmund W. Vaz, ed., Middle Class Juvenile Delinquency (New York: Harper & Row, 1967).

PART TWO
Delinquency
causation

The search for causes of undesirable behavior is an age-old activity. Every generation has assumed that the discovery of what causes misbehavior will enable society to rid itself of the behavior and bring harmony among its members. Unfortunately, each generation has been constrained in its search by the amount of knowledge and the techniques available to analysts of criminal and delinquent behavior. Through the years, knowledge and technique have produced a variety of bases for theory, from a belief in demons to scientific methods. Because knowledge and techniques follow patterns of cumulative development, the field of juvenile delinquency theory has come a long way.

This section begins with an examination of the requirements of theory in Chapter 6. An analysis of these criteria suggest that much of the speculation about crime and delinquency in the past does not qualify as scientific theory. Careful attention to the needs of an effective theoretical framework is suggested for current attempts at theory construction to avoid the mistakes and pitfalls of the past.

Chapter 7 deals primarily with historical attempts to explain criminal and delinquent behavior. Although many of the "theories" discussed in this chapter may appear simplistic and even absurd, they alert us to the mistakes of the past and suggest some of the foundations of modern theories and practices. If we can use an equally critical eye in regard to modern theories, the miscalculations of the past may not seem so glaring.

Psychological and psychiatric theories of delinquency are introduced in Chapter 8. Although some of the psychological and psychiatric theories of Freud and others are not readily amenable to empirical verification, they have exerted a tremendous influence on modern conceptions of delinquency. A great many prevention and treatment programs have been designed from this perspective.

Chapters 9 and 10 deal with sociological theories of delinquency causation. The emphasis of Chapter 9 is placed on the individual delinquent and the factors that may have led him or her to commit delinquent acts. Sutherland's differential association theory, which suggests that the individual learns delinquent attitudes, values, techniques, skills, and rationalizations through associations with others, is the first major theory examined. A second major theoretical framework is labeling. Here the emphasis is on the processes by which an individual acquires the label of juvenile delinquent and the individual's response to the stigma associated with that label. Other theories, which investigate the effects of the culture, society, social structure, and other factors on producing delinquency, are also presented.

The emphasis in Chapter 10 is on collective, or gang, delinquency.

Cohen's theory of delinquent gangs is the first perspective investigated. Cloward and Ohlin's differential opportunity structure is the second theoretical framework discussed. Other theoretical perspectives on collective delinquency are also presented. In Chapters 9 and 10, criticisms, reformulations, and the presence or lack of research support are discussed for each of the major theoretical frameworks.

Chapter 10 notes the lack of interdisciplinary approaches to juvenile delinquency causation. Certainly, theories of this nature are essential if all possible causes of delinquency are to be exhausted. Juveniles are multifaceted human beings; biological, psychological, and social characteristics may all be essential to a comprehensive understanding of the juvenile delinquent and his behavior.

Popular conceptions about the causes of delinquency are examined in Chapter 11. The influence of the family, broken homes, schools, and the mass media are among the topics discussed. Evidence for the validity or lack of validity of popular theories is noted for each topic.

The interplay of history, theory, and empirical research is a common emphasis in each of the chapters in Part Two. The implications of theory for the development of adequate conceptualizations of juvenile delinquents and their acts, as well as for policy decisions, make knowledge of theory essential to the student and practitioner alike.

CHAPTER 6
Problems of causation

Definitions, typologies, and statistics suggest the content and give evidence of juvenile delinquency, but they do not indicate *why* delinquency and juvenile delinquents exist. The causes of juvenile delinquency or child crime have long been a focal concern for society. Explanations of behavior relieve the tensions and fears associated with the unknown and provide security based upon the assumption that there is a link between cause and "cure." While the desirability of finding adequate explanations for behavior generally goes unquestioned, the requirements of causation place a number of restrictions on the theories that are presented as viable explanations of delinquent behavior.

FACING THE UNKNOWN

In the absence of carefully documented evidence to explain juvenile delinquency, many theories have been developed and programs suggested to alleviate the problem. Since theories reflect the knowledge and sophistication of the period in which they are developed, many of the early theories presented to explain delinquency seem naive and uninformed by today's standards. The evolution of criminal and delinquency theories mirrors the shift from an emphasis on the supernatural to a reliance on science to explain everyday occurrences.

Evolution of Theory

The earliest theories of delinquency, or child crime, were based on superstition. Lack of knowledge about the nature of the physical world and social life prompted much speculation. Probably the first attempt to explain crime and delinquency was provided by the *demon theory*. Demonology suggested that deviant behavior was caused by demons, spirits, or other invisible forces that possessed the offenders' bodies and made them do bad or evil things.[1] The belief in demonology remained in fashion longer than any other theory for deviant behavior. Even after its decline in popularity, occasional surges in support for the theory were, and still are, apparent. Remnants of these old beliefs are evident in our language today. For example, we occasionally hear some people ask "What got into him?" when confronted with a person who deviates from the norm.

The first attempts to explain crime and delinquency on the basis of scientific observation focused on the external characteristics of the body. Early theorists believed that brain size, head shape, protrusions or "bumps" on the head, and other, similar factors could lead to crime and delinquency. Although the focus of study shifted from the mind, or soul, of the individual to his physical characteristics, the basic premises underlying these theories did not differ significantly from the earlier belief in demons. The common elements of predestination and lack of individual responsibility were evident. While spirits entered the willing or unwilling body according to the demon theory, unknown forces also determined the body characteristics of the physically deformed individual. The individual's fate was determined by forces outside him.

Theories that were developed to replace these earlier, unsophisticated ones often did not offer entirely revolutionary premises. Mysterious, unknowable external forces were basic underlying causes of crime and juvenile delinquency, according to the earliest theories. Later theories relied on similar mysterious but knowable external forces, such as social or economic systems, to explain the same type of behavior. New theories did not repudiate all the elements of earlier explanations. On the contrary, new theories were developed through the modification and expansion of the basic premises of earlier works to reflect the knowledge and sophistication of the period in which they were developed.

Policy Implications

Logic suggests that there is an intimate relationship between cause and cure. If the necessary prior conditions for an event are removed, it is reasonable to expect that the event cannot and will not occur. This logical link between cause and cure has spurred the search for the causes of crime and delinquency in an effort to develop solutions to these problems.

Early theories focused on evil supernatural forces as the underlying cause of criminality. Because these forces were more powerful than man, he could not eliminate them. The individual offender as the

instrument of evil, however, could be controlled. Social policies based on the demon theory attempted to reduce and control crime through exorcism, exile, and execution. It was believed that an individual could be relieved of evil spirits through exorcism by transferring the spirit to an inanimate, and therefore more harmless, object. The evil spirit would not be eliminated completely but would be in a position to cause a minimum of damage. If exorcism was impractical or did not work, exile might be imposed on the individual to remove him or her from an area where he could cause harm to the populace to an environment where his evil actions would be no problem. When all else failed, execution was considered.

The common-sense solutions to the problems of crime in a simple society presented no serious problems. However, as the rights of man were given greater emphasis and the theories of crime and delinquency grew more complex, social policies designed to prevent and control crime became less well defined. The complexity of cause and solution in modern society does not, fortunately, negate their relationship. If we can locate the causes of delinquency by modern theory and methodology, and if these causes are subject to manipulation, it should be possible to develop social policies that might prevent or control juvenile delinquency. The profusion of modern delinquency theories and their varied policy implications nevertheless suggest serious questions regarding the limits of social control.

Social Control and Juvenile Delinquency
Societies will never be free of deviant behavior. Some crime and delinquency will always confront them. Whether or not this is a nega-

tive situation is a matter of debate. Emile Durkheim suggests that criminal behavior (and juvenile delinquency, which shares some of its characteristics) serves positive functions for a society. He contends that crime is both normal and necessary to society because it has a role in promoting cohesion, setting boundaries of acceptable behavior, and facilitating social change.[2] The general consensus, however, appears to be that the amount of crime and delinquency present in American society is far more than is "normal" or "necessary" to the society and that controls need to be instituted.

Ethics of Control

Practical and ethical problems arise in the development of programs of intervention, prevention, and control.[3] Ethical problems are encountered when decisions must be made regarding who is to be controlled and who is to make control decisions. We may eventually be able to predict delinquent behavior before people commit criminal acts by learning a great deal about their backgrounds. Moreover, we may be able, by working with schools or other institutions, to change the situations that produce delinquent behavior. Social policies of this nature, however, require a shift in emphasis to a programed society and a turning away from a primary concern for individual rights.

Even if a programed society were desirable, a number of questions would still remain to be answered. Who would make these decisions? Who would be affected most by these decisions? Also, who has the right to intervene in the life of another in the belief that he might one day commit a delinquent act? These questions suggest that even though we may someday gain the knowledge to prevent or reduce delinquency, there may be ethical, legal, or moral problems that would prevent the widespread application of effective programs. This is not to say that the search for causes should be abandoned because of their possible consequences. Social control will be exerted to reduce or prevent juvenile delinquency whether or not the causes are actually known. Verified knowledge of the causes of juvenile delinquency may well prevent abuses of social-control authority based on unfounded or invalid beliefs.

Current beliefs about the causes of delinquency are valuable and should not be discarded until they have been exhaustively studied. Beliefs in themselves do not provide a sufficient foundation for explanation and social policy, but they do provide a starting point for building theories which can be tested by various verification techniques. Extensive testing of the theories derived from current beliefs may lead to the modification, extension, or discarding of various theories. Adequate theories resulting from these verification processes may suggest programs to effect intelligent methods for prevention and control.

THEORY AND EXPLANATION

The search for explanations of juvenile delinquent behavior has produced a voluminous literature. The difficulty of separating fact and valid ideas from supposition and fallacy in these diverse writings has created a great many different views of juvenile delinquency. In order to explain juvenile delinquency in light of the divergent perspectives, a number of theories have been proposed. It is generally assumed that theories explain phenomena or behavior, but a careful examination of what theory is and what theory does indicates that theories do not explain but rather provide a framework for explanation.

Theory: Definition and Explication

Most scientists agree that theories are useful, and even necessary, for explaining any phenomenon; there is less agreement on what qualifies as theory. Some scientists define theory very narrowly and suggest that statements that do not meet these stringent requirements do not qualify as theory. Others are willing to concede a broader definition of theory.

Some scientists equate theory with description. The theoretical task is to identify, define, and describe concepts. Much can be learned about the nature of a phenomenon when this approach is used. However, a description of a phenomenon does not constitute theory. It does not indicate why or how the phenomenon is perpetuated. Certainly, theory involves concepts and their definitions. However, concepts in themselves are not theory but are rather the "building blocks" of theory.[4] They are only one of the necessary elements of theory.

A few sociologists equate theory with the works of the classical writers. If a book or article is old and yet remembered and read, some individuals believe its contents should be called theory. Modern theorists need to be cognizant of the contributions of early writers, but dependence on their writings may obscure more recent but important contributions and result in the stagnation of knowledge in the area.

A third group of sociologists define theory in a more narrow and precise sense to include only formal systems from which testable hypotheses can be derived.[5] The narrowness of this definition may lead to the unnecessary rejection of some useful conceptual schemes or potentially valuable, but less clearly delineated, ideas about explanation, and it allows the scientist to ignore some of the assumptions he must make about his methods and data.[6]

A compromise between the philosophical and narrowly scientific views about what qualifies as theory has been suggested by Sjoberg. According to him, theories are ideas about explanations that have a "broad logical structure" and generally involve content that includes "generalizations or propositions [hypotheses] concerning the patterning of the empirical world."[7] This broad definition of theory retains the assumptions ignored by strict scientific definitions of theory and broadens the scope of theory.

What constitutes a theory, and what its appropriate scope and content are, are extremely difficult questions to answer, but the nature and purpose of theory may be more clearly delineated. Theories are speculations about why and how events or phenomena occur. They are not facts. If it can be demonstrated that events will occur precisely as stated, without exception, the statement is no longer theory but law.[8] The statements of relationship (hypotheses) found in delinquency theories do not mysteriously explain why and how juvenile delinquency occurs. Only laws have this capability, and there are no scientific laws of juvenile delinquency. Theories merely provide a framework through which juvenile delinquency can be analyzed and predicted. In other words, a theory does not explain why and how one event leads to another but suggests possible relationships between a phenomenon and other phenomena. Where the relationships stated in the theory can be verified, causal inferences can be made.

Theories, by their statement of relationship, provide logical perspectives for examining or studying juvenile delinquency. Their validity and utility for prediction and explanation, however, are demonstrated only through verification research examining the stated relationships. One result of an increasing emphasis on research in juvenile delinquency has been an attempt to structure or restructure delinquency theories with an eye toward verification requirements.

SCOPE AND CONTENT

Delinquency theories vary in scope and content. The scope of theories varies with the inclusiveness of the phenomena under study. Some theories attempt to explain all delinquent behavior; others are limited to certain types of delinquent behavior (such as gang behavior). The scope of a theory is also determined by its power of explanation. A theory may seek to explain a phenomenon in its entirety or it may be addressed to only one facet of a phenomenon. While a few theories attempt to delineate and clarify the relative importance of all factors involved in the genesis of juvenile delinquent behavior, others have a more limited application and attempt only to identify some of the factors leading to delinquent behavior.

The content of a theory reflects the interests of the theorist. The subject chosen, the features emphasized, and the approach taken are expressions of a perspective. Where a phenomenon is not fully understood, it is subject to a variety of interpretations; there is no single explanation that satisfies all. Speculation about what causes an event is in part determined by the speculator's past experience and interests. If, for example, a diverse group of individuals wished to speculate on why dogs bite, many explanations may be given. Individuals interested in motivation may suggest psychological explanations. Those trained in animal biology may suggest explanations related to the animal's physical condition. Still others may suggest that the nature of the relationship between the animal and his victim is paramount. Each of these theories is based upon the perspective of the individual. Speculation about what causes delinquency is subject to the same processes.

Because theories vary in scope and content, imprecise statement of a theory may result in its misinterpretation and limit its utility. The types of hypotheses stated or implied in a theory influence the choice of verification techniques and even the type of data employed in its validation. If misunderstanding or misinterpretation suggests improper research techniques, the intended theory may not receive an adequate test. The researcher can only attempt to verify his interpretation of the theory which may or may not coincide with the intent of the theorist. Clear and precise statements of a theory give the researcher adequate clues, however, to accurately estimate the intended scope and content of a theory. A precise specification of the theoretical hypotheses contributes to clarity but does not negate the need for verification or justify ignoring the requirements of causal inference.

Causal Inference

One of the major problems encountered in the search for causes has been the vague manner in which cause itself has been defined. Everyone believes that he knows what *cause* means until he is asked to define it. We know, for example, that yeast causes a cake to rise. Few problems about the meaning of *cause* are encountered in everyday life,[9] and we readily use causal language in our day-to-day speech, with terms such as *produce, leads to, influences,* and so on.[10] In a more scientific sense, however, *cause* is not so readily amenable to definition.

DEFINITION OF CAUSE

A search of the sociological literature indicates that sociologists often disagree on the definition, as well as on the usefulness, of the concept of cause. Some writers state that it may not be necessary to use the concept of cause in delinquency theory or in other areas of sociology,[11] but others point out that it is useful as a language convention.[12] The concept of cause might be defined after an extensive study of Kant and Hume and more recent social scientists, but it does not appear necessary or profitable to get extensively involved with this old problem here. One method used to avoid this difficult definitional problem is to take the position of Costner and Blalock, who suggest treating *cause* as a primitive or undefined term in any theory.[13] As they point out, "causes can never be observed empirically, nor can they be defined theoretically. . . ." The concept of cause can be defined as a convention used to suggest that a change in one phenomenon produces or leads to change in another.[14]

REQUIREMENTS OF CAUSATION

Causation can be inferred in the following situations:

1. An independent variable (the phenomenon that produces change) is prior to the dependent variable (the phenomenon being changed) in a time sequence.
2. The dependent and the independent variables are associated; a change in one variable makes a change in the other.
3. The association between the variables remains even if the influence of other independent variables is controlled (no spurious relationship).[15]

It is often easier to establish noncausality than to infer causality. Causal inference requires that all three of the conditions listed above (association, temporal order, and lack of spuriousness) be met. The absence of any one of these conditions, however, is sufficient ground for establishing noncausality. Hirishi and Selvin point out that some frequently cited causes of delinquency, such as broken homes, poverty, poor housing, and lack of recreational facilities, are associated with juvenile delinquency and may appear in required causal order but nevertheless are not causes of delinquency.[16] In addition to association and causal order, a finding of no spurious relationship must be indicated. In the case of broken homes and juvenile delinquency, for example, juvenile delinquency is not eliminated when homes are held intact nor does the relationship between delinquency and broken homes remain the same when other factors are changed or removed. Thus, broken homes alone do not cause delinquency.

PROBLEMS IN THE CAUSAL SITUATION

Even if the conditions necessary to infer causation are present in a situation, unknown factors may make the assumption of causation invalid. An illustration of this problem can be shown in the story of the old maids and the honey supply:

A stranger in town remarked to a gray-haired old man that the honey in the region was the best he had ever tasted. The stranger suggested that honey-producing conditions must be exceptional. The old resident smiled, nodded, and replied that the next year's honey crop would be even better and more abundant because two old maids had moved into town in the past month. The stranger chuckled at the foolish old man and indicated that he didn't understand his reasoning. He was sure that the old fellow was senile and that his mind had wandered off the subject at hand. There could be no connection between old maids and a honey crop; bees, not old maids, produce honey. Being familiar with the limited logic of strangers from the city, the old man asserted that there was a definite connection between old maids and a good supply of honey. You see, said the old man, when old maids move into town they are very lonely and they acquire cats to keep them company. The impatient stranger got annoyed with the old man's slow explanation of the situation and demanded to know what difference old maids and their cats made. The old man explained that cats eat a lot of mice. Mice have a peculiar craving for clover seeds, and if there weren't enough cats to eat the mice, there wouldn't be enough seeds to make a good clover crop. The old man asserted that everybody knows that bees thrive on clover, and clover makes the best honey in the world. So, if you have more old maids, you have better honey!

As Simon has pointed out, you are well advised to "get to know all about the circumstances surrounding the causal relationship you seek to establish."[17] There may be much more to a situation than the apparent relationships, and these must be understood for a full explanation.

Closely related to the problem of lack of relevant information is the problem of the hidden third factor. The hidden third factor involves the presence of a factor that is not perceived to have relevance but nevertheless must be present before the causative situation will occur. Simon illustrated the problem of the hidden third factor by referring to the classic case of the drunk gentlemen who after drinking "brandy and soda, whiskey and soda and bourbon and soda, concluded that the soda caused their inebriation."[18] While their logic was sound in respect to causal ordering (they were drinking soda before they became incapacitated) and appeared to be sound in regard to association (they drank soda each time), they did not test for spuriousness (this could have been done by removing other factors and drinking soda alone). Furthermore, this example suggests that lack of information or too great specificity may result in the rejection of important factors in the causal chain. Although it may appear common-sense reasoning to us that brandy, bourbon, and whiskey are all alcoholic beverages and should not have been rejected as unimportant in the causal chain, such distinctions are not always apparent.

Confounding factors may also present a problem in the causative situation. In this instance, the apparent cause and the phenomenon that is caused are both related to, and possibly caused by, a third factor. For example, an association between delinquency and home environment might be caused by a third factor—poverty, in the event that poverty causes both home environment and juvenile delinquency. Although confounding factors are closely related to the hidden third factor, these factors are not the same problems. As you remember, in the case of the drinking gentlemen, while alcohol consumption (the hidden third factor) was the apparent cause of the incapacitation, it did not appear that it also caused the drinking of soda. The problems of confounding are particularly striking when the factors under consideration are not clear. In the case of home environment and poverty as causes of juvenile delinquency, it is well to examine whether they are separate phenomena or whether home environment is just an indicator of poverty.

The dependent variable (the variable to be changed or explained) may not be caused by one, or even two, variables. Delinquency, for instance, may be produced by numerous factors (multivariate causation). Several modern sociological theories stipulate the circumstances under which the major causal factors may be considered. In Sutherland's theory of differential association, contact with individuals who have definitions favorable to violation of law is considered to be the major factor in the genesis of delinquent behavior. Sutherland indicates, however, that an individual having these associations must be presented with an opportunity to commit such acts and know the techniques for committing the acts.[19] Multivariate statistical techniques[20] are available to determine how much influence is exerted by each factor in a complex causal scheme involving numerous variables. Multivariate techniques have enjoyed considerable respect, but the problem of determining whether all relevant variables have been considered still remains.

Although a number of problems in the causal situation result from a lack of all relevant information, even a knowledge of all of the relevant information (including hidden and confounding factors) does not assure that valid statements about cause can be made. Aside from the problems created by the lack of information, feedback between the variables must also be considered. The variables may influence each other. Consider the problem of the association between home environment and juvenile delinquency; a poor home environment may provide a fertile ground for the genesis of delinquent behavior, but at the same time delinquent behavior in the home may result in an even poorer home environment. When the feedback element is present in the causative situation, special efforts must be made to establish causal relationships and to separate direct causative effects from the effects of feedback.

THEORETICAL VERIFICATION: RESEARCH METHODS

Empirical research allows the sociologist to assemble, organize, and interpret facts about juvenile delinquency and other social behavior.[21] The ultimate goal of research, however, is the verification of theory through the use of a variety of methodological techniques. Theory and research methods are intimately related. The development of complex methods of verification makes it possible to test complex theoretical relationships and allows the theorist to state relationships in new and different ways. Conversely, new statements of theory may demand revised or new research methods to test the theory. Furthermore, research allows the scientist to correct, modify, extend, or generate new theoretical relationships. Because theory and research methods are so closely linked, it is necessary to become acquainted with research methods in order to understand the intricacies involved in the evolution and verification of theory.

Research Methods

Detailed presentations of current research methods are presented in a number of sources;[22] therefore, detailed description is not necessary here. A brief overview of two major types of research strategies—exploratory and explanatory research methods—is sufficient at this point to suggest the nature and extent of the relationship between theory and research methods. Although both major types of research methods are useful techniques, their purposes and the utility of the information gathered varies (see Table 6.1). The type of analysis chosen for any given research project depends on the research question being asked, the clarity and precision of the theoretical statement, and the purpose of the inquiry.

EXPLORATORY RESEARCH METHODS

Hypotheses (statements of relationship between independent and dependent variables) are not tested in exploratory research. Instead, several variables are specified, but the nature of the relationships among the variables generally is not stated in advance. Data is collected and ordered in convenient categories or presented with the aid of graphs and tables for ease of understanding. An explicit relationship of the data to an existing theory is usually not attempted. The purpose of the exercise is to illustrate existing situations accurately and discover relationships without being bound by the formal rules of logic characteristic of explanatory research.

The practical application of these methods is found in the standardized crime statistics reported in the *Uniform Crime Reports* and in the decennial reports of the U.S. Census Bureau. These publications utilize reports of events or demographic characteristics of individuals but do not refer to theoretical constructions. Another commonly used descriptive technique is the case study. Participant observation or available records are often used to describe and summarize the characteristics of some sociological phenomena by reference to isolated cases. Emerson's study of the juvenile court is one example of the use of this technique,[23] and Whyte's *Street Corner Society* is another.[24]

Exploratory research may be a necessary first step to verification, because case studies, in-depth interviews, and accurate descriptive statistics may contribute significantly to constructing theories that can be verified with more quantitative research methods. It may be necessary to obtain a practical knowledge of delinquent behavior through these techniques so that theoretical relationships can be developed for testing with explanatory techniques.

TABLE 6.1 COMPARISON OF EXPLORATORY AND EXPLANATORY RESEARCH STRATEGIES

TYPE OF RESEARCH	MAJOR VARIANTS	UTILITY	RELATIONSHIP TO THEORY	EMPHASIS ON MEASUREMENT	STATISTICAL METHODS
Exploratory	participant or unknown observer life histories case studies in-depth interviews descriptive statistics (summary and description)	description, discovery, suggest hypotheses, build theory	often weak but could be first step to verification in developing theory	often weak	some methods do not require statistics but if used they include measures of central tendency, standard deviation, and summary tables and figures
Explanatory	experiments nonexperimental (statistical inference, tests of hypotheses) mailed questionnaires structured interviews, etc.; dynamic and longitudinal design	test hypotheses	often strong	strong	statistical tests of hypotheses (regression, analysis of variance, correlation)

EXPLANATORY RESEARCH METHODS

Explanatory research methods are more directly linked to sociological theory. An attempt is made to apply research findings to earlier research and theoretical efforts. In other words, the work is not isolated but integrated into a larger enterprise. Various techniques are used to state hypotheses more explicitly, define concepts, and analyze the findings in view of what would be expected if the theory proved valid. If theory allows the researcher to account for variations in the data, verification of the theory may be possible.

Both exploratory and explanatory techniques are useful, but explanatory techniques have the advantage of allowing scientists to test some of the ideas found in the theory to see if they fit with the data that is collected. Science becomes self-correcting in the sense that research can suggest that portions of a theory do not account for regularities in the data and may indicate modified statements of relationship for further testing. Explanatory research helps move theory from the realm of speculation and ideas into the realm of knowledge and even sociological law.

Although exploratory techniques have predominated in the study of juvenile delinquency in the past, explanatory studies are rapidly increasing. Recent examples of the use of explanatory techniques include Chilton and Markle's study "Family Disruption, Delinquent Conduct and the Effect of Subclassification"[25] and Griffin and Griffin's studies of drug and marihuana use.[26]

DELINQUENCY THEORIES

In the chapters that follow, a number of different and often competing theories are presented and discussed. These theories are drawn from different time periods and represent the accumulation of thinking about the causes of child crime or delinquent behavior. Because juvenile delinquency was not separated from adult crime until the twentieth century, some early theories were applied to both juveniles and adults. Many of the theories are still mere speculation, but others have varying degrees of empirical support. You might find many of the theories simplistic, inadequate, or both.

A comprehensive theory of juvenile delinquency might include biological, psychological, sociological, and economic factors. However, there has been little interest in pursuing an interdisciplinary approach. The trend is toward disciplinary separatism.

Perhaps an adequate understanding of delinquency causation cannot be developed by a single discipline such as sociology or psychology. Interdisciplinary approaches might be stressed, but there is little evidence that this approach has produced more adequate explanations than intradisciplinary efforts.

Classification of Delinquency Theories

A typology, or classification scheme, is used in the chapters that follow to facilitate an understanding of the various theories of juvenile delinquency. The basic features of the typology are introduced to suggest how the theories are compared and contrasted even across schools of thought and disciplines in the social sciences. The typology is believed to be useful because it allows the summary and description of relatively large amounts of information even though it may not be a universally accepted classification. Each chapter on theory contains one or more tables that summarize the information discussed in the text about the theories of delinquency causation it examines. These tables are designed as summaries, but they should also allow you to compare, contrast and describe each theory.

Within each of the major divisions of delinquency theory (early theories of child crime, psychological and psychiatric theories, sociological theories, and interdisciplinary theories) there are various schools of thought comprising the writings of scholars who are believed to exhibit similarities in terms of their approaches to delinquency causation. For example, included under the heading of early approaches to child crime are six different schools: demonology, physiognomy, phrenology, environmental determination, economic determinism, and the classical school (see Table 7.1).

The first major criterion for comparing these schools is the general *approach* taken to delinquency, and this category would give an idea of the major or general causal factors that were considered. For example, the physiognomy school's approach emphasized the personality and the body as major factors. The *focus* of the theory is the second criterion for comparison. In this category we look more closely at the major variables that the theorists considered relevant. For example, the physiognomy school considered facial features and other external attributes to be important elements to focus on in their research. The third criterion of comparison looks at the major *concepts* that the theorists used in formulating their theories. In the classical school, for instance, the pleasure-pain principle and the "penal pharmacy" were relevant concepts. Under our fourth criterion for comparison, the *leading writers* are listed for each school.

By reading across a row in the typology table, it is possible to see at a glance the major characteristics of a school or theory in approach, focus, concepts, and leading writers. Furthermore, schools can be compared regardless of the discipline toward which the school is oriented. The typology can also be used in a variety of others ways— as a check list of the variety of factors that have been advanced as possible causes of juvenile delinquency, as a study aid or mnemonic device to help recall salient features of each theory, and as a means of determining what factors, if any, have been omitted from consideration.

THEORY AND CAUSATION IN PERSPECTIVE

A theory of delinquency may consist of a series of interrelated propositions (or statements of relationship) that are used to explain the causes of delinquency. A good theory tends to inspire research to verify or test its hypotheses. The review of the theories of delinquency presented in the next five chapters makes it apparent that there is no single theory that adequately accounts for all delinquent behavior. It is important to examine these theories, however, as well as the presence or absence of research support for them. Science proceeds by building on the work of earlier scholars, and future theories should not make the mistake of attributing great importance to a factor or variable that has been demonstrated to have little effect. One of the major tasks of a scientific discipline is to build adequate theories and not defend existing theory. The emphasis should be on finding or building adequate explanations based on previous efforts rather than merely listing old and often outdated research hypotheses and encouraging their acceptance.

Even though a valid theory may be developed in the sense that it is not rejected by research, there are still problems because of the limitations in scientific explanation. Some theories are limited or partial in the sense that they explain only a portion of delinquency. It may be necessary to link partial theories to eventually obtain a general theory of delinquency or link partial delinquency theories to a more general theory of human behavior. Even though a theory may appear to have considerable research support, it should still be approached with a critical and somewhat skeptical eye. The theory that appears adequate today may, through the self-correcting nature of science, become less than acceptable in the future.

A well-systematized science of human behavior has not yet been developed, and we will find many beliefs, guesses, and descriptions of behavior as well as a few efforts to produce systematic theories. Sociologists are just beginning to discover and verify complex interrelationships so that more adequate prediction, explanation, understanding, and control of delinquency may be possible. There is still a need, however, for the development of new systematic causal explanations of delinquent behavior.

In the absence of an adequate theory of human behavior, a practitioner is reduced to the ad hoc field diagnosis of problems on which decisions are made about the futures of individuals. Field workers or caseworkers must make thorough investigations of delinquents and get relatively complete statements about their backgrounds and past delinquent behavior. Without a uniform framework, the social caseworker is left to seek and interpret information in a situation where his or her idiosyncrasies and preconceptions may help determine what is reported and the eventual outcome for the client. Because there is no widely accepted theory to inform and suggest to the practitioner which factors might be emphasized to modify behavior, the building and verification of adequate theories is especially important. The application of scientific knowledge to social problems is, after all, of vital concern and contributes to the welfare of a society.

NOTES

[1] See Harry Elmer Barnes and Negley K. Teeters, *New Horizons in Criminology*, 3d ed. (Englewood Cliffs, N.J.: Prentice-Hall, 1959), pp. 119–120.

[2] George Simpson, *Emile Durkheim: Selections from His Work* (New York: Crowell, 1963), p. 62.

[3] See Gideon Sjoberg, ed., *Ethics, Politics, and Social Research* (Cambridge, Mass.: Schenkman Publishing, 1967), for a discussion of ethical and political problems in research.

[4] A discussion of theory and theory construction can be found in Arthur L. Stinchcombe, *Constructing Social Theories* (New York: Harcourt Brace Jovanovich, 1968); Robert Dubin, *Theory Building* (New York: Free Press, 1969); Nicholas C. Mullins, *The Art of Theory: Construction and Use* (New York: Harper & Row, 1971); Hubert M. Blalock, Jr., *Theory Construction* (Englewood Cliffs, N.J.: Prentice-Hall, 1969); Jack P. Gibbs, *Sociological Theory Construction* (New York: Dryden Press, 1972).

[5] Hans L. Zetterberg, *On Theory and Verification in Sociology* (Totowa, N.J.: Bedminister Press, 1965), pp. 9–29.

[6] See Gideon Sjoberg and Roger Nett, *A Methodology for Social Research* (New York: Harper & Row, 1968), pp. 29–32.

[7] *Ibid.*, p. 30.

[8] Julian L. Simon, *Basic Research Methods in Social Science* (New York: Random House, 1969), pp. 360–361.

[9] *Ibid.*, p. 434.

[10] *Ibid.*

[11] Jack P. Gibbs, "Causation and Theory Construction," *Social Science Quarterly* 52 (March 1972): 815–826.

[12] Herbert L. Costner and Hubert M. Blalock, Jr., "Scientific Fundamentalism and Scientific Utility: A Reply to Gibbs," *Social Science Quarterly* 52 (March 1972): 827–844.

[13] *Ibid.*, p. 830; also see Blalock, *op. cit.*

[14] Costner and Blalock, *op. cit.*

[15] Travis Hirschi and Hanan C. Selvin, "False Criteria of Causality in Delinquency Research," *Social Problems* 13 (winter 1966): 254–268.

[16] *Ibid.*, pp. 255–256.

[17] Simon, *op. cit.*, p. 153.

[18] *Ibid.*, p. 154.

[19] Edwin H. Sutherland and Donald R. Cressey, *Criminology*, 8th ed. (Philadelphia: Lippincott, 1970), pp. 71–92.

[20] The student is referred to one or more of the following statistics books for a discussion of multivariate statistics: Hubert M. Blalock, Jr., *Social Statistics* (New York: McGraw-Hill, 1972); John H. Mueller, Karl F. Schuessler, and Herbert L. Costner, *Statistical Reasoning in Sociology*, 2d ed. (Boston: Houghton Mifflin, 1970); George W. Snedecor and William G. Cochran, *Statistical Methods*, 6th ed. (Ames: Iowa State University Press, 1967).

[21] Matilda White Riley, *Sociological Research* (New York: Harcourt Brace Jovanovich, 1963), p. 3.

[22] The student is referred to the following texts for a detailed discussion of sociological research methods: Riley, *op. cit.*; Simon, *op. cit.*; and Claire

Selltiz, Marie Jahoda, Morton Deutsch, and Stuart W. Cook, *Research Methods in Social Relations* (New York: Holt, Rinehart and Winston, 1959).

[23] Robert M. Emerson, *Judging Delinquents: Context and Process in Juvenile Court* (Chicago: Aldine, 1969).

[24] William Foote Whyte, *Street Corner Society* (Chicago: University of Chicago Press, 1943).

[25] Roland J. Chilton and Gerald E. Markle, "Family Disruption, Delinquent Conduct and the Effect of Subclassification," *American Sociological Review* 37 (February 1972): 93–99.

[26] Brenda S. Griffin and Charles T. Griffin, "Marijuana Use Among Students and Peers," *Drug Forum* (forthcoming, 1978); Brenda S. Griffin and Charles T. Griffin, "Drug Use and Differential Association," *International Journal of Addictions* (forthcoming, 1978).

CHAPTER 7
Early theories of child crime

Almost everything from acne, the family, divorce, and big ears to poverty, poor housing, race, demons, and bumps on the head have been listed as determinants of crime and delinquency. What now appear to be the results of simplistic and faulty reasoning were at one time serious attempts to understand and describe the causal processes of crime and delinquency. The single-factor or single-cause explanations developed in the past have, for the most part, been discarded by trained criminologists. However, the remnants of some of the early theories remain embedded in our culture and provide the simple, uncomplicated explanations so often desired and sought by laymen.

It may not be readily apparent why early theories of crime and delinquency have an important place in a text on juvenile delinquency. Many of the early theories do not contribute to a greater understanding of modern juvenile delinquency. On the other hand, a knowledge of fruitless searches for causes, blind alleys, and inaccurate or even seemingly ridiculous explanations is valuable because it illustrates the mistakes of the past and projects trends for the future. If nothing else, a review of the earnest efforts of the past can give us a more realistic perception of modern approaches and their value. One day the theories of the twentieth century may also be placed in the category of pre-scientific theories and criticized for their simplicity and faulty reasoning.

The earliest theories developed to explain norm-violating behavior did not distinguish between adult and juvenile offenders. The consideration of delinquency as a separate and distinct type of behavior is a relatively recent development. Thus the factors used to explain adult crime were also applied to youths. Some evidence suggests that juveniles were subjected to the same treatment given adults to eliminate the causes of disapproved behavior and thus the behavior itself. A summary of the various early theories is presented in Table 7.1.

PRESCIENTIFIC THEORIES

A number of the very early theories of crime were of a prescientific nature.[1] They were not developed from systematic observation and careful analysis of criminal behavior but instead were based on the moralist ideologies present in the society. Forces opposed to the natural order were blamed for problems that surfaced and resulted in conflict. Prescientific theories have been prominent throughout human history.

Demonology

Probably the oldest theory used to explain crime and delinquency involved possession by devils, evil spirits, or demons. "The devil made me do it" and "God will get you for that" are now comic phrases, but diabolical possession has been seriously accepted in a broad range of societies throughout most of recorded history. Where religious ideology dominated society, criminal conduct and sin were viewed as one and the same. The criminal was an offender against both God and man. Speculation about the causes of crime centered on belief in the power of good and evil spirits. Man was no match for the forces of nature; it was apparent that the power of God was dominant over the lives of individuals. Only when devils took possession of a body was that power challenged by the appearance of evil.

The belief in demons was prevalent in the United States as recently as the eighteenth century. The persecution of witches in New England was based on this belief. Relatively harmless individuals were burned to death or disposed of in other ways because they were believed to be possessed by devils. The purpose of individual persecution was to rid the community of devils or exorcise evil spirits. Unfortunately, this seems to have required the death of some of those possessed by the spirits. Marion Starkey's book The Devil in Massachusetts describes the impact of demonology in the persecution of witches in Massachusetts.[2] The Christian concept of original sin often became linked with demonic possession, resulting in a view of man as naturally perverse.

Demonic theories suggested a number of simple and straightforward treatments or "cures" for criminality. The devils might simply be driven from the society. This could be accomplished by exorcism to expunge the evil spirit. More certain and swift cures involved exile of the possessed individual or putting him or her to death. All of these

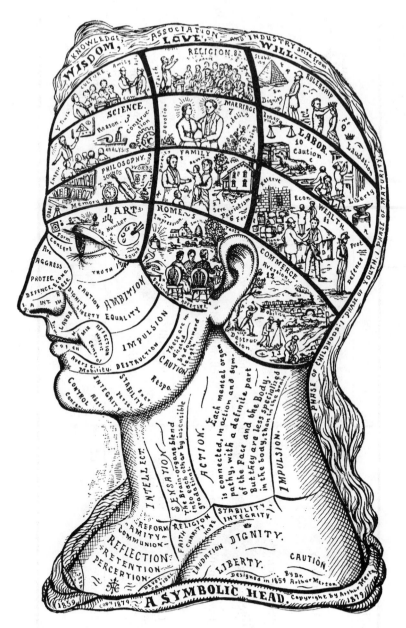

measures were designed to protect the society from contamination by possessed individuals.

Demonology no longer commands the attention of experts in criminology, but remnants of its influence still remain a part of the tradition of the criminal justice system and popular folklore. Many people still believe in the influence of devils, accept numerous superstitions, and use good luck charms and rituals to ward off evil spirits. Certainly the idea that devils influence behavior and that man is nat-

TABLE 7.1 EARLY THEORIES OF CHILD CRIME

	SCHOOL	APPROACH	FOCUS	CONCEPTS	LEADERS
Prescientific theories	Demonology	predestination	invisible forces	spirits demons possession	
	Physiognomy	personality and body	facial features and shape of skull	physiognomical fragments	della Porte Lavater
	Phrenology	personality and body	shape of skull and brain	organs faculties	Gall Spurzheim
	Environmental	geographic determinism	climate and topography	thematic law homicide formula	Quetelet Lacassagne Kropotkin
Rationalism	Classical	rational decision making	free will	pleasure-pain	Beccaria
			hedonism	hedonistic calculus	Bentham legal system
Determinism	Economic determinism	social structure	poverty		de Verce Bonger
			social class	strict law of causality	Marx and Engels

urally evil and perverse has not completely disappeared. Movies and books such as *The Exorcist, Rosemary's Baby,* and *The Omen* receive widespread acclaim and attention. Devil-worship cults have reappeared in recent years along with renewed interest in witches and magic. The clergy still give "hellfire and brimstone" sermons emphasizing the terrible reality of forces beyond our comprehension and understanding. Suggestions for handling delinquents often appear in keeping with this perspective. Popular belief suggests that delinquency might be contained if the delinquent had gone to church, come from a Christian home, or had the devil beaten out of him.

Physiognomy

The perceived relationship between body characteristics and criminal behavior captured the attention of a variety of philosophers and criminologists. Early philosophers such as Aristotle and Galen noted the possibility of such a relationship. The work of J. Baptiste della Porte (1535–1615) is probably the most representative of this early approach. Della Porte's theory of physiognomy was not actually a causal theory but was instead a method of predicting individual criminality. During his school years, he began to notice that personality appeared to be associated with facial features. Comparing the facial features of ordinary men with those of dead criminals, della Porte concluded that their basic physical features were different. He claimed that thieves, for example, could be identified by reference to their little ears, bushy eyebrows, small noses, thin lips, shifty eyes, and long fingers. Because these traits were inborn and intimately associated with criminality, della Porte believed that it was impossible to change or reform criminals. The physiognomy approach did not become widely accepted; however, it did draw a number of steadfast adherents through the years.

The ideas of della Porte would probably have had little impact had it not been for the work of John Casper Lavater about two hundred years later. His book *Physiognomical Fragments* focused attention on the head and skull once again. While the approach did not become popular, it did have significance as an influence on phrenology and the constitutional approach to criminology.[3]

Phrenology

Phrenology went a step beyond physiognomy by attempting to explain the connection between physical characteristics and criminal behavior. Franz Joseph Gall (1758–1828) dismissed the importance of facial features and concentrated instead on the shape of the skull. Believing that the mind controlled the body, Gall claimed that different types of minds were contained in differently shaped skulls. Studies of the shape and size of skulls of criminals seemed to provide evidence for this belief. Different bumps and irregularities in skull shape appeared to be associated with different types of criminal activity. Spurzheim, a student and collaborator of Gall, popularized and spread his teacher's ideas through his writing and lectures. Basically Gall's theory held that the skull takes the shape of the brain. Different areas of the brain, according to his theory, controlled distinct faculties or functions. By examining the shape of the skull, a trained observer could spot which areas, and thus faculties, were overdeveloped or underdeveloped. Gall's "cranioscopy" enabled him to map the skull into 27 areas which provided cues about individual behavioral tendencies. Spurzheim refined and elaborated Gall's theory, discovering 35 faculties.

Phrenology was widely accepted during the nineteenth century. Even leading social scientists such as William James and Auguste Comte were influenced by it. The theory was further legitimized when several public prisons began keeping cranial measurement records for their inmates. Phrenology began to lose popularity when it could not satisfy its critics. They pointed out that many noncriminals also possessed unusual skull configurations. Furthermore, the elementary development of psychology began to point out that the simple mapping procedure was not highly enough developed to explain the complexities of human behavior.

The biological base of physiognomy and phrenology is obvious. Suggestions that these approaches should be classified with the constitutional school are not without foundation; however, the quasi-scientific nature of the approaches argues for classification as prescientific theory. The relationship of phrenology with the constitutional approach discussed later in this chapter is direct and close. Phrenology did not just disappear; rather, it provided a foundation for the work of Lombroso and other constitutional theorists.

OTHER PRESCIENTIFIC THEORIES

Around the end of the eighteenth century, interest in the scientific method began to take hold in the social sciences. Before this time, speculation on the causes of crime had been little more than social philosophy. The development of statistical techniques represented a significant advance in the field of criminology. Many modern-day theories have their roots in prescientific theories developed and first tested more than a hundred years ago.[4]

Environmental and Geographic Determinism

Broadly defined, environment includes all factors that originate from forces external to the individual. Other persons, organizations, the neighborhood, housing conditions, weather, and geographic factors may be included under this interpretation. Early environmentalists were primarily concerned with spatial arrangements and characteristics of the physical ecological environment. Although their statistical and methodological techniques were crude by today's standards, they developed procedures that are still used in the collection of delinquency data. For example, social area analysis techniques used by early environmentalists were later adopted by modern ecologists.

The earliest environmental theories involved climate and topography. Geographers have often proposed that climate and topography affect human behavior. Temperature, altitude, humidity, and other features of the physical environment were blamed for high rates of crime and vice. Montesquieu, in his *Spirit of Laws*, suggested that criminality increased near the equator and drunkenness was more prominent as one approached the earth's poles.

Adolph Quetelet (1796–1874), the reputed father of statistics, was a leading figure in the development of geographic determinism and the statistical approach to crime. Rather than relying on intuition and casual observation as others before him had done, Quetelet systematically collected and analyzed data on homicide and other crimes. He reported his findings in several books which were distributed widely. One consistent finding was that property crimes were more likely to be found in cold northern areas, while crimes against the person were more prevalent in warm southern climates. Quetelet called this relationship between climate and crime the *thermatic law*. Quetelet's ideas inspired much research analyzing the influence of climate on crime. Lombroso, Ferri, and others observed similar relationships between crime and weather conditions. Lacassagne noted that December had a disproportionately high property crime rate and attributed the cause to climate. High crime rates are still noted for the month of December, but modern explanations suggest that social expectations regarding Christmas gift giving may be more important than the weather.

Prince Peter Kropotkin carried the environmentalist position much further than most geographic theorists. He developed a precise formula to predict the number of homicides that might be expected in a month in a given location:[5]

Number of homicides = (average temperature) (7) +
(average humidity) (2)

The application of his formula can result in comic conclusions. Because population size is not considered, the formula suggests that hot rural areas with few people may have a greater number of homicides than large cities in mild climates. Other geographic determinists and climatologists have attempted to discover a "spring urge" associated with biological body rhythms to explain the observed increase in sex crime rates that occurs in the spring. Despite the existence of spring fertility festivals such as Easter and university spring celebrations, most people discount the possibility of a spring urge.

The major weakness of geographic determinism was its failure to explain why weather and topographical features had an effect on some individuals living in a particular area and not on others. This defect was probably a result of the focus on crime rates rather than criminal offenders. The old theories were not totally without merit; they raised issues that required answers from modern sociologists. Merton, Cloward and Ohlin, Park and Burgess, and others can trace elements of their theories to the issues and questions raised by Quetelet and the geographic determinists.

THE CLASSICAL PERSPECTIVE

The classical approach, exemplified by the writings of Jeremy Bentham (1748–1832), represented a dramatic departure from early deterministic perspectives on criminal behavior. The classical theories were based upon the rationality of the individual. Rational people were not believed to be prisoners of external forces; they were free to make their own choices and behave as they wished. Unfortunately, free individuals were not endowed with inherent goodness. Hedonistic tendencies made them desirous of forbidden but pleasurable activities. They had to be taught to conform to societal rules. Through guidance and the application of sanctions for misbehavior, the individual developed a conscience and the ability to make distinctions between right and wrong. The rational person would seek to minimize pain and maximize pleasure. Programs to control crime, based on this theory, were simple. The society must provide sanctions for crime that would outweigh the possible pleasure to be gained from their commission. Some classical writers attempted to develop a "hedonistic calculus" wherein specific amounts of pleasure and pain were calculated for each violation. A penal pharmacy which provided the proper dose of punishment for each crime was suggested.

Classical writers developed their theories out of concern for problems in the legal system. At the end of the eighteenth century, punishments for crime were very severe and inequitably applied. Agitation for reform in the legal system needed an ideology or a justification. The classical perspective offered a rallying point. The idea gained a number of powerful supporters, and reform was implemented. The philosophy was retained along with reform. It continues, even today, to provide the basis for the American criminal justice system; its elements are embedded deeply in the American culture.

Criminals are not, according to this perspective, sick or controlled by external forces. They are normal, rational people capable of making their own decisions and carrying them out. The classical approach, as originally developed, was applied to both adults and juveniles. However, the juvenile court philosophy adopted at the end of the nineteeth century signaled the beginning of a new approach to delinquent behavior. The major change involved a turning away from the conception of the juvenile as a rational, responsible being.

ECONOMIC DETERMINISM

The economic determinists produced some of the earliest scientific theories to survive intact to modern times. Many people are willing to believe that crime and delinquency may result from economic necessity, and a wide variety of social welfare programs have been developed to relieve the burdens of poverty. Studies comparing the rates of crime and delinquency for different economic strata appear to provide evidence to support theories based on economic deprivation.

One of the earliest "scientific" studies on the relationship between poverty and crime was conducted by di Verce in 1894. His analysis of convicted criminals in sections of Italy indicated that the poor were disproportionately represented in the prison population. According to his findings, the poor constituted only 60 percent of the country's population but constituted 85 to 90 percent of all convicted criminals.[6] He concluded that poverty must be a major cause of criminality. Similar work was carried out by William Bonger, who used European data to link practically all social problems to crime. Under the influence of Marxist doctrine, Bonger attempted to develop a theory of crime based on economic deprivation and class cleavages within capitalist societies. A favorite technique used to support his theory involved the comparison of fluctuations in the prices of grain and other commodities with the amount of crime.[7]

Marx and Engels had laid the foundation for Bonger's attack against the capitalist system. Marx suggested that all social phenomena, whether they be political, ethical, or material, are products of economic conditions. All behavior, he believed, had an economic basis. According to the strict law of causality, an individual's economic position determined the character of his conscience and this in turn determined behavior. Economic reality was the first cause of all human behavior.

The economic determinists came to be associated with the Marxian school of thought which placed negative evaluations on the capitalist system. As a result, it did not enjoy widespread popularity among social philosophers in America. New scientific theories soon overshadowed this perspective. However, poverty and deprivation remained a popular explanation for crime among laymen. Charles Loring Brace and other reformers remained convinced of the association between poverty and misery and crime.

Although economic determinism did not develop into a major branch of criminology, it has not been totally ignored. Some modern theories of delinquency appear to have an economic base. Cloward and Ohlin's "differential opportunity structures" tends to parallel some of the structural ideas of the Marxists.[8] The class and economic background of offenders has been the focus of many studies of juvenile delinquency.[9]

The economic model of criminality was recently resurrected in the field of economics. The modern theories combine elements of the historical economic determinism with a new interest in the rational model of the individual. Gary Becker wrote in 1968 that criminals and delinquents are essentially rational and calculating individuals who seek to maximize their satisfaction within the constraints of the economic system.[10] Becker's theory has been elaborated and modified by a number of scholars. Gordon, for example, suggested that the character and extent of crime reflects the economic structure of a society. Systems that promote competition do not guarantee economic security to each and every individual. Each must strive to make his or her own way in a marketplace characterized by the unequal distribution of rewards. Driven by the fear of economic insecurity and the likelihood of failure, many individuals become criminals.[11] Once again, economic deprivation appears as an explanation of criminal behavior. Sullivan specified all of the calculations that may be made by the potential thief in coming to a rational decision to commit a crime: "(1) all his practical opportunities of earning legitimate income, (2) the amounts of income offered by these opportunities, (3) the amounts of income offered by various illegal methods, (4) the probability of being arrested if he acts illegally, and (5) the probable punishment should he be caught."[12]

Using the *opportunity cost* theory of crime, several economists have suggested policy to reduce the amount of crime and delinquency in society.[13] The new economic view suggests that rehabilitation approaches are ineffective because they assume the offender is abnormal, sick, or irrational. Since normal, rational people commit crimes, it is suggested that programs that reduce the benefits and increase the costs of crime would be more effective.

BIOLOGICAL AND CONSTITUTIONAL APPROACHES

Biology was one of the earliest systematic sciences to deal explicitly with the human being. As a result of its early successes, popularity, and prestige, scholars seeking the causes of human behavior were not hesitant to apply its principles and techniques to the question of crime. The work of phrenologists and physiognomists was not ignored by the new criminologists. Some of the theories that grew out of the application of biology to the explanation of human behavior can be recognized as extensions and modifications of the earlier views. New interpretations in the infant field of psychology suggested that the time was right for the association of mind, body, and behavior.

A great number of theories grew out of the biological perspective. Theories that use the techniques of biology as well as those that attempt to establish a connection between the body and behavior are often included under the biological or constitutional approach. An overview of a selected sample of these theories is shown in Table 7.2.

TABLE 7.2 BIOLOGICAL AND CONSTITUTIONAL APPROACHES TO DELINQUENCY

SCHOOL	APPROACH	FOCUS	CONCEPTS	LEADERS
Positivist	physical stigmata	atavism	born criminal insane criminals criminaloids morally insane	Lombroso
	social responsibility	crime rates	criminal diathesis law of criminal saturation and super-saturation social accountability penal substitutes	Goring Ferri
	moral deficiency	adaptation	natural crime pity, probity elimination	Garofalo
Constitutional	heredity	physical abnormality	low-grade organisms	Hooten
	body type	body build and temperament	mesomorph endomorph ectomorph index of disappointness	Kretchmer Sheldon
		temperament, body build, and environment	physique	
Heredity and pathology	mental degeneracy	family trees		Dugdale Goddard
	physical defects	cosmetic abnormalities		Banay Baker
		endocrine gland		Schlapp
		genetic complement	XYY double male	Price Jacobs Jarvik
		eugenics	sterilization	
		hyperactivity or hyperkinesis	minimal brain dysfunction	

The Positivists

Some of the theorists working on the causes of crime adopted the techniques and language, if not the content, of biology. By examining the characteristics of the criminally deviant organism, measuring differences and similarities, systematically correlating the findings, and publishing detailed reports, these theorists raised criminology from a speculative art to a scientific endeavor. The shift in emphasis from the crime to the criminal was to have a lasting influence on criminology.

The positivists were not always in agreement on the basic underlying causes of crime. The earliest of the positivists, Cesare Lombroso, choose to believe that biological anomalies were at the root of criminal behavior. Other positivists rejected biological explanations in favor of social or environmental influences. They were all in agreement, however, that the techniques of biology—the scientific method—offered the greatest opportunity for an understanding of crime and the criminal.

THE CRIMINAL INDIVIDUAL

Cesare Lombroso (1836–1909), traditionally called the father of modern criminology, was probably the first theorist to systematically analyze the link between biology and criminal behavior. As a physician in the Italian army, Lombroso had the opportunity to observe the physical differences between troublesome and conforming soldiers. He noted that troublemakers had atypical physical characteristics. Many of the soldiers had tattoos. Lombroso noted that the content of these body pictures also varied with the temperament of their owners. Troublemakers often displayed vulgar or threatening tattoos; wild animals were not uncommon. Decent soldiers, on the other hand, were more likely to wear harmless and simple tattoos with hearts or flowers and the name of a loved one. From these observations, Lombroso concluded that physical attributes, psychological characteristics, and behavior were in some way related. An autopsy on the brain of an Italian brigand appeared to confirm Lombroso's speculation.[14]

From his many observations, Lombroso developed a theory of criminality that focused on the physical stigmata of the individual. He believed that criminals represented a biological throwback to primitive, uncivilized man. This process he called atavism. Homo sapiens evolved, according to Lombroso, from "homo delinquents" who exhibited antisocial behavior. A delinquent or a criminal was a reversion to this primitive stage. The presence of atavistic or degenerate tendencies could be identified by certain physical stigmata, such as extremely long arms, defects in the eye, an unusual size of the ears, facial asymmetry, and other peculiarities. Differing degrees of atavism were also reflected in an individual's temperament and behavior.

Like many other criminologists, Lombroso developed a classification of criminals. His included born criminals, insane criminals, criminaloids, and criminals by passion. The classification suggests that not all of Lombroso's criminals were victims of atavism to the same degree. Different combinations of physical stigmata and psychological traits characterized the different types. For example, the born criminal had pronounced abnormal physical characteristics and an immoral temperament. Other types had less severe handicaps.

Although many of Lombroso's contentions have not stood the test of scientific investigation, his contributions to modern criminology are great. His emphasis on the scientific approach, multiple causation, and the value of studying the criminal rather than the crimes were to be adopted by many generations of criminologists and delinquency analysts. The movement away from free-will doctrines also suggested that treatment rather than punishment might be used as a means to reduce crime and protect the society.[15]

The popularity of Lombroso's theory declined after the turn of the century when Charles Goring accepted Lombroso's challenge to test his theory.[16] Enlisting the aid of the statistician Karl Pearson and others, Goring conducted a massive study of the English prison population. He and his associates took detailed measurements of the physical features of 3000 repeat offenders. The data collected were analyzed by Pearson's correlation technique to discover whether certain types of criminal behavior were related to the physical stigmata of the offenders. As a result of his study, Goring rejected physical characteristics as clues to criminality. Goring believed that a combination of both social and constitutional factors was responsible for criminal behavior. He suggested that all people possessed a natural tendency (mental, moral, or physical) that was strong enough to determine behavior. This proclivity he called a *criminal diathesis*.[17] When a particular set of circumstances presented itself, the individual would follow his natural tendencies.

After the publication of Goring's research, few writers continued work in the Lombrosian vein. The repudiation of his theory had been accomplished, but his manner of studying the criminal with a scientific approach lingered on.

SOCIAL ORGANISMS

Enrico Ferri, another prominent member of the positivist school of criminology, disagreed with the idea that the criminal was morally responsible for his acts. He replaced moral responsibility with the concept of social accountability. Biologists had shown that cells, tissues, and organs have no independent existence outside a body. Using the organic analogy, Ferri claimed that the individual has no existence except as a member of society. Each and every human (organ) has to function properly in order to preserve the society (body). The rules or laws of the society prescribe the proper behavior. It is the responsibility of each individual to follow the rules in order to preserve the society and thereby preserve himself. Because their actions affect others, people are held accountable to society and to other people when the law is broken. Crime, then, is a social problem that disrupts the orderly relationships between people.

Ferri was probably the most modern of the three major positivists of the Italian school. He believed that crime was a product of a combination of anthropological, psychological, geographic, economic, and sociological factors. Because a number of these factors could be changed, Ferri proposed a treatment approach. Criminals were to be separated from other members of the society for an indefinite period of time until they could be rehabilitated and take a responsible position in the community. The state was expected to compensate the victim for injuries inflicted by the criminal and to repair any damaged property.[18] Because punishment did not provide a solution to the crime, Ferri offered *penal substitutes* to protect society from crime. Foster homes for young offenders, schools for neglected youths, and legalized divorce were among these penal substitutes. In addition, Ferri believed that technological, legislative, and other factors could affect the incidence of crime and delinquency in society. For example, smuggling was believed to be more easily reduced by lowering the import tariffs than by cutting off the hand of a smuggler. Steam power for ships helped reduce piracy, and other scientific discoveries might help reduce or prevent other crimes.[19]

Ferri compared criminal behavior to a chemical reaction. It occurs only when certain factors are brought together under a given set of conditions. The individual becomes criminal, according to Ferri, only when the environment contains all the factors needed to produce crime. Because these conditions will come together in the proper combination infrequently, only a certain number of crimes can be committed in a given period of time. Ferri's *law of criminal saturation* was little more than a prediction of official crime rates given a set of physical and social conditions. By *criminal supersaturation* he referred to the role of special factors, such as famines, wars, depressions, and other unusual societal conditions, which might increase or depress the crime rate.

Ferri attached great importance to crime statistics. He believed that the crime rates should be compared with changes in legislation, the number of police, and differences in punishment to provide information for policy decisions. After reviewing criminological studies he warned against the careless use and abuse of statistics. Statistics were considered especially important for documenting his laws of criminal saturation and supersaturation.

Ferri accepted Lombroso's assertion that the criminal was not a normal person and turned his attention to the criminal justice system. He classified the methods of handling criminals in three categories: hygienic measures, therapeutic measures, and surgical operations.[20] Hygienic measures were all the techniques that might be used in crime prevention. His penal substitutes, for example, were placed in this category. Although he did not have much faith in traditional punishments, he suggested that reparative and repressive means might have to be used as therapeutic measures in some cases. Where all other means failed, the death penalty was proposed as the ultimate surgical operation to eliminate criminal behavior.

THE IMMORAL INDIVIDUAL

A third major figure of the positivist school was Raffaelo Garofalo. Unlike Lombroso, Garofalo believed that criminals could not be understood apart from their crimes. Because they did not take into account the natural types of crime, Garofalo believed that popular ideas about the criminal were incomplete and scientifically unacceptable. He further rejected the notion that crime was the violation of man-made laws. Instead, he introduced the idea of *natural crime*—unacceptable behavior that exists at all times and places regardless of the actions of particular legislatures. Natural crimes were acts that violated "probity" (the respect of property rights) and "pity" (revulsion over the infliction of harm and suffering on other people).[21] Garofalo argued that probity and pity were basic moral attributes in any society, and he believed that they were essential to social order.

Garofalo believed that criminality was a result of moral inadequacy. The true criminal lacked probity or pity and thus felt no remorse after committing a criminal act. The true criminal had a moral "anomaly" or a "psychic variation" characteristic of "primitive or inferior races." Thus while minimizing Lombroso's conception of physical atavism, Garofalo offered a psychological, moral variant. The criminal was believed to lack the moral development characteristic of civilized people.

Garofalo developed a classification scheme to describe and distinguish among the four kinds of criminals.[22] The first type was identified as the *endemic* criminal, or murderer, and the second referred to "criminals deficient in probity," or thieves. A third category distinguished lascivious criminals, or "cyniques" who commit sex crimes. The fourth type included "violent criminals" influenced by situational factors; few of these criminals could be found because moral considerations were more important than opportune circumstances. Because crime was determined by moral anomalies inherent in the individual criminal, the idea of deterrence was rejected.

Influenced by the writings of Darwin, Garofalo suggested that morally deficient individuals should be eliminated from society just as maladapted organisms were eliminated by natural selection in nature. Three means of elimination were recommended: (1) death for criminals with a moral anomaly, (2) partial elimination in the form of long-term or life imprisonment for criminals who are only fit to live in nomadic hordes or primitive tribes, and (3) reparations or restitution for crimes by those who lack probity or respect for property.

The Constitutional Approach

The positivists influenced many criminologists by providing a scientific model to follow. Their theories, however, did not have lasting appeal. Following the publication of Goring's research, the biological approach fell into disfavor. Little theoretical or research attention was directed to clarification or modification of the biological approach for some time. Theories based on the conception of the law violator as a distinct biological type did not reemerge until serious attention was given to an explanation of juvenile delinquent behavior.

The work that signaled the demise of the Lombrosian perspective was, ironically, influential in giving biological explanations a second chance. In refuting Lombroso's work, Goring dismissed the idea that physical stigmata were predictive of criminal behavior. However, he suggested that the overall body dimensions of certain types of criminals differed significantly from that of the general population, and the constitutional approach was launched.

CONSTITUTIONAL INFERIORITY

Goring's research prompted a great deal of criticism. Among the most systematically presented was the work done by Ernest Hooten.[23] His worked paralleled that of Lombroso, whose theory was the target of Goring's work. Hooten studied the physical characteristics of over 13,000 criminals and compared them with the physical characteristics of some 3,000 noncriminal controls. As a result of his study, he concluded that the criminals were "organically inferior." Crime was said to result from "the impact of environment on low grade human organisms."[24]

Although Hooten's critics suggested that his work did not provide evidence that inferiority was inherited, he was not defeated. Research on identical twins, which appeared about this time, seemed to provide "proof" that heredity was important to an explanation of nonconformist behavior.[25]

BODY TYPE AND CONSTITUTIONAL INFERIORITY

A new type of biological research attracted attention in the 1940s. Drawing on the earlier work of the German Ernest Kretschmer, who related body type to mental illness, and endocrinology theorists, William H. Sheldon and his associates at Harvard developed a classification scheme to distinguish among the different body types found in juveniles. Sheldon identified three basic body types, or somotypes: (1) the endomorph, with a soft, round, fatty body exhibiting small bones and short limbs; (2) the mesomorph, with a large, muscular trunk and chest and large wrists, hands, and bones; and (3) the ectomorph, who shows a delicate, skinny frame; small, slender face; drooped shoulders; and small bones. Each of the body types was then related to specific expected temperamental tendencies.[26] Both body type and temperament were believed to be symptoms of basic inherited physical disorders.

Sheldon measured the somotypes of 200 boys between the ages of 15 and 21 residing in an institution in Boston. "Disappointing performance" was the criterion used for assessing the delinquency of youths involved in the study. When asked "disappointing to whom?" Sheldon answered, "disappointing to you" as the observer.[27] A seven-point "index of disappointedness" or "index of delinquency" was used to summarize each boy's shortcomings. Most of the disappointing, or delinquent, boys in Sheldon's study were judged to be mesomorphs with slight ectomorphic or endomorphic tendencies.[28] Unfortunately, Sheldon failed to recognize that mesomorphic tendencies are also found in a large number of police officers, army officers, football players, and political leaders. Thus the evidence for a relationship between delinquency and body types is not convincing and does not offer a causal explanation for delinquency. Some support, however, has been provided by Sheldon and Eleanor Glueck.

TEMPERAMENT AND ENVIRONMENT

Sheldon and Eleanor Glueck extended the work of William Sheldon in an attempt to explain the perceived relationship between body type and juvenile delinquency. Using Sheldon's somotypes, they found that 60 percent of their juvenile delinquents were mesomorphs, but only 31 percent of the nondelinquents could be so classified.[29] While the Gluecks found support for the contention that body type was related to juvenile delinquency, they also offered additional insights in linking temperament to their findings on body type. The mesomorph was seen as a muscular man of action who acted aggressively and assertively in meeting the problems encountered while growing up. The law may be broken by the mesomorph, and he may be seen as delinquent. The ectomorph, by contrast, reacts to a problem by either living with the problem or brooding over it rather than acting it out in delinquent behavior. Thus each physical or body type is believed to be associated with a different temperament, and the resulting combination of factors is supposed to help explain juvenile delinquency.

Additional research conducted by the Gluecks suggested that different types of delinquent behavior are committed by individuals with different temperaments and body types.[30] In contrast to the mesomorph, the ectomorphs are sensitive and introverted individuals who tend to be tense and inhibited but exhibit intense mental conflicts. If the inhibition against expression of conflict is released, destructive and even sadistic acts may result. A "balanced physique," on the other hand, has characteristics of all three types coupled with a balanced temperament and is not prone to commit delinquent acts.

In more recent years, the Gluecks have appeared to back away from a strict biological approach to delinquency. They cite evidence to suggest that environmental factors, such as the family, the community, and socialization, are potential causes of delinquent behavior.[31] The social factors, according to the Gluecks, operate selectively by affecting different body and temperament types differently. Both the critical body type and the environmental factors must be present for delinquency to surface. They conclude that delinquency is a complex phenomenon which is not easily understood.

A number of criticisms can be directed at the Gluecks and at the constitutional approach to explanations of delinquent behavior. It is, for example, interesting to speculate about the applicability of the constitutional approach to female delinquency. It is hard to imagine that the majority of females populating juvenile correctional institutions have large muscular trunks and chests or large hands, wrists, and bones. Perhaps the relatively lesser frequency of female delinquency is due to the fact that females are less likely to have these mesomorphic body features? It is apparent that Sheldon developed his classification scheme for boys only. Of course, if the constitutional approach can only be applied to boys, it cannot possibly provide an explanation of all delinquent behavior.

The constitutional approach is subject to other, and possibly more serious, criticisms. For example, the scale developed by Sheldon to measure delinquency is open to severe criticism because of its subjective nature and because it may not include serious offenses. Instead of law-breaking behavior, irritating, obnoxious, or other disruptive but legal behavior may be heavily weighted on the Sheldon scale. Much of the research support for Sheldon's hypotheses, including that of the Gluecks, is open to methodological criticism. Supportive research studies often lack adequate samples, control groups, or theoretical guideposts. The Gluecks, for example, did not seem to have a theory to guide them in their massive research efforts. Instead, they seemed to be engaged in "dust bowl empiricism," which seeks to measure everything that might possibly be related to delinquency. Many of the statistical relationships they found in their research may be due only to chance and have little or no theoretical significance.

Another basic criticism of the constitutional approach is that it relies on biological factors which are basically unchangeable. Even if we did discover that mesomorphs were more likely to become delinquent, the question becomes "so what?" What are the policy implications of such a discovery? How could we change body type or temperament? The answer, of course, is that we could do nothing to change the body type or the temperament of individuals if they are, as the theorists claim, biologically determined. We are essentially left with the implication that "boys will be boys" or "mesomorphs will be mesomorphs," and there is little society can do to change this. Only by discovering more important and changeable factors can we hope to develop effective strategies for the prevention and control of juvenile delinquency.

Heredity and Pathology

The constitutional approach to crime has inspired a wide variety of perspectives on criminal and delinquent behavior. Biological factors and heredity have often been given preeminent roles in explaining human behavior. A great deal of energy has gone into sorting out the influence of various biologically determined factors on both crime and delinquency. The underlying assumption is that the criminal or delinquent is different and perhaps even a degenerate biological entity. Among the biological and constitutional factors that have been considered as causes of delinquency and crime are mental abnormality, physical abnormality, endocrine gland abnormality, genetic abnormality, and, more recently, minimal brain dysfunction.

MENTAL DEGENERACY

Richard Dugdale and Henry Goddard were among the proponents of the mental degeneracy hypothesis. The mental degeneracy explanation of crime and delinquency suggests that an individual may inherit defective biological characteristics which weaken his resistance to antisocial conduct. To show support for the hypothesis that the tendency toward criminal and other disapproved behavior is inherited, a number of theorists have conducted extensive studies of genealogy. Mental retardation, crime, and deviance of members of a single extended family have been traced over several generations.[32]

The family studies of Dugdale and Goddard stimulated interest in mental retardation as a cause of crime and delinquency, but little evidence has been found to link retardation definitely to crime and delinquency. In spite of the lack of evidence to support the mental degeneracy hypothesis, popular opinion still holds remnants of the theory. The ideas that mental deficiency may lead people to commit crimes and that criminal behavior "runs in the family" are difficult to dispel.[33]

Research carried out to support the mental degeneracy hypothesis created considerable interest in mental disturbances as a possible cause of criminal behavior. The approach was influential in bringing psychology and psychiatry into the field of criminology. Because some of the researchers (such as Goddard and Dugdale) overlapped fields, their work will be discussed in greater detail in the next chapter to emphasize the biological base from which the psychological and psychiatric theories were evolved.

PHYSICAL DEFECTS

One popular biological approach stresses physical handicaps or abnormalities as a cause of delinquent behavior. Physical defects, such as blemishes, acne, a club foot, a large nose, poor eyesight, obesity, crippled limbs, big ears, or a disfiguring birthmark have all been listed as possible indirect causes of delinquent behavior.[34] The physical defects may lead to emotional or personality problems that produce delinquent behavior. A fact often overlooked by adherents of this approach is that most individuals with physical handicaps make an adjustment to their physical problems without resorting to either juvenile delinquency or adult crime. Thus physical defects do not necessarily lead to delinquency. This approach has little scientific justification.

ENDOCRINE GLAND DYSFUNCTION

Some endocrinologists claim that delinquency is produced by malfunctioning of the endocrine gland or other ductless glands in the body.[35] Early studies conducted by Schlapp and his associates to explain the behavior of gamblers, thieves, and murderers by investigations of glandular malfunction was influential but probably misdirected. If a parent, teacher, or other adult finds a child with atypical behavior problems, a consultation with a physician might locate glandular problems. Medication, however, is available to help relieve problems associated with glandular imbalance. An important point is that it has never been demonstrated that delinquents suffer more glandular malfunctioning than nondelinquents.

GENETIC ACCIDENT

The genetic approach to criminal and delinquent behavior has generally not been well received in anthropology, sociology, or criminology. This modern version of the biological approach suggests that genetic heredity may play a role in the development of delinquent tendencies. In recent years, the role of human chromosomes has received considerable attention.[36] A chromosome is a thin thread of genetic material containing the instructions for the growth and development of every part of an organism. In normal men and women there is one pair of sex chromosomes among the 23 chromosome pairs in a body cell. In women the sex chromosomes are alike (both are X chromosomes), but the male has one X and one Y chromosome. Therefore a normal woman has an XX chromosome pair and a normal man an XY chromosome complement (the Y chromosome is believed to determine maleness).

Jacobs and Strong have demonstrated the significance of the chromosome complement in sexual development and suggest that several different chromosome complements are possible. Some individuals possess an XXY, XXX, XYY, XXXX, XXXY, or XXYY complement. The XXY individual is believed to be a male with female characteristics, while the XXYY is called the *double male*. The double male has been described as being very tall with a low IQ which borders on imbecile level, but the XXYY male is extremely rare. The XYY chromosome grouping has probably received the greatest attention in criminology. Jacobs and her associates report that an outstanding characteristic of the XYY male is his height; he is at least 6 inches taller than the average male in the general population.[37] Richard Fox reports that the XYY individual has male sex organs, is sterile, has a degree of mental retardation, and may show extensive breast development.[38]

Several attempts have been made to relate criminal behavior to chromosomal complement abnormalities.[39] For example, Casey and his colleagues discovered that a larger percentage of XYY individuals were located in a prison population than in the general population. Amir and Berman found the XYY complement more frequently among criminals than among the general population, and reported that the XYY group exhibited higher rates of violent crime. Research reporting the incidence of violence and aggression by XYY individuals has led some writers to claim that they represent the closest thing to the born criminal that has yet been discovered.[40] Others remain unconvinced that there is a direct relationship between chromosome complement and criminal behavior.[41]

There is no reason to assume that possession of the XYY complement must necessarily lead to violence just because these individuals are more highly represented in the prison population. Even the height distinction has been questioned, because chromosomally normal brothers who are as tall as their XYY brothers have been found. In addition, differences in personality characteristics for the XYY group have not been convincingly established. Some individuals with the XYY chromosome pattern have presumably managed a reasonably normal adjustment in society. Thus research studies report inconsistent and often conflicting evidence.

EUGENICS

A closely related approach, and probably not a separate category, is eugenics, which involves improving the hereditary stock of the race. If a person believes that delinquency is inherited, a eugenics program may appear logical. Castration or other forms of sterilization would prevent a criminally inclined person from reproducing and thus cut off the criminal strain at an early stage. Execution would accomplish the same purpose. Programs of this type have generally not attracted widespread support, although occasional reports of sterilization programs in prisons do appear in the press.[42]

HYPERACTIVITY OR HYPERKINESIS

In the last few years, there has been increasing interest in the effects of minimal brain dysfunction on the behavior of preadolescents. Youngsters who exhibit a variety of symptoms, including troublesome behavior in school, extreme activity, selfishness, amorality, learning problems, uncontrolled bowel and bladder problems, listlessness, and extreme verbosity, may be classified as hyperactive or hyperkinetic. A link with delinquency has been claimed because their extreme activity and troublesome behavior may lead to contact with the police. Controversy exists regarding whether the conditions will be outgrown as the youngster reaches puberty. Authorities who claim that it can be outgrown point out that the difficulties experienced by the hyperactive child may contribute to delinquency and even adult crime. Those who claim that it is not outgrown see a more direct link with delinquency.

The causes of hyperactivity have not been established, but speculation centers around birth injury and heredity. Hyperactivity can be controlled, however, with amphetamines or ritalin. Surprisingly, these drugs, which are stimulants for the more normal individual, have a calming effect on the hyperactive youngster. Most authorities recommend, however, that drug therapy be supplemented with counseling, especially in the more extreme cases. A definite link between hyperactivity and delinquency has not been established, but the discomfort that a hyperactive youngster can cause his family and himself should not be doubted. Case 7.1 documents the history of a troublesome, hyperactive youth.

EARLY THEORIES IN PERSPECTIVE

Early theories of crime and delinquency often appear to have little foundation. Belief in devils and mysterious bumps are, for the most part, discounted by scientific evidence. Certainly, it is easy to look back at the old prescientific theories and point out their absurdities; however, they may prove valuable in indicating the temporal nature of ideas on crime, delinquency, and human behavior in general. Each of the early theories was based upon the best knowledge and information available at the time. Who is to say that current theories will not also appear simplistic and even absurd in the future?

The early, prescientific theories are still important to modern criminology. Current theories rely to a great extent on many of the assumptions of the determinist and free-will doctrines.[43] The classical perspective, which stressed free will and hedonism, provides a base for modern criminal justice. Free will and its development through learning was also taken into account in the development of the juvenile court system. Various social programs have arisen out of this perspective as well. Several of the determinist theories have been modified and restructured to serve as a foundation for modern theory and research. And there are indications that one or more of the old theories may be resurrected for modern analysis.

Knowledge about human behavior is still incomplete, and a total disregard of the biological and constitutional approaches to human behavior is probably not warranted. An underlying assumption of most of the early biological approaches to crime and delinquency was that criminals were degenerate or inferior by reason of heredity, physique, temperament, or mental equipment. Care must be taken when dealing with this approach. A researcher might be able to demonstrate that left-handed people are disproportionately found among a training school population of delinquent boys. For some this fact might be sufficient for them to claim that left-handedness leads to delinquency.

THE HYPERACTIVE YOUNGSTER

M. L. was born about two months premature and weighed 4 pounds, 2 ounces at birth. The birth was extremely difficult. At 2 months, the boy acquired bilateral hernias when trying to roll over and lift himself up in his crib. He cried constantly and had difficulty sleeping. M. L. learned to walk and talk at an early age, but never crawled. He enjoyed talking to adults and seemed to be a charming but surprisingly active youngster for his age. Most young boys are expected to be active and "get into things," so his parents at first thought little was wrong with his behavior. M. L. was an only child, and there was no point of reference for judging his problem behavior.

As M. L. got older, he began to play outside with other youngsters. At this point, some behavior problems were noticed by neighbors who frequently complained to M. L.'s parents. Even at the age of 5, for example, M. L. refused to return home to use the bathroom, preferring to relieve himself in the open air. At the age of 4, he fell off a building that he was attempting to climb by putting his fingers and toes in the spaces between the bricks. He succeeded in reaching the top but fell when he tried to get down. He scattered the trash from neighbors' cans over the entire block.

M. L. was allowed to play outdoors with explicit instructions about boundaries for activity. Unfortunately, the boy seemed almost incapable of remembering or following directions. More than once he was brought home by the police or neighbors for wandering too far from home. The police recorded the fact that he was found, at age 5 years, 4 miles from home and still going. His parents had taken him to a lake a week before, and he reported that he just wanted to return for a visit.

At home M. L. was a terror. He seemed to vibrate with energy. He stood on top of the television, literally climbed the walls, leaving footprints and destroying furniture. He could not sit still and in fact walked on tiptoe most of the time. He was frequently seen turning in circles. He had a peculiar fascination for sugar and would eat it by the spoonful or demand or steal candy.

By age 6, M. L. had set his bed on fire. After being admonished for this incident, he burned his blackboard and set fires in trash containers in his room in protest. He seemed incapable of

learning from mistakes. By age 7, M. L. was
discovered breaking windows in a neighbor's house.
He was kept inside his own home for several days
following this incident. During this period, he
ruined the family television by rapidly and
repeatedly rotating the tuning knob.

In kindergarten, M. L. was a continual behavior
problem. He fought with other children in the
classroom. He yelled, cried, and threw temper
tantrums. He had difficulty learning because he
could not complete a series of actions in the
proper sequence. The school psychologist ran a
series of tests on the boy. He was found to be
intelligent, but it was suggested that the child
might have some brain damage. He was referred to
a doctor.

The doctor recognized the problem as hyperactivity and prescribed medication. With the first
dose, M. L. visibly reacted. He sat down calmly
and even took a nap. He had never napped before.
It took time and experimentation to adjust M. L.'s
medication. But soon he began to adjust to school
requirements, neighborhood demands, and parental
guidance. By age 11, M. L. had friends, excellent
school grades, a good home adjustment, and no
further contacts with the police.

Certainly, left-handedness would become labeled as inferior because
delinquents or potential delinquents possessed this trait. This belief
might even help create a situation in which left-handed people have
difficulty avoiding situations that might result in delinquency because
people expect them to be delinquent. In fact, any physical trait that is
linked to delinquency may become suspect or "degenerate." Questioning the basic assumption of hereditary inferiority was not common
among the adherents of the biological or constitutional approaches;
even Sheldon and the Gluecks make this mistake. At least the biological
and constitutional approaches led to some of the first attempts to
explain delinquency rather than concentrating wholly on adult crime.
Thus, the approach has been influential on both psychology and
sociology.

The early development of the biological approach exemplified by
the positivist school of criminology by Lombroso, Ferri, and Galofaro
helped debunk free will and perverse will as causes of crime. Attention was directed to the individual, and criminal acts began to be
recognized as being caused by forces beyond the conscious control, or
will, of the individual. Thus the individual could no longer be fully
blamed for his or her acts. We did not blame people for catching the
flu or other illnesses. Yet criminals were still viewed as less than
human—a lower species, degenerate or biologically inferior.

Much of the research conducted on the body-type theories of Sheldon and others received serious methodological criticism. Sampling inadequacies and lack of controlled comparisons are frequently mentioned. The index developed by Sheldon can be criticized as being subjective, unreliable, and relatively useless. In addition, most of the researchers have not ruled out environment as a factor in delinquency. Personality, family influence, diet, age, sex, race, and so on are often mentioned as social factors related to juvenile delinquency. Contradictory findings weaken the strength of the biological argument. For example, Sheldon saw the criminal as an athletic type, but for Hooten the criminal was an underdeveloped runt.

In the 1960s and 1970s, some psychologists, such as Skinner, Ellis, and others, have been arguing that the individual's inborn biological traits have been deemphasized and neglected in the social sciences. However, renewed attention has been given to inborn tendencies and genetic structures. The recognition that people are not born with identical biological equipment and potential has again come in vogue. Few people believe that delinquent behavior is inherited, but the belief that certain inherited traits increase the potential for delinquent behavior is common. Constitutional or biological explanations may be considered useful, and they may make a contribution to an understanding of delinquency. These approaches are not sufficient if used by themselves, and links with other explanations are essential if an adequate explanation of delinquency is to be achieved.

NOTES

[1] A more detailed discussion of these theories can be found in Harry Elmer Barnes and Negley K. Teeters, New Horizons in Criminology, 3d ed. (Englewood Cliffs, N.J.: Prentice-Hall, 1959).

[2] Marion L. Starkey, The Devil in Massachusetts (New York: Knopf, 1949).

[3] George Vold, Theoretical Criminology (New York: Oxford University Press, 1958), p. 45.

[4] A more detailed discussion of these approaches can be found in Stephen Schafer, Theories in Criminology (New York: Random House, 1969).

[5] Barnes and Teeters, op. cit., p. 143.

[6] Ibid., p. 147.

[7] Marshall Clinard, Sociology of Deviant Behavior (New York: Holt, Rinehart and Winston, 1963), p. 101.

[8] Richard A. Cloward and Lloyd E. Ohlin, Delinquency and Opportunity (New York: Free Press, 1960).

[9] A few examples of this approach are contained in the following: John P. Clark and Eugene Wenninger, "Socio-economic Class and Area as Correlates of Illegal Behavior Among Juveniles," American Sociological Review 27 (December 1962): 826–834; Albert J. Reiss and Albert L. Rhodes, "The Distribution of Juvenile Delinquency in the Social Class Structure," American Sociological Review 26 (October 1961): 720–732; Charles V. Willie, "The Relative Contribution of Family Status and Economic Status to Juvenile Delinquency," Social Problems 14 (winter 1967): 326–335; Belton M. Fleischer, The Eco-

nomics of Delinquency (New York: Quadrangle, 1968); F. Ivan Nye, James F. Short, Jr., and Virgil J. Olsen, "Socioeconomic Status and Delinquent Behavior," American Journal of Sociology 63 (January 1958): 381–389.

[10] Gary S. Becker, "Crime and Punishment: An Economic Approach," Journal of Political Economy (March–April 1968): 169–217.

[11] David M. Gordon, "Capitalism, Class and Crime in America," Crime and Delinquency 19 (April 1973): 163–186.

[12] Richard F. Sullivan, "The Economics of Crime: An Introduction to the Literature," Crime and Delinquency 19 (April 1973): 138–144.

[13] Sullivan, op. cit.; George J. Stigler, "The Optimum Enforcement of Laws," Journal of Political Economy (May–June 1970), pp. 526–536; William M. Landes, "An Economic Analysis of the Courts," Journal of Law and Economics (April 1971), pp. 61–108; Robert G. Hann, "Crime and the Cost of Crime: An Economic Approach," Journal of Research in Crime and Delinquency (January 1972), pp. 12–30.

[14] A more comprehensive discussion of Lombroso and his theory can be found in Schafer, op. cit.

[15] Marvin Wolfgang, "Cesare Lombroso," in Pioneers in Criminology, Hermann Mannheim, ed. (New York: Quadrangle, 1960), p. 40.

[16] Barnes and Teeters op. cit., pp. 127–128.

[17] Schafer, op. cit., p. 186.

[18] Enrico Ferri, Criminal Sociology, trans. J. I. Kelley and Hohn Lisle (Boston: Little, Brown, 1917).

[19] Elmer H. Johnson, Crime, Correction and Society, 3d ed. (Homewood, Ill.: Dorsey Press, 1968), pp. 155–156.

[20] Schafer, op. cit., p. 131.

[21] Ibid., p. 135.

[22] Raffaelo Garofalo, Criminology (Boston: Little, Brown, 1914).

[23] Ernest A. Hooten, Crime and Man (Cambridge, Mass.: Harvard University Press, 1939); Robert K. Merton and M. F. Ashley-Montagu, "Crime ..nd the Anthropologist," American Anthropologist 42 (July–September 1940): 384–408.

[24] Schafer, op. cit., p. 187.

[25] Horatio H. Newman, Multiple Human Births: Twins, Triplets, Quadruplets and Quintuplets (New York: Doubleday, 1940); Vold, op. cit., pp. 96–98.

[26] This typology was discussed in greater detail in Chapter 5.

[27] William H. Sheldon, Varieties of Delinquent Youth (New York: Harper & Row, 1949), and The Varieties of Human Physique (New York: Harper & Row, 1940).

[28] Sheldon, Varieties of Delinquent Youth, p. 820.

[29] Sheldon Glueck and Eleanor Glueck, Unraveling Juvenile Delinquency (Cambridge, Mass.: Harvard University Press, 1951).

[30] Sheldon Glueck and Eleanor Glueck, Physique and Delinquency (New York: Harper & Row, 1956).

[31] Sheldon Glueck and Eleanor Glueck, Family Environment and Delinquency (Boston: Houghton Mifflin, 1962).

[32] Richard Dugdale, The Jukes (New York: Putnam, 1942); Henry H. Goddard, Feeblemindedness: Its Cause and Consequences (New York: Macmillan, 1923).

[33] Carl Murchusion, "American White Criminal Intelligence," Journal of Criminal Law 15 (August 1924): 254–257; for a discussion of mental retardation and crime, see Barnes and Teeters, op. cit., pp. 135–138.

[34] Ralph Banay, "Physical Disfigurement as a Factor in Delinquency and Crime," Federal Probation 7 (January–February 1943): 20–24; Harry J. Baker and Virginia Traphagen, The Diagnosis and Treatment of Behavior-Problem

Children (New York: Macmillan, 1935); E. W. Wallace, "Physical Defects and Juvenile Delinquency," *New York State Journal of Medicine* 40 (November 1940): 1586–1590; Barnes and Teeters, *op. cit.*

[35] M. G. Schlapp, "Behavior and Gland Disease," *Journal of Heredity* 15 (1924): 11 (quoted in Barnes and Teeters, *op. cit.*).

[36] Lissy Jarvik, Victor Klodin, and Stephen Matsuyama, "Human Aggression and the Extra Y Chromosome," *American Psychologist* 28 (August 1973).

[37] Patricia Jacobs, M. Brunton, M. Melville, and W. F. McClemont, "Aggressive Behavior, Mental Subnormality and the XYY Male," *Nature* 208 (December, 1965): 1351.

[38] Richard Fox, "The XYY Offender: A Modern Myth?" *Journal of Criminal Law, Criminology and Police Science* 62 (March 1971): 61.

[39] Menachem Amir and Yitzchak Berman, "Chromosomal Deviation and Crime," *Federal Probation* 34 (June 1970): 57–58; Jacobs, Brunton, Melville, and McClemont, *op. cit.*; M. D. Casey, et al., "Y Y Chromosomes and Antisocial Behavior," *Lancet* 2 (1966): 859; W. H. Price and P. P. Whatmore, "Behaviour Disorders and Pattern of Crime Among XYY Males Identified at a Maximum Security Hospital," *British Medical Journal* 1 (1967): 533.

[40] Edward Sagarin, *Deviants and Deviance* (New York: Praeger, 1975); Jarvik, Klodin, and Matsuyama, *op. cit.*

[41] *Ibid.*

[42] For a discussion of eugenic programs, see Johnson, *op. cit.*

[43] A summary of the free-will and determinist approaches is presented in Robert G. Caldwell, *Criminology* (New York: Ronald Press, 1956).

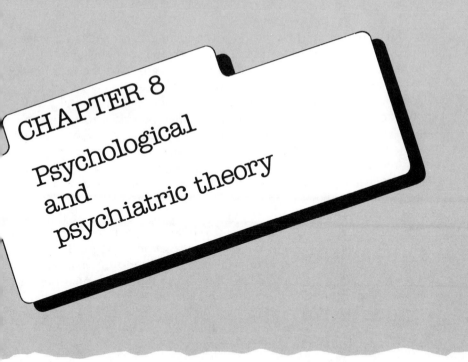

CHAPTER 8
Psychological and psychiatric theory

The shift in emphasis from the crime to the criminal prompted by the positivists changed the character of criminal explanation. For the early thinkers, demons were the answer. When the focus shifted to the individual criminal, the character of the solutions to the crime problem changed. The individual perpetrated crime and was not the victim; therefore the explanation was to be found in forces internal to the individual. The devil was still the primary "cause" of crime. However, demons no longer lurked about waiting for a victim. They took up residence in the personality, mind, or psyche of the weak individual, either with the consent of the individual (the free-will position) or without it (the determinist position).

The constitutional school looked for the "mark of the beast" on individuals convicted of crime. They searched for closely set eyes, low foreheads, swarthy skin, bumps on the head (horns?), and other features which were popularly believed to be characteristic of the devil. When these physical manifestations were not consistently found in all criminals, less outwardly evident biological structures became the focus of attention. The weak mind, which could not resist evil temptations, was one of the first nonphysical structures to be examined and analyzed. From this point it was only a matter of time until the workings of the mind would become the primary concern.

Much of the work done by the psychological and psychiatric theorists has focused upon the mind of the individual as it works to achieve a balance between impulse and disciplined behavior. The individual who commits criminal or delinquent acts is believed to have internal conflicts which are acted out in disapproved behavior. It is sometimes assumed that such acting out is a signal that the individual needs or wants help to solve his or her conflicts and achieve balance. According to this belief, maladjusted, pathological, or abnormal minds are the "cause" of juvenile delinquency. When outside forces are considered, they are generally given credit for precipating emotional or personality reactions in the individual. The environment thus does not cause the imbalance but only provides the opportunity for acting out.[1]

The distinction between the brain and the mind is not always clear. These terms have sometimes been used interchangeably in delinquency theories, particularly in the early days. Therefore it is practically impossible to separate early psychological theories from their roots in the biological approach. Mind explanations entered the theoretical arena by way of the brain analyses of the constitutional school. It is not surprising that some of the theories in this transitional period overlapped both schools. Therefore some theorists must be given attention in discussions of both the constitutional and the psychological or psychiatric schools. An overview of a selected sample of psychological and psychoanalytic theories of delinquency is shown in Table 8.1.

MENTAL DEFICIENCY

The earliest psychologically oriented theories focused on the mental capacity of the individual criminal. Whether the workings of the mind or its physiological structure was the primary concern is open to question. A number of theorists made reference to general constitutional characteristics of the criminal and stress heredity but also indicate that the mind has a function in determining behavioral tendencies which cannot be predicted by its physiological makeup. These theorists stood on the threshold of psychological and psychiatric explanation. A discussion of their theories suggests that the roots of modern theories about the mind are firmly based in human biology.

Degeneration

Vaschide Vurpas was among the first to emphasize the role of mental degeneration in the production of criminal behavior. His work therefore represents one of the first attempts to construct a psychiatric or psychological theory of crime and delinquency. Vurpas's grounding in the biological and constitutional approaches is evident in his descriptions of the criminal as "constitutionally weakened" and lacking in the biological conditions necessary for success in the struggle for existence. Permanent stigmata mark the criminal, according to Vurpas, but a constitutionally and psychically weakened resistance to crime determines his behavior. Mental degeneracy—a throwback to an earlier mental type—counteracts the effects of civilization and leaves the mind weakened and subject to the acceptance of antisocial behavior pat-

terns. Once a weak strain appeared in a family, the degeneration grew progressively worse, until the family died out through natural selection.

Family trees or genealogy charts were used to provide evidence for the presence of degenerate strains and their association with criminal behavior. The use of the family tree technique became very popular around the turn of the century, when reports on several degenerate families were circulated.[2] Of these, Dugdale's description of the Juke family probably sparked the greatest enthusiasm for degeneration theory. Dugdale traced the family tree of one Ida Juke, supposedly an illegitimate individual. Among the 1200 descendents who could be traced, Dugdale found 60 thieves, 280 paupers, 300 premature births, 7 murderers, 50 prostitutes, 440 veneral disease carriers, 140 other assorted criminals, and a variety of other deviant types. Dugdale estimated that the family had cost the public over a million dollars from the first half of the eighteenth century until 1876.[3] Estabrook traced the same family up to 1915 and located 2094 members. He found an additional "170 adult paupers, 118 criminals, 378 prostitutes, 86 brothel keepers, and a number of other deviants."[4]

Another well-received study using family trees was completed by Herbert Goddard, who described the Kallikak family. A purportedly feeble-minded girl had an affair with Martin Kallikak during the American Revolution. An illegitimate son resulting from the affair had 480 known descendents. After the Revolution Kallikak married a woman from a "good" family, and 496 descendents resulted from the marriage. Of the descendents of the marriage, only one was judged abnormal, two were alcoholics, and there were no criminals. Among the descendents of the illegitimate son, however, there were 24 alcoholics,

TABLE 8.1 PSYCHOLOGICAL AND
PSYCHOANALYTIC THEORIES OF DELINQUENCY

SCHOOL	APPROACH	FOCUS	CONCEPTS	LEADERS
Psycho-logical and psycho-analytic	mental degen-eration	family trees	hereditory degen-erations	Vurpas Dugdale
	mental abnor-mality	psychoses	crime as a substitute for mental illness	Maudsley Ray
	psycho-logical disorders	personality develop-ment	id, ego, superego	Freud
			collective unconscious	Jung
			inferiority complex, will to power	Adler
			birth trauma	Rank
			anxiety	Horney
			sibling studies	Healy Bonner
	intelligence	general intel-ligence	feeble-mindedness, IQ	Goddard
		social intel-ligence	adjustment to environment	
		personality inventory	personality inventory	
	learning	conditioning and social	modeling	Trasler
		experience	adversive control	
			extinction	

36 illegitimate births, 33 prostitutes, 8 brothel keepers, 143 feeble-minded persons, 3 epileptics, 3 criminals, and an assortment of other deviant individuals.[5]

These family studies lack methodological sophistication. They concentrate on the inheritance of mental degeneracy, but they differ from more recent research and theory which emphasizes the influence of the family on the production of delinquency. Instead, deviance was seen as something that was passed from one generation to another in a manner similar to hair color or nose shape. These studies were not far removed from the biological or hereditary influence of their prede-cessors. For this reason, the work of Dugdale, Estabrook, and Goddard probably should be listed as a biological approach to delinquency, except for their influence on psychological and psychoanalytic approaches to delinquency.

Abnormality

A more direct link between the biological approach and psychological theory was evident in the works of Henry Maudsley and Isaac Ray. Maudsley, for example, accepted the mental degeneracy theory of criminal causation during the early part of his career. Inheritance was given an important role in the production of delinquency. Maudsley noted that many criminals did not exhibit degenerate stigmata; their criminal tendencies therefore must be produced by mental abnormalities. It was the mental abnormality, not physical stigmata, that produced criminal behavior. Maudsley saw crime as an outlet for pathological energies of the degenerate mind. Unknown forces which impinged on the mind required release through crime, sin, or insanity. Although Maudsley never directly related crime to mental illness, his conception of the impact of known forces on the minds of the unaware was influential in the development of later psychological and psychiatric theories.[6]

Some theorists' careers reflected the developments in criminology. Ray, for example, started his career as a phrenologist but later became interested in psychiatry and medical jurisprudence. His early training in constitutional theory was combined with his new interests, and he proposed that criminals were products of moral insanity. Mental abnormalities compelled them to engage in behavior that they knew to be wrong. Ray believed that the criminal justice system was of limited use in helping criminals unless medical aid was also provided.[7]

Others have suggested variations on the basic mental abnormality framework. Aschaffenburg, for example, proposed that crime was caused by psychosis or other mental abnormalities, but he suggested that social factors were also essential to a full understanding of the genesis of crime and delinquency.[8] Still others have leaned toward a physiological perspective on mental abnormality and its relationship to crime. Marro believed that defects in the central nervous system of an individual may result in criminal behavior.[9] Kovalensky stressed the importance of injury to brain centers that inhibit socially unacceptable behavior, thereby producing crime.[10] Abnormality does not always affect the entire mental process, according to Galton. He suggested that an individual may have a normal intellect but display other types of mental abnormality.[11]

PERSONALITY OR CHARACTER DISORDERS

Psychiatry and psychoanalysis do not constitute a single well-defined and coherent approach to juvenile delinquency. Rather, there are a variety of theorists and competing theories. A common thread that has bound most of these diverse theories is the immense influence of Sigmund Freud.

Freudian Theory

Freudian psychoanalytical theory generally breaks with explanations of delinquency based on heredity and biology. Instead, it is proposed that each child "enters the world as a criminal, i.e., socially not adjusted."[12] The child must become a normal social being by successfully passing through several critical life stages. A child is born with an id, which is the unconscious source of biological needs and drives common to all people. The id seeks only selfish pleasure; it does not take into account the consequences of actions. It is said to be the seat of antisocial drives and motivations which give rise to delinquent or criminal behavior. The ego develops somewhat later in life, and it represents the conscious portion of the personality. The ego includes the attitudes, ideas, and habit patterns that are acquired in associations with other people. The third component of the personality is the superego, which arises out of the conflicts and tensions between the id, the ego, and relationships with other people. The superego reflects the norms and values of the groups that significantly affect an individual's social life.[13]

Biological drives, according to psychoanalytical theory, are reflected in the id. While the biological factors are still accorded a degree of importance as unconscious drives and motivations, psychoanalysts have recognized that, at least for man, biology is affected by social and psychological experience. Biological factors are relatively constant, affecting behavior only after mediation through the ego and superego. The alteration in the natural or criminal state of a child takes time and develops through a series of stages.

The first year and a half of a child's life is often referred to as the *oral* stage. The youngster is driven by oral urges at this primitive stage in his development, and some psychoanalytical writers have called the urges exhibited by the infant sadistic and cannibalistic. Of course, this stage is usually associated with bottle or breast feeding and the sucking impulse.

The second stage for the child is the *anal* or *anal sadistic* phase, which may last until sometime in the third year of life and is associated with toilet training. During this stage the child may become cruel, stubborn, or spiteful. For the first time the child begins to learn that he or she can influence and even control the behavior of other people. The child can sit on the training potty and reward or punish adults according to whim. A desire to hurt and destroy are believed to be common during this training period.[14]

The anal phase is followed by the *phallic* stage. This stage may last until the age of 6 years. An interest in one's own body is common. Strong erotic feelings may be directed toward the opposite-sex parent; hostility and jealousy are directed toward the same-sex parent. Freud called this phenomenon the Oedipus complex. The resolution of the Oedipus complex by age 6 is partially due to the development of the superego with associated moral prohibitions against incest and the killing of a parent.[15]

Only the id exists at birth, and the child must successfully pass through several stages in order to fully develop the personality, or self, which is composed of the id, ego, and superego. At birth the child operates on the pleasure principle. The infant seeks immediate gratification and pleasure and the minimizing of pain and discomfort. Time and reality do not exist for the infant. The pleasure principle is gradually altered in favor of the reality principle. When the ego develops in the first years of life, it represents the portion of the self in closest contact with external reality. Behavior is directed toward the satisfaction of biological and social needs through the operation of the reality principle. This means that the child still seeks pleasure, but gratification of selfish demands may sometimes be delayed although not forgotten or abandoned.[16]

Only when the superego develops does the child feel any guilt or remorse over acts he may have committed. The superego brings with it a set of abstract moral principles which help govern the behavior of the child even in the absence of the parents or others who may have aided in his development. Thus even if the child acts on an id impulse, he may feel guilt or remorse if the superego has been developed.

Shortly before puberty, oral, anal, and phallic conflicts are thought to be revived. Behavioral problems may arise during puberty if the superego fails in its struggle to maintain control over antisocial urges. In most adolescents, only the "normal" problems of puberty are found, but some youngsters develop symptoms characteristic of neurosis, psychosis, or delinquency. The youth without proper inner controls is the most likely candidate for delinquency. However, the youth with an overdeveloped superego may also become delinquent. Severe guilt feelings may produce a need to be punished by authority figures such as the police or the juvenile court. Disturbance in the ego may also result in delinquent behavior.[17]

Psychoanalytical approaches attribute delinquency to emotional problems, personality conflicts, and the unconscious. According to many theorists, delinquency is only a symptom of deep, unconscious problems. The phallic stage of childhood development with the Oedipus complex is fundamental for a psychoanalytical explanation of juvenile delinquency. Males are believed to develop hostility toward their fathers while naturally loving and desiring their mothers. The healthy youngster successfully resolves the Oedipus complex, but some youngsters are believed to repress the hostility toward the father. Substitutes for the father are aggressively and violently attacked because the superego controls prevent a direct attack on the father.[18]

Psychoanalytic theory suggests that individuals are not fully responsible for their delinquent acts because the acts are partially the product of unconscious motivations. The use of a rifle or pistol in a robbery attempt, for example, may be a reflection of feelings of impotence. Breaking and entering is merely an unconscious attempt to violate one's mother. Psychoanalysts suggest that a judge should attempt to understand and diagnose the underlying problems of a delinquent if sentencing or disposition is to reflect the juvenile's needs.[19]

Psychiatrists claim that the first "crime" committed by all children is violation of prescriptions for cleanliness. For the first time the child faces sanctions provided for violating a norm. "Sphincter morality" becomes the foundation upon which to build all morality.[20] Toilet training is the child's first contact with societal demands. As the child begins to control his sphincter muscles, he develops inhibitions against disapproved behavior. It is suggested that problems or disturbances during this period may cause delinquency in later life. A youth who persists in committing delinquent acts despite continued efforts by parents and the juvenile justice system is analogous to the baby sitting on his training potty refusing all demands to complete his business while feeling superior to all.[21] Delinquency, from the psychoanalytic perspective, results primarily from problems associated with the early life experiences of the individual.

In Freudian psychoanalysis, the delinquent is helped by allowing him to freely discuss his problems with the analyst. Slips of the tongue, dreams, and other cues are used to obtain a window to the unconscious. The personality of the delinquent is restructured in analysis by uncovering the unconscious and associating these urges with the repressed complexes of the individual. The analyst can help only if he is free from repression himself, so the analyst must be psychoanalyzed before he or she begins to practice. Freudians are usually convinced of the validity of psychoanalysis, and they usually believe that helping agencies for juveniles should be similar to mental hospitals.

Variations on Freud's theory have been proposed by several writers. Carl Jung placed less emphasis on sex than did Freud. His *analytic psychology* stressed the *collective unconscious*. Alfred Adler's *individual psychology* emphasized the individual's desire to be part of, and obtain status within, the group. Status striving in the group was viewed as a reflection the "will to power" or an inferiority complex, and these concepts were used to explain various forms of behavior. Modern gang theorists, such as Albert Cohen, James F. Short, Cloward, and Ohlin were apparently influenced by Adler. Gang delinquents are often described as status seekers. Otto Rank stressed the trauma of birth and the individual will as factors important to the explanation of human behavior.

Another Freudian, Karen Horney (1885–1952), introduced the concept of anxiety. She suggested that the world provides hostile restrictions on individual behavior which results in personal feelings of helplessness. Helplessness leads to anxiety, and juvenile delinquency presumably results from efforts to relieve anxiety, gain attention from others, and elicit response from a cold and rejecting environment. Case 8.1 suggests that this theory may have some validity.

William Healy and Augusta Bronner studied the relationship between delinquency and emotional problems. Their research was primarily concerned with psychoanalytic theory and practice. They chose to examine same-sex siblings where one youngster was delinquent and the other was nondelinquent; each sibling was within two years of the same age to control for the environmental differences that might exist if they were of widely differing ages. Excluded from the study were youngsters lacking in English language fluency, intelligence, or a willingness to accept treatment. The researchers compared 105 and found that 91 percent of the delinquents, but only 13 percent of the nondelinquent siblings, exhibited emotional disturbances. Even while controlling for the effects of child-rearing practices within a family, the delinquents exhibited more emotional problems than their nondelinquent siblings.[22] Sutherland and Cressey suggest that Healy and Bronner found emotional problems in most delinquent youths because they believed they were there but did not demonstrate that emotional disturbance was the causal factor in producing juvenile delinquency.[23]

Schuessler and Cressey reviewed numerous studies of criminal personality characteristics. They found that the claims of personality differences between criminal and noncriminal individuals were of doubtful validity. Results from their 113 comparisons led them to conclude that inconsistent results made it impossible to determine whether personality and criminality were related.[24] If these findings can legitimately be applied to juvenile delinquency, we might be led to conclude that the delinquent and the nondelinquent are not radically different in personality.

Waldo and Dinitz reviewed the personality research completed between 1950 and 1965. They found little evidence for a relationship between personality factors and delinquency or crime.[25] Hakeem also reviewed a number of research studies and concluded that some diagnostic labels used by psychologists and psychiatrists had little validity. He believes that diagnostic labels, when applied to delinquents, reflect the biases of the expert and not the emotional problems exhibited by the juvenile delinquent.[26]

Social Work and Psychoanalytic Theory

Social work has traditionally been oriented toward psychological or psychoanalytical theory. Social workers who come in contact with juvenile offenders may have considerable impact on their handling and disposition. The psychoanalytically oriented social worker usually expects juveniles to help themselves by becoming self-reliant. The potential for self-reliance, according to this perspective, lies within the individual personality and is amenable to development through ther-

CASE 8.1

THE ANXIOUS ADOLESCENT

An adolescent girl resident of a juvenile
correctional institution is confused about her
motivation for committing delinquent acts. Her
record suggests problems with excessive drinking,
running away from home, and sexual promiscuity.
The following account suggests psychological
problems developed in her formative years:

> My father gave me such a beating when I was
> little that I was black and blue from the
> beating. All the time he was an alcoholic and
> he beats us all the time. My mother married
> when she was fifteen years old. There are
> fourteen children.

> My mother married and divorced several times.
> My mother beat me terribly. My mother did
> awful things when she was drunk. . . . She
> pulled my arm completely out of its socket and
> broke it. . . . She choked me. I will never
> forget some of the awful things. . . .

> How can I drink when I hated my mother for
> drinking so much?

> I have a terrible father. I hate him. He was so
> strict. He was always beating us. . . . I want
> discipline. My father doesn't give me the right
> supervision. . . . Mother is okay but she
> doesn't do anything.

Source: Gisele Konopka, The Adolescent Girl in Conflict
(Englewood Cliffs, N.J.: Prentice-Hall, 1966), p. 51.

apy, guidance, and supervision. The role of social workers in probation, parole, and aftercare programs will be discussed in subsequent chapters, but it is important to note that their orientation may introduce a psychological approach to delinquency prevention and rehabilitation in the local community.

Social workers often occupy leadership positions in local community agencies that work with juvenile delinquents or administer delinquency prevention programs. They are frequently instrumental in establishing programs that provide financial support, counseling, or therapy to youngsters in trouble. The social worker is often a contact point or the community coordinator for obtaining resources from social welfare agencies. Social workers are given responsibility for determining the particular needs of individual juveniles. They must locate and refer the juvenile to the appropriate agency so that his or her needs may be met. Many young people are diverted from official contact with the juvenile justice system into individual psychologically-oriented programs by the skillful work of a social caseworker.

Most large communities have a variety of organizations and agencies that provide services to youths in trouble. These include the YMCA and YWCA, Big Sister and Big Brother, public and private welfare agencies, Youth Services, foster home programs, and many others. Social workers can provide a useful service if they are familiar with these organizations. Whether the individual is a person in need of supervision, a youth in trouble, a youngster who has been adjudicated delinquent, or someone in need of aftercare services following release from an institution, one organization might not be in a position to provide adequately for all the individual's needs. Instead, the effective coordination of a variety of community service organizations may be essential for providing help for a youngster. Well-trained social work personnel have some advantages over those employing the kindly or fatherly approach and emphasizing religious conversion, as was so often used in the past.

Intelligence

The relationship between intelligence and delinquency drew much attention in the latter part of the nineteenth century. Most of the early work was a matter of unsystematic speculation. However, with the development of psychology, more and more work was directed toward studying the relationship between innate mental ability and deviant and law-violating behavior. Sophisticated learning studies grew out of some of the early work on mental capacity.

Intelligence Testing

Psychological tests to measure innate intelligence were used extensively during the First World War. The results of studies on large numbers of soldiers suggested that humans display varying degrees of intelligence. Because human behavior is also wide-ranging, many early researchers concluded that intelligence might provide useful cues to predict and explain variations in behavior.[27]

Henry H. Goddard was an outspoken early proponent of the idea that feeble-mindedness, or low intelligence, caused delinquency. As the director of the research laboratory of the Training School for Feeble-minded Girls and Boys, he believed that every feeble-minded child was a potential delinquent. Inherited mental ability precluded their control of impulses. According to Goddard, the feeble-minded child's judgment and ability to distinguish right from wrong was seriously impaired by low mental capacity. Goddard had some difficulty supporting his beliefs with research and spent much time explaining away his own findings.[28] Impaired intellect may explain the situation described in Case 8.2.

INNOCENT BABES

Two 12-year-old boys, Peter and George, were referred to the juvenile court for stealing from a store. It was winter, and the boys had stolen a pair of gloves each. Store detectives presented the evidence to the court. Court personnel felt that the boys were retarded. The following exchange took place between the boys and the juvenile judge:

Judge: What's the idea, George?
George: My hands were freezing. My hands were freezing. My gloves has all holes in them.
Judge (sarcastically): Your hands were freezing. . . . What makes you think you can take property that belongs to someone else?
(Neither boy answered.)

The boys were providing a childlike solution to what appeared to be a pressing problem confronting them. Like infants, they acted on impulse.

Source: Robert M. Emerson, Judging Delinquents (Chicago: Aldine, 1969), pp. 184-185.

General intelligence as measured by standardized intelligence tests has long been discussed and studied by experts in the field of delinquency. A number of studies have sought to clarify the relationship between intelligence and juvenile delinquency.[29] Some research tends to suggest that delinquents score somewhat lower on intelligence tests than nondelinquents. Critics point out, however, that most IQ tests do not take into account variable factors, such as family background, English language ability, number of years of schooling, or cultural heritage. It is suggested that the tests are standardized to middle-class, white, Protestant expectations; any individuals not meeting the prescribed standards are judged inferior.

Most youths have committed offenses for which they could be adjudicated and found delinquent. This group could not be much different from the youth population as a whole. Only 5 percent of all youths, however, are actually adjudicated and found delinquent. It is possible that this group differs in intelligence, but it is doubtful if intelligence is the factor that led to the commission of delinquent acts, since it does not deter others. Possibly the "dumb" ones are more likely to get caught, but it appears that we need to look elsewhere for an explanation of delinquency. We may wonder why only a small portion of the total number of youths committing delinquent acts are

TABLE 8.2 INTELLIGENCE QUOTIENTS FOR
WARDS IN ILLINOIS STATE JUVENILE INSTITUTIONS, 1974

		BOYS			GIRLS		
	TOTAL WARDS	TOTAL BOYS	COOK COUNTY BOYS	DOWN-STATE BOYS	TOTAL GIRLS	COOK COUNTY GIRLS	DOWN-STATE GIRLS
Under 65	3	2	2	—	1	1	—
65–74	27	25	25	—	2	2	—
75–84	48	47	40	7	1	1	—
85–94	95	92	64	28	3	1	2
95–104	84	82	59	23	2	—	2
105–114	45	43	18	25	2	1	1
115–124	9	9	6	3	—	—	—
125–134	—	—	—	—	—	—	—
Untested	108	94	38	56	14	5	9
Totals	419	394	252	142	25	11	14
Median	93.2	93.3	91.3	98.5	90.0	75.0	97.5

Source: Illinois Department of Corrections, Juvenile Division, *Semi-annual Statistical Summary, 1974* (July 1 to December 31), prepared by Garland A. Kingery, Judie Egelhoff, and Rick Nehoff (Springfield, 1974).

arrested and sent to juvenile court and how they differ from all those who committed delinquent acts. It is possible that juveniles from deprived or culturally different neighborhoods and family backgrounds, who would tend to score somewhat lower on IQ tests, are more likely to be arrested and sent to correctional facilities. These factors may help account for any IQ differences between delinquents and non-delinquents.

Despite the fact that most experts do not accept the idea that low IQ causes juvenile delinquency, the results of intelligence tests are sometimes reported for institutionalized offenders. For example, the Illinois Department of Corrections reports the IQs for boys and girls in the youth correctional institutions in the state, as shown in Table 8.2. In 1974 the report indicated that most of the boys achieved below-average scores (95 to 104 is considered the average intelligence level). These figures probably reflect differential enforcement of the law and the lower-class backgrounds of the boys, but it does not necessarily suggest that individuals with low IQs are more likely to be involved in delinquency.[30]

Social Intelligence

The ability of an individual to adjust to his social environment and exhibit maturity in social relationships is sometimes called *social intelligence*. Intelligence tests, which measure general intelligence, do not appear to measure social adjustment. The Vineland Social Maturity

Scale, used to measure social intelligence, is one of the few available. The results of its use have not been very encouraging. Work in this area is based on the idea that it would be possible and useful to develop measures of individual adjustment to social environments. An underlying assumption of these devices is that conformity is beneficial to society. This approach ignores the fact that a delinquent may be well adjusted in his particular social milieu but maladjusted from a societal perspective. For example, the individual urban gang member may be effectively adjusted to his local social environment but from a broader perspective seems maladjusted. There is no evidence that the social intelligence approach can provide adequate explanations of juvenile delinquency.

Personality Testing

Psychologists have been adept at developing tests used to diagnose emotional and personality problems. Research using devices such as the Minnesota Multiphasic Personality Inventory (MMPI) and other tests to locate and describe the differences between delinquent and nondelinquent youths has been common. The results, unfortunately, have often been inconsistent and disappointing. Hathaway and Monachesi claimed that the MMPI had some power to discriminate delinquents from nondelinquents.[31] Waldo and Dinitz argued, however, that social factors correlated higher with delinquency than personality factors, and there were problems in interpreting the data from personality studies.[32]

Psychological tests have also been used to establish indirect links between personality and delinquency. Guy Swanson, for example, studied the relationship between family dissatisfaction and juvenile misconduct. His research, however, did not provide conclusive evidence for a link between the two variables.[33] Conger and Miller claim to have found a relationship between personality and delinquency. Their studies of third-grade teacher evaluations and psychological test results suggested that these may be important in predicting delinquent or deviant behavior in youths.[34] Research based on the Jesness Inventory has also been used and cited as evidence of a link between personality and delinquency. According to this research, delinquents exhibit more hostility toward authority figures than do nondelinquents. However, delinquents and nondelinquents do not differ significantly on neuroticism scales, orientation to the family, or value orientation. The studies indicate that institutionalized delinquents are more likely to feel isolated, deny the existence of problems, be less mature, and exhibit more concern about whether they are normal.[35] Of course, the institutionalized delinquents studied by Jesness could have developed problems as a result of their misconduct and institutionalization whether or not a personality problem actually created the delinquent behavior.

LEARNING THEORIES

Learning and conditioning theories have also been used to explain delinquent behavior. Psychologists have developed learning principles for studying human behavior as it is influenced by positive and negative reinforcers. According to this approach, when a juvenile's behavior is positively reinforced, the behavior will be repeated when the individual is again in a similar situation. The probability of a given behavior being repeated is said to be influenced by the frequency, intensity, and consistency of the reinforcing stimulus.

The learning theorists suggest that different procedures can be used to change a juvenile's undesirable behavior. For example, the behavior might suffer "extinction" if positive rewards are eliminated. New behavior patterns might be learned through *modeling* or *adversive control*. Modeling requires observation and emulation of individuals who engage in rewarded conformist behavior. Adversive control, on the other hand, involves the use of punishment to provide negative sanction for undesirable behavior. Punishment is applied immediately following the inappropriate act, and attempts are made to insure that the juvenile delinquent understands the reason for the sanction. Trasler suggests that punishment is essential to learning conforming behavior patterns. According to his theory, punishment promotes the development of healthy anxiety in children. The fear produced by the threat or application of punishment in childhood inhibits deviant or disapproved behavior impulses in later life. According to Trasler's theory, those who are disposed to commit delinquent acts have not been adequately punished at an early age and therefore have not developed anxiety or adversion to potential sanctions for rule-violating behavior.[36]

A number of sociologists have been learning theorists. Gabriel Tarde was probably the first to suggest that criminal and delinquent behavior results from social learning rather than inherent biological tendencies. Tarde emphasized the importance of imitation. He believed that people select admired individuals and model their behavior on them.[37] This focus on the influence of the behavior of others on the individual was developed more fully by Edwin Sutherland.[38] Because his theory is basically sociological, it will be discussed in greater detail in later chapters.

PSYCHOLOGICAL AND
PSYCHOANALYTIC THEORIES IN PERSPECTIVE

The psychoanalytic approach is interesting and has many adherents, but there are many problems associated with its empirical verification. Theories that cannot be tested and verified are more akin to ideology than to science, and they probably should be excluded from a discussion of delinquency causation. Many studies have searched for the emotional and personality disturbances that would separate the delinquent from the nondelinquent, but most of these studies have failed to locate major differences. The preponderance of evidence suggests that delinquent youths are psychologically similar to non-delinquents. They do not appear to have more severe emotional or personality problems than their nondelinquent peers. It has been argued that emotional problems found in delinquents may be as much a consequence of delinquent behavior as a cause of it.[39]

Mental deficiency, personality, and intelligence have not offered adequate explanations of juvenile delinquency. However, the integration of psychological or psychiatric theory with social and environmental theory has begun to show promising results.[40] Further development of the learning theories may provide hope for discovering the causes of juvenile delinquency from a multidisciplinary perspective.

NOTES

[1] Stephen Schafer, *Theories of Criminology* (New York: Random House, 1969), pp. 204–206.

[2] *Ibid.*

[3] Richard L. Dugdale, *The Jukes: A Study in Crime, Pauperism, Disease and Heredity* (New York: Putnam, 1910).

[4] Authur Estabrook, *The Jukes in 1915* (Washington, D.C.: Carnegie Institute, 1916) (quoted in Schafer, *op. cit.*).

[5] Henry Herbert Goddard, *The Kallikak Family: A Study on the Heredity of Feeblemindedness* (New York: Macmillan, 1919) (quoted in Schafer, *op. cit.*, p. 206).

[6] Henry Maudsley, *Responsibility in Mental Disease* (London, 1874). Other books include *The Physiology of Mind* (London, 1867), *The Pathology of Mind* (London, 1870), *Body and Mind* (London, 1870), and *Natural Causes and Supernatural Seemings* (London, 1886), as referenced in Schafer, *op. cit.*

[7] Isaac Ray, *A Treatise on the Medical Jurisprudence of Insanity*, 3d ed. (Boston, 1855). Also see Winfred Overholser, "Isaac Ray," in *Pioneers in Criminality*, ed. Hermann Mannheim (London: Routledge and Kegan Paul, 1960), pp. 113–134, and Schafer, *op. cit.*

[8] Hans von Hertig, "Gustav Aschaffenburg," in Mannheim, *op. cit.*

[9] Schafer, *op. cit.*, p. 209.

[10] *Ibid.*

[11] Francis Galton, *Inquiries into Faculty and Its Development* (London, 1883).

[12] Franz Alexander and Hugo Staub, *The Criminal, the Judges and the Public* (New York: Free Press, 1956), p. 30.

[13] C. G. Schoenfield, "A Psychoanalytic Theory of Juvenile Delinquency," *Crime and Delinquency* 17 (October 1971): 469–480.

[14] *Ibid.*

[15] *Ibid.*

[16] *Ibid.*

[17] *Ibid.*

[18] Alexander and Staub, *op. cit.*

[19] Martin Haskell and Lewis Yablonski, *Juvenile Delinquency* (Skokie, Ill.: Rand McNally, 1974), pp. 341–342.

[20] Sandor Jerenczi, "Psychoanalysis of Sexual Habits," in *Sex in Psychoanalysis*, trans. Ernest Jones (New York: Basic Books, 1950).

[21] Alexander and Staub, *op. cit.*, p. 55.

[22] William Healy and Augusta Bronner, *New Light on Delinquency and Its Treatment* (New Haven, Conn.: Yale University Press, 1936).

[23] Edwin H. Sutherland and Donald R. Cressey, *Principles of Criminology*, 7th ed. (Philadelphia: Lippincott, 1966); see Schafer, *op. cit.*, chap. 9, for a discussion of psychoanalytic approaches to crime.

[24] Karl Schuessler and Donald R. Cressey, "Personality Characteristics of Criminals," *American Journal of Sociology* 60 (March 1950): 476–494.

[25] Gordon P. Waldo and Simon Dinitz, "Personality Attributes of the Criminal: An Analysis of Research Studies, 1950–1965," *Journal of Research in Crime and Delinquency* 4 (July 1967): 185–202.

[26] Michael Hakeem, "A Critique of the Psychiatric Approach," in *Juvenile Delinquency*, ed. Joseph S. Roucek (New York: Philosophical Library, 1958).

[27] George B. Vold, *Theoretical Criminology* (New York: Oxford University Press, 1958), provides a summary of some research on intelligence tests and theoretical explanations of the data.

[28] Henry Goddard, *Human Efficiency and Levels of Intelligence* (Princeton, N.J.: Princeton University Press, 1920).

[29] See Cecil M. Charles, "A Comparison of the Intelligence Quotients of Incarcerated Delinquent White and Negro Boys and a Group of St. Louis Public School Boys," *Journal of Applied Psychology* (August 1936), pp. 499–510; Harry Shulman, *A Study of Problem Boys and Their Brothers* (Albany, N.Y.: State Crime Commission, 1929); Sheldon Glueck and Eleanor Glueck, *Delinquents in the Making* (New York: Harper & Row, 1952), pp. 118–129.

[30] Illinois Department of Corrections, Juvenile Division, *Semi-annual Statistical Summary*, 1974, prepared by Garland Kingery, Judie Egelhoff, and Rick Nehoff (Springfield, 1974).

[31] Starke Hathaway and Elio D. Monachesi, eds., *Analyzing and Predicting Juvenile Delinquency with the Minnesota Multiphasic Personality Inventory* (Minneapolis: University of Minnesota Press, 1953).

[32] Waldo and Dinitz, *op. cit.*, pp. 185–207.

[33] Guy E. Swanson, "The Disturbances of Children in Urban Areas," *American Sociological Review* 14 (October 1949): 676–678.

[34] John Janeway Conger and Wilber C. Miller, *Personality, Social Class and Delinquency* (New York: Wiley, 1966).

[35] Carl F. Jesness, *The Jesness Inventory: Development and Validation*, Report no. 29 (Sacramento: California Youth Authority, 1962). Also see Don Gibbons, *Delinquent Behavior* (Englewood Cliffs, N.J.: Prentice-Hall, 1970), pp. 83–84, for a description of the research by Jesness.

[36] Gordon Trasler, *The Explanation of Criminality* (London: Routledge and Kegan Paul, 1962).

[37] Gabriel Tarde, *Penal Philosophy* (Boston: Little, Brown, 1912).

[38] Sutherland and Cressey, *op. cit.*, p. 75.

[39] Gibbons, *op. cit.*, p. 87.

[40] Walter Reckless, Simon Dinitz, and Barbara Murray, "Self-concept as an Insulator Against Delinquency," *American Sociological Review* 22 (1957): 744–746; David Feldman, "Psychoanalysis and Crime," in *Mass Society in Crisis*, ed. Bernard Rosenberg, Israel Gerver, and F. William Howton (New York: Macmillan, 1964), pp. 50–58.

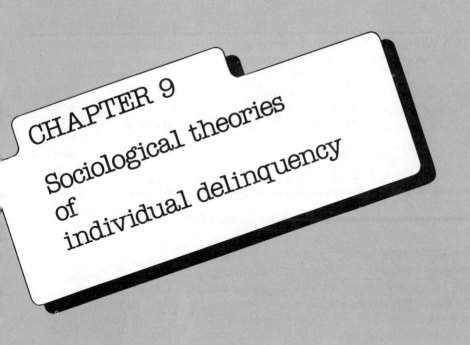

CHAPTER 9
Sociological theories of individual delinquency

Several disciplines have been involved in the search for the causes of juvenile delinquency; but of all the disciplines, sociology has produced the greatest amount of theory and research on the subject. The theories developed from the sociological perspective have all incorporated the basic sociological assumption that human beings are shaped by their social environments. An individual becomes a delinquent, then, because his social environment contains delinquency producing elements.

The social world is complex and complicated. A social environment consists of all elements that govern or structure human relations. Norms, values, location in the social structure, and many other factors may be important to the individual's development and behavior. The complexity of the social world is such that no single theory can deal effectively with all its various aspects. As a result, sociologists have tended to focus on one or a few of its many aspects.

Some theorists look to the social structure itself for an explanation of the genesis of juvenile delinquency. An individual's position in the social world, it is said, may limit his or her alternatives for action, thereby determining the individual's behavior. Other sociologists examine the norms and values that impinge on the individual and suggest that conceptions of proper behavior vary. According to this approach, the individual may become a conformist and a delinquent at the same time. Still other theorists look at the nature and content of an individual's interactions, suggesting that these may be sufficient to produce delinquent behavior in the individual. Some sociologists concentrate

TABLE 9.1. SOCIOLOGICAL THEORIES
OF INDIVIDUAL JUVENILE DELINQUENCY

SCHOOL	APPROACH	FOCUS	CONCEPTS	LEADERS
Sociological	individual behavior	learning	imitation differential association	Tarde Sutherland Cressey De Fleur and Quinney
			reinforcement	Burgess and Akers
		societal reaction	tagging	Tannenbaum
			deviance by definition	Lemert
			labeling	Becker
		culture	culture conflict	Sellin
			cultural values	Taft
		structure	anomie, moral density	Durkheim
			cultural goals, structural means	Merton

on statuses and corresponding role behavior. This approach attaches a great deal of importance to the self-concept and its role in creating delinquent expectations in the individual.

Each of these types of approaches offers valuable insights into the nature of delinquent behavior. Each has made valuable contributions in one way or another. Taken together, they demonstrate the versatility and comprehensiveness that can be attained by a single disciplinary perspective. An overview of some of the major sociological theories of individual delinquency is shown in Table 9.1.

LEARNING THEORIES

A number of sociological theories have taken a learning approach to juvenile delinquency. According to these theories, all social behavior is learned through the process of socialization. Delinquent behavior and "normal," conforming behavior are believed to be learned in much the same manner. While most of the learning theorists suggest that delinquent behavior results from misdirected learning, a few believe that delinquency results from flaws in the socialization process itself.

The forerunners of learning theory dealt only with crime, but more recent theory has concentrated on basic principles that are sufficiently general to apply to both crime and juvenile delinquency.

Sutherland's differential association theory, for example, applies to both crime and juvenile delinquency, and it has become one of the most influential theories in the field of juvenile delinquency.

The Pioneers

Tracing the origins of learning theory is a difficult task; however, there are indications that Benoit Morel (1809–1873) was the first theorist to argue systematically that crime was a form of learned behavior. Newspaper reports, Morel claimed, produced "moral contagion" in readers, resulting in their repetition of the criminal behavior of others. Following Morel, Paul Aubrey studied the "contagion of murder." He introduced the concepts of *imitation* and *suggestion* to explain how reports of murder could lead to repetition of the act by other people using similar techniques. Learning was believed to occur through the imitation of the activities of other people, who provided the suggestion to receptive minds. Aubrey's approach appears to have had greater applicability to collective behavior, and his work has been more influential in that area than in the field of juvenile delinquency.

The theories developed by Morel and Aubry were heavily influenced by the biological perspective so popular at the time. They deviated from the general pattern, however, in that they viewed biology as little more than a base from which to discuss more important social factors involved in the development of criminal behavior.[1] The theories of Morel and Aubry provide a point of departure for important theoretical developments in sociology.

The Law of Imitation

Gabriel Tarde (1843–1904) was, like the pioneers, concerned with the impact of newspapers on the spread of crime. He noted that when a crime occurred it was not an isolated event; other crimes involving similar techniques soon followed. Tarde believed the subsequent crimes were a result of imitation. After studying the cases of a number of persons involved in crime, Tarde commented on the similarities that he could find through the imitative process. These principles Tarde called the *law of imitation*.

According to Tarde's theory, imitation observed several universal laws. First, people tend to imitate the fashions and customs of others. Among homogeneous groupings, fashions and customs will be somewhat uniform and slow to change. However, if diverse groups come in contact with each other, there will be increased imitative behavior. Second, subordinates tend to copy the behavior of their superiors. Tarde reported that some types of crime originated in the upper classes and eventually came to be adopted by the lower classes by identification and imitation. Third, people tend to copy the newer form of behavior when two or more patterns conflict. Tarde felt that imitation is a common form of learning and that some types of imitation may result in criminal behavior.[2] Criminal behavior spreads in much the same way that fashions in other types of behavior spread. There are fashions in crime as well as in clothing and hair style.

Gabriel Tarde's theory does not fully explain how the first crimes were committed, except by reference to individual creativity and spontaneity. Once the criminal behavior is initiated, it may be imitated by others. Only a minority of the people will imitate criminal conduct. Questions remain because Tarde does not fully explain the process of imitation or why some acts are imitated and not others. However, he contributed to criminology by describing how criminal behavior results from learning through interaction and association with other people. His work also helped to lay to rest the old biological explanations of crime and delinquency.

Differential Association

The differential association theory, first presented by Edwin Sutherland in 1939, represented a modification and extension of the early learning theories. Like Tarde, Sutherland focused on the genesis of crime in the individual.[3] However, Sutherland, working during a later time period, claimed that his theory was applicable to all kinds of criminal behavior, including juvenile delinquency.

In the initial formulation of his theory, Sutherland stressed the importance of social disorganization as a broad underlying cause of juvenile delinquency. He suggested that delinquency occurs as a result of a breakdown in the individual's normative controls. Where control is weak, individuals are likely to accept the deviant values and attitudes of individuals around them. Sutherland was not referring to the individual's inner controls but rather to societal controls that inhibit deviant behavior. He believed that disorganization in the society contributed to a breakdown of societal controls and enabled deviant norms and values to gain a foothold. In highly disorganized areas, individuals would have a greater chance of coming in contact with deviant norms and behavior, which might be adopted in the same manner that "normal" behavior is learned.

Shortly after the publication of his theory, Sutherland was attacked by Arthur Leader. Leader charged that Sutherland's theory was incomplete or inadequate on five points. He claimed that Sutherland had failed to (1) define important concepts, (2) consider the meaning of the behavior for the individual who adopts it, (3) explain why people differentially associate with one another, (4) explain why people who associate with one another may commit different types of crimes involving a variety of diverse techniques, and (5) explain why some individuals who come in contact with criminals do not become criminals.[4]

Leader suggested that a comprehensive theory of juvenile delinquency must take into account all of the links in the causal chain that produces this behavior. Sutherland had not taken into account the personality factors so important to Leader's conception of juvenile delinquency. Leader believed that personality patterns and need satisfaction were the basic causal elements in the production of behavior. He indicated that the individual's reaction to associations were more important than the content of the associations themselves. When a person's needs are not met, Leader claimed, alternative forms of behavior consistent with the personality are sought. Therefore criminal behavior was a product of the personality and its attempt to achieve satisfaction, and not merely a result of differential association.[5]

In a reply to Leader, Sutherland defended his own version of the theory, but he also introduced modifications apparently taking some of Leader's criticisms into account. Significantly, Sutherland argued that mere exposure to delinquent attitudes and techniques could produce delinquency unless inhibiting mental or physical conditions were present.[6] Imitation and suggestion were important features of the differential association theory. Sutherland rejected Leader's argument that personality factors were essential to an explanation of behavior. He suggested that these factors were only indirectly related to criminality in that they described the setting of criminal activity.

MODIFICATION OF THE THEORY

In Sutherland's revision (1947) of differential association some significant changes were introduced to refine the theory.[7] Differential social organization replaced social disorganization as an underlying cause of delinquency. While the change may seem minor or only a semantic alteration, this is not the case. When associations with other people occur within the context of differential social organization, an individual associates with people who are members of diverse social groups holding differing norms, attitudes, and values. Some of these groups may have attitudes that are favorable to violating the law, while others do not. Thus because of association with disparate groups, an individual may experience conflict over which group norms, attitudes, and values to accept. Social disorganization, on the other hand, implies that groups have not accepted or internalized norms that provide guides for action.

An examination of the hypotheses underlying the substance of the revised differential association theory suggests that juvenile delinquency is a result of a differential socialization process. Sutherland believed that individuals learned their attitudes and behavior as a result of face-to-face interaction with others. Some of the individual's associates may be accepting of criminal attitudes and behavior; others are not. Whether the individual adopts delinquent or nondelinquent behavior depends on the nature of the relationships and the ratio of nondelinquent to delinquent associations, the strength of the influence depending on the frequency, priority, duration, and intensity of the associates' relationships with the juvenile. The juvenile learns the attitudes and values that characterize the preponderance of his associates. If the balance of the definitions a juvenile learns is favorable to the violation of law, the youngster will become delinquent. Where criminal and delinquent influences are predominant, rates of delinquency will be high.[8] Case 9.1 suggests the importance of peer influence on adolescent behavior.

Sutherland's theory has received a great deal of attention. Some of the early critics suggested that it was not applicable to a wide range of criminal behavior, for instance, middle-class crime. However, Sutherland applied his theory to white-collar crime,[9] and Cressey studied the validity of the theory for explaining the genesis of criminal behavior in individuals convicted of embezzlement. Cressey reported that several conditions were necessary for embezzlement to occur: the possession of appropriate information and technical skills and the learning of rationalizations that justify embezzlement or violation of trust. Cressey's analysis sought to "determine whether or not these conditions can be present in individual cases without the person's having had an 'excess' of associations with criminal behavior patterns."[10] Cressey found that the learning of technical skills was independent of association with criminals, but association was needed for rationalizations to justify trust violation through embezzlement.

Other critics suggested that the differential association theory would not explain the activity of compulsive criminals. Cressey replied that delinquency and crime that result from compulsion is not a proper subject for sociological investigation, and Sutherland's theory should not be expected to apply. Cressey contended that volition, or choice, is a necessary component in the commission of a delinquent or criminal act, and this component is missing in compulsive behavior. Acts that result from compulsion are insane acts, and they can be better studied by psychology, not sociology.[11]

CASE 9.1

THE HIPPEST GUY AROUND

Adolescents often emulate the activities of their heroes. The choice of heroes and associates can have a lasting influence on a youngster. Such was the situation in this case. Johnny D., the neighborhood idol, had been involved in a number of illegal activities—murder, rape assault, con games, numbers, prostitution, and dealing in stolen property. Some of the neighborhood kids followed in his footsteps. One of his admirers gave the following account of his influence:

Although I was tighter with the guys who had been with me at Wiltwyck [a juvenile correctional institution], I was still close to Danny and Butch and Kid. I just didn't look up to them as much as I did before I went to Wiltwyck. . . . One of the reasons was that they weren't the hippest guys around anymore. Johnny D. was the hippest cat on the scene now. . . . Everybody used to listen when he said something. It made sense to listen—he was doing some of everything, so he must have known what he was talking about. Sometimes we used to sit on the stoop or up on the roof and talk to Johnny or just listen to him talk shit. He sure seemed to know a lot of things. Johnny just about raised a lot of the cats around there, and I guess I was one of them. To me, what he said was truer than the Word of God.

Source: Claude Brown, <u>Manchild in the Promised Land</u> (New York: New American Library [Signet], 1965), p. 113.

Probably the most often stated criticism of the theory is that it is too broad or vague. Cressey, one of its leading proponents, admitted that the theory was "neither precise nor clear" and attempted to clarify its major assertions and implications.[12] Again asserting that the theory applies to all forms of criminal or delinquent behavior, he suggested that it had been misunderstood. The theory was not limited to an explanation of single individual criminal acts; it could also be applied to explain crime rates.[13] He suggested that tests of the theory be expanded to account for variations in crime rates.[14]

EMPIRICAL TESTS
The first study to use the differential association theory as a base was Sutherland's study of trust violators.[15] Since this first study in the 1940s, a number of other research efforts have been directed toward testing the validity of the theory.

James F. Short, Jr., focused on the frequency, priority, duration, and intensity dimensions of primary group associations in a test of Sutherland's theory. Institutionalized and noninstitutionalized boys and girls were asked to identify their friends in terms of delinquency-producing or -inhibiting characteristics. Short sought to determine whether access to delinquent values was greater in the institutionalized youngsters. The results of the test were supportive of the theory.[16] In a later article based on the same study, Short isolated the intensity, priority, frequency, and duration variables for in-depth analysis. He concluded that these variables were important to the explanation of juvenile delinquency.[17] A replication of the study by Harwin Voss supported Short's conclusion.[18]

Reiss and Rhodes focused on a small-group relationships for their test of differential association. The basis for their research was their finding that less than 20 percent of the individuals coming before the juvenile court were lone offenders; the usual size of the groups involved was two or three participants. The purpose of the study was to demonstrate that Sutherland's theory could differentiate between associations that were formed on the basis of value similarities and those that resulted in delinquent behavior. Reiss and Rhodes collected data from 299 triads (three-person groups) and 79 dyads (two-person groups) which were formed among male high school students. They found that boys chose friends whose delinquent or law-abiding behavior was similar to their own, but they were not able to support or refute the differential association hypothesis. The extent of the association of boys with the same kinds of delinquent behavior in close triad groups was greater than could be attributed to chance, but Reiss and Rhodes felt that it was well below what was expected by the theory. Furthermore, the results were not independent of social class. Thus only limited support was found by Reiss and Rhodes for the differential association theory.[19]

REFORMULATION AND REVISION
The lack of clarity in Sutherland's theoretical statement and the problems associated with its empirical testing led a number of scholars to suggest revision and reformulation of the differential association theory. James F. Short focused on the problems of empirically testing the theory. He contended that much of the support claimed for the theory was based on a limited application of a broad principle of differential association. While a fragment of the theory centering around the intensity, duration, priority, and frequency dimensions had been documented, the theory as a whole had not been tested. Previous research, according to Short, illustrated the need for reformulating the theory into a series of verifiable hypotheses.[20] Short suggested a logical transformation of the theory.

Daniel Glaser also reviewed Sutherland's theory and suggested a reconceptualization in which role taking and reference group imagery were taken into consideration. Glaser claimed that this conception would make the theory clearer and more specific. Glaser's formulation recognized that "a person pursues criminal behavior to the extent that he identifies himself with real or imaginary persons from whose perspective his criminal behavior seems acceptable."[21] Glaser believed that this type of revision in the differential association theory would focus attention on interaction in which role model choice occurs. According to Glaser, both prior identification and present circumstances determine the choice of role models or reference groups for an individual.[22] The focus on role models and reference groups may, however, already be found in Sutherland's theory as a result of his specification of the interactions that occur in intimate face-to-face groups. Members of the groups chosen as associates constitute both role models and reference groups for the imitation and learning of behavior.

A promising reformulation of the differential association theory was presented by De Fleur and Quinney. The nine basic assertions of this theory were logically analyzed for content and importance to the overall theory. As a result of their analysis, using symbolic logic, De Fleur and Quinney demonstrated that only five of the nine assertions were basic to Sutherland's theory. The five hypotheses that remained were translated into a clearly stated and logical theoretical model. The essence of the theory was stated as follows:

> Overt criminal behavior has as its necessary and sufficient conditions a set of criminal motivations, attitudes, and techniques, the learning of which takes place when there is exposure to criminal norms in excess of exposure to corresponding anticriminal norms during symbolic interaction in primary groups.[23]

De Fleur and Quinney stated that the propositions that were not logically central to the theory "offer important qualifications and suggest links with more general behavioral concepts."[24]

Cressey praised the De Fleur and Quinney article for revealing unexpressed relationships and clarifying the theory. "Their English translation of set theory language," asserted Cressey, "states the theory more beautifully and more efficiently than it has ever been stated before."[25] This approval is particularly relevant since Cressey had worked closely with Sutherland on various aspects of differential association theory.

Following the Quinney and De Fleur reformulation, a series of studies were conducted by Griffin and Griffin to test Sutherland's theory.[26] Upon reexamining the theory and Sutherland's exchanges with his critics, they suggested that the theory makes reference to two distinct types of differential association processes. The first, differential attitude association, involves the learning of attitudes, values, and norms that are favorable to the violation of law. This process involves the internalization of attitudes. The individual must come to believe

and verbalize deviant attitudes which are expressed in his overt behavior. A second process, *differential action association*, involves the
recognition and imitation of behavior displayed by associates. The
juvenile may perform delinquent acts along with his friends even
though he has not internalized the corresponding delinquent attitudes.[27] Either or both of these processes may be involved in the
development of individual delinquency. Of course, if delinquent behavior results from internalized attitudes and values, the behavior will
be resistant to change, and treatment will be more difficult.[28]

Griffin and Griffin tested the De Fleur and Quinney version of the
differential association theory, first using marijuana use[29] and then drug
use[30] as forms of delinquent behavior. While the findings differ somewhat, the results are supportive of Sutherland's theory. Their research
represents the most comprehensive test of Sutherland's theory to date.

DIFFERENTIAL REINFORCEMENT

Sutherland's differential association theory has been influential in
inspiring a number of attempts to produce additional revisions and
extensions of the basic theory. One extensive revision was produced by
Clarence Jeffrey, who discussed the relationship between differential
association and modern learning theory. Jeffrey suggested that *differential reinforcement* rather than differential association was the key
to explaining delinquent behavior. Differential reinforcement implies
that delinquents pursue their behavior because it has been rewarded
in the past. If negative sanctions had been applied to the delinquent
behavior following its initial appearance, the behavior would not have
been repeated.[31]

Building on the reinforcement theory formulated by Jeffrey,
Burgess and Akers proposed another revision of the differential association theory. They included a more detailed specification of the learning
processes that were involved in the genesis of delinquent behavior.
Modifications in Sutherland's theory were suggested which they believed would bring the theory up to date with advances in learning
theory.[32]

The work of Jeffrey as well as that of Burgess and Akers alters the
differential association theory at its base. In fact, the central focus of
the theory, which represents an emphasis on learning through differential associations with groups and individuals with differing definitions
of the legal code, is altered. Reinforcement theory has received only
limited support in explaining juvenile delinquency, but the reinforcement may have found practical application with the development of
behavior modification techniques used to treat juvenile delinquents.

PRACTICAL APPLICATIONS

Cressey discussed the application of Sutherland's theory to diagnosis and treatment. Cressey reminded us that the popular clinical

approaches to the treatment of delinquents had concentrated on re-forming the individual. Differential association theory, however, sug-gests that attempts to change an individual's behavior patterns will be unsuccessful unless efforts are directed at changing the behavior and attitudes of the delinquent groups in which the individual is involved. Treatment based on a group perspective may involve the use of non-delinquent groups as a medium of change, or it might involve the delinquent's group as a target of change. Cressey suggested that differ-ential association provides a valuable framework on which to build effective prevention and rehabilitation programs.[33]

The practical application of differential association theory was also the focus of an article by Henry McKay.[34] Three types of interven-tion programs were suggested as a means to control or change the individual's participation in delinquent behaviors. The first technique involves direct intervention in the life of the individual, the second requires intervention in the social situation and group relationship, and the third revolves around unplanned and almost accidental inter-vention into the lives of other people. McKay asserted that successful delinquency-prevention programs should be based on increasing the participation of the individual in conventional groups and decreasing the individual's association with delinquent groups.

Glaser was also concerned with the practical application of dif-ferential association. His interest, however, centered on its predictive utility. The differential association theory was compared with alterna-tive theories to see which was most effective in predicting delinquent behavior. The differential association theory was chosen as superior because it served as a source of valid prediction of delinquent be-havior. Glaser found that the frequency, duration, priority, and in-tensity variables specified by Sutherland were effective in predicting the involvement of individuals in delinquent behavior. While the theory was judged to be superior to existing theories, Glaser suggested that a *differential anticipation* theory would meet the standards employed in his analysis even more adequately.[35]

Summary

The learning approach to delinquency has occupied a prominent place in the area of juvenile delinquency causation. Early theories placed the primary emphasis on the role of contagion or imitation in producing criminal (and delinquent) behavior. Although they lacked sophistication and rigor, these theories played an important role in bringing out the importance of social interaction in developing indi-vidual behavior.

Modern conceptions of social learning as a factor in delinquency causation have developed primarily as reactions to Sutherland's differ-ential association theory. His theory has generated controversy and renewed interest in social learning. As a result of its intense scrutiny, it has provoked a great deal of research and stimulated attempts to modify and improve the theory. This theoretical approach has probably inspired more new and fruitful theoretical work than any of the other recent approaches to juvenile delinquency.

SOCIETAL REACTION THEORIES

Most delinquency theories that focus on the individual delinquent stress conditions in the social environment that make delinquency a desirable alternative behavior. Individuals commit delinquent acts because of these conditions and are thereby considered delinquent. The proponents of the societal reaction perspective, however, reject this traditional view. Instead, they claim, it is society's reaction to the individual that produces "delinquent" behavior. A deviant label is attached to particular individuals who are thereby stigmatized and left little opportunity to be rewarded for conformist behavior.

Precursors and Pioneers

The first statement of societal reaction theory came from Lemert in 1951,[36] but Howard S. Becker popularized the perspective in sociology and provided the impetus for further development with the publication of *Outsiders* in 1963.[37] The theoretical roots have been traced all the way back to the Inquisition by Ned Polsky.[38] Others have traced its beginnings to Lombroso, W. I. Thomas, Merton, and Ruth Benedict. However, Frank Tannenbaum is usually given credit for having directly anticipated the labeling perspective when he used the term *tagging* rather than *labeling*. Tannenbaum illustrated how the treatment of offenders could create delinquency by producing commitment to delinquent careers.[39]

Tagging

The first systematic application of the societal reaction approach to juvenile delinquency was proposed by Tannenbaum in his textbook *Crime and the Community*. In this book he sketched out the process by which a juvenile becomes delinquent through the definitions of others. A juvenile may, through misadventure, disobey a norm which brings him under the scrutiny of the community. Once this occurs his personality, companions, hangouts, social background, speech, and behavior are brought into question. He is perceived not as a youth who has misbehaved but as a delinquent. His entire being is defined as bad, not just his specific act. In this process the individual is tagged, and his subsequent behavior is determined. He is seen as bad; therefore none of his behaviors can be described as anything but bad. Attempts to change behavior and thereby societal conceptions are futile. The juvenile, then, accepts the definitions of those around him and becomes the delinquent they expect.

Tannenbaum summarized this delinquency-producing process in

the following words: "The process of making the criminal, therefore, is a process of tagging, defining, segregating, describing, emphasizing, making conscious and self-conscious; it becomes a way of stimulating, suggesting, emphasizing and evoking the very traits that are complained of. . . . The person becomes the very thing he is described as being."[40] Although Tannenbaum's approach was apparently used only to describe the process whereby occasional offenders were turned into committed delinquents, later theories taking this approach used it to describe virtually all juvenile delinquency.

Labeling

Modern theories that developed from the societal reaction approach have followed and extended the basic premises of Tannenbaum's theory. Edwin Lemert, the pioneer of the modern labeling perspective, believed that acts are not in and of themselves delinquent. Instead, acts acquire delinquent character by society's conception of them.[41] Because societies change, ideas of what is deviant also change.

Lemert proposed that two kinds of deviance or delinquency could be found in a society. The first he called *primary deviation*. Acts that fall into this category are relatively minor; they involve little more than risk taking, testing of societal behavior limits, or flirting with danger. Individuals who engage in these behaviors are not committed to pursuing careers of disapproved behavior. They do not associate their acts with their own self-concepts and thereby have little or no criminal intent. If left unattended, their deviant acts will soon cease. If, on the other hand, these relatively harmless behaviors become a focus of attention, *secondary deviation* may result.

When a juvenile is detected, labeled, and treated as a juvenile delinquent, his self-concept is changed. The stigmatizing delinquency label is picked up and reinforced by those people who come in contact with the youth. Efforts to counteract the delinquency label fail, and the juvenile becomes committed to additional and more serious delinquency. The delinquency that results from the effects of labeling and societal reaction Lemert called secondary deviation.[42]

Another labeling proponent, Becker, suggested that the individual does not have to engage in primary deviation in order to be initially labeled delinquent. Rule breaking is not sufficient to establish a delinquent label for an individual; many juveniles break laws, but only a few are labeled and treated as delinquent. From Becker's perspective, the delinquent label and therefore delinquency result from the differential application of the rules to particular individuals. The application of the delinquent label, not behavior, is the cause of individual commitment to a delinquent life style. Even if helpful, interested, and well-intentioned people are involved in applying the label, the result is the same. In fact, the harder people work to help the youngster, the more difficult the problem becomes for him or her. Avoidance of delinquency becomes more difficult precisely because the label has been applied.[43]

For any act, there exists a wide range of labels. *Rip off, borrow, steal, swipe, lift,* and *theft* are all terms that apply to the same behavior patterns. The audience of powerful individuals and groups decides which label is relevant. Terms such as *ripped off* or *borrowed* have less severe consequences than *steal* or *theft.* The juvenile justice system itself becomes a primary causal agent in the production of juvenile delinquency because this system discredits, taints, and spoils the identity of the individual. Detention, court appearances, and training schools involve a series of degradations by which a self-image as a good and worthwhile person is torn away. The juvenile is seen by others in terms of the acts he may or may not have committed. If, for instance, a boy is seen as a thief or a mad attacker, he may come to define himself in the same way. Even if a delinquent act was committed, it constitutes only a small part of the behavior of an individual, but because of that act the individual may be seen as a thief and a "bad" person; he is not seen as a loving son, a brother, or a good student.[44] The youngster is defined in terms of the act he or she committed and the definitions that other people have about what characteristics an offender should possess. Case 9.2 suggests the effect of stereotyping.

The labelist takes a relativistic view of delinquency. Delinquency varies from place to place, from time to time, and from one culture to another. Even within the United States legal norms vary from state to state and often from one area of a state to another. The reactions of powerful groups and individuals also vary. A case in point are laws that regulate the sale and possession of marihuana. This drug has been in relatively widespread use in the United States for some time, and it has been cultivated as a cash crop for other purposes. At one point in time, it was in the interest of a powerful group of individuals to begin regulation of the drug. Marijuana use then became an illegal or criminal behavior. However, as powerful middle- and upper-class people accepted and used marijuana, it became more and more acceptable. A demand for change in the laws surrounding marijuana use has been noted, and many state laws have been changed so that the penalties for possession have been reduced and decriminalized.

IMPLICATIONS OF LABELING[45]

The labelist neglects juvenile delinquency to focus attention on the labelers, not the juvenile. The labeling proponent contends that no act is either good or evil, but the act may become evil if people attribute evil to it. The reactions of powerful people are crucial. Delinquency is imposed on some people but not on others. If identical acts are committed by two boys, the reaction to the first may be characterized by the phrase "boys will be boys," but the second boy may

DELINQUENTS ARE PEOPLE TOO

The tendency of people to stereotype (or label) offenders may produce hostile reactions in the juvenile. Innocent remarks, meant to soothe and promote a sense of relatedness, may motivate the offender to commit additional crimes. One such incident is reported in the following passage:

> You know, he didn't see this as an insulting remark at all: in fact, I think he thought he was being honest in telling me how mistaken he was. And that's exactly the sort of patronizing you get from straight people if you're a criminal. "Fancy that!" they say. "In some ways you're just like a human being!" I'm not kidding, it makes me want to choke the bleeding life out of them.

Source: T. Parker and R. Allerton, *The Courage of His Convictions* (London: Hutchinson, 1962), p. 111.

be referred to the police and declared delinquent by the juvenile court. The difference between the two outcomes reflects the reactions of powerful groups in society. One of the problems with labeling is that the delinquent is seen as a passive creature who has done nothing "bad"; he is the victim of an evil and unjust juvenile justice system. The labelist seems to have lost sight of the fact that some juveniles do steal, destroy property, and assault and even kill other people. There are victims who cannot be pushed into the background as abstractions and ignored.

Because powerful groups create delinquency by the application of rules to particular people, some labelists have apparently concluded that in the absence of all labels and rules, there could be no juvenile delinquency and no negative consequences to be derived, because secondary deviance would not exist. This type of reasoning creates confusion; it suggests that in the absence of laws against murder, there would be no murder. Without personal property, there would be no theft. Of course, even if the rules were eliminated, it does not mean that the activities involved in taking a life or stealing the property of other people would disappear. We may, however, call these behaviors by some other label or tag.

Disturbing questions arise when the labeling perspective is applied to juvenile delinquency. For example, murder and rape could be perceived as not bad in themselves; the acts are only bad because they have been so defined by powerful groups, and when they occur the groups react strongly to them. Even slavery and genocide could be said to be not inherently evil if the society in which they occur does not define them as bad. An extreme cultural relativist position is proposed by labeling theorists by which imposing labels on people becomes improper because the individual is imposing his morality on others. Most sociologists seem to accept the view that there are some acts—such as murder—that are inherently undesirable. Certainly, laws, morality, and individual values differ from one society to another, but it is probably possible to locate universal principles defining some acts as inappropriate because they are harmful to others and have been viewed as such by most people in most societies through different time periods. Labeling is probably most applicable to minor acts that do not have victims, and it probably does not have many applications to serious delinquencies.

IDEOLOGICAL FRAMEWORK

Labeling adherents create an ideology that supports the delinquent as a victim of the system. The delinquent requires sympathy as an underdog who has been victimized by society. Because the delinquent has been cruelly wronged, labeled, and misunderstood, he needs someone to take his side. Becker claims that it is impossible to avoid taking sides, but we must be concerned with which side is chosen.[46] Rather than taking the side of officialdom, social control, or the victim (who exists only as an abstraction anyway), the labelist chooses to take the side of the juvenile. Side taking, of course, introduces an ideological element into the analysis which may seriously impede understanding. It creates an ideology supporting the underdog in opposition to the "overdog."[47] Decision makers including the police, welfare workers, judges, and other officials are said to create delinquency by supporting established rules.

At this point the labeling perspective runs into problems. If a young woman is raped, who is the victim? Who deserves the sympathy of the labelist? Should the labeling proponent take the side of the rapist and view his victim as only an abstraction? Should he take the side of the rape victim against the rapist, the courts, and the legal system? Possibly the labeling perspective can be useful in allowing the sociologist to understand the offender from his perspective, but if the labelist sees only the viewpoint of the delinquent, it is not helpful even for the offender.[48]

Labeling stresses the delinquency label as a hindrance that leads to secondary deviance. An individual who is labeled a delinquent is the victim of discrimination, stigmatization, and degradation and is pushed toward more delinquency. This process may occur in some situations, but some sociologists question whether secondary deviance always results from the application of a label. The label may be a form of hitting bottom from which some improvement can be expected.[49] Instead of sinking into more delinquency as a result of the label, a youngster may end his offending behavior and begin to take responsibility for it. Thus labeling may actually help produce socially acceptable behavior and efforts to escape the label.[50]

UNDETECTED DELINQUENCY

Adherents of labeling seem to accept the view that an individual is not delinquent unless his illegal acts have been detected and condemned. Detection, official handling, and adjudication are essential elements in the labeling process. Labelists thus have difficulty explaining undetected delinquency. A youngster may commit rape, but unless he is detected and officially handled, he is not perceived as a delinquent. The secret rapist may fear reprisal, exposure, and public censure, and this knowledge may create further problems for him. Yet official detection and the application of a stigmatizing label by official agencies is a central part of the labeling perspective. If the labeling perspective only applies to detected delinquency, the perspective and its ability to account for delinquency is severely limited. Labeling adherents, with the possible exception of Lemert,[51] have overemphasized visibility, apprehension, and official handling, or they have ignored a large part of the delinquency problem.[52] Unofficial handling and labeling can be a powerful force in controlling behavior in the absence of legal controls and protection for the procedural rights of juveniles. But the neglect of informal labeling is unfortunate no matter what the reason.

VERIFICATION

Testing and verification of the labeling theory has proceeded at a slow pace. The lack of precision and clarity in statements of the theory has been a major stumbling block to systematic analysis. Other problems of verification center around its ideological content. Because labeling is basically a critique of the establishment rather than a systematic set of interrelated hypotheses, the usual research and verificational techniques are frequently not applicable.

Research cited as evidence to support labeling theory as an explanation for juvenile delinquency has taken several directions. Some proponents point to the good boy-bad boy studies of Reckless and Dinitz as illustrations of the effects of a labeling process in creating undesirable behavior. These studies suggest that youngsters who are characterized as "bad" by parents and teachers are more likely to become involved in delinquent behavior than those judged "good."[53] These studies have come under a great deal of critical scrutiny. Several writers have pointed out methodological problems which might cast doubt on the validity of the bad boy findings.[54] Conflicting results in later studies have proved inconclusive.

More frequently, research has focused on official attention to juvenile misbehavior. Proponents cite studies that suggest differential handling of juveniles throughout the juvenile justice system. Police bias[55] and juvenile court organization[56] or politics[57] are emphasized by a variety of analysts. Here again, the critics point out conflicting evidence which lessens the impact of supportive findings. It might also be pointed out that evidence of differential handling is not incongruent with other theories of juvenile delinquency.

Another approach used to study the effects of labeling on juvenile delinquency has involved the study of treatment programs. Official and informal treatment outcomes are compared to assess the impact of institutionalization on the juvenile offender. The labeling perspective suggests that more formal, institutionalized treatment would reinforce delinquent behavior. Most of the available evidence, however, suggests that training schools have a neutral influence.[58] Furthermore, studies comparing community-based treatment and institutional alternatives have produced conflicting evidence.[59]

A number of case studies have been developed to illustrate the labeling theory. Most of these studies, however, have focused on deviant behavior other than juvenile delinquency. Although Tannenbaum studied incorrigibles,[60] Lemert worked with prostitutes, Communists, stutterers, and the mentally ill.[61] Becker studied musicians and marihuana users.[62] The cases chosen for analysis are often ones for which a reasonable case can be made for labeling. The acts often do not appear to be inherently evil, bad, wrong, or antisocial, and the reactions of powerful groups can be shown to provide negative consequences for the individual labeled. There have been few attempts to start with a labeling perspective and design research to apply the theory to delinquency and serious crime. Quinney[63] and Hartjen[64] are among the notable exceptions. Much more research is needed to assess the utility of the labeling perspective for explaining juvenile delinquent behavior.

PRACTICAL APPLICATION

From the labeling point of view, delinquency is not an inherent quality of an act or an actor; thus suggestions to alleviate the problem focus outside the offender. The question of how or why a particular individual comes to engage in misbehavior is not a primary concern.[65] In fact, it doesn't matter whether the individual violated the law or not; the reactions of others constitute the primary emphasis. Efforts to reduce crime and delinquency lie in educating the public and public officials about the consequences of labeling and stigmatization of the offender.

Proponents of the labeling perspective suggest that several methods can be used for reducing the incidence of crime and delinquency in society. Some of the programs proposed focus on the law. It is suggested that many laws are outdated or that they regulate behavior that is not damaging to society. If these laws were repealed or the acts decriminalized, individuals would be protected from governmental invasion of privacy, and law enforcement officials could focus their attention on more important matters. Several communities have followed the advice of the labeling theorists and have begun to review some minor offenses. Marihuana use has been decriminalized in some areas, and some juvenile status offenses have been eliminated in others.

Other programs to reduce juvenile delinquency focus on the relationship between the offender and the juvenile justice system. It is suggested that informal handling, diversion from the juvenile justice system, or even benign neglect may result in the abandonment of delinquent behavior by the juvenile offender. Community-based treatment programs developed from this perspective have been readily accepted by officials of the juvenile justice system. Most large cities have diversion programs as treatment alternatives.[66] Though there is not a great deal of evidence to support their effectiveness, it is unlikely that these programs will be abandoned in the near future.[67]

Summary
The societal reaction theories are relative newcomers to the field of juvenile delinquency causation. Because they have not had a long history of development and modification, these theories have not been separated from their ideological roots. As a critique of the establishment, labeling has focused scrutiny on methods of handling lone offenders. This has led to a reassessment and modification of existing structures that deal with misbehaving youth in American society.

Labeling has become a theory of policy rather than of individual delinquency causation. As such, it cannot speak to the question of why and how illegal acts are committed. Its influence is most keenly felt in its humanizing effect on legal processes. The perspective will not soon be dismissed or forgotten.

CULTURAL THEORIES
Although learning and societal reaction theories provide the leading sociological perspectives on individual juvenile delinquency causation, other theoretical approaches have enjoyed considerable acclaim at one time or another. Cultural and structural theorists laid the foundation for modern theories of group delinquency. Their pioneering work, however, was concentrated on conditions in the society that might lead a juvenile to accept deviant modes of behavior. Many of their theories may still be adapted to explain individual behavior.

Several sociological theories have taken a cultural approach to explain the presence of juvenile delinquency in society. Under this approach, it is suggested that the norms and values of an individual are shaped by the general values of his or her social environment.

Some theorists have argued that crime is a normal and necessary feature of every society. Others claim that certain societies have more crime and delinquency than others because their national values promote receptive attitudes toward novel alternatives to legitimate activities. A third approach suggests that the culture of a society may not be uniform and that the conflicts that result from the clashes of its various cultures create delinquent situations.

Culture Conflicts

Thorsten Sellin approached crime from a culture conflict perspective. Looking at a society, Sellin noted that its values, norms, and beliefs were not uniform throughout the population. Identifiable groups had divergent customs, traditions, and perspectives on what constituted right and proper attitudes and behavior. In isolation each of these groups lived in harmony; however, when they came in contact, conflict ensued. Sellin indicated that group antagonism can develop in several ways. A new group may migrate into an area occupied by another, more established group. Or contact between cultures may occur on common boundaries. If one of the groups possesses the power to extend its rules over the entire territory occupied by the joint population, individuals from the subordinate group may be punished for violating "foreign" rules. They are treated as delinquents even though their behavior is approved by members of their own group. Conflict and a high rate of delinquency can be expected to persist until the subordinate group becomes acculturated.[68]

Sellin's theory may be applied even more specifically to juvenile delinquency. Juvenile delinquency is defined by a body of rules that prohibit certain types of conduct and provide remedies for violation of them. Although the prohibited behavior reflects the character and interests of the groups that legislate them, the rules are applied to an age group having little influence over their content. While some youths find that the legal norms reflect their life experiences, others belong to groups that hold conduct rules that are at variance with the officially instituted codes. Conflict results when youths are committed to a subculture that differs in important respects from the formally instituted norms of society.[69] Behavior considered correct by the norms of the slum neighborhood or conforming by the norms of a teen-age subculture might be considered delinquent by the laws of the broader society.

Sellin's theory was initially developed to explain the fluctuations of crime rates in a society. However, his ideas have become very important in the field of juvenile delinquency. His theory provided a lasting contribution in that it has influenced a number of subcultural theories of juvenile delinquency. Some of these theorists suggest that juvenile delinquency is a reaction against societal standards; others believe that delinquency results from conformity to subcultural standards. Several of these theories are discussed in Chapter 10.

The Criminal Culture

Donald Taft developed a theory that attempted to explain high rates of crime by examining the "standard" culture prevalent in some types of societies. He suggested that crime is inevitable in societies characterized by particular cultural traits. Although the complexity and stability of the society were considered, Taft believed that the content of the society's value system was even more important to the production of high crime rates.

Taking the United States as a model of a high-crime society, Taft analyzed the culture for values that might contribute to disrespect for the law and high rates of crime. He concluded that materialism, individualism, status striving, group loyalty, and frontier values were the prime crime-producing values.[70] These values contributed to a tolerance for quasi-criminal exploitation and corruption by entrepreneurs, thereby legitimizing some types of crime. Case 9.3 illustrates the role of one type of American belief that has been used to justify delinquent behavior.

Taft suggested that some cultural values may be crime inhibiting. A society that emphasizes self-control, for example, may have lower crime rates. The United States did not appear to adhere to many inhibiting values. Instead, it stresses acquisition of property, prestige, success, and other scarce resources without controls on the means that should be used. The result is often the achievement of success at any price with any means.[71] With this cultural emphasis, success is shown by what a person has and not by what he is. Consumption of material goods is more important than integrity. In such a culture, it may not matter how the material goods, prestige, or status was obtained. The most important thing is that success is achieved at any price and with whatever means are available.

There appears to be some validity to Taft's analysis of American cultural patterns and their role in producing crime. The theory does not, however, explain why all Americans are not criminals or delinquents. Some people are able to resist the tendency to greed, corruption, and materialism which are such obvious features of American cultural patterns. Some Americans rise above materialism and the low points of politics and business. The theory may explain some crime, but it does not explain all of it.[72] Additional problems include the fact that Taft's theory does not allow ready comparisons across cultures and thus it may only be applicable to the United States. Taft's theory was developed to explain adult crime, but it can be applied to some types of juvenile delinquency as well.

STRUCTURAL THEORIES

A few theories have been developed to explain crime and delinquency by reference to the social structure. These theories call attention to the fact that societies are stratified. Not all their members are

NATIVE BELIEFS

The attitudes of the dominant society may be used to justify delinquent activities. One adolescent rationalized his behavior (vandalism) in terms of prejudices found in the larger society:

The neighborhood was old and filled with all kinds of people. . . . Mexican and niggers came and everything changed. Niggers and an Indian family lived next door to us and we fought them all the time because we didn't like niggers. The boys would break their windows, holler in their doors, and throw tin cans into their houses. . . .

Source: Andrew L. Wade, "Social Processes in the Act of Vandalism," in Criminal Behavior Systems, ed. Marshall B. Clinard and Richard Quinney (NewYork: Holt, Rinehart and Winston, 1967), p.181.

offered the opportunities needed to achieve societal ideals. The very structuring of the society, it is believed, creates disturbance and conflict among its members.

The Division of Labor

Emile Durkheim was probably among the first theorists to make a systematic attempt to locate the causes of crime in the social structure. According to Durkheim, the moral attitudes of a society are a reflection of its social structure. As the society increases in size and "moral density," the ideas about what constitutes proper behavior change. Criminality is not inherent in any behavior but rather it is perceived as criminal because it shocks the collective conscience.[73] As a society increases in size and complexity, the laws that govern it change.

In a rapidly changing social structure, the norms may conflict or break down completely. Individuals may be unsure of the proper modes of behavior. Crime and delinquency may result from such anomie.[74] Case 9.4 is an example of this. Social disorganization which results from rapid changes in the social structure is given as the basic underlying cause of deviant behavior.

Durkheim believed that crime is a normal and necessary phenomenon. It serves as an example which reinforces morality and it promotes change in both the laws and conceptions of morality. In the simple society, shared moral beliefs, traditions, and moral sentiments brought harmony. However, as society became increasingly complex,

ANOMIE

The case of Dorothy, a resident of a juvenile correctional facility, illustrates the sense of helplessness experienced by the anomic individual:

> I feel terribly lonely. No, I don't talk about it to anyone. It's no use. . . . I think its no use to even try. I will always get into trouble. I learned the things here about prostitution, and I will continue. I don't care. . . . I am a prostitute, and I don't think that is so terrible. No it doesn't bother me. I just don't care. I learned it here, and I make a good living with it. I started out by writing bad checks. Now I prostitute. I do it for money. Money is good. You need money. . . . Dangerous? It makes absolutely no difference to me if I live or die. I don't like this life but there is no other.

Source: Gisele Konopka, *The Adolescent Girl in Conflict* (Englewood Cliffs, N.J.: Prentice-Hall, 1966), pp. 115–116.

individuals grew different, and their beliefs and traditions became more disparate. Because they pursued different labors, their experiences were different, and the rules needed to maintain harmony grew more complex. The laws and thereby the crimes and punishments took on a different complexion. The laws grew broader and the punishments less repressive. Thus there were more possible crimes and less understanding of, and commitment to, the specialized body of laws. Crime would increase with the growing complexity and increased division of labor in a society.

Durkheim's theory did not inspire an appreciable amount of research on crime or juvenile delinquency. His concept of anomie, however, provided a base from which later theories of juvenile delinquency were developed.

Anomie

Robert K. Merton also concentrated on the social structure to develop a theory of deviant and law-violating behavior. He believed that the social structure may exert a pressure on some individuals, pushing them into criminal behavior.[75] Two features of social life are essential to an understanding of deviant behavior, according to this theorist. The first is content of the cultural values. The cultural values define the goals that are socially acceptable for individuals in a given society. Success, as evidenced by material and economic achievements, is given a high rating in the hierarchy of cultural goals in American society. Individuals are judged on the basis of their ability to achieve the valued goals. The cultural values also provide prescriptions for reaching these goals. Some means are not acceptable; others are highly valued. In American society, for example, thrift, hard work, and education are perceived as proper modes for mobility. The cultural values suggest that pursuit of the valued means will result in achievement of sought-after goals. Where the means and goals are not mutually compatible, the goals are given priority.

In stable social structures, according to Merton, there is an interdependence between the goals prescribed by the culture and the structural means provided to achieve them. However, the social structure may suffer severe dislocations. Where this occurs, individuals do not all have equal access to the approved means of reaching the goals of success. Individuals from the lower classes, for example, may have considerably fewer opportunities to pursue an education or to save money. Their only avenue to success may be through the use of illegitimate means. Crime or delinquency may provide the individual an opportunity to gain the symbols of success and enhance his or her sense of worth.[76]

The primary source of crime and delinquency, then, is in the dislocations of the social structure which produces discrepancies between culturally defined goals and socially structured means for achieving them. Merton did not suggest that these discrepancies always resulted in law-violating behavior. Crime or delinquency was only one alternative. Unfortunately, Merton did not specify the circumstances under which criminality would consistently be selected as the alternative.

Merton's theory has served as a base for research and theoretical development. Much of his influence, however, has been concentrated in explanations of group delinquency. Therefore his theory and its implications will be discussed in Chapter 10, which focuses on explanations of gang delinquency.

INTERDISCIPLINARY APPROACHES

Most of the theories of delinquent behavior have developed within a single discipline. Where this has been the case, the content of the theory is determined by the subject matter of the discipline. Sociologists tend to look to social factors to explain delinquent behavior; psychologists rely on psychological factors. And so it goes, each discipline focusing on its own natural subject matter. A recognition of the multifaceted nature of juvenile delinquency has prompted suggestions from many quarters that it will not be fully explained by a single factor or a single theory drawn from a specialized discipline. These criticisms have prompted attention to two somewhat different approaches which attempt to introduce a more inclusive approach to juvenile delinquency. The first of these is the *multiple factor approach* and the second is called the *interdisciplinary approach.*

A multiple factor theory is one that uses more than one variable to develop an explanation of delinquency. Many early theories of delinquency relied on one factor, such as poverty, the free will, demons, or biology. With the multiple factor approach, a variety of variables may be introduced to explain delinquency. However, the variables are usually drawn from within a single academic discipline. For example, Cohen, Miller, and Sutherland might all be classified as multiple factor theorists. In fact, most of the recently developed theories in sociology and psychology involve a variety of factors to explain delinquent behavior, the assumption being that delinquent behavior is too complex to be explained by a single cause.

An interdisciplinary approach to delinquency recognizes that a variety of academic disciplines may have developed insights useful to an understanding of juvenile delinquency. Theorists involved in the interdisciplinary approach attempt to synthesize, or at least draw together, these insights for a more comprehensive approach to juvenile delinquency. Proponents of the interdisciplinary approach point out that a child's behavior is not easily separated into its sociological, psychological, medical, legal, or biological aspects. A youngster does not divide his behavior or problems into neat categories just because academic disciplines are so organized. In fact, discipline boundaries are believed to frustrate and limit an understanding of juvenile delinquency and crime. Individuals who choose to work within this area need a broad background in law, social work, psychology, sociology, criminology, police science, and biology so that insights from these areas can be combined and integrated. The approach is eclectic because it involves a willingness to draw from a broad theoretical base, and it recognizes that disciplinary boundaries are artificial constructs. These disciplinary barriers must be broken down if the various theorists are to understand and appreciate each other's work. After this is accomplished, they can get on with joint efforts to solve common problems.

The Importance of an Interdisciplinary Framework

No single theory has been shown to provide a comprehensive explanation of all juvenile delinquent behavior. Nor has a program been developed to eliminate all kinds of illegal acts. This does not mean that nothing has been learned about juvenile delinquency. A number of theories from diverse disciplines have offered some promise in uncovering some of the factors that appear to be related to the genesis of juvenile delinquency. However, each of these theories provides only a partial explanation.

Juvenile delinquency is an extremely complex phenomenon. It may involve minor misbehavior, such as curfew violation, or serious

TABLE 9.2 INTERDISCIPLINARY
APPROACHES TO JUVENILE DELINQUENCY

SCHOOL	APPROACH	FOCUS	CONCEPTS	LEADERS
Multiple causation	inter-disciplinary	all factors	global science social pathological crime	Liszt
			classified multiple causative factors	Healy
			conspicuous, inoperate, minor, and cooperating factors	Burt
			push, pull, containment, self-concept	Reckless

offenses up to the very act of homicide. Each of these behaviors must be accounted for. Theories have been developed to describe and explain some of the special types of delinquent behavior. Studies based upon the various theories suggest that some delinquencies are more readily explained by social factors, while others appear to be rooted in individual psychology. Certainly, we might expect that different explanations may be applied to the gang delinquent and the young arsonist who must stay at the scene of the crime to watch the property burn. If all the various perceived causes of a variety of delinquent behaviors were listed and compared, several disciplines would be represented. A combining of the efforts of several disciplines might provide a comprehensive overview of all that is currently known about juvenile delinquency and thereby contribute to an understanding of the area.

There have been a number of attempts to develop both multiple factor and interdisciplinary theories. The multiple factor approach has been widely accepted within the various disciplines. The interdisciplinary approach, on the other hand, has not gathered a great number of adherents. Most of the interdisciplinary efforts have attempted to bring together such a broad and diverse range of theories that extensive integration and synthesis is unlikely. The result has often been overgeneralization and misinformation. Perhaps when this area becomes more highly developed and sophisticated, it will provide more fruitful results than have been seen in the past. For an overview of this area, see Table 9.2.

The Pioneers

Franz Von Liszt (1851–1919) was one of the earliest social scientists to pursue a systematic effort to develop an interdisciplinary approach to criminal causation. His work with Van Hamel (1842–1917) and Prins (1845–1919) in establishing the International Association of

Penal Law brought together a broad range of thinkers from sociology, psychiatry, psychology, biology, and other disciplines involved in the delinquency problem.[77] The stimulation of his contact with thinkers from the many disciplines provided Liszt an opportunity to develop and hone his own interdisciplinary approach to criminal causation.

In the early period of his career, Liszt was interested primarily in social explanations of crime. As his career developed, however, he became interested in personality and other variables as potential explanatory factors. Liszt conceived of criminology as a global science which would combine biology, sociology, and psychology for a full explanation and understanding of crime.[78] He did not propose radically new theories to explain crime and delinquency. Instead, he and the other early pioneers proposed a compromise among existing but competing theories. The strong points of each of the competing views were to be combined for a new perspective on crime. While these early writers proposed a synthesis of biological, psychological, psychiatric, sociological, and other varieties of theory, most of their works involved the combination of theories from only two or three disciplines.

THE AMERICAN INFLUENCE

The earliest American interdisciplinary effort was initiated by a psychiatrist. William Healy and his associate Augusta Bronner constructed a series of studies in 1936 that drew from several disciplines but focused primarily on personality factors. As a result of his studies of over 800 juveniles referred to the juvenile court during a five-year period, Healy listed about 140 factors that he believed might lead to juvenile delinquency. He categorized this long list of factors and produced an elaborate typology that contained 15 major categories.[79]

Healy and Bronner conducted a series of research studies to sort out the causes of juvenile delinquency. Their work probably made its greatest contribution in eliminating certain factors as direct causes of delinquency. They found, for example, that serious delinquents were not below average in intelligence and that mental retardation was not a cause of juvenile delinquency.[80] Furthermore, they reported that poverty could explain only a small percentage of all delinquency cases. They also noted that many delinquents came from normal homes.[81] Healy and Bronner suggested that unsatisfactory human relationships resulting from poverty, poor neighborhoods, and other impoverished conditions was a critical factor in the production of juvenile delinquency.[82]

Healy and Bronner were critical of the ecological approach to delinquency, which was gaining popularity at the time of their studies. They contended that the ecological approach produced very little new theory or information. Rather, they believed, the approach merely stated what every policeman already knew. Healy and Bronner's approach became less interdisciplinary over the years as they began to lean toward a more psychoanalytic approach. Their influence was probably greatest in the psychoanalytic field.

THE APPROACH IN ENGLAND

Cyril Burt identified about 170 potential causal factors to explain juvenile delinquency. In his 1938 book *The Young Delinquent*, Burt concluded that the cause of juvenile delinquency could not be located in a single factor or even in a single discipline.[83] He attributed delinquency to a multiplicity of diverse factors from an array of sources. Furthermore, he believed that the particular combination of causes would differ from one juvenile to another. Burt classified his causative factors into four major categories: (1) primary or conspicuous influences, (2) cooperating factors, (3) minor factors, and (4) inoperative factors.[84] In applying his classification to juveniles, he emphasized the importance of evaluating the individual case. A delinquent might display one or all of the various factors in his classification.

During Burt's time, poverty was a popular factor for explaining delinquency. He conducted a study to ascertain the influence of this factor and discovered that a majority of delinquents did indeed come from economically deprived homes. He concluded, however, that this did not mean that poverty necessarily causes crime. Burt suggested, instead, that the figures on crime reflected the differential handling afforded members of the various economic classes.[85]

Modern Interdisciplinary Efforts

Although the interdisciplinary approach has not gathered a great number of followers, several examples can be found in modern juvenile delinquency theory. Most of the recent work, however, involves a smaller number of disciplines than was popular among the pioneers. Sociology and psychology appears to be the most popular combination.

CONTAINMENT THEORY

Reckless's containment theory represents a fairly recent example of the interdisciplinary approach to delinquency causation. His theory attempts to explain how delinquent acts are caused by a multiplicity of factors drawn primarily from sociology and psychology. Reckless contends that a hierarchical arrangement of forces affects all individuals. These forces push some individuals toward delinquency and pull others away from nonacceptable and nonconforming behavior. *Pull* factors are personal characteristics, such as age, ethnic group identification, family background, and other factors that exert pressure for nondelinquency. *Push* factors are external forces in the environment that predispose the individual to delinquent behavior, including associations with peers who accept delinquent norms and attitudes and commit delinquent acts, membership in a delinquent gang, and others.[86]

According to the containment theory, the family, school, and other conforming groups may surround the individual with a structure of *external containment* which is effective in preventing juvenile delinquency. On the other hand, ineffective or nonconformist groups in the individual's environment may fail to provide the external controls needed to prevent delinquent behavior. Delinquency may also be inhibited by *inner containment*, which constitutes another layer of social pressure on the individual. According to Reckless, the primary agent of inner containment is the self-concept, which is a product of socialization.

A "good" self-concept will contain delinquency by isolating the individual from the values, attitudes, and associations that support violation of the law. The "good" concept is supposed to develop in youths from intact families that provide emotional support for the child. A "bad" self-concept, on the other hand, is more likely to develop in youngsters from broken or nonsupportive families. A child with a "bad" self-concept is not insulated from delinquent acts, values, or attitudes. Because the youngster believes he is not a worthwhile person, he or she may be more likely to commit delinquent acts. The individual may be pushed toward delinquency because of an inadequate self-concept. Because a poor self-concept is associated with hostility, aggression, inferiority feelings, tension, and family conflict, it may be sufficient to push the child into delinquency in the absence of strong external controls.[87]

If the inner and outer controls (containment factors) are adequate, delinquency will not surface. According to Reckless, inadequate outer containment is indicated where there is a lack of parental or other controls on the behavior of a youth. Even where there is inadequate outer control, though, youngsters may not become delinquent if they have developed sufficient inner controls over their own behavior. Reckless stresses inner controls because these factors allow the individual to avoid situations and individuals that might involve the youngster in delinquent activity. The self-concept plays a major role in the genesis of inner controls that inhibit delinquent behavior. Therefore it is important to understand more fully how the self-concept develops and influences delinquent behavior.

Reckless and his associates conducted a series of studies on boys to test the containment theory.[88] After examining the data, they concluded that the nondelinquent boy has school, peer, and family reference groups that define the boy as good, while the delinquent youth has reference groups that define him as bad and potentially delinquent. The potential delinquent and the good, nondelinquent boy play previously defined roles. The good boy develops an image of himself as good, while the delinquent comes to define himself as bad. The good boys were satisfied, and the potential delinquents dissatisfied, with their respective roles. But the good boys avoided behavior and contact with others that might lead to trouble with the police and the courts. The delinquency-prone boys, partially because of their self-image and partially because of the definitions of significant others, were unable to avoid the behaviors and contacts leading to delinquent behavior and trouble with police and courts. Sociologists, however, have not enthusiastically accepted Reckless's findings. They point out methodological problems and the use of unwarranted assumptions in his research.[89]

INDIVIDUAL THEORIES IN PERSPECTIVE

Modern sociological theories of individual juvenile delinquency generally take one of four major approaches. Of these, the learning approach has probably been the subject of greatest scrutiny. Differential association, the most prominent of the learning theories, has received considerable support. The societal reaction approach is a more recent development. Nevertheless, it has acquired a number of enthusiastic supporters. While it has not been investigated as widely as the learning theories, it has been influential in the development of treatment programs for juveniles. Diversion and policies of benign neglect often have their roots in the labeling approach. Unfortunately, many of the basic assertions of labelists are not supportable and lack both clarity and precision. Major cultural and structural theories have also been developed to explain the genesis of delinquent behavior. These theories have not been popular in describing delinquency-producing processes in the individual, however. Their influence has been generally limited to the development of theories to explain subcultural and gang delinquency.

There are numerous avenues for theoretical development that need to be explored. One revolves around the need for developing theories to explain delinquency by the individual. An adequate theory, when it is developed, will probably depend on some variant of learning theory. Sutherland pointed the way, but the full implications of learning theory for explaining juvenile delinquency have not been explored.

Interdisciplinary approaches to delinquency are probably needed if a full understanding of delinquency is eventually to be created. The interdisciplinary approach suggests a solution to the problem of finding a middle ground between overgeneralized, abstract, and even irrelevant statements on the one hand and overspecialization and trivia on the other. The major obstacle to the development of this approach is the difficulty of breaking down the barriers that separate the various disciplines. Until this goal is accomplished, interdisciplinary theory will continue to be a rarity. Perhaps it is too early in the life of this young discipline to branch out into other areas. Development of theory in the separate disciplines may be necessary before a coherent, integrated multidisciplinary approach is possible.

The development of an interdisciplinary theory would be a valu-able addition to the literature on juvenile delinquency. Because so many theories include a variety of factors, it is often difficult to tell which ones are multiple factor theories and which are interdisciplinary approaches. We have found few interdisciplinary approaches, but other experts may classify theories somewhat differently. Yet it seems that interdisciplinary theory has been a relatively ignored area that might offer a fruitful avenue for further investigation.

NOTES

[1] See Stephen Schafer, *Theories in Criminology* (New York: Random House, 1969), pp. 238–239.

[2] Gabriel Tarde, *The Laws of Imitation* (New York: Holt, Rinehart and Winston, 1963); Gabriel Tarde, *On Communication and Social Influence* (Chicago: University of Chicago Press, 1969).

[3] Edwin H. Sutherland, *Principles of Criminology*, 3d ed. (Philadelphia: Lippincott, 1939), pp. 4–9; Edwin Sutherland, *Principles of Criminology*, 4th ed. (Philadelphia: Lippincott, 1947).

[4] Arthur L. Leader, "A Differential Reinforcement Theory of Criminality," *Sociology and Social Research* 26 (September–October 1941): 45.

[5] *Ibid.*, pp. 45–48.

[6] Edwin H. Sutherland, "Rejoinder," *Sociology and Social Research* 26 (September–October 1941): 50–52.

[7] Sutherland, *Principles of Criminology*, 4th ed., *op. cit.*

[8] Edwin H. Sutherland and Donald R. Cressey, *Criminology*, 8th ed. (Philadelphia: Lippincott, 1970), pp. 75–77.

[9] Edwin H. Sutherland, *White Collar Crime* (New York: Dryden Press, 1949).

[10] Donald R. Cressey, "Application and Verification of the Differential Association Theory," *Journal of Criminal Law, Criminology, and Police Science* 43 (May–June 1952): 44.

[11] Donald R. Cressey, "The Differential Association Theory and Compulsive Crimes," *Journal of Criminal Law, Criminology and Police Science* 45 (May–June 1954): 29–40.

[12] Donald R. Cressey, "The Theory of Differential Association: An Introduction," *Social Problems* 8 (summer 1960): 3.

[13] *Ibid.*

[14] *Ibid.*

[15] Sutherland, *White Collar Crime*, op. cit.

[16] James F. Short, Jr., "Differential Association and Delinquency," *Social Problems* 4 (January 1957): 233–239.

[17] James F. Short, Jr., "Differential Association with Delinquent Friends and Delinquent Behavior," *Pacific Sociological Review* 1 (spring 1958): 20–25.

[18] Harwin Voss, "Differential Association and Reported Delinquent Behavior: A Replication," *Social Problems* 12 (summer 1964): 78–85.

[19] Albert J. Reiss, Jr., and A. Lewis Rhodes, "An Empirical Test of Differential Association Theory," *Journal of Research in Crime and Delinquency* 1 (January 1964): 5–18.

[20] James F. Short, Jr., "Differential Association as a Hypothesis: Problems of Empirical Testing," *Social Problems* 8 (summer 1960): 14–25.

[21] Daniel Glaser, "Criminality Theories and Behavioral Images," *American Journal of Sociology* 61 (March 1956): 440.

[22] *Ibid.*

[23] Melvin L. De Fleur and Richard Quinney, "A Reformulation of Sutherland's Differential Association Theory and a Strategy for Empirical Verification," *Journal of Research in Crime and Delinquency* 3 (January 1966): 1–22.

[24] *Ibid.*, p. 8.

[25] Donald R. Cressey, "The Language of Set Theory and Differential Association," *Journal of Research in Crime and Delinquency* 3 (January 1966): 23.

[26] Brenda S. Griffin and Charles T. Griffin, "Marijuana Use Among Students and Peers," *Drug Forum* (1978, forthcoming); Brenda S. Griffin and Charles T. Griffin, "Drug Use and Differential Association," *International Journal of Addictions* (1978, forthcoming).

[27] *Ibid.*

[28] *Ibid.*

[29] Griffin and Griffin, "Marijuana Use Among Students and Peers," *op. cit.*

[30] Griffin and Griffin, "Drug Use and Differential Association," *op. cit.*

[31] Clarence Jeffrey, "Criminal Behavior and Learning Theory," *Journal of Criminal Law, Criminology and Police Science* 61 (September 1965): 294–300.

[32] Robert L. Burgess and Ronald Akers, "A Differential Association-Reinforcement Theory of Criminal Behavior," *Social Problems* 14 (fall 1966): 128–147.

[33] Donald R. Cressey, "Changing Criminals: The Application of the Theory of Differential Association," *American Journal of Sociology* 61 (September 1955): 116–120.

[34] Henry McKay, "Differential Association and Crime Prevention: Problems of Utilization," *Social Problems* 8 (summer 1960): 25–37.

[35] Daniel Glaser, "Differential Association and Criminological Prediction," *Social Problems* 8 (summer 1960): 6–14.

[36] Edwin M. Lemert, *Social Pathology* (New York: McGraw-Hill, 1951).

[37] Howard Becker, *Outsiders* (New York: Free Press, 1963).

[38] Ned Polsky, *Hustlers, Beats and Others* (Chicago: Aldine, 1967), p. 195.

[39] Frank Tannenbaum, *Crime and the Community* (Boston: Ginn and Co., 1938).

[40] *Ibid.*, pp. 19–20.

[41] This point of view is not unlike that held by Emile Durkheim, whose theory was discussed earlier in this chapter.

[42] Edwin M. Lemert, *Human Deviance, Social Problems and Social Control* (Englewood Cliffs, N.J.: Prentice-Hall, 1967); Edwin M. Lemert, *Social Action and Legal Change: Revolution in the Juvenile Court* (Chicago: Aldine, 1970); Edwin M. Lemert, *Social Pathology* (New York: McGraw-Hill, 1951).

[43] Becker, *op. cit.*

[44] Kai T. Erickson, *Wayward Puritans* (New York: Wiley, 1966), pp. 6–7.

[45] This section draws heavily on the excellent critique of the labeling perspective found in Edward Sagarin, *Deviants and Deviance* (New York: Praeger, 1975), pp. 129–142.

[46] Howard S. Becker, "Whose Side Are We On?" *Social Problems* 14 (1967): 239–247.

[47] David Bordua, "Recent Trends: Deviant Behavior and Social Control," *Annals of the American Academy of Political and Social Sciences* 338 (1967): 119–136.

[48] Sagarin, *op. cit.*, p. 134.

[49] Harold Garfinkel, "Conditions of Successful Degradation Ceremonies," *American Journal of Sociology* 61 (1956): 420–424.

[50] Milton Mannkoff, "Societal Reaction and Career Deviance: A Critical Analysis," *Sociological Quarterly* 12 (1971): 204–218.

[51] Lemert, *Social Pathology, op. cit.,* p. 51.

[52] Sagarin, *op. cit.,* pp. 140–141.

[53] Walter Reckless, Simon Dinitz, and Ellen Murray, "Self-concept as an Insulator Against Delinquency," *American Sociological Review* 21 (December 1956): 744–756; Walter Reckless, Simon Dinitz, and Ellen Murray, "The 'Good Boy' in a High Delinquency Area," *Journal of Criminal Law, Criminology and Police Science* 48 (May–June 1957): 18–25; Walter Reckless, Simon Dinitz, and Barbara Kay, "The Self-component in Potential Delinquency and Potential Nondelinquency," *American Sociological Review* 22 (October 1957): 566–570; Simon Dinitz, Barbara Kay, and Walter Reckless, "Group Gradients in Delinquency Potential and Achievement Scores of Sixth Graders," *American Journal of Orthopsychiatry* 28 (July 1958): 598–605; Jon Simpson, Simon Dinitz, Barbara Kay, and Walter Reckless, "Delinquency Potential of Preadolescents in a High Delinquency Area," *British Journal of Delinquency* 10 (January 1960): 211–215; Frank R. Scarpitti, Ellen Murray, Simon Dinitz, and Walter Reckless, "The 'Good Boy' in a High Delinquency Area: 4 Years Later," *American Sociological Review* 27 (August 1962): 555–558; Simon Dinitz, Frank Scarpitti, and Walter Reckless, "Delinquency Vulnerability: A Cross Group and Longitudinal Analysis," *American Sociological Review* 27 (August 1962): 515–517; Walter Reckless and Simon Dinitz, "Pioneering with Self-concept as a Vulnerability Factor in Delinquency," *Journal of Criminal Law, Criminology and Police Science* 58 (December 1967): 515–523.

[54] Michael Schwartz and Sandra S. Tangri, "A Note on Self-concept as an Insulator Against Delinquency," *American Sociological Review* 30 (December 1965): 922–926; Sandra S. Tangri and Michael Schwartz, "Delinquency Research and the Self-concept Variable." *Journal of Criminal Law, Criminology and Police Science* 58 (June 1967): 182–190; James D. Orcutt, "Self-concept and Insulation Against Delinquency: Some Critical Notes," *Sociological Quarterly* 2 (summer 1970): 381–390.

[55] See Chapter 12 for a discussion of some of these studies.

[56] David Matza, *Delinquency and Drift* (New York: Wiley, 1966).

[57] Robert Emerson, *Judging Delinquents* (Chicago: Aldine, 1969).

[58] Don Gibbons, *Delinquent Behavior,* 2d ed. (Englewood Cliffs, N.J.: Prentice-Hall, 1976), p. 257.

[59] See Gibbons, *op. cit.,* for a review of some of these studies.

[60] Tannenbaum, *op. cit.*

[61] Lemert, *Social Pathology, op. cit.*

[62] Howard S. Becker, "The Professional Dance Musician and His Audience," *American Journal of Sociology* 57 (1951): 136–144; Becker, *Outsiders, op. cit.*

[63] Richard Quinney, *The Social Reality of Crime* (Boston: Little, Brown, 1970).

[64] Clayton A. Hartjen, *Crime and Criminalization* (New York: Praeger, 1974).

[65] John I. Kitouse, "Societal Reaction to Deviant Behavior: Problems of Theory and Method," *Social Problems* 9 (1962): 247–256; John I. Kitouse, "Deviance, Deviant Behavior and Deviants," in *An Introduction to Deviance,* ed. W. J. Filstead (Chicago: Markham, 1972), pp. 233–243.

[66] See Chapter 14 for a discussion of some of these programs.

[67] Don Gibbons, *Society, Crime and Criminal Careers,* 2d ed. (Englewood Cliffs, N.J.: Prentice-Hall, 1973), pp. 526–528.

[68] Thorsten Sellin, "The Lombrosian Myth in Criminology," *American*

Journal of Sociology 42 (May 1937): 898–899; Thorsten Sellin, "Culture, Conflict and Crime," *Social Science Research Council Bulletin* 41 (1938); Thorsten Sellin, "Common Sense and the Death Penalty," *Prison Journal* 12 (October 1932): 12.

[69] Sellin, "Culture, Conflict and Crime," *op. cit.*

[70] Donald Taft and Ralph England, Jr., *Criminology*, 4th ed. (New York: Macmillan, 1964).

[71] Donald Taft, *Criminology*, 3d ed. (New York: Macmillan, 1956).

[72] Harry Elmer Barnes and Negley K. Teeters, *New Horizons in Criminology* (Englewood Cliffs, N.J.: Prentice-Hall, 1959), pp. 159–160, 169.

[73] Emile Durkheim, *The Division of Labor in Society* (New York: Free Press, 1933).

[74] Emile Durkheim, *Suicide*, trans. John A. Spaulding and George Simpson (New York: Free Press, 1951).

[75] Robert K. Merton, *Social Theory and Social Structure* (New York: Free Press, 1968).

[76] *Ibid.*

[77] Schafer, *op. cit.*, p. 221.

[78] *Ibid.*, p. 222.

[79] William Healy and Augusta Bronner, *The Individual Delinquent* (Boston: Little, Brown, 1915).

[80] William Healy and Augusta Bronner, *Treatment and What Happened Afterward* (Boston: Judge Baker Guidance Center, 1939), p. 22.

[81] Healy and Bronner, *The Individual Delinquent, op. cit.*

[82] William Healy and Augusta Bronner, *Delinquents and Criminals* (New York: Macmillan, 1926).

[83] Cyril Burt, *The Young Delinquent* (London: University of London Press, 1938).

[84] *Ibid.*

[85] *Ibid.*

[86] Walter Reckless, *The Crime Problem* (Englewood Cliffs, N.J.: Prentice-Hall, 1961).

[87] *Ibid.*

[88] The studies are summarized in Reckless, *op. cit.*, pp. 346–353, and in Ruth Shonle Cavan and Theodore N. Ferdinand, *Juvenile Delinquency*, 3d ed. (Philadelphia: Lippincott, 1975), pp. 135–138.

[89] Schwartz and Tangri, *op. cit.*; Tangri and Schwartz, *op. cit.*; Orcutt, *op. cit.*

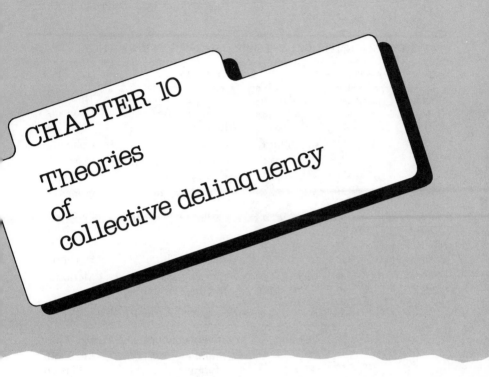

Most theories of delinquency have attempted to explain how *individuals* become delinquent. However, research suggests that delinquency is largely a group phenomenon. From 60 to 90 percent of all juvenile offenses have been attributed to groups.[1] Often the theories advanced to account for the delinquent behavior of individuals carry assumptions that do not apply to collective or gang delinquency. Furthermore, theories that seek an explanation for delinquent behavior in individuals may be too limited to account for group delinquency.

Several sociological theories explaining gang delinquency have been developed in recent years. For the most part these theories relegate biological and psychological factors to the background. Instead, social factors are considered the primary causal agents of delinquency. The social nature of the gang and its relationship with the surrounding social environment provides the focus for a number of gang theories. Some theorists look to the ecological environment to find an explanation for the development and maintenance of gangs. The early gang theorists noted that gang delinquency appeared to be most prevalent in deteriorated, unstable areas where social disorganization was apparent. Other theorists examined the value systems of the gang and the broader society. They suggested that gang delinquency was a consequence of the misinterpretation of the cultural values or was a reaction to them. Another approach sought answers to the problem of delinquency in the social structure. According to this view, the juvenile may become delinquent because it is one of only a few alternatives

TABLE 10.1 SOCIOLOGICAL THEORIES OF GANG DELINQUENCY

SCHOOL	APPROACH	FOCUS	CONCEPTS	LEADERS
Socio-logical	gang be-havior	social disor-ganization	the gang zones of transition slum	Thrasher Shaw and McKay
		subcultures	nonutilitarian neutralization, drift commitment generating milieu striving to manhood	Cohen Matza Hirschi Miller Bloch and Nieder-hoffer
			teen-age culture	England
		social structure	cultural goals structural means differential opportunity	Merton Cloward and Ohlin
		learning	reference groups commitment to con-formity	Haskell Briar and Piliavin

open to the youth. An overview of a sample of these theories is presented in Table 10.1.

Whatever the theoretical approach used to explain gang delinquency, one thing is evident: The gang evolves a distinct set of norms and values, and what appears to be deviant behavior from the point of view of society might be perceived as highly conformist to the internal membership of the gang.

SOCIAL DISORGANIZATION

Much of the early sociological analysis of delinquent gangs was associated with the "Chicago school" of urban sociology. In studying the relationships between residential areas and the groups that inhabit them, social ecologists discovered that gang delinquency was concentrated in slum areas—"zones of transition"—of Chicago and other cities. Burgess identified five areas that characterized the city:

Zone I—central business district
Zone II—transition area
Zone III—workers' residential area
Zone IV—residential zone
Zone V—commuters' zone[2]

Each of these areas was occupied by natural groups that were drawn to the area. Poor, new arrivals were concentrated in low-rent, deterio-

rated areas near the center of the city in Zone I or II. Burgess noted
that these areas were characterized by a high degree of social disorganization. In these areas, overcrowded and substandard housing,
poverty, low education levels, unstable residential populations, and
crime were facts of life.

Probably the most comprehensive early work on gang delinquency and delinquent subcultures was Frederic M. Thrasher's The Gang
(1927).[3] Noting that gangs frequently develop in transitional areas of
the city, characterized by conflict, disorganization, and weak family
and neighborhood controls, Thrasher developed a multifaceted approach to gang delinquency. In a thorough and systematic study of
1313 gangs, Thrasher was able to demonstrate the effects of both
psychological and social factors on the development and maintenance
of gang structures.[4]

Thrasher suggested that gangs develop as children seek to satisfy
a set of basic, universal needs. All children strive for security, positive
response, recognition, and new experiences. Gang members, in this
sense, are no different from other children. Only the way in which
these needs are satisfied sets them apart. Where family and neighborhood controls are weak, children form spontaneous play groups to
satisfy their needs. Because of the relatively uncontrolled nature of
these groups and the presence of many opportunities for fun, groups
engage in a wide variety of activities, both legal and illegal. Activities
are selected and performed by the play group without conventional
adult supervision. Thrasher emphasized the fun and adventurous quality
of many illegal acts, particularly in the early stages of the ganging

process. However, it is apparent that illegal acts may also have more rational and utilitarian bases. For example, much theft is instrumental in maintaining the independence of the group from adult authority. If a group of children are to live away from home for extended periods of time, there must be a means of obtaining essentials such as food. Thrasher gave a number of examples in which petty theft of food or marketable goods were used to satisfy such requirements.[5]

Play groups inevitably come into conflict with each other over the nature of the activities to be performed. Rival groups may attempt to coopt the play group; adult authorities try to control or convert the group to more conventional behavior. If these efforts by outsiders fail, the group survives and becomes part of a network of similar groups. It is thereby transformed into a gang. Continued external opposition serves to strengthen group values and elaborate the previously informal structure. By middle adolescence, the group has become a gang with a distinctive name, ethnic or racial identity, and technology for support and survival. One such group is described in Case 10.1.

Even though most of the gang's activities are not illegal, and much time is spent in athletic activities and other conforming behavior, the gang structure facilitates delinquent activity. As Thrasher put it:

> It would be more accurate to say that the gang is an important contributing factor facilitating the commission of crime and greatly extending its spread and range. The organization of the gang and the protection which it affords, especially in combination with a ring or syndicate, makes it a superior instrument for the execution of criminal enterprises. Its demoralizing influence on its members arises through the dissemination of criminal technique, and the propagation, through mutual excitation, of interests and attitudes which make crime easier (less inhibited) and more attractive.[6]

Even where the disruption potential of the gang is recognized, the social environment in disorganized areas is permissive, attractive, facilitative, and supportive of the ganging tendency. The social environment is permissive in that conventional controls are weak or non-existent. In a highly disorganized area, family controls are often minimal, and children are expected to display a high degree of independence at an early age. Other agencies of social control, such as the school and police, have less influence as a result of the lack of support from parents. In such a milieu, the gang tends to flourish.

The apparent success of adult criminals in the neighborhood offers a vivid contrast to the drab existence of parents or other conventional characters in the slum. The fact that the adult criminal has a lot of money, free time, and prestige does not go unnoticed or unappreciated by the adolescent. The very presence of the criminal is an indication that opportunities are available. Delinquency and crime are

GANGS IN A DISORGANIZED AREA

The Lawndale area of Chicago had long been the breeding ground for delinquent and gang behavior. Polish and Jewish groups in the area had organized gangs before the area became predominantly black. The Clovers were one of the first fighting gangs in the area. As its charter members began to drift away (at about age 20), the Vice Lords entered from St. Charles. At the same time, the Clovers were already being pressured by a newer group called the Cobras who had started in "Jew Town." A branch of this gang moved to the West Side near "K-Town" (where all the street names began with a K) and were known as the K-Town Cobras. The Cobras established supremacy over the Clovers following a humbug.

The members of the Vice Lords began moving into the area vacated by the Clovers. The club's original activity centered around parties and just hanging around together. The group grew slowly, and gradually came into conflict with the Cobras and the Imperial Chaplains. An alliance with the El Commandoes provided a boost in membership. Both the Vice Lords and the El Commandoes were social, and not fighting, clubs. The El Commandoes were eventually absorbed by the Vice Lords as the latter grew in membership.

Accounts vary, but it appears that Cave Man was one of the original Vice Lords from St. Charles. Some claim that he was the founder of the club. Cave Man's mother is reported to have allowed the use of her basement for club parties and meetings, but the group had to locate other facilities after several fights forced them from Cave Man's home.

After winning fights with both the Cobras and the Imperial Chaplains, membership increased. At this point, the club had about 25 members but was still primarily a social club without a formal leadership structure. After a break-in and fire (arson) at Cave Man's house and threats from the Cobras, the gang began to change. A recruitment drive was initiated. Special attention was directed to boys who did not belong to either the Cobras or the Imperials. Smaller groups,such as the Spanish Counts, were absorbed. The fact that the Spanish Counts were known as good fighters enhanced the "rep" of the Vice Lords.

By 1962 the Imperials had begun to break up, but the Cobras intensified their conflict with the Vice Lords. As the Vice Lords grew, the organization was formalized and subdivided into Seniors,

Juniors, Midgets, and even Pee-Wees. Branch
organizations and female auxiliaries were
developed. Gang fights continued intermittently.

Source: R. Lincoln Keiser, The Vice Lords: Warriors of the
Streets (New York: Holt, Rinehart and Winston, 1969), pp. 1-12.

attractive because they are fun and profitable. Being a "good kid"
does not offer adequate compensation for many youngsters.

✓   Tolerance of adult criminal activity in a neighborhood provides
implicit moral support for illegal activity. Furthermore, explicit and
concrete approval is evidenced by the willingness of conventional,
"honest" adults to buy stolen goods at discounted prices. Local politics
also contributes to gang delinquency. The use of political pull and
"under the table" deals provides a means of filtering benefits from
the elite to the poor, but it also creates an atmosphere in which influence is considered more important than conforming behavior. The
political machine may create structures that provide an organizational
framework for the development of organized gangs. The neighborhood
environment, in short, provides supportive values, attitudes, and "successful" role models which are readily identifiable by potential delinquents.

Clifford Shaw and Henry McKay conducted extensive studies in
Chicago and 21 other cities during the 1930s and 1940s and found
support for the relationship between social disorganization and juvenile delinquency.[7] Shaw and McKay described the relationship between
residential area and delinquency as follows:

> In the process of city growth, the neighborhood organizations, cultural
> institutions and social standards in practically all of the areas adjacent
> to the central business district and the major industrial areas are subject
> to rapid change and disorganization. The gradual invasion of these
> areas by industry and commerce, the continuous movement of the older
> residents out of the area and the influx of newer groups, the confusion
> of many divergent cultural standards, the economic insecurity of the
> families, all combine to render difficult the development of a stable and
> efficient neighborhood organization for the education and control of
> the child and the suppression of lawlessness.[8]

McKay's continued research on delinquency within the tradition of the
Chicago school produced additional support for social disorganization
theory. McKay reported that the trends in officially recorded delinquency from 1927 to 1962 revealed that the rapidly rising delinquency
rates were found in neighborhoods that had experienced an influx of
black settlers, while the most rapidly falling rates were found in stable
black areas.[9] He concluded that the invasion of neighborhoods by
socially and economically disadvantaged groups weakens traditional

institutions of social control. However, when the neighborhood stabilizes, the traditional institutions become stronger and more effective.

For nearly three decades after the publication of Thrasher's pioneering work on gangs, the social disorganization approach dominated the study of gangs. The postwar increase in delinquency, however, stimulated new interest in gang behavior. By the mid 1950s, new research on gangs began to bear fruit and produce new approaches to the problem.[10]

SUBCULTURAL THEORIES

A number of the theories developed to explain or describe collective delinquency rely on the presence of alternative value systems in a heterogeneous society. There is not unanimous agreement on how the competing value systems develop; however, there is consensus that a delinquent gang's members will share a common value system.

Problem Solving

Albert Cohen recognized that an understanding of people, and not places or biology, was basic to the analysis of gang delinquency.[11] In studying why people act as they do, Cohen concluded that behavior is problem solving. In other words, whenever people act, they do so in response to problems that confront them. In seeking a solution to problems, an individual's alternatives are conditioned by the nature of the problem. Some problems are trivial and are automatically solved with little thought; others are more difficult and unusual. How a person defines a situation as a problem is dependent upon a number of influences, from early childhood on.[12]

Noting that an inordinate proportion of official delinquency is concentrated in the lower classes, Cohen suggested that class background is an important determinant of delinquent behavior. According to Cohen, early socialization in the working class does not adequately prepare the youth to compete in a world dominated by middle-class individuals. A knowledge of the skills and conduct necessary for successful status achievement in a middle-class setting is lacking in the working-class environment. Thus when the child reaches school, he is destined to fail. The disapproval, rejection, and punishment he encounters in his efforts to achieve status produce frustration. His reaction is an acting out of status frustration by reversing middle-class norms in "non-utilitarian, malicious and negativistic" behavior.

Contact with other youths with similar experiences suggests a common bond centering on the rejection of middle-class values. An informal counterculture develops through interaction among the "failures," and it provides an alternative set of criteria for assessing success. In Cohen's words "The delinquent subculture takes its norms from the larger subculture, but turns them upside down. The delinquent's conduct is right by the standards of his subculture precisely because it is wrong by the norms of the larger culture."[13] In the gang, the norms of the larger society are reversed so that nonutilitarian, deviant, or delinquent behavior is the preferred mode.

Cohen's theory provoked a great deal of critical response. Wilensky and Lebeaux, for example, questioned its application to middle-class youths. They claimed that middle-class boys were more likely to be affected by status anxiety than by the masculine identity problems described by Cohen.[14] Kitsuse and Dietrick claimed that Cohen had not presented a convincing argument that lower-class youths are concerned with middle-class views about them. They suggested that the motives for participation in delinquent gangs are varied. Once the delinquent gang is established, however, it persists because it creates the very problems that it was organized to counteract.[15]

David Bordua raised questions about subcultural theories in general and Cohen's theory in particular. Bordua claimed that the general image of the delinquent presented by Cohen was different from the one originally presented by Thrasher. Thrasher described individuals seeking fun, thrills, and kicks. But Cohen pictures the gang member as a youth driven by stress and anxiety; the delinquent behavior of the gang is nonutilitarian. Bordua, on the other hand, believed that the behavior of juveniles in gangs was often of a utilitarian character. In addition, the subcultural approach did not assign sufficient importance to other variables in explaining gang behavior. Family patterns were believed to be relevant, especially the absence of a father or loose ties with the family members. These variables were important for the delinquency of lower-class males.[16]

Cohen responded to some of the criticisms directed against his theory in an article written with James F. Short, Jr. They suggested that there are several different subcultural patterns for lower-class delinquency—the conflict, drug addict, and parent-male subcultures. The parent-male pattern was the one discussed in Cohen's *Delinquent Boys*. The other patterns represented variations on that basic theme.[17] Cohen and Short relied heavily on an earlier article by Kobrin in replying to the critics.[18] Gangs were reported to arise in areas where adult crime was integrated into the social organization. In these areas, criminals mix openly with respectable entrepreneurs, community leaders, and others. In fact, adult criminals were viewed as potential heroes to many youngsters. The adult criminal may become a role model who is worthy of imitation. On the other hand, Cohen and Short admitted that there were some lower-class areas where criminals were not tolerated, in which case delinquency may result from a youth's alienation from the social organization of the area.

Cohen's theory has received a great deal of reaction from a variety of delinquency analysts. Several theorists have used critiques of Cohen's theory as a foundation for developing theories of their own. Because his theory was influential in spurring the development of a wide range of theories, he has made an important contribution to the area of juvenile delinquency.

NEUTRALIZATION

Cohen's initial portrayal of gang delinquency was broad and imprecise; thus a number of criticisms, revisions, and alternative explanations followed the publication of his work. Gresham Sykes and David Matza presented criticisms and advanced an argument in favor of the techniques of *neutralization*. According to their approach, juveniles do not subscribe to norms that directly oppose those of the larger society. Instead, they are wise to the norms of the conforming sphere and use these norms and values to justify law-violating behavior. Sykes and Matza list five techniques developed by delinquents to neutralize their responsibility:

1. *Denial of personal responsibility.* Juveniles use popular conceptions of the determinist causes of delinquency to shift responsibility to others. They may claim that they could not resist delinquent activity because they come from broken homes or impoverished environments or because of some other delinquency-producing problem. Case 10.2 illustrates this technique.

2. *Denial of harm.* Juveniles may claim that no one was harmed. Property returned or restitution is believed to set everything right and erase the troublesome behavior.

3. *Denial of victims.* In this case, the victims of the juveniles' behavior are blamed for their part in the act. A victim of assault was "asking for it"; a store was robbed because the owner overcharged customers.

4. *Condemnation of condemners.* Youths may accept the idea that their behavior was wrong but insist it is much less corrupt than the behavior of others. Examples of worse behavior may be so exaggerated that delinquents look innocent and good in comparison.

5. *Appeal to group loyalties.* Youths may claim that they have only committed law-violating behavior in the interests of others. Loyalty to the gang may take precedence over all other considerations.[19]

The use of these techniques does not, according to Sykes and Matza, suggest that the delinquent's value system lies in opposition to that of the broader society. Instead it may indicate that "the delinquent has picked up and emphasized one part of the dominant value system, namely, the subterranean values that coexist with other, publicly proclaimed values possessing a more respectable air."[20]

Matza, further pursuing the effects of subterranean values, theorized that juveniles "drift" between criminal and conventional action.[21] Because the norms are not clear and unambiguous, juveniles may alternately adopt criminal and conventional responses depending on the perceived requirements of a particular situation. Commitment to one culture or the other—criminal or conventional—is not set until late adolescence.

IT'S NOT MY FAULT

In recent years, sophisticated delinquents have begun to shift the responsibility for their behavior to other individuals. Awareness of popular explanations of juvenile delinquency has produced a new breed of "innocent youth." One example is provided by Virginia Held:

> A 15 year old boy came here the other day with a handful of clippings that said that delinquency is the fault of the parents, and that parents should talk with and try to understand their children. He said his parents didn't understand him, so it wasn't his fault that he held up a store. Another youngster claimed that his mother was neurotic: she forced him to clean his room. Thus, she was responsible for his delinquent behavior.

It is not unusual for authorities in the juvenile justice system to support the reasoning of the juvenile sophisticates. Hartung cites the case of a juvenile court hearing in Iowa. In this instance, a 12-year-old boy was accused of stealing purses, taking the money, and then disposing of them. In the court hearing, the judge praised the young man's physical appearance and his smile. The judge told him that he was a "good boy." With the boy still in the room, the judge began to berate the boy's parents. They were blamed for his bad behavior. The parents' divorce was called "thoroughly selfish." The judge accused the parents of thinking "only of their own bodies." The judge stated that the parents should have been horsewhipped and claimed that if the law had allowed, he would set up a whipping post and do it himself.

The judge declared the boy a ward of the court not because he was delinquent but because he came from an unfit home. In fact, the judge repeated the term "unfit home" several times in an emotional tone while the young boy was still in the courtroom. The parents were told that they were responsible for the boy's theft and that they should be ashamed of themselves. The parents were threatened with jail sentences if they attempted to interfere with the court or the foster parents. The boy was told that he had a friend in the

court and that he was a good boy. At the end of
the hearing the boy was still smiling.

Source: U.S. Congress, House Committee on the Judiciary, The
Formless Years: What Can We Do About J.D.: Hearings Before the
Subcommittee to Investigate Juvenile Delinquency, by Virginia
P. Held, 86th Cong., 1st sess., 1959, p. 474; and Frank E.
Hartung, "A Vocabulary of Motives for Law Violations," in
Delinquency, Crime and Social Process, ed. Donald R. Cressey
and David A. Ward (New York: Harper & Row, 1969), pp. 458–459.

SOCIAL CONTROL

Travis Hirschi offers a subcultural approach similar to that of
Matza. However, Hirschi believes that the juvenile's detachment from
conventional behavior is relatively permanent. The family, conforming
peers, and other successful conformist models provide ties that bind
juveniles to the conventional world. As long as juveniles maintain
attachments to conforming individuals and groups, their commitment
to, and belief in, the rightness of conformity will prevent involvement
in delinquent activities. When these ties are weakened or broken, delinquency will result. According to Hirschi, delinquent activity may be an
exciting and rewarding experience, and many youths would resort to
it if they were not restrained by social bonds that tie them to conforming behavior.[22]

Hirschi conducted a research study to test his theory. In a sample
of youngsters from a California community, he found that the involvement in delinquency was about the same regardless of social class.
The findings from the research were basically consistent with his theory.
Delinquents were found to be not as attached to parents, schools,
peers, and teachers as nondelinquents. In addition, the delinquents
were less involved in conventional activities, had less-positive attitudes,
and were less conforming than nonoffenders.[23] Hindelang, in another
study, was able to partially duplicate the findings of Hirschi.[24]

Natural Growth

A number of subcultural theorists have taken the point of view
that delinquent subcultures develop out of existing subcultures. The
gang is used as a mechanism for gaining entry and acceptance into
the larger, focal culture. The values and norms of the reference culture
may be exaggerated or otherwise distorted, but they nevertheless provide a foundation for the development of a specialized juvenile subculture.

THE GENERATING MILIEU

One prominent view of gang delinquency as a natural subcultural
phenomenon was elaborated by Walter B. Miller.[25] Miller suggests that

delinquency is not a reaction to the middle class culture but rather grows directly out of the lower-class male experience. In the lower class, many families take on a female-based form. Most of the key figures are female; there is little expectation of stable economic or emotional support by an adult male. As a result of this family structure, young males in the female-oriented household must seek out role models outside the home. Leaders of the adolescent street gang provide such models. Furthermore, participation in the adolescent male subculture gives the young male an opportunity to prove that he is a "real man." Proof, however, requires bigger-than-life evidence. Therefore the lower-class male emulates an exaggerated picture of the concerns and behavior of the unstable lower-class adult male culture.[26] Case 10.3 suggests a concern for toughness.

The lower-class way of life is characterized by a set of "focal concerns," or values, according to Miller. These include trouble, toughness, smartness, excitement, fate, and autonomy. Trouble is the dominant concern in the lower-class culture. It is what life gets you into; it is "a situation which results in unwelcome or complicating involvement with official authorities or agencies of middle class society."[27] There are only two types of behavior to pursue—law abiding or law violating. The individual's position in regard to trouble is crucial to his evaluation by others.

Toughness refers to physical prowess, skill, fearlessness, bravery, and daring. It is the measure by which masculinity is assessed. Everything soft and feminine is rejected to prevent feminine identification. Toughness is one of the ways boys get into trouble. Smartness is the ability to con or manipulate people or things with a minimum amount of labor. It does not include education; study is considered feminine and therefore undesirable. A good efficient "line" is considered a valuable asset for lower-class youths. Excitement refers to kicks, fun, and diversity of experience. As an activity, delinquency involves precarious excitement whose outcome is unexpected or out of the ordinary. The weekend drinking spree, sexual escapades, and group fighting exemplify this concern. Excitement is also a goal; it makes life interesting by putting aside responsibility for the mundane tasks of daily living.

The lower-class experience does not offer a sufficient example of success through hard work and tenacity to provide an incentive for acceptance of this type of goal. Those people who have worked hard and steadily within the community are perceived as failures. Material success is something one happens onto. Fate, events, and forces over which there is no control are important to lower-class youths and adults. Although there is the expectation that things will just happen, autonomy is highly valued. The amount, source, and severity of control by others puts the lower-class youth in an ambivalent position.

GROWING UP TOUGH

Some areas seem to be breeding grounds for juvenile gangs. A new crop of toughs is constantly emerging, so that the neighborhood is never free of gang activity. An older Vice Lord gang member describes the younger generation:

The roughest boys I ever met, they was between the ages of 13 and 15—Lil' Lord, Rough-head and them. They was the Midgets—the Midget Lords. And these were the baddest boys I ever went up against! What happened, they beat up one of the Senior Lords, a stud called Dough Belly. And Cave Man wouldn't even mess with the Midget Lords cause they had so many guns. We didn't know where they got the guns from, but they used to bring them around and give them to us.

Source: R. Lincoln Keiser, The Vice Lords: Warriors of the Streets (New York: Holt, Rinehart and Winston, 1969), p. 16.

Autonomy can mean independence—a trait particularly important for establishing masculinity—but at the same time it can also mean that nobody cares.

Miller maintains that the values, or concerns, of the lower class produce delinquency because they are naturally in discord with the larger society. The adolescent who readily conforms to lower-class values is automatically delinquent.[28]

STATUS STRIVING

Bloch and Niederhoffer focused their attention on the adolescent subculture. Citing evidence from other societies, they suggested that the adolescent period is "a phase of striving for the attainment of adult status" which is common to all cultures.[29] The extent to which the child in this stage is socially disruptive depends to a large extent on whether the society has provided satisfactory rites of passage to ease the transition to adulthood. Where these rites are not available the youths design seemingly appropriate ceremonies within the peer culture. Certain activities, such as fraternity initiations, club participation, and so on, serve as rites of passage to relieve the anxiety-producing absence of adult-sponsored rites.

Many of the subcultural theorists assume that gang delinquency is almost exclusively a lower-class phenomenon. Bloch and Niederhoffer, however, reject this assumption and cite evidence indicating that gang delinquency is also found in the middle class in the form of cliques. The gang, or some variant of it, is viewed as a vehicle for accomplishing the desired adult status in all social classes.[30]

THE TEEN-AGE CULTURE

Ralph England also focused on the subculture of youth. Noting that much of the recent increase in juvenile delinquency was contributed by "normal," middle-class youngsters, England pursued a theory to explain this phenomenon. His explanation suggests the development of a hedonistic teen-age culture in the United States.

According to England, a combination of events have combined to produce a teen-age culture that is at odds with broad societal norms. First, industrialization and the accompanying urbanization of American society has had a profound impact. For the first time, large numbers of youths were brought together in a small geographic area. Many of them worked side-by-side in factories, and networks of communication were established. The family unit no longer determined the youngsters' possible range of relationships. Second, the passage of protective labor measures and compulsory education legislation effectively removed youths from productive roles without a clear redefinition of their status and function.

The resulting ambiguity of status produced conflicting expectations for those too young to be adults and too old to be children. Teen-agers are expected to be both independent and dependent; they are not expected to engage in productive labor but neither are they encouraged to loaf. Teenagers are expected to be responsible and civic-minded, but they are not given serious responsibility. They cannot vote, serve on a jury, or hold public office.[31] England concluded that delinquency arises out of the attempts of juveniles to adapt to these conflicting expectations and find an appropriate function in society. He summarized his theory in these words:

> Delinquent motivations among middle class teenagers arise from this adaptive process in which the teenage world, peopled by immature and inexperienced persons, extracts from the adult world those values having strong hedonistic possibilities, with the result that the values of the teenage culture consist mainly of distorted and caricatured fragments from the adult culture. These highly selected and altered values then serve to motivate and give direction to members of the youth world, sometimes in ways adults define as delinquent.[32]

England believed that lower-class delinquency had its roots elsewhere. Lower-class youngsters enter the labor market and marriage, both of which enable them to acquire recognized adult roles and responsibilities, sooner than middle-class youths. For these youngsters, discrimination and utilitarian motives may prove more forceful in producing delinquency.[33]

The Implications of Subcultural Theories

Subcultural approaches basically provide a description of juvenile collectives. Although some attempts have been made to provide an evolutionary framework to indicate how the groups formed, little attention has been given to their link with delinquent behavior. There is little recognition of the fact that many youth groups do not engage in delinquent activities. An explanation of juvenile delinquency must go beyond the suggestion that youths are different from adults. Not all youths are delinquent, and many adults are not honest. It is important to discover under what circumstances an individual or group of either lower- or middle-class culture deviates from the institutionalized norms.[34]

STRUCTURAL THEORIES

A number of theories have taken a structural approach to an understanding of gang delinquency. Their basic underlying theme is that the growth and development of societies contributes to the presence of delinquent patterns of behavior and makes other patterns less likely to occur. The structure of a society itself is used to account for the general lawlessness of its members or to explain why some segments are more lawless than others. Few theories are devoid of influence from other approaches, and the structural theories are no exception. It will become apparent that these theories often overlap with cultural or learning approaches to individual juvenile delinquency.

Structural Discrepancies

Robert K. Merton's theory of criminal and delinquent behavior was developed primarily to explain individual deviance.[35] However, the implications of his theory for the development of approaches to the gang make it a proper topic for discussion here. Merton believed that the nature of the social structure exerted pressures on certain segments of society to commit crimes and engage in delinquency. An analysis of the American system, according to Merton, suggests that the dominant cultural values emphasize success as a goal for all, no matter what their social background. Rich or poor, healthy or unhealthy, bright or dull—each and every individual is expected to find his niche. Winning the game is all-important. The socially approved methods of attaining the goal, however, are somewhat limited. Hard work, education, and thrift are the major approved avenues. Unfortunately, access to the legitimate means for success is not equally available to all. When individuals have limited opportunities, they may deviate to attain the success goal through illegitimate means.[36]

Many individuals are caught in the bind between cultural goals and structural means that are not compatible. Not all of these persons become criminals. Merton described five different adaptive techniques that may provide alternatives for individuals troubled by structural discrepancies:

> 1. *Conformity.* Individuals continue to strive for success by legitimate means. They work hard, struggle for an education, and save for the future. They may even appear to be "getting ahead" and find satisfaction with the cultural mode. This is probably the most common mode of adaptation in every society.
> 2. *Innovation.* Individuals accept the success goal but reject the means prescribed by their society. Conventional patterns of work are eschewed for more novel modes. New behavior patterns are invented to provide the maximum return for the minimum of effort. Some innovators may choose illegal means and become criminals. When legitimate means are blocked, this mode may be particularly attractive. Case 10.4 illustrates this adaptive mode.
> 3. *Ritualism.* Some individuals perceive the futility of getting ahead and emphasize the merits of conformity to approved societal means. These individuals redefine their goals in directions that may be achieved through adherence to social norms. Thus, the "poor but honest" person can be proud and feel his or her rank is higher than that of those who are less conforming.
> 4. *Retreatism.* Retreatists reject both the success goal and the work ethic means. They withdraw from the mainstream of society by joining a subcultural group or becoming drug addicts, alcoholics, or cultists.
> 5. *Rebellion.* As in retreatism, individuals reject both means and goals. However, rather than quietly withdrawing from a discrepant society, they seek to change the social structure. A new order—a contraculture or subculture—is established with like-minded individuals.[37]

Several of these adaptations have implications for gang delinquency. In those adaptations where the means or goals are rejected, new subcultures may arise in opposition to, or at variance with, the institutionalized norms of society.

There have been a number of criticisms directed at Merton's theoretical framework. For example, Clinard expressed doubt about the theory's ability to explain all delinquent acts.[38] Questions were raised by Johnson about whether the framework was capable of explaining delinquency in a culture that was markedly different from that of the United States, which was used as the analytical base for developing the theory.[39] Nye, on the other hand, claimed that Merton's theory did not account for middle- and upper-class juvenile delinquency.[40] Cohen criticized the theory because he did not believe it accounted for the violence found in delinquent subcultures.[41]

The importance of Merton's theory, however, rests in the influence it had on subsequent theorists and not on its ability to withstand criticism. Cloward and Ohlin, for example, appear to have combined Taft, Durkheim, and Merton in their discussions of opportunity structures and gang delinquency.

CASE 10.4

FIFTY DOLLARS A DAY

Delinquent activity is not always done for the hell of it. In some areas it may provide the only sure means of economic success. It is hard to "reform" the successful delinquent without offering him alternative, legal success routes. The following exchange occurred between a social worker and a gang member:

Q: Why don't you get a job?
A: Oh come on. Get off that crap. I make $40 to $50 a day selling marijuana. You want me to go down to the garment district and push one of those trucks through the streets and at the end of the week take home $40 or $50, if I'm lucky: Come off it. They don't have animals doing what you want me to do. There would be some society to protect animals if anybody had them pushing those damn trucks around. I'm better than an animal, but nobody protects me. Go away mister. I got to look out for myself.

Source: President's Commission on Law Enforcement and Administration of Justice, The Challenge of Crime in a Free Society. Quoted in Daniel Katkin, Drew Hyman, and John Kramer, Juvenile Delinquency and the Juvenile Justice System (North Scituate, Mass.: Duxbury Press, 1976), p. 56.

Opportunity Structures

Cloward and Ohlin's theory of differential opportunity structures appears to be an attempt to apply Merton's theory directly to delinquent behavior patterns. Their basic postulate is: "pressures toward the formation of delinquent subcultures originate in marked discrepancies between culturally induced aspirations among lower class youth and the possibilities of achieving them by legitimate means."[42]

The widely shared view that success is available for anyone willing to reach for it puts lower-class youths in an undesirable position. Their lack of opportunity for education and of an advantageous social position put them at a competitive disadvantage in the legitimate channels for success. Failure, or the anticipation of failure, to succeed leads them to seek some explanation for their inability to move up. Some will blame themselves for the failure and seek personal adjustment. Others, however, blame the system that stresses success while restricting access in arbitrary and unjust ways. Adjustment to perceived injustices may result in the rejection of the legitimacy of formal, institutionalized norms or laws, and the lower-class youth may turn toward available alternative means for success. The juvenile does not automatically turn to crime, however. The opportunity to utilize illegitimate means is limited in much the same way that legitimate channels are. The successful criminal, as well as the successful physician, must be provided opportunities for learning the profession. Entrance or tutelage in crime is as limited as entrance into medical school.

According to Cloward and Ohlin, criminal opportunity structures are not always available. They are most likely to appear in neighborhoods "characterized by close bonds between different age-levels of offenders and between criminal and conventional elements."[43] Such an institutionalized criminal structure provides a "college" for the learning of criminal techniques. Given the small number of available vacancies in the criminal ranks, competition develops between the potential "students." The competitors tend to overconform to deviant standards to show their fitness for a position in the mature criminal structure. A small number of youths are accepted by the criminal structure and are processed and tutored eventually to take their place in the structure. Not only are new techniques learned, but the old, undisciplined, aggressive behavior is discouraged.

Disorganized and unstable neighborhoods provide neither legitimate nor illegitimate channels for success nor their attendant social controls. Under these conditions, adolescents seize upon violence as a route to social status. The conflict subculture arises not only because it provides a means of expressing anger and frustration but also because the qualities needed for success are available to all. "Guts" and the ability to endure pain can be cultivated by any who wish to do so. The conflict subculture is somewhat unstable; Cloward and Ohlin indicate that as new opportunity structures become available, the conflict subculture loses members. Conflict subcultures frequently exist alongside the adult criminal structures. Youngsters who fail to find a place in the criminal structure may continue the aberrant patterns of behavior used to capture the attention of criminal elements. After a time, violent behavior may become an end in itself.

Cloward and Ohlin distinguish a third type of subculture. The retreatist subculture "emerges among some lower class adolescents because they have failed to find a place for themselves in criminal or conflict subcultures."[44] There is considerable competition for membership in conflict gangs. Status in the conflict structure is as scarce as positions in the criminal hierarchy, and not all competitors find a niche. Some of these "double failures" revise their aspirations downward and adopt a law-abiding lower-class life style. Others retreat into the hazy world of drugs, where failure can be forgotten.

RESEARCH AND CRITICISM
Spergel's research was initiated in reaction to Cloward and Ohlin's claim that different patterns of delinquency are found in neighborhoods with differential opportunity structures. Spergel identified three

subcultural neighborhoods in New York City and studied organized groups to determine whether different types of subcultures produced different illegitimate opportunity structures for its youths. He reported that Slumtown, characterized by a low socioeconomic status and a high index of social disorganization, supported a conflict opportunity structure. Haulberg, which had the highest socioeconomic status rating and lowest disorganization index of the three neighborhoods, had an identifiable theft opportunity structure. The third neighborhood, Racketville, supported a racketeering structure.[45] This study, as well as his earlier Chicago study,[46] was taken as support for Cloward and Ohlin's theory.

Palmore and Hammond studied children in the Aid to Dependent Children welfare program. The youngsters were followed from age 6 to age 19. By age 19, about 34 percent of the children had experienced contact with the police or the juvenile court. Palmore and Hammond stressed that these youngsters were cut off from legitimate opportunities for success and at the same time lived in neighborhoods where illegal behavior was frequent. Delinquency was found to be more common in sections of the city where school failure was frequent and where family and neighborhood disorganization was common. Delinquency rates were lower in areas where school success was common and the neighborhood exhibited stable family patterns and low disorganization and crime rates.[47]

James F. Short, Jr., and his associates collected a vast amount of data on juvenile misconduct and gang behavior.[48] They found that delinquents exhibited discrepanies between their aspirations and their expectations for fulfillment by legitimate means. Short suggested that juvenile delinquents often believed that opportunity through education is closed to them. The findings are not clear-cut, however. Short found that blacks experienced the greatest discrepancy between aspirations and achievement expectations, but they were also the least delinquent. This finding appears to run contrary to the expectations of Cloward and Ohlin's theory. Short found that boys with low educational aspirations became more delinquent in their behavior patterns when their achievement was blocked by the school. The youngsters with high aspiration levels remained less delinquent, even though their educational aspirations were blocked when compared to youths with low aspiration levels.[49] In an attempt to account for their findings, Short claimed that high achievement aspirations suggest an identification with conventional society and behavior patterns. Thus the youth who aspires to achieve develops a stake or vested interest in conformity which helps to insulate the youth from delinquent behavior.[50]

Short also investigated the value commitments of delinquent youths. He reported that delinquents are not rebels against middle-class values. In fact, Short reported that the lower-class youth verbally accepts middle-class values associated with stable families, good jobs, and conformity. The gang structure, however, prevents or discourages the expression of these values to other gang members. Members may not know that their peers also accept these values. The members exist in "pluralistic ignorance" of each other. Social status for the gang delinquent is important, but Short reported that the critical factor is a status threat, either real or imagined. The youth grows up in a hostile environment which may threaten the status of the youth and lead to gang formation or gang membership to counter the threat or seek protection. Especially important are threats to a boy's conception of masculinity and his membership in the gang.[51]

Related to the status threats that significantly affect the youth are the limited social skills exhibited by gang members. Short and Strodbeck reported that the delinquent has not learned adequately to play social roles, and the delinquent is not able to shift roles quickly or easily—a social skill that is taught to middle-class children early in life. Because of various background factors, the lower-class child is raised with a limited range of experience which limits the child in contacts with other people and institutions in the community. The same factors may lead to a lack of assurance or confidence in his relationships with other people. As a result of these and other factors, the youth may experience problems in school which lead to a lack of job success and an inability to get along with others. The lower-class youngster has limited opportunities for upward social mobility because of these and other factors. In this context of failure and limited social skill, status within a gang or status achieved by other means can be important.[52]

LEARNING THEORIES
The learning approach has been used primarily to account for individual delinquent behavior. When gang delinquency is discussed, there is an attempt to discover how particular individuals become members of the ongoing group. Questions involving the evolution of the gang and how it becomes delinquency oriented are often left unanswered. Most of the theories in this perspective seek to show how or why individuals become group members but rely on Sutherland's theory of differential association or some variant of it to account for individual delinquent behavior.[53] One recent theory, however, explains both individual and group delinquency by reference to learning processes.

Reference Groups
The process by which a juvenile becomes committed to a delinquent subculture is the central concern of Martin R. Haskell's reference group theory of delinquency.[54] Although he devotes most of his attention to lower-class families, the middle class is also incorporated into his theory. The process by which a youth becomes a member of a street group involves several steps, according to Haskell.[55]

Before a child begins school, the family is the primary reference group. It is the circle of acquaintances from which the individual receives recognition and approval. It provides the normative patterns for the individual's behavior and insists on conformity. Mutual respect and obligation pass between the child and the other family members. All goes well until the lower-class child starts school and begins to become aware of alternate standards which devalue his parents' background. Goals presented in this setting are accepted as appropriate but appear unattainable in view of his background. He resents his lower-class parents for their failures and begins to discount their guidance and advice. Having no earnings, few skills, and no prestige, he also acquires feelings of social incompetence. The individual then begins to seek out other groups in the streets in which his competence can be demonstrated. In his desire for approval and acceptance, he begins to take on the attitudes and behavior of his new reference group.

Haskell's discussion of the role of reference groups does not come to terms with some very important questions which need to be answered in an adequate theory of gang delinquency. First, there is no suggestion of why some youths follow through the process while others do not. We might ask why particular individuals conceive of themselves as potential failures. If this conception is common to all lower-class students in middle-class school systems, perhaps an explanation of how failure is perceived would clarify why some youths become alienated from their parents.

Another flaw in the theory involves the choice of reference groups. Haskell appears to assume that a street group is the logical choice and that it may be delinquent. It is hard to believe that a youth just wanders into the street for satisfaction or that only one group is available. Much research needs to be done on the opportunity for membership in various groups and why an individual becomes a member of one rather than another. New gangs appear and old gangs disappear over time. An effort to explain the genesis and evolution of the group is essential. Otherwise we continue to study only the "sheep"—the peripheral followers—and forget the "goats," who lead and make the group viable.

Commitment to Conformity

Briar and Piliavin's essay on delinquency suggests a unique way of looking at delinquent behavior. Rather than seeking an explanation of why youths deviate, they asked why they conform.[56] Many situations arise in which individuals are exposed to pressures, temptations, and opportunities for deviant behavior. The extent to which an individual is able to suppress his desires for deviant behavior, according to Briar and Piliavin, is dependent on his commitment to conformity.

Several bases for commitment were identified—relationship with parents, aspirations, fear of deprivation or punishment, and belief in God. Briar and Piliavin cited a number of findings that lend an air of plausibility to their theory. The fact that delinquent behavior is an episodic and noncompulsive activity suggests that it is the result of breakdowns in social controls which generally produce conforming individuals. The presence of delinquent tendencies among most youths and their decline in early adulthood results from increased learning and internalization of conforming attitudes as the child reaches maturity. Applied to gangs, Briar and Piliavin's theory suggests that members are recruited only if they lack strong commitments to conformity. In other words, individuals seek out their own kind for sustained interaction. Even when a marginal commitment to conformity is present, the expectations of peers influence the youth tremendously. Occasionally the individual will forego commitments to conformity in response to peer pressure.

GANG THEORY IN PERSPECTIVE

Theories to describe or explain the development of collective crime or delinquency did not make an appearance until the 1920s, when Thrasher published his comprehensive study of over a thousand juvenile gangs in Chicago. His social disorganization approach dominated the area until the 1950s and the appearance of Cohen's book on delinquent boys.

Many of the recent gang theories were developed in response to Cohen's subcultural approach. Several critics attacked Cohen's position by offering subcultural theories which were directly contrary to his position. Unfortunately, research findings on Cohen's and other theorists' works have been conflicting or ambiguous. Other than providing descriptive material on existing gangs, the subcultural approach has not been extremely fruitful. The approach is open to charges of middle-class bias and needs some modification if it is to produce a greater understanding of all collective delinquency.[57]

Several other approaches have also been developed. Structural theory provides some valuable insights into gang delinquency. Probably its greatest contribution is its recognition that individuals do not always have an opportunity to become gang members. Beyond this, the approach has not been all that its proponents had hoped. The newest approach in the area of collective delinquency lies in learning theory. This new approach has not yet been subjected to extensive and intensive research, but it may provide a new departure needed to develop a better understanding of this vital area.

NOTES

[1] Lamar Emprey, "Delinquency Theory and Recent Research," *Journal of Research in Crime and Delinquency* 4 (January 1967): 28–42.

[2] Robert E. Park, Ernest W. Burgess, and R. D. McKenzie, *The City* (Chicago: University of Chicago Press, 1925).

[3] Frederic M. Thrasher, *The Gang* (Chicago: University of Chicago Press, 1927).

[4] *Ibid.*

[5] *Ibid.*

[6] *Ibid.*, p. 381.

[7] Clifford R. Shaw and Henry McKay, *Juvenile Delinquency and Urban Areas* (Chicago: University of Chicago Press, 1942); Clifford Shaw and Henry McKay, *Report on the Causes of Crime*, vol. 2, no. 13 (National Commission on Law Observance and Enforcement) (Washington, D.C.: Government Printing Office, 1931), p. 387.

[8] Shaw and McKay, *Report on the Causes of Crime, op. cit.*

[9] Henry D. McKay, "Criminal Careers of Male Delinquents in Chicago," in *Task Force Report: Juvenile Delinquency and Youth Crime* (President's Commission on Law Enforcement and Administration of Justice) (Washington, D.C.: Government Printing Office, 1967), pp. 107–118.

[10] James F. Short, Jr., ed., *Gang Delinquency and Delinquent Subcultures* (New York: Harper & Row, 1968).

[11] Albert K. Cohen, *Delinquent Boys: The Culture of the Gang* (New York: Free Press, 1955).

[12] *Ibid.*

[13] *Ibid.*, p. 19.

[14] Harold L. Wilensky and Charles N. Lebeaux, *Industrial Society and Social Welfare* (New York: Russell Sage Foundation, 1958), pp. 187–207.

[15] John I. Kituse and David Dietrick, "Delinquent Boys: A Critique," *American Sociological Review* 24 (April 1959): 208–215.

[16] David J. Bordua, *Sociological Theories and Their Implications for Juvenile Delinquency*, Juvenile Delinquency, Facts and Facets, no. 2 (Children's Bureau) (Washington, D.C.: Government Printing Office, 1960); David J. Bordua, "Delinquent Subcultures: Sociological Interpretations of Gang Delinquency," *Annals of the American Academy of Political and Social Science* 338 (November 1961): 119–136; David J. Bordua, "Some Comments on Theories of Group Delinquency," *Sociological Inquiry* 32 (spring 1962): 245–260.

[17] Albert R. Cohen and James F. Short, Jr., "Research on Delinquent Subcultures," *Journal of Social Issues* 14 (1958): 20–37.

[18] Solomon Kobrin, "The Conflict of Values in a Delinquency Area," *American Sociological Review* 16 (October 1951): 653–661.

[19] Gresham M. Sykes and David Matza, "Techniques of Neutralization: Theory of Delinquency," *American Sociological Review* 22 (1957): 665.

[20] David Matza and Gresham M. Sykes, "Juvenile Delinquency and Subterranean Values," *American Sociological Review* 26 (October 1961): 717.

[21] David Matza, *Delinquency and Drift* (New York: Wiley, 1964).

[22] Travis Hirschi, *Causes of Delinquency* (Berkeley: University of California Press, 1969). Also see the discussion of Hirschi in Don C. Gibbons, *Delinquent Behavior* (Englewood Cliffs, N.J.: Prentice-Hall, 1976).

[23] *Ibid.*

[24] Michael J. Hindelang, "Causes of Delinquency: A Partial Replication and Extension," *Social Problems* 20 (spring 1973): 471–487.

[25] Walter B. Miller, "Lower Class Culture as a Generating Milieu of Gang Delinquency," *Journal of Social Issues* 14 (1958): 5–19.

[26] *Ibid.*

[27] *Ibid.*, p. 8.

[28] *Ibid.*

[29] Herbert A. Bloch and Arthur Niederhoffer, *The Gang: A Study in Adolescent Behavior* (New York: Philosophical Library, 1958), p. 7.

[30] *Ibid.*

[31] Ralph W. England, Jr., "A Theory of Middle Class Juvenile Delinquency," *Journal of Criminal Law, Criminology and Police Science* 50 (April 1960): 535–540.

[32] *Ibid.*, p. 539.

[33] *Ibid.*

[34] Marvin Wolfgang, "The Culture of Youth," in *Task Force Report: Juvenile Delinquency and Youth Crime* (President's Commission on Law Enforcement and Administration of Justice) (Washington, D.C.: Government Printing Office, 1967), pp. 145–154; Robert C. Bealer, Fern K. Willits, and Peter R. Maida, "The Myth of a Rebellious Adolescent Subculture: Its Detrimental Effects for Understanding Rural Youth," in Lee G. Burchinal, *Proceedings of a National Conference on Rural Youth in a Changing Environment* (Washington, D.C.: Government Printing Office, 1965).

[35] Merton's theory is also discussed in Chapter 10.

[36] Robert K. Merton, *Social Theory and Social Structure* (New York: Free Press, 1957).

[37] *Ibid.*, pp. 141–156.

[38] Marshall Clinard, "Criminological Research," in Robert K. Merton, Leonard Broom, and Leonard Cottrell, eds., *Sociology Today* (New York: Basic Books, 1959), p. 514.

[39] Elmer Hubert Johnson, *Crime, Correction and Society* (Homewood, Ill.: Dorsey Press, 1968), p. 244.

[40] F. Ivan Nye, *Family Relationships and Delinquent Behavior* (New York: Wiley, 1958), p. 2.

[41] Cohen, *Delinquent Boys, op. cit.*

[42] Richard A. Cloward and Lloyd E. Ohlin, *Delinquency and Opportunity* (New York: Free Press, 1960), p. 36.

[43] *Ibid.*, p. 171.

[44] *Ibid.*, p. 183.

[45] Irving Spergel, *Racketville, Slumtown* and *Haulberg* (Chicago: University of Chicago Press, 1964).

[46] Irving Spergel, "Male Young Adult Criminality, Deviant Values and Differential Opportunities in Two Lower Class Negro Neighborhoods," *Social Problems* 10 (winter 1963): 237–250.

[47] Erdman B. Palmore and Phillip E. Hammond, "Interacting Factors in Juvenile Delinquency," *American Sociological Review* 29 (December 1964): 848–854.

[48] James F. Short, Jr., and Fred L. Strodbeck, *Group Process and Gang Delinquency* (Chicago: University of Chicago Press, 1974); Ramone Rivera and James F. Short, Jr., "Occupational Goals: A Comparative Analysis," in *Juvenile Gang in Context: Theory, Research and Action*, ed. Malcolm W. Klein (Englewood Cliffs, N.J.: Prentice-Hall, 1967), pp. 57–69; James F. Short, Jr., "Gang Delinquency and Anomie," in *Anomie and Deviant Behavior*, ed. Marshall B. Clinard (New York: Free Press, 1964), pp. 98–127.

[49] Short, "Gang Delinquency and Anomie," *op. cit.*

[50] *Ibid.*

[51] *Ibid.*, pp. 115–127. For similar findings, consult Edward Rothstein, "Attributes Related to High School Status," *Social Problems* 10 (summer 1962): pp. 75–83.

[52] Short and Strodbeck, *op. cit.* Similar findings are reported in Robert A. Gordon, "Social Level, Disability and Gang Interaction," *American Journal of Sociology* 73 (July 1957): 42–62; Scott Briar and Irving Piliavan, "Delinquency: Situational Inducements and Commitment to Conformity," *Social Problems* 13 (summer 1965): 35–45; James F. Short, Jr., "Youth Gangs and

Society: Micro and Macrosociological Processes," *Sociological Quarterly* 15 (winter 1974): 3–19.

[53] This theory is discussed in detail in Chapter 10.

[54] Martin R. Haskell and Lewis Yablonski, *Crime and Delinquency* (Skokie, Ill.: Rand McNally, 1974), p. 373.

[55] Martin R. Haskell, "Toward a Reference-Group Theory of Juvenile Delinquency," *Social Problems* 8 (winter 1960): 220–230.

[56] Briar and Piliavin, *op. cit.*

[57] Thio, *op. cit.*

A long tradition of popular government and a belief in the value of self-reliance and individualism in the United States has produced a nation of problem solvers who are not afraid to speak their minds. They have opinions about solutions to many problems, and crime is an area of concern to most people. Many Americans believe that crime is on the increase in the United States. The crime problem is perceived to be grave. Most citizens, especially women, believe they are not safe on the streets of their own cities after dark.[1]

Although most Americans agree that crime is an increasingly serious problem, there is somewhat less consensus on what causes individuals to become criminals. When asked in a 1968 government survey "What are the main reasons why people become criminals?" a wide range of causes were given (see Table 11.1). Fifty-nine percent of the people questioned believed that lax parents were the primary cause of crime. No other reason received such widespread support.

Most Americans report a willingness to support tough measures to deal with crime and delinquency. In a 1972 opinion poll, Americans were asked if the police should be tougher in dealing with lawlessness. Eighty-three percent stated that the police should be tougher, 14 percent said that they should not be tougher, and 3 percent had no opinion.[2] A large percentage of the American people appear to be willing to vote for candidates who support tough responses to lawbreakers.[3]

A number of the popular conceptions about what causes crime

TABLE 11.1 PERCEIVED MAIN REASONS
WHY PEOPLE BECOME CRIMINALS, 1968

	TOTAL PERCENTAGE[a]
Lax parents	59
Bad environments	16
Poverty	16
Unemployment	12
Lack of education	12
Lack of morals in young people	12
Alcohol	10
Drugs (narcotics)	10
Broken homes	9
Lack of recreation for the young	9
For kicks	9
Being spoiled and having too much	7
Excessive public welfare	7
Lack of religion	7
Leniency in the courts	5
Living in a time of unrest	4
Violence on television	4
Mental illness	3
Too many restrictions on police	3
Other	8
Not sure	3

[a] Figures do not add to 100 percent, as some respondents gave more than one answer.
Source: Derived from Law Enforcement Assistance Administration, *Sourcebook of Criminal Justice Statistics, 1974* (Washington, D.C.: Government Printing Office, 1975).

and the effectiveness of popular solutions have been the subject of scientific investigation at different times. The results of various studies have often been cited as support for including these factors as important contributors to juvenile delinquency. A great deal of concern has been focused on the quality of family life, drugs, education, and the mass media.

THE FAMILY

The family is one of the primary agents for the socialization of children. The family provides role models, attitudes, values, and potential protection from a harsh environment. A child's first experience with social life usually comes from within the family. The quality of this experience helps determine whether the child will engage in normal or delinquent behavior patterns. The types of behavior exhibited by youngsters as they come in contact with other community institutions often reflects patterns learned in the home. Family membership helps determine the child's economic position, social class, neighborhood, school, social acceptability, and access to medical care. The family has more influence when the child is young. As the child reaches adolescence, the peer group becomes increasingly important as an influence on behavior.[4]

The family's influence on the child is studied by several disciplines. Psychologists, for example, often search for early childhood experiences and disruptions which affect personality development. Emotional problems and disturbances in parent-child relationships or toilet-training practices are believed by some psychologists and psychiatrists to lead to adjustment problems for adolescents. Severe deprivations and emotional problems directly related to delinquent behavior may be traced to childhood deprivations in the family.[5]

Parental rejection and lack of parental love creates emotional problems for a youngster. According to psychologists, delinquent behavior has meaning apart from its illegality. Delinquent behavior is seen as an acting out of early childhood experiences and problems in the family. Delinquent behavior expresses motives, needs, and values learned in the home. The behavior may be a symptom of underlying emotional problems. If family relationships have been positive, the child will make a ready adjustment to the community. On the other hand, when the family experience has not been positive, the child will face adjustment problems because the family fails to help the youth develop an ability to solve problems.[6] This situation is illustrated in Case 11.1. Berman reported that delinquents have more difficulty in early experiences with their parents than nondelinquents.[7]

August Aichhorn stressed the family's importance in providing love, security, and acceptance for the child.[8] Hostility, rejection, harsh discipline, and harsh toilet training creates emotional and behavioral problems which are expressed in a variety of ways. One of these may be juvenile delinquency. If the child cannot respond to community pressures, it is because the family has failed to prepare the child for problem solving.[9] Aichhorn contends that family problems can be located in outwardly normal and well-adjusted families if the investigator searches hard enough. These deep-seated problems might create juvenile delinquency. Hostility, shallow family relationships, little concern for the child, and the absence of adequate role models are expected in such families.[10] Thus even in the absence of obvious family pathology, some psychologists insist that it remains the prime cause of delinquency. They seem to say that the cause is really found in family relationships and maladjustment. If we only look hard enough, the problems will eventually be found. Of course, almost all families have some problems, but the hard question remains unanswered. Did the family cause delinquent behavior? It is probably safe to conclude that not all delinquent behavior is caused by the delinquent family.

The sociological approach to the family has generally taken one of two directions. The family may be taken as the determinant of the child's environment. It determines the child's social class, geographic

CASE 11.1

THE FAMILY SCAPEGOAT

Berman describes a situation in which a boy's problem with his family led to delinquent behavior. Although the boy's father was near death with heart disease, the family did not discuss the problem or its potential impact on the family group. Instead, the boy was relegated to the role of family scapegoat. Essentially, the boy became the family victim; other family members would not speak or acknowledge his presence. The boy believed that he was being blamed for the illness and impending death of his father. Because the young boy was not able to strike back at the rest of his family, frustrations were expressed outside the home. The local community reacted as if the boy had done something wrong. Berman suggests that the problem is, in fact, a reflection of the family's obvious difficulties.

Source: Eric Berman, Scapegoat (Ann Arbor, Mich.: University of Michigan Press, 1973).

location, and many other aspects of the environment which may have an effect on behavior. The family may also be viewed as the primary socializing agency for the child. Sociologists study the process and content of socialization to gauge the family's effect on the child's behavior. Unlike psychologists, sociologists focus their attention on societal institutions rather than the needs, desires, and perceptions of the individual. The investigation of the existence and transmission of norms that guide and regulate social behavior is a special field of interest for sociologists.

According to the sociological perspective, the family is an appropriate focus of attempts to understand juvenile delinquency. Because it is the major socializing agency for the child, it may be effective in building social controls that inhibit delinquent behavior.[11] The controls exerted by the family may be either internal or external. Families build internal controls against undesirable behavior by teaching the child to know, appreciate, and respect proper behavior. If a juvenile comes to believe that conforming behavior is more desirable than its alternatives, he or she will conform. The development of a conscience and an adequate self-concept are often taken as signs that a child has adopted inner controls. Families exert external controls on a youngster by supervising and guiding the child's behavior. Family members may impose curfews, forbid undesirable activities, and use punishment to enforce the rules.

Because an effective socialization process is believed to inhibit delinquent behavior, delinquent activity is often attributed to an ineffective or misdirected socialization process. When this occurs, the family and the quality of family life come under close scrutiny. A number of conditions have been given credit for contributing to delinquent behavior.

Broken Homes

Divorce, death, separation and, desertion break and disrupt family ties. The unstable, disrupted family has often been cited as an important contributor to juvenile delinquency. Glueck and Glueck investigated the relationship between broken homes and juvenile delinquency. They reported that over half of the delinquents in their sample were raised in single-parent families, while only 10 percent of the nondelinquents had such a background.[12] The Gluecks predicted that 60.4 percent of all delinquents and 34.2 percent of all nondelinquents will have experienced family disruption sometimes during their childhood.[13] A number of other studies reported similar findings.[14]

Some researchers suggest that the broken family is only part of the problem. Gordon agreed that many delinquents come from broken homes but claimed that factors other than the removal of a parent are determinant.[15] Koutrelakos made a similar point; he contended that young children (3 to 6 years of age) are affected more than older youngsters by a break in family ties.[16] All the children in a family are not affected in identical ways when the family is broken. Kvaraceus, for example, found that most of the brothers and sisters of delinquents did not become juvenile delinquents.[17]

Family Tension

McCord, McCord, and Thurber did not find support for the popular belief that broken or single-parent homes contribute to juvenile delinquency.[18] Nye reported that unhappiness in an intact but tense and unhappy home was an important factor in delinquency. Unhappiness was found to have a stronger relationship to juvenile delinquency than the broken home.[19] It may not be the broken home that creates delinquency. The fighting, bickering, and unhappiness in the damaged family may be a prime factor in the production of juvenile delinquency. Sterne agreed that it is not the breaking apart of the home that creates delinquency. He claimed that divorce and separation are preceded by tension and intense family battles. Negative influences exist in the life of the child prior to the break in the home. Sterne reported that these tensions and problems are one of the major causes of juvenile delinquency and not just the broken home per se.[20]

The family tension factor in delinquency has frequently been overlooked; however, there is considerable evidence to support it. For example, Abrahamsen, Audry, McCord, and Zola reported that the well-integrated and cohesive family produces fewer delinquents than less well-adjusted families.[21] Nye added a qualifier to his support for family tension as an important factor in producing juvenile delinquency: He claimed that quarreling and family tension is more important for explaining delinquency in females than in males.[22] The Gluecks, Aichhorn, and Slocum and Stone also reported support for the relationship between family tension or conflict and juvenile delinquency.[23]

Considerable research support has been presented for the contention that family tension and conflict produce delinquency. Thus the theorists who contend that the broken home or the absence of a parent causes delinquency may be somewhat incorrect. Instead, the tension and conflict that precedes or accompanies the departure of a parent may be the relevant factor. Furthermore, these factors may be more important for female delinquents than for males. The problems to be faced by a child in such a home are very real. For example, the child may become trapped between warring factions or become a pawn played by one parent against the other. The child may be adversely affected, but juvenile delinquency is only one of a variety of possible avenues for the expression of the anger and frustration of the child.

Family Discipline

All parents must use discipline with their children to facilitate the process of socialization. Some researchers contend that the type of discipline used may contribute to delinquency. The consistency of the application of discipline seems to be the relevant factor. When parents are inconsistent in their approach to the child, adequate behavioral controls are not established, and the child may reject efforts to impose effective controls on his behavior.[24] McCord, McCord, and Zola identified several types of discipline that might have unintended, negative effects on the child.[25] Erratic and ineffective discipline is evident when punishment is unevenly applied. It may involve inconsistent application, where the child is disciplined only occasionally for a particular misdeed, or it may involve the use of inconsistent methods for a single type of disapproved behavior. Vacilliation between spanking, lecturing, confinement, and other methods may be confusing to the child. Erratic punishment may also involve the inability of parents to agree on proper disciplinary techniques. One parent may be lax, while the other administers severe punishments.

The researchers reported that erratic discipline practices are associated with delinquency in the child. Nondelinquent behavior was common among children who had experienced consistent, well-reasoned, love-oriented disciplinary measures, such as the withholding of privileges. Delinquent children, on the other hand, were more likely to have received erratic discipline. McCord, McCord, and Zola concluded that the erratic nature of the punishment and not the type or amount of discipline was the determinative factor in delinquency.[26]

Discipline may also indirectly affect juvenile delinquency. The type and nature of discipline may be important to the development of the self-concept or values and attitudes that serve to insulate the child from delinquency. These may help the child develop inner controls on his own behavior. The potential threat of discipline may exert effective outer controls against delinquent activity.

Parental Rejection

Gibbons is critical of theories of delinquency based on studies of family relationships; however, he admits that "scientific candor compels us to conclude that the link between parental rejection and aggressive conduct is one of the more firmly established generalizations concerning delinquency."[27] Both psychologists and sociologists report that open rejection and hostility may produce juvenile delinquency. Hostility and rejection make it difficult for youngsters to accept parents as role models from whom to learn appropriate behavior patterns. As a result, the child may not learn or develop the inner controls needed to avoid delinquency or develop a positive image of himself as a person.[28]

Glueck and Glueck reported a relationship between hostile, rejecting fathers and delinquent behavior in their offspring. They also stated that the absence of the father or the father's unwillingness or inability to spend time with the child was a delinquency-producing factor.[29] Audry reported that juvenile delinquents are more likely to believe that they received too little love and affection from their parents than nondelinquent youths.[30] Nye suggested that more research is needed on the attitudes of children toward their parents. The best available information, however, indicates that mutual rejection of parents and children results in aggressive behavior on the part of the child.[31]

The transmission of parental attitudes and values to children has been the topic of considerable discussion in the delinquency literature. Parental problems with discipline, emotional stability, rejection, and hostility may contribute to delinquent behavior.

Family Finances

Howard James said of delinquents: "Too often their parents are 'losers,' unable to make a marriage go, unsuccessful in business or alcoholics, emotionally unstable, or have other problems."[32] Most delinquents come from homes with multiple problems. Not only are the homes characterized by personal and family problems, but financial problems are frequently evident.[33] Most of the juveniles who are arrested and committed to juvenile institutions are from low-income or poverty-stricken backgrounds. This fact does not mean, however, that poverty necessarily produces juvenile delinquency. These findings may only reflect differential law enforcement, whereby middle- and upper-class families are able to get their children off the hook when they come in contact with the juvenile justice system.

Many youngsters from poverty-stricken families and high-crime areas of American cities do not resort to delinquency despite the pressures that inadequate incomes place on their families. In fact, the rate of delinquency does not appear to be much different when the middle and lower classes are compared on self-reported delinquent activity. On the other hand, the subculture of violence with which many poor families are associated may lead to more serious and more violent crimes if delinquency is an avenue of response chosen by the youngster.

The Family Problem in Summary

The family often plays an important role in sociological and psychological theories of juvenile delinquency. Parental rejection, emotional instability, authoritarianism, inconsistent discipline, poverty, and broken homes may be factors in creating juvenile delinquency. However, these factors do not tell the whole story. Some youngsters, especially older youths, are influenced by other groups and circumstances. The peer group may replace the family as the primary agent of socialization at a relatively young age, especially in urban industrial societies such as the United States. Parents may not be held accountable for some delinquent acts. The youngster of 16, 17, or 18 years of age is relatively free of direct parental influence and control. The automobile and numerous activities outside the home take the youth away from parental supervision. The sociologist may be able to fall back on the self-concept or conscience to explain the genesis of delinquent behavior as a result of family-related factors, but there are many influences on a youngster other than family.

No space has been devoted to such topics as the working mother and the stable single-parent family and its effect on delinquency. These factors do not seem to have much effect. If the family produces juvenile delinquency, it is not because only one family member is present. Delinquency is not due to working or career-oriented mothers. Variables such as rejection, discipline, and family tension may be the contributing factors, but they cannot, by themselves, be used to explain delinquency. Beyond that, it does little good to blame the family of a delinquent youngster.

If the child is already being neglected, if the parents are nearing divorce, or if the parents are emotionally unstable, the intervention of juvenile authorities into the family may do more harm than good, no matter how well intentioned. If family problems cause delinquency, one solution is to remove the youngster from his family. But most people are not willing to go that far in attempts to control delinquency. Thus if the family is a major cause of delinquency, problems of preventing and rehabilitating the delinquent result.

Shifting the burden of guilt from the shoulders of the juvenile to his parents may be counterproductive for both the child and the family. The child may not be able to distinguish between proper and improper modes of behavior. In later years, as an adult, he may continue deviant behavior patterns, unwilling to accept responsibility. Where the parents accept sole responsibility for a youth's behavior, they encounter a dual problem. They cannot change the youngster's behavior unless he is willing to cooperate. However, cooperation will not be forthcoming unless the child accepts some responsibility for his behavior.

DRUG USE AND ABUSE

The possession, sale, and use of a variety of illegally obtained prescription drugs accounts for a large share of juvenile delinquent activities.[34] Strictly speaking, illegal drug use is not a *cause* of delinquency, because it is a delinquent act itself. However, a sizable number of people believe that drug use is a major cause of crime and delinquency.[35] It is suggested that the use of drugs may provide motives for additional, secondary delinquency. There are situations in which drug use may lead to other types of delinquent activity. For example, a young heroin addict may need up to 150 or 200 dollars a day to support his or her habit. Most young people do not have that amount of readily available cash. As a result, some youngsters resort to prostitution, theft, or burglary to support their habits (see Case 11.2). Drug use may explain why they engage in these activities, but it does not explain why the individual originally resorted to the use of drugs. In a similar way, delinquency may result from alcohol use by teen-agers. The purchase and consumption of alcohol is controlled in all states, especially where minors are concerned. The use of alcohol may lead to other offenses, such as driving while under the influence, public intoxication, disorderly conduct, assault, and vandalism.

The *Uniform Crime Reports* lists a large and growing number of arrests of persons under the age of 18 for narcotic drug law violations, liquor law violations, driving while under the influence, and public drunkenness.[36] Drug use and abuse is not a phenomenon found only in the large city or ghetto; it is found throughout American society and has become a national problem.

Americans have a drug-oriented society. There are drugs and patent medicines for all sorts of complaints and ailments. Drugs are readily available to help Americans deal with their aches, pains, and problems. Aspirin and Bufferin are taken for a headache; Digel and Maalox are useful if the tummy gets upset. Alka Seltzer is taken if there has been too much to eat or drink. Flavored Tums neutralize excess acid, and Chlorets help hide the odor of alcohol. Cold tablets are available for colds, and sinus tablets help with a runny nose. There are concoctions for constipation and others to help calm the bowels, but if all else fails, Preparation H soothes the damage. Coffee, tea, and cola perk us up, No Doz keeps us up, and Sominex puts us to sleep at night. Alcohol relaxes and frees inhibitions for a party. There are pills that contribute to weight loss, others that promote weight gain. Through it all, a pipe, a cigarette, or a cigar seems to help some people face the day. Does America have a drug problem? Is it any wonder that young people turn to drugs to solve their problems? How can the drug problem be resolved when most Americans depend to varying degrees on some chemical substance to solve their problems and keep them happy and alert?

Drug Types

Drugs include a variety of chemical substances which are introduced into the body by inhalation, swallowing, or injection. These substances are classified into three general categories—depressants, stimulants, and psychedelics. The depressant drugs include a variety of substances such as alcohol, barbituates, tranquilizers, inhaled chemicals (airplane glue, freon, amyl nitrite, and nitrous oxide), and narcotics (opium derivatives such as heroin, codeine, and morphine and synthetic narcotics such as methadone). The stimulants are the second drug category and include such substances as nicotine, caffeine, cocaine, amphetamines (Dexedrine, Benzedrine, and Methedrine), and antidepressants (Elavil, Ritalin, and Tofranil). The third drug category refers to psychedelic drugs, which include cannabis (marihuana, hashish, and THC) and the hallucinogens (LSD, DMT, psilocybin, STP, and others).[37]

Some of these drugs are in widespread use in American society. Depressants such as alcohol and stimulants such as caffeine and nicotine are so widely accepted and used that many people do not wish to consider them drugs. Attitudes toward cannabis may be changing in this direction, and it may become as widely accepted and used as the more common drugs. The trend is toward decriminalization and reduction in the penalties for possession. On the other hand, Americans are not likely to approve the free use of cannabis by minors when it is illegal for the same young people to purchase and possess alcohol or cigarettes.

Extent of Illicit Drug Use

Marihuana use has been an activity with widespread appeal to American youth. The National Commission on Marihuana and Drug Abuse conducted a survey on a representative sample of youths between the ages of 12 and 17 to determine the extent of the problem among juveniles. Their findings, reported in Table 11.2, indicate that a sizable number of children under the age of 14 have tried the drug. By age 17, nearly one-third of the youngsters have used marihuana.[38] A 1971 survey of college students indicated that at least 51 percent of the college population was using or had used the drug.[39] These figures, however, may underestimate current use. The increasing availability and acceptability of the drug may have resulted in increased use since 1971.

Marihuana is obtained by youths from a variety of sources. In the government survey, youngsters between the ages of 12 and 17 who had tried marihuana reported that a friend had been the direct source of the drug in about 80 percent of the cases. The youngster was introduced to marihuana by a friend (62 percent), an acquaintance (9 percent), or a family member (9 percent). Only 4 percent had their first experience with marihuana alone.

The youngster's first experience with the drug is generally not planned in advance, however similar the reasons given when they are asked why they tried marihuana. The most frequent of these reasons are out of curiosity, for excitement, to try a new experience, to expand their awareness, to experience a high, to relieve boredom, or because

TABLE 11.2 REPORTED MARIHUANA
USE AMONG THE YOUTH POPULATION, 1971

DEMOGRAPHIC CHARACTERISTICS	PERCENTAGE
Male	14
Female	14
Age	
12	5
13	7
14	7
15	13
16	23
17	33
Grade	
Eighth or less	8
Ninth and tenth	17
Eleventh and twelfth	30

Source: National Commission on Marihuana and Drug Abuse, *Marihuana: A Signal of Misunderstanding*, Technical Papers of the First Report of the National Commission, vol. 2, 1972, appendix, p. 947; and Law Enforcement Assistance Administration, *Sourcebook of Criminal Justice Statistics, 1974* (Washington, D.C.: Government Printing Office, 1975), tab. 3.4, p. 2281.

of peer pressure. Curiosity seems to be the major reason for trying marihuana. The search for a new and exciting experience seems to be the second most frequently cited reason for the use of the drug.[40]

A large number of studies have been conducted on marihuana use among youths. However, the findings have often been conflicting or inconclusive. More work is needed to develop a fuller understanding of the marihuana problem and its causes.[41] More students report the use of marihuana, but the use of cocaine, heroin, and amphetamines is also relatively high among American youth. Unfortunately, the data are not available to allow a comparison of the use of these drugs with the use of marihuana among the 12-to-17 age group. Information on college students suggests that there is a hierarchy of drug use. Some drugs draw more individuals than others. Eighteen percent of the college student respondents admitted to having tried hallucinogens.[42] However, only 7 percent reported the use of cocaine, and 2 percent indicated that they had tried heroin.[43] A larger number—22 percent and 15 percent, respectively—had used amphetamines and barbituates.[44]

All states have laws that regulate the possession and sale of alcohol, but the public, including youths, consumes large quantities of it. Alcohol is addictive for some people, and it can lead to physical, social, and psychological problems for youths. The social cost for widespread alcohol abuse among youth can be high.

Other drugs, such as barbituates and amphetamines, can be quite harmful if abused, but these drugs have medical uses and are sometimes found in the home. A doctor's prescription is usually required for their legitimate use, but these drugs are often diverted into illegitimate uses and may be readily available on the street. The possession and sale of these drugs is illegal. In some states, the possession of drug apparatus, such as a syringe, is illegal. In other states it is illegal to be in a place where illicit drugs are used. It may also be against the law to associate with known addicts. Because of these and other laws, a drug user is placed in a situation in which violation of state and federal law is frequent, and he or she may be arrested.

THE SCHOOL

Virtually all juveniles attend school for an extended period of time. The individual may spend 10 to 20 years in educational institutions. A large share of the youth's waking hours are occupied by the school or school-related activities. As a result, the school is an important socializing agency. In some ways it may be more important in inhibiting or producing delinquency than the family. It brings together children from a wide variety of backgrounds, introduces skills essential to the legitimate pursuit of success goals, and is given responsibility for instilling community values and norms.

Schools are expected to do many things to, and for, a heterogeneous student body and the community itself. The school is expected to be an agent of change to rid society of social problems such as sexism, racism, and delinquency. At the same time, the school is also expected to be a conservative influence by transmitting cultural patterns from one generation to the next. Schools are expected to provide a liberal education, but they also train youngsters for success in specific work roles and provide marketable job skills. Generally the goal of education is to create educated, responsible, and well-adjusted citizens. With such broad and conflicting demands on the school, it should not surprise anyone if everything is not done perfectly. Few institutions can be all things to all people.

All states have compulsory attendance laws; children are required to attend school until a specified age is reached. The goal of universal education has been approached if elementary school attendance is considered. Almost all American children get at least an eighth-grade education. Although the trend is for more and more students to graduate from high school, some youngsters continue to drop out of school as soon as the law allows.

Most schools have organized the curriculum so that college-bound students are more effectively handled. These youngsters are often drawn from the middle classes, and their backgrounds are usually similar to the backgrounds of the teachers. Vocation oriented youths find the college-bound programs unsuited to their needs, interests, and job prospects. Some youths aspire to become either skilled or unskilled workers, not college graduates. Such youngsters usually have parents with limited educations who aspire for only a high school diploma for their children. The school may be seen as inappropriate or even antagonistic to the values and goals of many lower-class children. Some of these children do not adjust to school and present behavior and discipline problems for school personnel. Many middle-class children do not adjust to the school routine, but the middle-class child tends to come from a family that supports the goals of education and the teacher's efforts to teach and control the child.[45]

Compounding the school problems for lower-class youths is the fact that most teachers are drawn from the middle class. The teacher may not understand or appreciate the values, attitudes, or needs of lower-class students. Teachers usually accept middle-class orientations toward dress, appearance, teaching methods, proper school behavior, and what the child should want and need to learn. Because of a bias in favor of middle-class children who exhibit the "proper" approved behavior in school, the middle-class child is favorably received and rewarded. Lower-class children, on the other hand, are often judged to be lacking in appearance, motivation, attitude, and behavior. The lower-class child is, in a sense, rejected by teachers who have inappropriate expectations for the child. The lower-class youth may find school and extracurricular activities dominated by the middle class. He or she may react by rejecting the school and dropping out prior to graduation. The school may, in a sense, reject the child by developing inappropriate programs and expectations.

Programed Failure

Schafer and Polk criticized school programs that group, or "track," children from poor families. These tracking systems usually assign youngsters to a vocational training or low-ability track where they receive little attention or training. In addition, few of the children receive adequate vocational or academic counseling. Case 11.3 illustrates this point. Lower-class children often find themselves in inner-city ghetto schools with inferior teachers and a conspicuous lack of remedial or compensatory educational experiences.[46]

Not infrequently, teachers blame the culturally deprived child for his or her educational difficulties. Academic and behavior problems, it is believed, result because the youngster is bad, stupid, sick, or a combination of these. The role of the school in producing these problems is often overlooked, while the balance of the blame is placed on the child.[47]

Delbert Elliott investigated 743 tenth-grade boys in San Diego high schools. He found that the delinquency rate was high for lower-class boys whether they remained in school or became dropouts. On the other hand, the rate of delinquency involvement was lower for middle-class boys who were in school and for middle-class dropouts.

CASE 11.3

SCHOOL AND WORK

Frequently the lower-class child does not get
adequate training for job placement. One ex-
delinquent articulated his problem in the
following way:

(What kind of school program were you doing?
Vocational education?) Yeah, vocational training. (Did that prepare you for a job?) It was
supposed to prepare me for a job but it didn't.
(Did you try to get a job?) Yeah, I tried to get
a job. The men said I wasn't qualified. (Did
you think while you were in school that you
would get a job?) That's right—that's why I
stayed in school so I could get a job upon
completion of high school because they put so
much emphasis on getting a high school diploma.
"If you get a high school diploma, you can do
this and you can do this, without it you can't
do this." And I got one and I still can't do
nothing. I can't get a job or nothing after I
got one.

Source: President's Commission on Law Enforcement and the
Administration of Justice, The Challenge of Crime in a Free
Society (Washington, D.C.: Government Printing Office, 1967),
p. 71.

Elliott's research suggests that the school may have a role in producing
juvenile delinquent behavior.[48]

School Misconduct

Schools concentrate a large number of youngsters in a small area
for a major part of their day. Much juvenile misconduct occurs either
within or near the school. The school itself handles most of the misconduct through relatively well-developed discipline and policing
policies. Only after serious delinquency does the school official consider calling the police or other agencies for aid. Traditionally, school
personnel have preferred to discipline their pupils and provide services
such as vocational and psychological counseling rather than to admit
defeat with a youngster and call other agencies for aid.

Misconduct in school ranges from discourtesy to teachers to vandalism, assault, drug use, and alcohol abuse. Some schools report that
physical attacks by students on teachers and other school personnel
is a growing problem, but most schools have minor juvenile conduct
problems, such as the use of obscene language, cheating, lying, petty
theft, fighting, or destroying and defacing property. An especially

serious and expensive problem for most schools is vandalism. Broken windows, destruction of school property, and damage to school buses costs the American taxpayer millions of dollars each year. Many of these acts, even if detected by school officials, are never reported and seldom lead to a juvenile court referral.

Serious acts are also committed in or near the school. The physical attack on a teacher, fighting, drug use, weapons possession, and vandalism must be considered serious behavior problems that deserve the attention of school personnel or other social control agencies.

Neighborhood Misconduct

Youthful misconduct can occur on the way to school, near the school, or while the youngster is waiting for or riding a school bus. Here again, most of these activities are handled by school authorities; others are handled informally by parents and neighbors. Breaking windows, destroying property, fighting, and stealing are relatively common, but more serious delinquent acts may occur. These acts might result in police or court action if they occur in the absence of school officials. When the school is involved, the cases tend to be handled either within the school system or by the parents or neighbors. Of course, the child who gets into trouble in school may also get into trouble in the community, and the youngster who is in trouble in the local community may have intensified problems in the school atmosphere. The child may eventually end up in a situation in which a court referral or some other official action is contemplated.

Aspirations

Schafer and Polk are highly critical of the school's role in delinquency. They stress that schools are especially important for producing delinquency in lower-class youths who lack commitment to educational goals. Lower-class youngsters are seen as attempting to succeed, but their attempts are blocked by the school's failure to provide legitimate alternative avenues to success.[49] In addition, the labeling perspective seems to suggest that the school might play a role in producing delinquency by labeling some youngsters as "bad," thereby stigmatizing the youth and encouraging secondary deviance.

The lower-class youth frequently experiences educational failure in school.[50] When educational success is considered essential by the lower-class child, his or her success drive coupled with failure may lead to intense frustration.[51] Because the child's educational goals are blocked, the student's self-concept and belief in the future and his or her own self-worth are negatively affected. The youth may become both bitter and cynical, and delinquency may result. The middle-class youth who fails in school tends to be kept in conventional society by parental and peer support. The lower-class youth is seldom provided with similar supports.[52]

Truancy

Truancy refers to the illegal absence of a child from school. The child may be absent with or without the knowledge of parents. An absence without parental knowledge is the traditional truant case, but some parents keep children at home to work, to baby-sit for younger siblings, or for reasons other than illness. An occasional absence is usually not considered a major problem. A pattern of unexcused absences, on the other hand, may set school and legal machinery in action to force the child back to school.

The number of absences necessary to define the child a truant varies from place to place. Most schools have their own disciplinary and investigatory procedures for a determination of truancy.[53] Although absence from school seldom results in delinquency declarations from the courts, the chronic truant may become involved in a variety of delinquent activities. While most truants are males between the ages of 14 and 16, truancy is reported even in the first grade. After age 16, truancy drops significantly, since most of the chronic truants simply drop out of school.[54] The truants tend to have personal characteristics that are similar to the rest of the school population except that they are not as well adjusted academically.[55] There is some evidence that habitual truancy is associated with adult crime, but the evidence is weak.[56] It is not suggested that truancy is either a cause of delinquency or adult crime. But in some cases truancy may indicate a broader pattern of maladjustment which may be expressed in either adult crime or delinquency.

School Discipline

Whether misconduct occurs near school, in the school building, or in the community as a result of truancy, the school may react to the behavior. Teachers and other school officials are often expected to handle infractions of school rules and state or national laws without bringing either the police or other agencies into the case. The tendency of schools to handle misconduct on an internal basis may place some teachers in an untenable position. Some students are unwilling participants in the school, and others become openly defiant and belligerent. Nevertheless, teachers are expected to discipline youths without resorting to corporal punishment or other strict and punitive forms of discipline. Recent court rulings may permit corporal punishment in school, but most schools have given up such harsh procedures or use them only in extreme cases. Teachers, principals, and school boards claim that it has become difficult to maintain order in the schools. Police officials, welfare agencies, and schools need to work more closely together for the control of juvenile misconduct.

Delinquency Prevention Programs

The school is probably not directly responsible for producing juvenile delinquency. It is perceived as a more or less effective mechanism for inhibiting antisocial behavior.[57] Because education has come to be praised as a solution for a wide variety of social problems, it is not surprising that it has been used in delinquency prevention efforts. Drug education, sex education, police-school liaison, and many other programs are offered to guide the youngster's behavior. Most of these programs are not proposed or justified as delinquency prevention efforts, however. Instead the programs are encouraged as a means to develop a student both academically and socially. Many of these school programs reach youths who are likely to get into trouble with the police, courts, or school officials. Indirectly, at least, these programs may help treat, prevent, or control delinquency.

School counselors, psychologists, social workers, and similar personnel have become relatively commonplace in American educational systems. Efforts are frequently made to diagnose childrens' problems and help them within the school or refer them or their families to appropriate community service agencies before problems become serious enough to result in juvenile delinquency. Unfortunately, there has been little research to determine how effective such programs are in preventing delinquency.[58]

In some areas, special programs have been developed to prevent truancy and keep potential dropouts in school. For example, some efforts have been made to integrate work and practical experience with formal education so that the educational experience may become more relevant for low-income and vocation oriented youths. Vocational education programs are valuable for a number of reasons, whether or not they prevent delinquency. In addition, summer work programs, Project Head Start, Upward Bound, Job Corps, and other special programs involve efforts to prevent delinquency by contributing to the social and educational adjustment of lower-class youths.

The Contribution of the School

The school may serve as more than a location for juvenile misconduct and social control. The school experience may frustrate lower-class youths and negatively affect their self-concepts by labeling some individuals "bad" or "problem" children. As a result, the school is intimately tied to the delinquency problem in American society. There is little consensus about what the school can or should do to prevent or control juvenile delinquency, or even how it should discipline problem children. Even special programs, classes, and child-care workers may not be effective in preventing or controlling juvenile delinquency.

Americans must begin to realize that the schools cannot do everything—educate, prepare for jobs, solve personal problems, solve social problems, feed, clothe, and do all the other things we expect from our schools. Just because the family and other agencies of social control have failed to meet the needs of youth does not mean that the responsibility for resolving the delinquency problem can be dumped

on the school. Other agencies in the community may be better prepared to prevent delinquency or treat the offender.

THE MASS MEDIA
Many youngsters spend much of their time absorbed in a flicker-
ing image on a television screen positioned in the family living room
or in their own room. Television has a tremendous impact on children
and youths, but the precise nature of the influence is not fully understood. Most mothers of very young children can testify to the influence
of television. Just watching a child in a supermarket may be enough
to demonstrate that influence. Children help their parents choose
particular brand-name goods by pointing out their many virtues or
repeating catchy jingles learned from the ever-present television commercial. A child may recognize some cookies because elves made them
or sing a beer commercial for dad. If the child can walk or reach the
shelves, a particular package may be seized and carried to the parent
for purchase.

In addition to training a new generation of ferocious consumers,
television may have educational significance. The producers of "The
Electric Company" and "Sesame Street" have recognized the impact of
short but stimulating commercials on young children. These television
programs provide "commercials" for letters and numbers to capture
the relatively short attention span of youngsters. The presence of television in almost every home in America provides an unprecedented
opportunity for quality education that could capture and mold the
minds of even very young children. But there are few programs with
the quality of "Sesame Street" or "The Electric Company."

Program Content
Watching television in the early morning (before school), in the
early evening (after school), and on Saturday mornings can be instructive. These are the times when children watch television and when
children's programs are presented. "Thor," "The Hulk," "Popeye,"
"Superman," "Spiderman," "Batman and Robin," "Clutch Cargo,"
"Roadrunner," "Shazam," "Crazy Goolies," "Space Nuts," "Super-
friends," "House of Frightenstein," "Captain America," and "Captain
Kangaroo" are just a sampling of the shows presented for children.
With the notable exception of "Captain Kangaroo," most of these
shows are extremely violent in nature. The shows represent life as an
overly simplistic battle between good and evil forces. Often powerful
or superhuman forces battle with equally devilish and powerful forces
for supremacy. Good usually prevails over evil but only after a fantastic
battle. Reason is rarely used to solve the conflict between good and
evil. Might makes right on children's television; the hero is frequently
a killer who is not punished for his "justifiable" behavior.

A similar theme seems to characterize many prime-time or "family" television shows even though the message is presented in a some-

what more sophisticated manner. "Hawaii Five-O," "Kojak," "Cannon," and many other police and private detective shows serve as examples. The viewer is sometimes reminded of a John Wayne movie or early "Gunsmoke" westerns where the hero rarely needs to worry about the fine points of law as long as he has his trusty six-shooter. If a problem exists, it can be handled with a gun, a knife, or the fist. Violent action is the key to understanding how good prevails over evil on American television. The issues are simple and presented in easy-to-understand terms where good and evil are opposing forces. Powerful evil forces are overcome violently by the forces of goodness. Violence to obtain good ends is similar to violence to obtain evil ends. A child may be led to believe that all problems can be solved by violence. The hero kills or beats people to solve his problem. Should we be surprised if a youngster comes to believe that a gun, a knife, or a fist is an approved and acceptable method of solving his problems?

Media Impact

There is not sufficient evidence to conclude that television violence causes juvenile delinquency. There have been instances, of course, where a television or other media presentation contributed directly to a series of violent incidents. For example, the showing of a movie that depicted the dousing of helpless victims with gasoline and setting them afire was once followed by a rash of incidents using similar techniques. Of course, these incidents may be only isolated cases and not fully representative of the general impact of television.

American society is violent, and violence may be an integral part of our culture as one of the survivals of a pioneer past. It is not known whether television merely reflects the violence in society or helps create and perpetuate it. Americans watch and approve of violent shows on television; they might not watch nonviolent television if it were presented. Some people claim that mass media violence allows vicarious participation and serves as a safety valve for aggression so that it prevents even more real violence in American society.

A number of studies have been conducted to clarify the nature of the mass media's impact on youth. Although the studies have not been conclusive, they have succeeded in raising the question above the level of ideological conflict and speculation. The Surgeon General, under the auspices of an Advisory Committee on Television and Social Behavior, commissioned a number of research projects to investigate the content of television programing, who watches television, and the effects of televised violence. Several volumes and numerous research reports were presented to the commission.[59] Children's television was shown to contain more violence than adult programing. The leading character was frequently a killer who could not be killed himself. According to another government report, young children preferred violent shows or cartoons.[60]

Research on the relationship between televised violence and

youthful aggression suggests that there may be a relationship between a preference for violent television shows and ratings of high aggressiveness by peers. According to one study, a preference for violent television in the third grade appears to be related to ratings of high aggressiveness even ten years later; preference for violence at age 9 may be predictive of aggression at age 19.[61] The Surgeon General's report suggests that a preference for violent television is more important as an influence on aggression than factors such as intelligence, career aspirations, social class, religion, race, or family problems.[62]

Research evidence suggests that televised violence has a pronounced short-term effect, but there is less evidence for the long-term effects of television. Television may produce not only aggression but also hostile outbursts. Some evidence suggests that televised violence leads directly to violent outbursts from viewers, if the violence is presented as justifiable. Furthermore, shows appear to have greater violence-producing effects if the viewer was not angry prior to seeing the justifiable violence on the screen.[63]

Bandura conducted a suggestive but inconclusive psychological experiment with young children to test the effects of viewing violence. Children were divided into several groups and shown different types of violent presentations. The first group of children was shown an actual adult attacking a doll; the second group watched a movie of an adult attacking a doll; while a third group saw a television presentation of an adult attacking a doll. In the televised presentation, the adult was costumed as a cat. The fourth group served as the control group; these children did not see a violent presentation of any type. Bandura reported that the children were observed from behind a mirror after each presentation. Observation of violent behavior reportedly increased the amount of violent behavior exhibited by children. Bandura contended that the observation of violent behavior reduces a child's inhibition against expressions of violence and aggression. In addition, experiences with violent presentations determine what patterns the behavior will take when expressed. Youngsters in the experiment imitated the behavior of the adult and attacked the doll in much the same manner. Significantly, Bandura reported that violence on the screen was as influential as observation of violence by a real adult. Children were somewhat less likely to copy the cartoon character, but many children imitated the behavior of cartoon, movie, and real-life actors.[64]

The evidence for a relationship between violence on the screen and violent viewer behavior is tentative, but the best available data suggests that televised violence does have an effect on young people. Television may provide role models and techniques and contribute to the belief that violence is an approved, appropriate, effective, and rewarding response to life's problems. Of course, the youngster who is oriented toward violence and who has emotional or family problems may tune in more of the violent television shows, which have a more pronounced short- and long-term effect. American television, however, is so saturated with violence that it may be difficult, if not impossible, for even the normal child to ignore it completely. More research is needed to specify the precise nature of the impact of television on all types of young people.

CONTRIBUTING FACTORS IN PERSPECTIVE

The family, drugs, schools, and the mass media are all popularly believed to cause juvenile delinquency. Some of these factors may indeed contribute to delinquency, but probably not in the way envisioned by most laymen. More research and theoretical work is needed in most of these areas before any conclusive statements can be made.

Of the popular conceptions on the causes of juvenile delinquency, the relationship between family factors and delinquent behavior has been the subject of the greatest amount of research. While a number of family problems have been associated with delinquent youth, there is little evidence that the nature of family relationships alone provides an adequate explanation of delinquency. Certainly, family tension, broken homes, rejection, and disciplinary approaches cannot be ruled out as contributing factors.

Drug abuse is a delinquent act and therefore does not cause initial juvenile delinquency. However, drug use may be instrumental in explaining secondary delinquency. Examples of this type of delinquency are found in heroin addicts, who must turn to prostitution or theft for the support of their habits.

The influence of education and its role in causing delinquency is not well understood, and more research is needed. Disturbing questions about the role of the schools in delinquency control, prevention, and treatment have been raised, but few solutions can be provided. Education-related prevention and treatment programs will be discussed in subsequent chapters.

The influence of the mass media on violence and aggression has not been adequately studied. The available evidence suggests, however, that there may be a relationship between the media and societal violence. Television provides role models, techniques, and supportive attitudes for the expression of violent behavior. The mass media have become one of the prime agencies or instruments by which the young in American society are socialized. Television, in a very real sense, helps form the perspective from which the young view their world.

Each of these contributing factors has been discussed separately because these influences have not been integrated into a single theory that suggests the interrelationships between these factors and delinquency. Theory is not available to suggest, for example, how the influence of the mass media, the family, and the school might combine to produce juvenile delinquency. There is a need, therefore, for the development of such a theory. In addition, more research is needed on the relationship between the mass media and schools to describe in greater detail their respective contributions to juvenile delinquency.

NOTES

[1] Law Enforcement Assistance Administration, *Sourcebook of Criminal Justice Statistics, 1974* (Washington, D.C.: Government Printing Office, 1975), p. 172, tab. 2.3.

[2] *Ibid.*, p. 203, tab. 2.67.

[3] *Ibid.*, p. 207, tab. 2.74.

[4] Hyman Rodman and Paul Grams, "Juvenile Delinquency and the Family: A Review and Discussion," in *Task Force Report: Juvenile Delinquency and Youth Crime* (President's Commission on Law Enforcement and Administration of Justice) (Washington, D.C.: Government Printing Office, 1967).

[5] Robert C. Trojanowicz, *Juvenile Delinquency* (Englewood Cliffs, N.J.: Prentice-Hall, 1973), p. 65.

[6] *Ibid.*

[7] Sidney Berman, "Antisocial Character Disorder," in *Readings in Juvenile Delinquency*, ed. Ruth Cavan (Philadelphia: Lippincott, 1964), p. 142.

[8] August Aichhorn, *Delinquency and Child Guidance* (New York: International Universities Press, 1969).

[9] *Ibid.*

[10] *Ibid.*, p. 16.

[11] See Albert J. Reiss, Jr., "Delinquency as the Failure of Personal and Social Controls," *American Sociological Review* 16 (1951): 196–207; Trojanowicz, *op. cit.*, p. 66.

[12] Sheldon Glueck and Eleanor Glueck, *Delinquents and Nondelinquents in Perspective* (Cambridge, Mass.: Harvard University Press, 1968), p. 12.

[13] *Ibid.*

[14] Maude A. Merrill, *Problems of Child Delinquency* (Boston: Houghton Mifflin, 1947); Thomas P. Monahan, "Family Status and the Delinquent Child," *Social Forces* 35 (March 1957): 250–258; Roland J. Chilton and Gerald E. Markle, "Family Disruption, Delinquent Conduct and the Effects of Subclassification," *American Sociological Review* 37 (February 1972): 93–99; Charles J. Browning, "Differential Impact of Family Disorganization on Male Adolescents," *Social Problems* 8 (1960): 37–44; Walter Slocum and Carol L. Stone, "Family Interactions and Delinquency," in *Juvenile Delinquency*, ed. Herbert C. Quay (New York: Van Nostrand, 1965); Donald R. Peterson and Wesley C. Becker, "Family Interaction and Delinquency," in Quay, *op. cit.*

[15] I. J. Gordon, *Human Development: Birth to Adolescence* (New York: Harper & Row, 1962).

[16] James Koutrelakos, "Perceived Parental Values and Demographic Variables as Related to Maladjustment," *Perceptual and Motor Skills* 32 (1971): 151–158.

[17] William C. Kvaraceus, *Juvenile Delinquency and the Schools* (New York: Harcourt Brace Jovanovich, 1945), pp. 78–79.

[18] Joan McCord, William McCord, and Emily Thurber, "Some Effects of Paternal Absence on Male Children," *Journal of Abnormal and Social Psychology* 64 (May 1962): 361–369.

[19] F. Ivan Nye, *Family Relationships and Delinquent Behavior* (New York: Wiley, 1958).

[20] Richard S. Sterne, *Delinquent Conduct and Broken Homes* (New Haven, Conn.: College and University Press, 1964), pp. 21–28.

[21] David Abrahamsen, *The Psychology of Crime* (New York: Columbia University Press, 1960); R. C. Audry, *Delinquency and Parental Pathology* (London: Metheun, 1960); William McCord, Joan McCord, and Irving Zola, *Origins of Crime* (New York: Columbia University Press, 1959).

[22] Nye, *op. cit.*

[23] Glueck and Glueck, *op. cit.*, p. 8; Aichhorn, *op. cit.*, p. 33; Slocum and Stone, *op. cit.*

[24] Glueck and Glueck, *op. cit.*, pp. 15–16.

[25] McCord, McCord, and Zola, *op. cit.*

[26] *Ibid.*

[27] Don Gibbons, *Delinquent Behavior* (Englewood Cliffs, N.J.: Prentice-Hall, 1970), p. 202.

[28] Abrahamsen, *op. cit.*, p. 62.

[29] Glueck and Glueck, *op. cit.*, p. 62.

[30] Audry, *op. cit.*

[31] Nye, *op. cit.*, p. 73.

[32] Howard James, *Children in Trouble* (New York: McKay, 1969), p. 196.

[33] Gordon H. Barker and W. Thomas Adams, "Glue Sniffers," *Sociology and Social Research* 47 (1963): 298–310; Trojanowicz, *op. cit.*, p. 77.

[34] An excellent discussion of drug use and abuse is found in Trojanowicz, *op. cit.*, pp. 106–123.

[35] *Sourcebook, op. cit.*, p. 176 tab. 2.12.

[36] *Ibid.*, p. 347, tab. 4.13.

[37] Joel Fort, "Major Drugs and Their Effects," *Playboy Magazine*, September 1972, pp. 143–145. The article is also discussed in Martin R. Haskell and Lewis Yablonski, *Juvenile Delinquency* (Skokie, Ill.: Rand McNally, 1974), pp. 294–295.

[38] *Sourcebook, op. cit.*, p. 228, tab. 3.4.

[39] *Ibid.*, p. 230, tab. 3.8.

[40] *Ibid.*

[41] For a detailed discussion of marihuana use studies, see Stanley E. Grupp, *The Marihuana Muddle* (Lexington, Mass.: Lexington Books, 1973).

[42] *Sourcebook, op. cit.*, p. 231, tab. 3.10; the data were drawn from the American Institute of Public Opinion's *Special Drug Study* (1971).

[43] *Sourcebook, op. cit.*, p. 231, tab. 3.11.

[44] *Ibid.*, p. 232, tab. 3.12 and tab. 3.13.

[45] Ruth Shonle Cavan and Theodore Ferdinand, *Juvenile Delinquency*, 3d ed. (Philadelphia: Lippincott, 1975), p. 255.

[46] Walter E. Schafer and Kenneth Polk, "Delinquency and the School," in *Task Force Report: Juvenile Delinquency and Youth Crime* (President's Commission on Law Enforcement and Administration of Justice) (Washington, D.C.: Government Printing Office, 1967), p. 230.

[47] *Ibid.*

[48] Delbert S. Elliott, "Delinquency, School Attendance and Drop Outs," *Social Problems* (winter 1966): pp. 307–314.

[49] Schafer and Polk, *op. cit.*; Kenneth Polk and Walter Schafer, eds., *Schools and Delinquency* (Englewood Cliffs, N.J.: Prentice-Hall, 1972).

[50] Schafer and Polk, "Delinquency and the School," *op. cit.*

[51] James S. Coleman et al., *Equality of Educational Opportunity* (Washington, D.C.: Government Printing Office, 1966).

[52] Schafer and Polk, "Delinquency and the School," *op. cit.*

[53] Cavan and Ferdinand, *op. cit.*, p. 262.

[54] John L. Roberts, "Factors Associated with Truancy," *Personnel and Guidance Journal* 34 (1956): 431–436.

[55] Cavan and Ferdinand, *op. cit.*, p. 263.

[56] Henry D. McKay, "Report on the Criminal Careers of Male Delinquents in Chicago," in *Task Force Report: Juvenile Delinquency and Youth Crime* (President's Commission on Law Enforcement and Administration of Justice) (Washington, D.C.: Government Printing Office, 1967), p. 112.

[57] Cavan and Ferdinand, *op. cit.,* p. 124.

[58] William C. Kvaraceus and William E. Ulrich, *Delinquent Behavior, Principles and Practices* (Washington, D.C.: National Education Association, 1959), pp. 182–183, 215–219; Edward Stullken, "Chicago's Special School for Social Adjustment," *Federal Probation* 20 (March 1956): 31–36; Cavan and Ferdinand, *op. cit.,* pp. 270–271.

[59] Public Health Service, Surgeon General's Scientific Advisory Committee on Television and Social Behavior, *Television and Growing Up: The Impact of Televised Violence* (Washington, D.C.: Government Printing Office, 1972).

[60] Public Health Service, Surgeon General's Scientific Advisory Committee on Television and Social Behavior, *Television and Social Behavior,* 5 vols. Vol. 1: *Media Content and Control* (Washington, D.C.: Government Printing Office, 1972).

[61] *Ibid.,* vol. 3: *Television and Adolescent Aggressiveness.* Also see Haskell and Yablonski, *op. cit.,* p. 281, for a discussion of the reports.

[62] *Ibid.,* vol. 4: *Television and Day to Day Life: Patterns of Use.*

[63] David Lange, Robert K. Baker, and Sandra J. Ball, *Mass Media and Violence* (Washington, D.C.: Government Printing Office, 1969), p. 243.

[64] Albert Bandura, "What TV Violence Can Do to Your Child," *Look,* October 22, 1963, pp. 46–48.

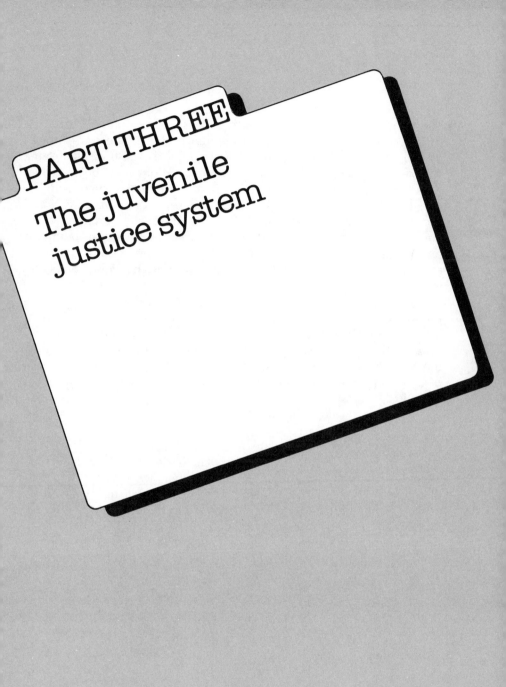

PART THREE

The juvenile
justice system

The behavior of a particular youth and the corresponding reactions of others may result in the youth's entrance and progression through official channels of the juvenile justice system established for dealing with delinquent youth. The complete sequence of events begins when the child engages in an act or series of acts that is perceived as delinquent and ends with his discharge from probation or parole and acceptance back into the community. Not all juvenile offenders progress through the entire sequence, however. At several points, a juvenile may be diverted to informal channels for less stigmatizing assistance. Youths who progress through official channels are subject to diverse disposition alternatives at all stages of the sequence.

A number of events determine the eventual outcome for the juvenile offender. Both the actions of the youth and the reactions of interested or concerned segments of society are important to his or her progress through the system. An interplay of circumstances surrounding the offender and members of the larger society as well as official personnel may result in the differential handling and treatment of juveniles.

Progress through the juvenile justice process generally involves seven stages:

1. Youngsters may violate municipal, state, or federal criminal codes or engage in other behavior that, if detected, results in disapproval. Children may attempt to conceal their actions or may participate openly. If they are not alone, their actions will be observed by others. Their referral to legal authorities will depend on the perceptions of those who observe or detect the behavior. Those observing the behavior may choose to ignore it, report the behavior to parents, complain to legal authorities, or report the behavior to other nonlegal authorities such as the school, the church, or community service agencies. These interested third parties may or may not make formal complaints to legal authorities.

2. If children are referred to, or incidentally come in contact with, the police, they may be handled unofficially or officially. Police are given wide discretion in encounters with juveniles. When an officer observes a youth committing an offense, in "suspicious" circumstances, or at the scene of a violation, he or she has several disposition alternatives: (1) outright release, (2) release and submission of a "field interrogation report," (3) outright release to a parent or guardian, (4) taking the child into custody for an "official reprimand" and release, (5) citing to juvenile court and release, or (6) holding in detention for further official action. The first three alternatives are generally considered unofficial handling or on-the-spot adjustments, and no official delinquency records are made for the offender. The remaining official

alternatives, however, result in the acquisition of a police record for the juvenile. When a child is referred on informal complaints from outside agencies or individuals, any of the above dispositions may be applied. However, if a formal complaint is filed, only official handling may be considered suitable.

3. Children referred to a juvenile court have their cases reviewed by an intake department, usually operated by probation departments. At this point, some children are released, referred to social welfare agencies, or placed on informal probation, while others are held under supervision for a hearing before the juvenile court. Although most cases are referred by police, this step may be short-circuited. Interested individuals, such as parents or school authorities may refer juveniles to the court without intervention by police.

4. If a period of time must elapse before the juvenile court hearing, the youths may be released to the custody of their parents or other interested, responsible individuals. When this is not feasible, children may be held in police custody, either in jail or in a juvenile detention center or shelter. Custody of the juvenile may be continued until final disposition of the case by a juvenile court. During the period prior to a hearing in juvenile court, a social investigation will be prepared to ascertain information about the child's background and facts surrounding any offense that may have been committed. Depending on the juvenile authority and its staff and their responsibilities, this report may include a superficial rundown of basic information or a full case history, which involves all aspects of the juvenile's life.

5. When the juvenile judge hears the case, he or she makes use of information provided regarding the alleged offense as well as the social investigation to come to a disposition decision. Several alternatives are open to the judge: (1) The case may be dismissed and the juvenile released. (2) The child may be placed on probation under the supervision of a probation officer or some other community agency. (3) The child may be placed in a foster home or a private institution. (4) In some cases the juvenile may be bound over to criminal court. If a child is believed to be mentally disturbed, he or she may be placed in a specialized institution. In cases of incorrigibility, parents have sometimes agreed to placement in private "military" schools. (5) The child may be sent to a foster home. (6) The youth may be placed in a state training school, group home, farm, or ranch.

6. When they are released from treatment, they may be placed under the supervision of a parole or aftercare officer, either for a specified time period or until attainment of majority age.

7. Eventually the juvenile is released unconditionally into the community.

Ideally, each case of alleged delinquency is handled on an individual basis. As indicated above, each step through the juvenile justice system may result in a wide range of outcomes. It is not sheer chance that produces a particular outcome for the youngster. Attributes of the juvenile offender, juvenile justice personnel, established (official and unofficial) policy, and tradition may interact to determine the disposition of the individual juvenile offender.

This section of the text will discuss the elements of the juvenile justice system. Chapter 12 deals primarily with police handling of juvenile offenders. The ways in which particular juveniles are brought to the attention of the police are outlined and discussed. Policies for the handling of juveniles are examined, and the factors that result in the preference of one disposition over another are analyzed. The mechanisms formally established for dealing with juveniles and detention practices will also be treated.

Chapter 13 focuses on the juvenile court. It examines three major aspects of the court: (1) philosophical stance, (2) scope and power, and (3) the court in practice. It become apparent that a broad gap has developed between the philosophy of the juvenile court and its actual workings. The modern juvenile court is examined in terms of the mechanisms and procedures used to process juvenile offenders and determine disposition outcomes. Chapter 14 presents the implications of disposition decisions made by the court. The meaning and effectiveness of suspension, probation, and institutionalization are studied.

The structure and philosophy of juvenile corrections is the focus of Chapter 15. The training school concept is examined as it is applied in modern correctional institutions. Significant trends in juvenile treatment in official circles suggest future development for this element of the juvenile justice system. Finally, Chapter 16 deals with the programs (or the lack of programs) that might prepare the juvenile for reentry into the community. The problems of a delinquent youth returning to the community are numerous. The lack of programs to smooth the transition from correctional institution to the community frequently results in a return to delinquency. The reasons for rehabilitation failure and the possible link between delinquency and adult crime are discussed.

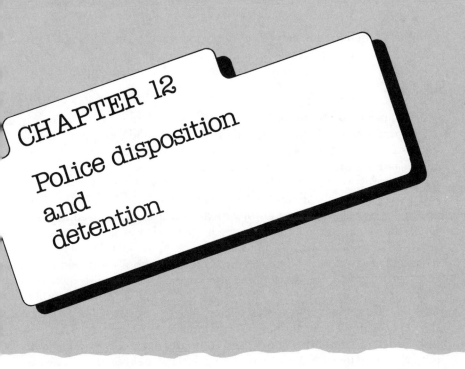

CHAPTER 12
Police disposition and detention

The juvenile court is often cited as the most significant of the agencies that deal with juvenile offenders. However, the juvenile court does not reach out into the community to recruit potential clients. Court action is initiated only after referral from individuals or agencies in the community. Most referrals are initiated by or channeled through the local law enforcement agencies such as the police department or sheriff's office. The initial police confrontation can be highly significant in determining the types and number of cases that come to the attention of the juvenile court for adjudication.

DETECTION OF OFFENDERS

Discovery and disposition of juvenile offenders is not a clear-cut task for law enforcement officers. Definitions of what constitutes juvenile delinquent behavior are sufficiently broad that most adolescents may be subject to attention and sanction at some point. The sheer volume of such law-violating behavior precludes direct detection and control of all offenders by agents of the juvenile justice system. It is apparent, then, that the commission of a delinquent act alone is not sufficient to insure the juvenile's entry into the official system.

Following the commission of a delinquent act, the first step in the determination of delinquent status is detection. Unless he or she is alone and leaves no traces of the act, the act is likely to be detected. Whether detection leads to official handling depends upon the actions and attitudes of those witnessing or discovering the event. A large number of delinquent acts go unreported each year. Some of these offenses are handled outside official law enforcement and judicial channels. There are a number of reasons why police might not be called in.

Community Discretion

Parents may differentially interpret their child's behavior. Some youths habitually stay away from home past the curfews set by parents or engage in other forms of behavior that are disapproved. While one parent dismisses the child's behavior as normal or makes some adjustment with the youth, another parent insists that the child is incorrigible and requests help from law enforcement officials or the juvenile court. Once the parent, police, other agencies, or individuals officially petition the juvenile court, the court must act. A merchant's willingness to accept restitution for damages or theft, the school's intervention in cases of truancy or vandalism, and the victim's compromise of assault cases provide examples of unreported acts and informal handling outside the system of juvenile justice. Private adjustments between the accused and the accuser are commonplace.

Broad community values and attitudes may result in under-reporting to officials, thereby deflating official delinquency statistics. A number of reasons are given for failure to report juvenile delinquent activity. Some individuals may regard youthful misbehavior as a family matter and fear reprisal for their interference. Others have little faith in the effectiveness of law enforcement agencies or the juvenile court and prefer to apply their own sanctions to bring juvenile behavior in line with accepted standards. A number of adults do not report detected delinquency because they know little about the procedures for reporting such activity. Still others do not report delinquency because they do not want the inconvenience of taking time to telephone authorities, file a petition, or spend hours at the juvenile court. Some people become concerned about the possible effects on the child if contact with the legal system is initiated.

Public pressure is a significant factor in determining which delinquency laws are enforced. Although a wide variety of juvenile behaviors may be legally sanctioned in a given community, the public is not concerned about all of them. A priority ranking of offenses and probable public response is understood by the opinion leaders in a city or a neighborhood. What is considered a serious offense by the residents of one area (i.e., staying out past parental curfew or production of graffiti) may be overlooked elsewhere.

The delinquency detection function is primarily lodged in the citizenry rather than the police. A recent study by Black and Reiss suggested that the large majority of youth-police encounters are initiated by interested citizens.[1] It appears that the selection process for the determination of delinquent status is operating even before any

official agency comes into play. Individuals are differentially treated so that some are more likely to receive official handling and others unofficial treatment following the detection of their actions.

THE ROLE OF POLICE

Whether or not a juvenile becomes involved in the juvenile justice system is generally dependent on the outcome of an encounter with police. Police-juvenile confrontations are initiated as a result of several different circumstances. A large majority of encounters result from citizen initiation. An individual witnessing a juvenile involved in questionable behavior may call the juvenile to the police's attention. Most of these complaints are not official, and no formal charges are drawn. Other citizens may report patterns of delinquency or dependence for a particular child. Citizen calls about particular offenses or evidence of wrongdoing may also result in confrontation at or near the scene of an alleged offense.

Confrontations may also be initiated by police officers. When police spot an officially "wanted" youth, confrontation is mandatory. Less frequently, police directly observe youngsters engaging in unlawful activity or in suspicious circumstances. A police officer may happen upon the scene of a crime in progress or a situation that leads him or her to believe that a crime has taken place. Observing a youth running away from a broken store window or expressing exaggerated enjoyment at the scene of a fire might be viewed as suspicious behavior. The *Challenge of Crime in a Free Society*[2] indicates that many encounters are initiated on less concrete grounds: "Many encounters are based on a relatively minor violation or not a specific crime at all but on the policeman's sense that something is wrong. He may suspect that a crime has happened or is about to happen. Or he may believe the juvenile's conduct is offensive, insolent, or in some other way improper."[3]

Disposition Decisions

Regardless of the type of encounter involved, the police have a wide range of alternatives for dealing with juveniles. Possible dispositions include outright release, release and submission of a field interrogation report, official reprimand, arrest, custody, detention, and referral to a juvenile court. The officer on the scene has broad discretionary powers, and a substantial portion of police-juvenile confrontations are handled unofficially. The President's Commission on Law Enforcement and Administration of Justice[4] listed some of the dispositional choices for the police officer when minor offenses or suspicious circumstances are involved: "He can pass by. He can stop for a few words of general banter. He can ask juveniles their names, where they live, where they are going. He can question them about what has been happening in the neighborhood. He can search them, order them to disperse or move on, check with the station for records and recent neighborhood offenses. He can send or take them home where he may warn their parents to keep them off the street. Suspicion, even perhaps without very specific grounds for it, may on occasion lead him to bring them into the station for further questioning or checking."[5] Police criteria for determining disposition of the juvenile is not uniform from one jurisdiction to another. While some police departments have written standards for adjustment and referral, others have covert understandings of a general policy toward the handling of youths.

THE OFFENSE AND THE OFFENDER:
ATTITUDE AS CRITERIA

It appears that type of offense is a major consideration in police handling.[6] Court or police department policy often requires that some offenses be handled officially, though this policy may not always be followed by individual police officers. More serious offenses seem to be adjusted by police relatively less often than minor ones. Nevertheless, a wide range of options have been exercised for almost every type of offense. The *Task Force Report* on juvenile delinquency revealed that "involuntary manslaughter, rape, serious assault and battery, armed robbery, burglary, and many other felonies are adjusted by police, frequently at significantly high rates."[7]

One study reported that a panel of police officers selected "offense" as the first piece of information needed to come to a disposition decision for handling juvenile offenders. However, the most critical information used by the panel to reach a final decision was attitude or demeanor of the offender.[8] Earlier studies have reported similar findings.[9] A high correspondence between poor demeanor and official handling is suggested by several researchers. Black and Reiss reported higher arrest rates for both the overly respectful and overly disrespectful.[10] Little information is generally available to an officer on the scene, according to Briar and Piliavin, and as a result character judgments are frequently based on outward appearances.[11] A juvenile's visible attitude toward the law, the police, and his or her own delinquent behavior were the most significant factors in the decision to officially process.

Some police officers believe that denial of guilt or defiance indicates an uncooperative attitude not amenable to informal treatment.[12] Often condemned as an inadequate criterion for disposition decisions, there are frequent questions about its objective use by law enforcement officers.[13] It is not appropriate to assume that real, as distinguished from feigned, attitudes can be accurately determined on the spot by police. Furthermore, attaching importance to attitude presupposes the juvenile's involvement in delinquent activities.

THE ROLE OF COMPLAINANTS

New evidence suggests that law enforcement officials are more highly influenced by the preferences of complainants in the making of disposition decisions than is generally believed. A study conducted by Black and Reiss indicated a tendency for police to comply with the preferences of complainants present on the scene.[14] While a significant number of complainants did not express a clear preference for disposition, a majority did indicate a preference. In this study, in no instance did the police arrest a juvenile when the complainant lobbied for leniency. Police arrested for misdemeanors in 60 percent of the cases in which complainants showed a preference for arrest. The implication is that the citizen complainant frequently performs an adjudicatory function in police encounters with juveniles. The patrol officer abdicates his or her discretionary power to the complainant. Hence the eventual action taken against the juvenile does not necessarily rest solely with the idiosyncrasies of individual police officers.

SOCIAL BACKGROUND FACTORS

Some of the criteria cited as factors that determine police disposition have included race, age, family status, prior record, availability of community programs for prevention or treatment of juvenile offenders, and police training. Data on the impact of race is contradictory and inconclusive. Several researchers have concluded that race is an important factor throughout the juvenile justice system. It has been reported that black youths are more likely to be questioned on the street.[15] If questioned, they are more likely to be arrested.[16] If arrested, they are more likely to be sent to court.[17] And if sent to court, the black youth is more likely to receive a severe disposition.[18] Other studies note the complexity of the decision-making process and suggest that other factors may enter into the final decision. Terry,[19] Bodine,[20] and McEachern and Bauzer[21] found evidence to support their contention that race is not a significant factor in disposition decisions. In a review of the systematic studies carried out in this area, Rosen concluded that racial discrimination could account for only a small number of differences in arrest rates.[22]

Goldman suggested that the kind of complaints that lead to arrest vary from neighborhood to neighborhood. In areas where serious criminal activities are frequent, police and citizens may ignore minor juvenile offenses. Hence, those youths who are confronted by police probably have committed more serious offenses.[23] Black and Reiss' findings indicated that the higher arrest rate for black youths, where complainants are present, is largely a consequence of the tendency for police to comply with the preference of complainants.[24] Black complainants are relatively severe in their expressed preference compared with white complainants. While police behavior may follow a similar pattern when handling black and white juveniles, differential treatment of black youths may arise from differences in citizen attitudes.

Age, family status, and prior record appear to be additional characteristics that affect disposition decisions. Case 12.1 illustrates the effect of family status.

POLICE ORGANIZATION AND TRAINING

The individual officer's training and the availability of alternative community services for young people may enter into the picture as factors influencing police handling of juvenile offenders. Police departmental structure and policy may also influence disposition. A number of police departments across the country have formulated guidelines that suggest appropriate disposition options for particular types of encounters, but the final decision is left to the discretion of police officers on the scene.[25] The impact of police training and departmental organization on handling was documented by Wilson, who concluded: "The training of a police force apparently alters the manner in which juveniles are handled. The principal effect of professional norms is to make the police less discriminatory but more severe."[26]

ATTITUDES AND EXPERIENCE

Within departments some variation in handling may also be found. Sullivan and Siegal reported that officers with more experience tend to make more decisions to arrest and adjust fewer cases on the street.[27]

A FAVORABLE DISPOSITION

Al had always been an active, upper-middle-class boy. He was a bit more chubby than was fashionable, but he was nevertheless well liked by adults and peers. Al enjoyed being a leader and was often the first to suggest prankish behavior to keep his friends interested.

At age 16, Al and several of his friends broke into a local swimming pool for after hours swimming and fun. Unfortunately, Al broke his arm while attempting to ride a bicycle off the high diving board. Another youth, a 15-year-old girl, cut her foot on a broken beer bottle and required medical attention. No police complaints or court referrals were initiated following police detection of the incident. It had just been a prank.

In the same year, Al was caught purchasing liquor from a package store. The owner of the store got into trouble with the police for selling liquor to minors. No action was taken against Al or his friends. Al also bought liquor from "bootleggers" who brought the illicit goods across state lines. It was cheap and a good deal for Al and his friends. On a lark, Al reported the bootlegger to the county sheriff. All Al got was a good laugh; the bootlegger got 30 days!

The next year, Al was caught driving while under the influence of alcohol. His friends in the car were incapacitated. One had passed out; another was sick. The police stopped the car and were ready to take the whole group to the station when one officer recognized Al—who happened to be the son of the local school board president and a prominent businessman. The other kids were also recognized as children of prominent townspeople—the local doctor, lawyer, and so on. The police took the kids straight home to their parents and took no further action.

Al's pranks continued in college. He and several friends "borrowed" a 6-foot long alligator from a city park during the winter hibernation period. With its snoot and tail tied up to prevent accidents, the animal was taken to a girl's dorm. The boys put the beast in a warm shower, bringing it out of its hibernating state. It was then released to wander the halls of the dorm. When Al and his buddies were caught, their parents intervened to prevent police action. The boys got a short suspension from school.

Another prank, never traced directly to Al by the authorities, involved one of the social clubs on campus. Because the school was a religious

institution, it had a chapel with a 6-foot
concrete cross on the front lawn. One Saturday
night (just before Easter) a nude boy was tied to
the cross to greet the worshippers the next
morning as they arrived at the chapel. When
discovered, the boy was unconscious and required
hospitalization as a result of exposure to the
rain and cold.
    After graduation, Al became a respected member
of his community. Through all his pranks, he never
acquired a police record.

Individual attitudes about the effectiveness of the juvenile court and
juvenile correctional institutions may also influence a police officer's
decision to pursue formal disposition. Concern with the stigmatizing
effect of a delinquent label may result in the outright release of juvenile offenders by "enlightened" police officers in the absence of alternative community treatment agencies.

The conventional view of the role of the police in juvenile delinquency—that it is restricted to the investigation of complaints and the
initiation of legal action—is far from realistic. Citizens and police exercise vast discretionary power over the final disposition of juvenile
offenders. Loose definitions of delinquency make most juveniles vulnerable to official action. This situation, however, should not blind us
to the fact that juveniles do commit unlawful acts which may result in
serious harm to themselves and others. Yet police and citizen discretion often limits the acts that are reported and influences who is to be
handled officially and who will be charged with more serious offenses.

Disposition Alternatives

Police handling of juveniles is conducted on a case-by-case basis.
Whether or not official disposition alternatives are chosen, each juvenile is to be given individual treatment. Unofficial handling can mean
several different procedures; official handling does not necessarily
mean that a child will appear for a juvenile court hearing. Police
handling falls into several distinct categories. An examination of these
categories will give a more intimate understanding of the role of the
police as gatekeepers of the juvenile justice system.

BENIGN NEGLECT

One alternative for police handling is benign neglect. If an officer
observes a juvenile engaged in minor misconduct (i.e., loitering, drinking, etc.), he or she may choose to ignore the apparent violation to
turn to more pressing matters. Where police-citizen relations are not
friendly, interference in minor infractions may be a volatile issue. The
ability to overlook minor offenses is considered essential to the devel-

opment of better community relations and the reduction of charges of harassment.[28] There is no way to assess the amount of all delinquent behavior detected by the police that falls into this category. If all self-reported delinquencies were handled by the police, their case loads would be enormous.

ON-THE-SPOT ADJUSTMENT

When police officers determine that juveniles requires attention, they have wide discretion in choosing an interrogation alternative. They may stop for general conversation: They may ask the juveniles who they are, where they live, where they are going, and what's happening in the neighborhood. After the police officers have satisfied themselves, they may move along with no further action. After brief questioning, officers may decide that further action may be useful. They may, then, search the juveniles, order them to move on, or check with the station for records and recent neighborhood offenses. Depending on the policy in the jurisdiction, a field interrogation report may or may not be filed. If the situation warrants it, police may also send or take the juvenile home. There they have the option of giving an unoffical reprimand or warning parents to keep the child off the streets.

Evidence or suspicion of juvenile misconduct often results in further action. When a complainant is involved, police officers sometimes act as arbiters to help the individuals settle their differences on the spot. A promise to discontinue the behavior and/or to pay restitution for damages may result in unwillingness of the complainant to pursue the charges further. Police have, at times, collected damage money from the juvenile and given it to the victim. Action by the police does not always end at this point. The officer on the scene may later conduct unofficial follow-ups to determine the satisfaction of all those involved.

STATION ADJUSTMENT

A juvenile may be taken to the police station under a number of circumstances. The visit may be official or unofficial. It is unofficial if the juvenile is not in custody or arrested. This type of visit is frequently used when parents cannot immediately be located, when evidence of misconduct is not clear enough to merit official handling, or if additional information is needed for a disposition decision. An unofficial visit might end with the outright release of the juvenile to parents, but other options are also available.

The juvenile may receive a reprimand at the station, after which he or she is released to parents. However, if there is reason to believe that a youth's parents need help to control their child, conditions may be attached to release. In Kansas City, for example, the police carry out an informal discipline program called grounding. A grounded juvenile must attend school, follow a study schedule, and adhere to stated prescriptions for dress and appearance; movements are to be limited in number and monitored by parents.[29]

Voluntary referral may also be used. Police have suggested that juveniles make use of the services of certain social agencies in the community as a "voluntary" condition of release. Unofficial treatment plans for the unadjudicated juvenile have included programs offered by voluntary associations, welfare agencies, family service agencies, and private or public institutions that purport to reach predelinquent or delinquency-prone youths. Unofficial handling of juveniles is varied and often haphazard. With few exceptions, the law is silent about permissible action toward nonadjudicated delinquents.

OFFICIAL HANDLING

If juveniles are officially taken into custody, they become record offenders. Their arrest and handling become a matter of public record, and delinquency files are established for them. Custody does not necessarily mean that a juvenile will be immediately referred to juvenile court. Police make a determination of final disposition through a screening and referral process. As in unofficial handling, disposition may range from outright release to referral to the juvenile court.

Procedure It is the duty of the officer who takes the child into custody to notify the youth's parents or guardian within a reasonable time. Most police training manuals provide procedural guidelines for the notification of parents and the conduct of interviews with the juvenile. Policies on records to be kept during processing vary considerably. Most juvenile court rules make provision for police to obtain authorization of the court to fingerprint and photograph a youth in custody or under investigation. However, this is not routine practice in most jurisdictions.

Investigation Report The processing of juvenile offenders varies from community to community. In jurisdictions where juvenile units have been established, this function is handled by the specialized unit. Here disposition is made after an investigation of the circumstances of the alleged misconduct and an examination of the social background of the youth. Such investigatory procedures are highly variable. The social investigation may be limited to a review of police records. In highly developed juvenile bureaus it may involve an attempt to establish a comprehensive background report through interviews with individuals from the school, family, neighborhood, and church and others.

If the offense is minor, if the evidence is not sufficient for referral to the juvenile court, or if the juvenile's record is reasonably good, he or she may be diverted from the system at this point for unofficial handling or outright release. Over 50 percent of all youths officially processed by the police in 1975 were referred to juvenile court, but many of these youngsters were eventually diverted from official or formal contact with the court.

Disposition Performance

The *Uniform Crime Reports* indicated that a total of 1,675,711 juveniles were taken into police custody in 1975 (see Table 12.1).[30] Forty-two percent of them were handled within the police department and released, but a greater number (52.7 percent) were referred to the jurisdiction of the juvenile court. Relatively small numbers were referred to a welfare agency, other police agencies, or the adult court.

The place of residence is an important factor in determining whether informal or official handling will be received by the juvenile. Rural police agencies are more likely to refer youngsters to the court and less likely to handle them in the department or release them. Suburban police departments are more likely to handle youths in the department and release them without court referral. City police department policy appears to be midway between those of the suburban and rural police departments. They are more severe in their handling than suburban departments but less severe than rural police agencies.[31]

JUVENILE DETENTION

When official handling is deemed necessary, juveniles may be released to parents pending a formal hearing. If youths have committed serious offenses or are perceived as threats to themselves or the community, the investigating officer may request a detention agreement pending a court hearing.[32]

Police have considerable discretionary power in the detention of juvenile offenders. In theory, decisions to detain are lodged in the juvenile court. In practice, however, court officials appear to be significantly influenced by police determination of a need for secure custody. The majority of cases brought to detention homes by police result in subsequent detention. *Standards and Guidelines for the Detention of Children and Youth*, prepared by the National Council on Crime and Delinquency (NCCD), suggests that detention be used only in those cases where "failure to do so would be likely to place the child or the community in danger."[33] In this category the NCCD includes runaways, those likely to commit additional serious offenses, and parole violators.

Juvenile detention is the practice of holding children of juvenile court age in secure custody until court disposition. A detention facility is any place for the temporary housing of children with locked outer doors, a high fence or wall, and screens, bars, detention sashes, or other window obstructions designed to deter escape.[34] Detention homes, juvenile shelters, and diagnostic and reception centers are such temporary care facilities. These facilities held 531,686 children in 1971. Most of the youngsters were held in detention centers (494,286). Table 12.2 reports the number of children held in shelters and diagnostic

TABLE 12.1 DISPOSITION OF JUVENILE OFFENDERS TAKEN INTO POLICE CUSTODY, 1975

POPULATION GROUP	TOTAL[a]	HANDLED WITHIN DEPARTMENT AND RELEASED	REFERRED TO JUVENILE COURT JURISDICTION	REFERRED TO WELFARE AGENCY	REFERRED TO OTHER POLICY AGENCY	REFERRED TO CRIMINAL OR ADULT COURT
Total all agencies						
Number	1,675,711	697,061	883,736	24,293	31,663	38,958
Percentage[b]	100	41.6	52.7	1.4	1.9	2.3
Cities[c]						
Number	1,375,424	588,098	711,456	18,821	24,871	32,178
Percentage	100	42.8	51.7	1.4	1.8	2.3
Suburban areas						
Number	720,877	357,689	325,397	7,986	14,245	15,560
Percentage	100	49.6	45.1	1.1	2.0	2.2
Rural areas						
Number	99,743	29,750	61,523	2,033	2,830	3,607
Percentage[b]	100	29.8	61.7	2.0	2.8	3.6

Source:: Federal Bureau of Investigation, *Uniform Crime Reports, 1975* (Washington, D.C.: Government Printing Office, 1976), p. 177.
[a] Includes all offenses except traffic and neglect cases.
[b] Percentages do not add up to total due to rounding off.
[c] Includes suburban, city, and county police agencies within metropolitan areas.

TABLE 12.2 ADMISSIONS TO AND DISCHARGES FROM TEMPORARY CARE FACILITIES BY SEX AND TYPE OF FACILITY, 1971

TYPE OF FACILITY	ADMISSIONS			DISCHARGES		
	TOTAL[a]	MALE	FEMALE	TOTAL	MALE	FEMALE
Detention centers						
Number	494,286	347,876	146,410	492,399	346,564	145,835
Percentage	100	70	30	100	70	30
Shelters						
Number	9,686	6,421	3,265	9,651	6,388	3,263
Percentage	100	66	34	100	66	34
Diagnostic and reception centers						
Number	27,714	22,384	5,330	27,445	22,381	5,064
Percentage	100	81	19	100	82	18
All temporary care facilities						
Number	531,686	376,681	155,005	529,495	375,333	154,162
Percentage	100	71	29	100	71	29

[a] There is a slight overlap in the total population movement into temporary care facilities, since most adjudicated delinquents entering a reception or diagnostic center have passed through a detention center or shelter. This overlap is less than 5 percent.

Source: Law Enforcement Assistance Administration, *Children in Custody: A Report on the Juvenile Detention and Correctional Facility Census of 1971* (Washington, D.C.: Government Printing Office, 1974), p. 11.

TABLE 12.3 NUMBER OF JUVENILES IN PUBLIC
DETENTION FACILITIES FOR JUVENILES, JUNE 30, 1973

TYPE OF FACILITY	NUMBER	PERCENTAGE
Detention centers	10,782	84.9
Shelters	190	1.5
Diagnostic and reception centers	1,734	13.6
Total	12,706	100.0

Source: Law Enforcement Assistance Administration, *Children in Custody: Advance Report on the Juvenile Detention and Correctional Facility Census of 1972–73* (Washington, D.C.: Government Printing Office, 1975), p. 8.

and reception centers as well as the number of discharges from such facilities in 1971. Although temporary care facilities are designed to hold youngsters awaiting court action, they also handle delinquents who are to be taken to correctional facilities as well as some dependent or neglected youngsters.[35]

On a single day, as many as 12,000 juveniles were housed in temporary care facilities in 1973 (see Table 12.3). These figures do not include children held in jails or other secure custody facilities used to house youths pending court hearing. A 1967 estimate of detention practices suggested that approximately 20 percent of all juveniles detained are held in jails.[36]

Facilities in Use

The National Jail Census reported 7,800 juveniles out of a total jail population of 160,863 in 1970. In addition, 2,104 juveniles were held for other authorities but not officially arraigned, and another 3,054 juveniles were held in jail while awaiting trial. There were 424 juveniles who had been convicted but were being held for further legal action. Furthermore, jails held 1,365 youngsters serving a sentence of one year or less and 853 serving a sentence of over one year.[37] Considering the inadequate condition of local jails and lockups in many communities in the United States, the practice of holding juveniles in jails should be further restricted. Detention centers should be provided to segregate adult from juvenile offenders while awaiting court action or transfer to a corrections facility following official action. Juvenile shelters could be used to house dependent and neglected youngsters. Some of the problems of jail detention are illustrated in Case 12.2.

The average daily population for detention centers was reported to be 10,782 in 1973, but it was only 190 for shelters and 1,734 for reception and diagnostic centers. The per capita yearly cost of a stay in a detention center was $7,541, compared with $7,738 for juvenile shelters and $8,347 for reception and diagnostic centers in 1971.[38] By 1973, the average per capita expenditure was $9,582.[39] The average

THE DETENTION NIGHTMARE

Over 90 percent of the nation's juvenile court jurisdictions have no place of detention other than the county jail. The depressing atmosphere and real dangers awaiting juveniles in these facilities can only be described as a nightmare:

- In Illinois, a 14-year-old boy was arrested on disorderly conduct charges and detained in jail. On his first night, he was the victim of a brutal homosexual rape. Although guards heard his screams, they did not interfere.
- In Arizona, four boys detained on suspicion of theft (of beer) died of asphyxiation. They had been left unattended for 11 hours near a defective gas heater.
- In Indiana, an alleged auto thief hung himself in his jail cell. He was 13.

Similar atrocities are not uncommon occurrences in the nation's outmoded jails. Unfortunately, we cannot take comfort in the trend toward an increase in juvenile detention centers. Many of these are little more than jails with fancy titles.

Source: Daniel Katkin, Drew Hyman, and John Kramer, Juvenile Delinquency and the Juvenile Justice System (North Scituate, Mass: Duxbury Press, 1976), pp. 231–232.

length of stay in 1971 for a juvenile was 11 days in a detention center, 20 days in a shelter, and 51 days in a diagnostic and reception center.[40]

Detention centers have been built throughout the United States; 319 such facilities existed in 1973. Over half of the detention homes have either been built since 1961 or have spent in excess of $50,000 in extensive renovation since 1961.[41] Detention centers often provide both educational and counseling programs for youngsters placed in their care. Of the 319 detention centers that existed in 1973, over half provided academic education. Many of the centers also provided vocational education. There were 57 centers providing no educational services to their inmates. Both shelters and diagnostic and reception centers generally provided educational services. Counseling services were usually provided by all types of temporary care facilities. Individual counseling for the juvenile offender is the type most frequently provided, but group counseling and even counseling for the juvenile and his family is provided in over half of the temporary care facilities.[42]

The temporary care facilities for juveniles often provide other services as part of their total program. For example, medical services are provided in most detention centers but not in juvenile shelters. Still, 128 detention centers out of the 303 existing centers provided no medical services in 1971. In addition, recreational services such as radio, movies, television, libraries, gymnasiums, and athletic fields were provided for most temporary care facilities, including detention centers, juvenile shelters, and the diagnostic and reception centers.[43]

Purpose of Detention

The youth's first experience in detention influences his or her attitudes toward society. The belief that a disagreeable experience will assure reform is not supported in practice. Removed from parents and friends, they may judge the larger society by the kind of substitute care, guidance, and control they receive in detention. Confinement with other alleged delinquents may result in identification with the delinquent group. And exposure to more sophisticated youths may encourage the development of techniques to defy authority. When short detention is used to "teach them a lesson," the lessons learned may not be those envisioned. The underlying purpose and intent of the facility and its design provide cues that may indicate its effectiveness.

Not all alleged delinquents need or are detailed in custody prior to adjudication. Approximately two-thirds of all juveniles referred to juvenile court are released to their parents or guardians during this period. The use of detention differs so widely from county to county and from state to state that the likelihood of a juvenile being detained is often a matter of geographic accident. Most statutes that attempt to regulate the use of detention are so broadly conceived that admission is wide open. In some jurisdictions, virtually all arrested youngsters are detained routinely; in others, less than 5 percent are held in secure custody facilities.[44] The lowest rates of detention are usually found where detention facilities are limited and where a low rate of detaining is considered satisfactory practice by local law enforcement and court officials.

DECISION TO DETAIN

The first decision to detain or release is made by police or probation officers. Unless an authorized court official is available to intervene shortly after arrest, a child may be detained overnight until a court official can be reached. In 15 states, youths may be detained without judicial review. The number of children admitted to detention is greater than the number referred to juvenile court for adjudication. Many of these youths are released within 24 to 48 hours. The conclusion emerges that detention is sometimes used not so much for the protection of the child and the community as for its shock value on the alleged delinquent.

Although it appears that detention has been overused and abused, some efforts have been made to alleviate these problems. A few jurisdictions control detention admissions through clearly written court policy, agreements with law enforcement agencies, and special 24-hour intake procedures. Metropolitan facilities using these methods have cut their detention rates considerably without evidence of damage to the community or the child.

Physical Facilities

In the early days of the juvenile court, private homes and alms-houses were used for the detention of children to avoid the use of jails. There is little information on what remodeling or alteration was required for adapting these facilities for secure custody. It is possible that makeshift rooms with barred windows and doors were installed on public property in the basements of courthouses and other inadequate places just as they were in the 1950s. Some early detention facilities were located within jails or institutions for dependent children, as they are today.[45]

HISTORICAL DEVELOPMENT

The first detention facility designed for dividing the population into separate age and problem categories was erected in 1932. Built with a congregate care design, it was the model for facilities constructed before World War II. The National Probation and Parole Association undertook a study of detention facilities for children and youths in 1945, and they proposed standards and guidelines for new construction. Although nearly all detention homes constructed since 1950 have used National Probation and Parole Association (now called the National Council on Crime and Delinquency) guidelines, only some of the facilities approach the model.[46]

LOCATION

The trend is toward locating detention homes on the outskirts of the community, convenient to main highways but far enough away to make the purchase of adequate amounts of land practicable. Occasionally neighborhood groups have objected to locating a detention center in suburban areas, because they fear for the safety of their children and are concerned about depreciation of property values. Where properly designed buildings and grounds have been established, these fears have been unsubstantiated. A few detention homes have been located in congested downtown areas, but in these locations, sufficient land has seldom been available for adequate outdoor activity areas and privacy.[47]

ORGANIZATION

Several types of detention facilities are in common use. Family-type detention homes are operated by a resident couple who rarely take care of more than eight children at a time. Usually the physical facilities are converted residences with bars or detention screens on the windows. These homes are not generally as secure as other types and are used to house less aggressive youths and first offenders. The single-unit home has been the most frequently built and the best designed, according to National Probation and Parole Association standards. A general living and activities area is usually located between a reception area in front and a service area in the rear. A wing of single bedrooms extends from each side of the living area. The premises are generally well secured. Multiunit facilities afford the additional advantage of separating children into age and problem categories. Each group has its own living and sleeping quarters, but administrative and casework services are shared by all groups. Security and service may be efficiently obtained in well-designed and well-staffed facilities of this type; however, only large caseload jurisdictions will find these facilities practical.

The majority of detention facilities for juveniles, regardless of the type of facility, do not separate the delinquents (adjudicated youths) from other juveniles who are being held for future court disposition. In addition, juveniles who are held pending court hearings for delinquent acts are not segregated from dependent and neglected youngsters, and these youngsters are not separated from adjudicated delinquents.[49] Some age segregation is practiced in detention facilities, but the juveniles are frequently not separated from each other on bases other than sex. Thus the adjudicated delinquent who may have committed serious offenses or adopted a delinquent career is thrown in with first offenders and neglected youngsters.

STAFFING

Staffing requirements vary with the type of facility. Whatever the type of facility, however, it must perform the eight basic functions outlined in the *Standards and Guides for Detention of Children and Youth:* (1) administration, (2) health, (3) casework, (4) clinical services, (5) group work, (6) education, (7) religious guidance, and (8) institutional or housekeeping services. For all these services to be adequately provided, a ratio of one full-time staff member per child is not excessive. This ratio is, however, seldom met. Volunteer workers are used in most detention homes, but it is the consensus of most experts that they should be used only to enrich the program and not to substitute for essential staff. Most untrained volunteers seek personal satisfaction from social work and bring patronizing attitudes to the job. However well-meaning the volunteer may be, attitudes of this nature give their work a doubtful value. Where they are used effectively, they have been well coordinated and used to provide services to supplement a well-organized program.

Use of Jails and Other Facilities

A variety of facilities have been and are being used for the secure custody of children prior to adjudication. Where special detention homes are not available, arrangements may be made to use facilities built for other purposes. Hospitals, old people's homes, courthouse facilities, and correctional institutions have been used for temporary care. These facilities often do not provide for the physical require- ments of children. When they do, there is little provision of services and counseling which might lay the foundation for rehabilitation after adjudication.

The county jail is the most frequently used alternative in the absence of a detention home. It is estimated that 75,000 to 100,000 children are housed in county jails (without special accommodations for children) annually.[50] Others may be detained in city jails for short periods of time. The typical jail is a series of small barred cells equipped with narrow cots and perhaps toilet and lavatory. Many are old, and most are small and with little or no area for exercise and fresh air. Personnel are untrained in handling children and provide minimum supervision.

THE POLICE AND DETENTION IN PERSPECTIVE

The proper exercise of police discretion in the disposition and detention of children suggests the need for a police force whose mem- bers are highly intelligent and educated and have had specialized training. Unfortunately, the conditions of recruitment and selection of police in the United States has not resulted in the attainment of such high standards, despite changes in these areas in recent years.

The President's Commission on Law Enforcement and Adminis- tration of Justice, in 1967, reported that on the average, cities were 10 percent below authorized personnel strength.[51] This shortage was not due to a lack of candidates but to an inadequate supply of successful ones. The standards used to qualify candidates fall into several cate- gories. Every department has detailed and rigidly enforced physical requirements and demands "good moral character" of its recruits. Many departments also require prior residence in the community. A high school diploma is required in 70 percent of the departments, but few require college credits. Salary and promotion schedules discourage a number of the best-qualified recruits. Most police are poorly paid and work under rigid promotion provisions. Lateral entry is not per- mitted in most departments, and patrol officers must serve several years before they are eligible for promotion to supervisory or command positions. Because most police officers, even in cities with special youth details, have regular contact with children, all police should have some training in procedures for disposition of youths and laws pertaining to youths.

In 70 percent of cities with a population of 500,000, new recruits receive at least eight weeks' training. In smaller jurisdictions, unfor- tunately, city and rural departments often provide little or no formal training at all, relying instead on in-service apprenticeship. Some de- partments have programs for continued education after the initial probationary period. Special youth officers provided in some areas should be given more extensive, specialized training. The Children's Bureau suggests that the following subjects be covered:

1. philosophy of police work with children
2. juvenile delinquency laws
3. delinquency causation
4. duties of juvenile control units
5. intradepartment relationship between the juvenile and other police units and personnel
6. interviewing, screening, and record keeping
7. dispositions
8. knowledge and use of community resources
9. developing good relations with related agencies and the public.[52]

This training is provided for through in-service apprenticeship programs in some of the largest departments, but comprehensive programs of this type are not available in many jurisdictions. A number of community colleges and universities sponsor institutes on juvenile law enforcement. A growing number of universities have initiated special degree programs in law enforcement and police administration which include courses applicable to youth police work. While requirements for training are still in flux, there are growing opportunities for formal training in this area.

The police officer plays an important role in the juvenile justice system, and it is especially important that adequate training be made available and utilized by police departments if the system is to be perceived favorably by the child and the community.

Many children do not need detention. Only those who pose a threat to themselves and/or the community are proper candidates for detention. A wide variety of places have been used for the detention of youths. Where specialized juvenile detention facilities are unavailable, jails have been used on a temporary basis. Foster homes, convalescent hospitals, and other public and private facilities have also been used.

Reliance on detention has increased with the proliferation of facilities specially built to house children. Unfortunately, most of these institutions are little more than holding pens for youths. The physical facilities have been improved over the years; however, they are, for the most part, understaffed and underfunded. Lack of rehabilitation programs or educational experiences within the facilities preclude a therapeutic function.

NOTES
[1] Donald J. Black and Albert J. Reiss, "Police Control of Juveniles," *American Sociological Review* 35 (February 1970): 63–77.
[2] President's Commission on Law Enforcement and Administration of

Justice, *The Challenge of Crime in a Free Society* (Washington, D.C.: Government Printing Office, 1967).

³ *Ibid.*, p. 78.

⁴ *Ibid.*

⁵ *Ibid.*

⁶ President's Commission on Law Enforcement and Administration of Justice, *Task Force Report: Juvenile Delinquency and Youth Crime* (Washington, D.C.: Government Printing Office, 1967), p. 13.

⁷ *Ibid.*, p. 12.

⁸ Dennis C. Sullivan and Larry J. Siegal, "How Police Use Information to Make Decisions: An Application of Decision Games," *Crime and Delinquency* 18 (July 1972): 253–261.

⁹ See Irving Piliavin and Scott Briar, "Police Encounters with Juveniles," *American Journal of Sociology* 70 (September 1964): 206–214; Aaron Cicourel, *The Social Organization of Juvenile Justice* (New York: Wiley, 1968); Nathan Goldman, *The Differential Selection of Juvenile Offenders for Court Appearance* (New York: National Council on Crime and Delinquency, 1963); David Bordua, "Recent Trends: Deviant Behavior and Social Control," *Annals of the American Academy of Political and Social Science* 369 (January 1967): 149–163; Black and Reiss, *op. cit.*; Thorsten Sellin and Marvin E. Wolfgang, *The Measurement of Delinquency* (New York: Wiley, 1964); Theodore N. Ferdinand and Elmer C. Luchterhand, "Intercity Youth, the Police, the Juvenile Court, and Justice," *Social Problems* 17 (spring 1970): 510–526.

¹⁰ Black and Reiss, *op. cit.*

¹¹ Piliavin and Briar, *op. cit.*

¹² *Task Force Report, op. cit.*, p. 13.

¹³ *Ibid.*, p. 18.

¹⁴ Black and Reiss, *op. cit.*

¹⁵ Piliavin and Briar, *op. cit.*

¹⁶ *Ibid.*

¹⁷ Goldman, *op. cit.*

¹⁸ Sidney Axelrod, "Negro and White Institutionalized Delinquents," *American Journal of Sociology* 57 (May 1952): 569–574.

¹⁹ Robert M. Terry, "Discrimination in the Handling of Juvenile Offenders by Social Control Agencies," *Journal of Research in Crime and Delinquency* 4 (July 1967): 218–230.

²⁰ George E. Bodine, "Factors Related to Police Disposition of Juvenile Offenders" (Paper read at American Sociological Association Annual Meeting, Montreal, August 1964).

²¹ A. W. McEachern and Riva Bauzer, "Factors Related to Disposition in Juvenile Police Contacts," in *Juvenile Gangs in Context*, ed. Malcolm W. Klein (Englewood Cliffs, N.J.: Prentice-Hall, 1967), pp. 148–160.

²² Lawrence Rosen, "Policemen," in *Through Different Eyes*, ed. Peter I. Rose, Stanley Rothman, and William J. Wilson (New York: Oxford University Press, 1973), p. 285.

²³ Goldman, *op. cit.*

²⁴ Black and Reiss, *op. cit.*

²⁵ Piliavin and Briar, *op. cit.*

²⁶ Cited in *The Challenge of Crime in a Free Society, op. cit.*, p. 79.

²⁷ Sullivan and Siegal, *op. cit.*

²⁸ See *The Challenge of Crime in a Free Society, op. cit.*, pp. 99–101.

²⁹ *Task Force Report, op. cit.*, p. 13.

³⁰ Federal Bureau of Investigation, *Uniform Crime Reports, 1975* (Washington, D.C.: Government Printing Office, 1976).

³¹ *Task Force Report, op. cit.*

[32] For a comprehensive survey of detention, see National Council on Crime and Delinquency, "Correction in the United States," *Crime and Delinquency* 13 (1967): 1–38.

[33] National Council on Crime and Delinquency, *Standards and Guides for the Detention of Children and Youth*, 2d ed. (New York, 1961), p. 15.

[34] *Ibid.*, p. 2.

[35] Law Enforcement Assistance Administration, *Sourcebook of Criminal Justice Statistics, 1974* (Washington, D.C.: Government Printing Office, 1975), p. 419.

[36] "Correction in the United States," *op. cit.*, p. 15.

[37] Law Enforcement Assistance Administration, *National Jail Census* (Washington, D.C.: Government Printing Office, 1971).

[38] Law Enforcement Assistance Administration, *Children in Custody: A Report on the Juvenile Detention and Correctional Facility Census of 1971* (Washington, D.C.: Government Printing Office, 1972).

[39] Law Enforcement Assistance Administration, *Children in Custody: Advance Report on the Juvenile Detention and Correctional Facility Census of 1972–73* (Washington, D.C.: Government Printing Office, 1975), p. 14.

[40] *Children in Custody* (1971), *op. cit.*, p. 4.

[41] *Ibid.*, p. 20.

[42] *Ibid.*, p. 15.

[43] *Ibid.*, p. 16.

[44] "Correction in the United States," *op. cit.*, p. 31.

[45] National Probation and Parole Association, *Detention Practice: Significant Developments in the Detention of Children and Youth* (New York, 1960), p. 23.

[46] *Ibid.*, p. 24.

[47] *Ibid.*, pp. 26–28.

[48] For a comprehensive overview of detention center developments, see National Probation and Parole Association, *op. cit.*

[49] *Children in Custody, op. cit.*

[50] National Council on Crime and Delinquency, *Directory of Juvenile Detention Centers in the United States* (New York, 1968).

[51] *The Challenge of Crime in a Free Society, op. cit.*, p. 108.

[52] Department of Health, Education, and Welfare, Children's Bureau and International Association of Chiefs of Police, *Police Services for Juveniles* (Washington, D.C.: Government Printing Office, 1954), pp. 42–43.

CHAPTER 13
The juvenile court

The juvenile court has been delegated responsibility for society's troubled children. Whether a youth's problem involves illegal behavior or a lack of adequate adult care, the juvenile court has jurisdiction. The identification of troubled or troublesome youths is not the responsibility of the juvenile court, however. Officers of the court do not have authority to reach into the community and select their clientele. Cases are referred to the court by parents, community agencies, and police. When referral occurs, the court is expected to perform a problem-solving function. Youths whose law-violating activities cause problems for the community are to be transformed into law-abiding citizens; neglected children are to be given parent substitutes. It is the responsibility of the court to outline plans of action that result in these outcomes.

Although the juvenile court frequently deals with individuals who violate criminal statutes, it is not a criminal court. It is a relatively new, judicially separate unit with special procedures and a distinct philosophy of treatment oriented to solving the problems of youths.

ORIGINS OF THE COURT
Prior to the late nineteenth century, children were tried and convicted in the criminal courts. Because English common law recognized the importance of maturity and knowledge as conditions of criminal responsibility, penalties for children were often reduced. Nevertheless, as miniature adults they participated in adversary proceedings and

suffered adult-type punishments for criminal activity. Children received special consideration in noncriminal matters, however.

The juvenile court was not the first institution to deal with the problems of children. Chancery courts were created in fifteenth-century England to deal with children whose parents failed to provide support, care, or supervision. The chancery court was commissioned by the king, acting as *parens patriae* (father of the country), to see that parents fulfilled their obligations to children. Where parents failed to comply, chancery courts typically operated *in loco parentis* (in place of parents). Parental custody was revoked in favor of the court. Chancery courts did not handle delinquency cases but dealt with what are now called neglected or dependent children or those in need of supervision. The court acted on behalf of the child to provide care or protect and administer property. The equity philosophy of the courts reflected the concepts of flexibility, guardianship, and the balancing of interests for the general welfare in order to achieve a fair result.[1]

The chancery court principle was adopted in the United States by way of the state courts. Some states established special chancery courts; others provided limited equity jurisdiction to the regular courts.[2] These courts, like the chancery courts of England, did not extend their jurisdiction to law-violating youths.[3]

Although the legal origins of the juvenile court are not clear, there is reason to believe that important forerunners of the juvenile courts included the equity jurisdiction of English chancery courts and common law doctrines that limited the criminal responsibility of children.[4] Nevertheless, the first efforts to provide distinctive treatment for delinquent youths rested in correctional reform.

Penal Reform

The early eighteenth century saw a move for reform of correctional institutions. Conditions of prisoners and prison facilities were appalling. Overcrowding, unsanitary conditions, and the mixing of children with adults concerned many civic-minded individuals. Recidivism rates suggested that the jails were no more than schools for crime. Little hope was expressed for the rehabilitation of older, hardened criminals, but there was some optimism that the children could be saved from a life of crime if they could escape the influence of older prisoners.

Beginning in 1825 with the founding of the New York City House of Refuge, some states began to provide separate correctional facilities for juveniles. In addition, a form of probation was first tried in 1841 as a way to treat children in the community while they were under the supervision of a court. By the end of the nineteenth century in the United States, criminal courts were sentencing more and more juveniles to training schools or placing them on probation rather than sending them to adult prisons.

The failure of the new juvenile correctional facilities to rehabilitate young law violators was a matter of concern to the reformers. It became clear that separate facilities was not the solution to the problem. Children continued to share facilities with adults while awaiting trial. The criminal trial and punitive orientation of the criminal court remained.

By the 1890s many reforms had been instituted to protect juveniles from criminal influences. Laws had been passed that provided punishments for adults who corrupted children. Separate correctional facilities for children was an idea that had found acceptance throughout the country. Probation was no longer an experiment in some areas. Separate court hearings for juveniles had been used in several states. Where these reforms had been fully instituted, attention was turned to cleaning up or revitalizing the juvenile correction facilities.

In this atmosphere of reform, it was only a matter of time before the innovations would spread, piecemeal, throughout the country. The fact that the juvenile court was created in Chicago, at a time when the entire system for juveniles had collapsed, enabled the reformers to guide the direction of this new institution. The system created by the Juvenile Court Act of 1899 was more than reform—it was a new invention.

COURT PHILOSOPHY AND PROCEDURE

The reformers pressed for significant changes in dealing with troublesome children. Many of the problems of youths were believed to be a direct result of immaturity and lack of guidance. They wanted an agency that would act as an understanding parent, assuming responsibility for the care, custody, and discipline of wayward youths. The juvenile court would be quite different from the criminal court. Because of their immaturity, children could not be expected to understand the punitive nature of the criminal justice system and the use of punishment as a deterrent. Each child was to be individually guided out of an undesirable situation and retrained to responsible citizenship free from the contamination of adult criminals.

The phrase *parens patriae* provides an adequate summary of the legal and social philosophy envisioned for the court by the reformers. Case 13.1 illustrates this philosophy in practice.

Court Proceedings

The new philosophy called for a new kind of court with new procedures, new personnel, and a treatment orientation. The juvenile court acts provided legal authorization and established guidelines for implementation. The new juvenile courts were to be distinctively different from criminal courts. Juvenile cases were to be heard in a separate designated courtroom under the direction of a judge appointed to hear juvenile cases. Informal summary proceedings were to be used rather than the formal adversary procedures that characterized the criminal court. Probation officers were to be provided to compile information that the judge might read for a better understanding of the child's background and problems. The probation officer was also to have responsibility for supervising children placed on probation.

The new procedures were designed to provide individualized treatment and prevent the stigmatization of adjudicated youths. Because the proceeding was conducted in the interest of the child, adversary procedures were abolished. A child could not be convicted of an offense. It was believed that this development reduced the stigma attached to the child. Furthermore, since the child had nothing to lose by admitting to his actions, communications channels were opened up between the child and the judge as a father figure. Understanding, diagnosis of problem areas, treatment, and child welfare were considered more important than mere guilt or innocence. This aspect of the court, considered of paramount importance to the reformers, has drawn a great deal of attention from modern critics of the court.

Treatment methods for juveniles under the new court were not significantly different from those levied on adult criminals. The court acts did specify that children be separated from adults in all stages of the justice system. However, the facilities to be provided for youths were not different in kind from those used by adults.

```
CASE 13.1
TROUBLE IN THE COURT

    Juveniles are not tried in juvenile court for
committing an offense. Underlying disturbances, not
offenses, are the defining characteristic of a
delinquent. Emerson indicates that court personnel
look for cues that might suggest that a child has
deeper underlying problems requiring specialized
treatment. He gives several examples in which this
orientation is present:

    • [A judge comments.] We look for tip offs that
      something is really wrong. We get some tip offs
      just from the face-sheet; truancy, school
      attendance, conduct, and effort marks . . .
      If you get something there, you know there's
      trouble. When you get truancy or bad conduct
      plus the delinquency, there's definitely
      something wrong.
    • [A probation officer speaks.] The first time a
      child appears in court no stone should be left
      unturned "to find out what the problem is." . .
    • [A judge dealing with two female delinquents.]
      There's something going on with them. I'm
      not worried about the stealing but that brings
      it to a head.

    Source: Robert M. Emerson, Judging Delinquents (Chicago:
Aldine, 1969), pp. 18, 84, 88–89.
```

GROWTH OF THE JUVENILE JUSTICE SYSTEM

The juvenile court idea spread across the country with unusual speed. Within 12 years, 22 states had adopted juvenile court measures. By 1925 there was provision for juvenile courts in all but two states.[5] Even these states fell in line by 1945. The passage of juvenile court statutes, however, did not provide a final effective solution to the problem of juvenile delinquency.

Enabling legislation for the juvenile courts was far from uniform from one jurisdiction to another. In most states, the county is the jurisdictional unit. Juvenile courts organized under the county system are generally a part of some other general court, usually a probate, county, or circuit court. The weakness of this type of system has been the financial inability of most counties to afford full-time juvenile court specialists. In rural areas, light caseloads make a full-time court impractical.[6]

In a few states, juvenile courts are created by special legislation with only city-wide jurisdiction. Juvenile courts established in this manner are often made a part of a family or domestic relations court having broad jurisdiction over an assortment of family matters.[7] Although these courts have been hailed as a significant advance in the protection of juvenile offenders, they have not been immune to criticism. These courts assume an even greater scope of jurisdiction over juveniles than do most courts on the county system. They may also impede the systematic development of state-wide systems of juvenile justice.

Only a few states have state-financed and state-administered juvenile court systems. In these systems, the juvenile courts operate in large districts with full-time judges and court personnel selected on the basis of qualifications in the area of delinquency.[8] The benefits and success of this type of jurisdictional system have been endorsed by the Council of Judges of the National Council on Crime and Delinquency.[9] The lack of standardization of juvenile courts has created many barriers to the creation of a true system of juvenile justice in the United States.

The juvenile court concept has as its primary goal the protection and treatment of wayward youths. The passage of the juvenile court statutes did not, however, automatically establish the juvenile court system the reformers had had in mind. A Children's Bureau survey in 1920 found that only 16 percent of the juvenile courts surveyed met the minimum criteria of separate hearings for children, a regular authorized probation service, and recorded social investigation.[10] A similar government-sponsored survey conducted in 1966 revealed that significant gaps still remained between the juvenile court ideal and actual practice.[11]

Although the juvenile court has not reached the expectations of the reformers, it has not stood still. Several developments have produced change in the juvenile court. Some of the changes have been substantial, while others have been more superficial.

Pressures for Change

Several developments brought the court philosophy under scrutiny and criticism. The first problem to surface was the condition of treatment facilities prescribed by the courts. During the 1940s the nation's training schools were nothing more than miniature prisons. Scandal after scandal was exposed, convincing many authorities that institutional treatment was ineffective. The gravity of possible court dispositions led some criminologists to scrutinize the implications of the treatment philosophy.[12] The treatment orientation of the court was criticized for its lack of concern with justice.[13] In the interest of treatment, children were found to be imprisoned for minor offenses such as truancy and disobedience.

Additional pressure for changes in court procedure and jurisdictional scope came from the United Nations. The Second United Nations Conference on the Prevention of Crime and the Treatment of Offenders recommended that the definition of delinquency be restricted to violations of the criminal law.

As a result of these developments, attempts have been made in some states to differentiate between juveniles who have committed offenses defined by criminal statutes and those who need guidance or supervision. Other jurisdictions have responded by restoring limited due process rights to juveniles. The President's Commission on Law Enforcement and Administration of Justice has recommended the use of informal diversion and the development of Youth Services Bureaus on a voluntary basis.[14] A few such agencies have been set up on an experimental basis. However, little systematic evaluation has been conducted to determine their effectiveness. There is some indication, however, that the existence of these agencies may result in an increase in the number of juveniles coming to the attention of official agencies.[15]

Other pressures for change have come from the Supreme Court. As recently as 1955 in the *Holmes* case, the Court took a noninterference stance on the philosophy of *parens patriae* embraced by the juvenile courts. However, in the years since World War II the Supreme Court has shifted its position in regard to juvenile justice. In 1967 the Court ruled in the *Gault* case that due process could not be denied juveniles in any court. Specifically, juveniles were to be given a notice of charges, the right to retain a lawyer, freedom from self-incrimination, and the right to confront witnesses and/or accusers. Even more significant in rejecting the juvenile court philosophy was the *Winship* decision in 1970. The Court ruled that delinquency must be proved beyond reasonable doubt. No longer was guilt to be assumed and treatment routinely dispensed. Rather, justice was to be the primary concern of the juvenile courts.

The Supreme Court reforms did not include the allowance of full rights to juveniles, however. Still denied is the right to jury trial and routine appeal. As a consequence of these omissions, the reforms drawn by the Court have not been fully implemented. No remedies are available to children whose judges refuse to implement the reforms.

Effects of Reform

The effectiveness of procedural reform is not clear. Evidence is contradictory. Lemert's study of the effects of procedural reform in California suggests that the use of a defense counsel in juvenile cases has resulted in larger numbers of dismissals and fewer removals from the home.[16] Duffee and Siegal, however, report that juveniles who had been represented by lawyers received more severe court dispositions.[17]

It is apparent that the juvenile court is in a state of flux at present. Despite recent changes in juvenile codes, many courts still conduct hearings in the old, informal way. The change is far from complete; the court continues to evolve.

TABLE 13.1 TERMINOLOGY OF THE JUVENILE JUSTICE SYSTEM

JUVENILE TERM	DEFINITION	ADULT EQUIVALENT
Summons	notice to appear for questioning and possible binding over to court	warrant
Take into custody	securing physical custody of an alleged offender by police	arrest
Initial hearing	meeting at which accused hears allegations against him or her and is assigned a court date	arraignment
Petition	document stating alleged violations of accused	complaint, indictment
Detention	holding in custody prior to judicial determination	pretrial jail
Hearing	court proceeding to determine disposition of case of accused	trial
Finding of involvement or adjudication	decision of court that accused has committed alleged offenses	conviction
Commitment or disposition	decision by judge that adjudicated individual be treated in a particular manner	sentence
Probation	supervision of an adjudicated individual after court hearing without prior commitment to an institution	probation
Aftercare	supervision of an individual after conditional release from a correctional institution	parole

The Language of the Juvenile Justice System

One of the major concerns of the juvenile court has been to reduce the stigmatization of youths coming under its jurisdiction. To this end a new "legalese" has evolved throughout the juvenile justice system to accentuate the noncriminal nature of juvenile proceedings. Some of these terms are given in Table 13.1 along with their definitions and equivalent adult terminology. Whatever the terms used, it is evident that the juvenile justice system is little more than an informal model of the criminal justice system minus significant procedural safeguards.

The judge may listen to evidence and social investigations and deliver a decision without a jury trial and, until recently, without provision for legal counsel to represent the juvenile. A juvenile is not arrested but rather taken into police custody. The juvenile is not sent to prison but to a training school, reformatory, forestry camp, or other institution that is often similar to a prison regardless of the term applied to it.

DISTINCTIONS BETWEEN CLIENTS

More important are the distinctions made between delinquent youths and PINS or MINS. The Second United Nations Congress on the Prevention of Crime and the Treatment of Offenders recommended that the term *juvenile delinquency* be restricted to violations of criminal law. Offenses that applied to juveniles but not to adults should not be created, even if the prohibited acts are minor offenses, seek to protect juveniles, or reflect maladjusted behavior. The United Nations further suggested that juvenile problems such as truancy and incorrigibility should be handled by the schools, the family, or social welfare agencies but not by the juvenile justice system, because acts of this type are not criminal.[18]

Several states began to revise their juvenile codes in the early 1960s. New York enacted the Family Court Act (1963), which distinguished between juvenile delinquents and PINS. The traditional authority of the juvenile court was reserved in the case of delinquents but restricted for PINS. Children who came under the PINS classification could not be detained by police or committed to a correctional institution. A similar statute was enacted in Illinois in 1966. This new juvenile court act distinguished between delinquents and MINS. MINS have a status and safeguards that are similar to those adopted in New York for PINS. California law no longer uses the delinquent category. Distinctions are made between dependent children (those neglected by their family or guardian or those without adult support) and wards of the court (those who constitute discipline problems or who have violated legal statutes).

EFFECTS OF THE NEW TERMINOLOGY

The different terms used in the juvenile justice system are sometimes merely euphemisms. For example, the distinction between a training school and an adult prison may be little more than a difference in terminology. On the other hand, some terms signify real differences in procedure and handling. The difference, for example, between a hearing and a trial for adults is often very real. Juveniles have been denied jury trial, representation by counsel (at least until the *Gault* case in 1967[19]), protection against self-incrimination, and other procedural rights normally provided to adults accused of a crime. Juveniles are committed to training schools on the "preponderance of the evidence" while adults are freed on "a reasonable doubt." A seemingly minor difference in language can often have important consequences for juveniles who find themselves in the clutches of the juvenile court.

New efforts to distinguish between law violators and dependent or neglected children may either represent a significant development in the evolution of the juvenile court or signal its end. There is little doubt that children need different types of care and treatment from adults. Some states have begun restructuring the court system in order to provide appropriate treatment for juveniles.

SCOPE AND POWER OF THE JUVENILE COURT

The juvenile court was designed to operate in the interests of the juveniles who come before it. Persons are not found guilty but are rather adjudicated delinquent, neglected, or in need of care and supervision. The ideal is individualized treatment tailored to the experience and needs of each child. The state assumes guardianship over the child where parental control is lacking or lax. All proceedings are initiated on behalf of, or in the interest of, the youngster, not against him. Immense authority is vested in the court, but it is not without limitation.

Jurisdiction

The line that separates jurisdiction in the criminal and juvenile courts is often blurred. Frequently their authority is overlapping. Juvenile courts hold several types of jurisdiction. The applicable jurisdiction is defined for the juvenile court by the type of offense and/or age of the offender.

EXCLUSIVE JURISDICTION

The juvenile court has exclusive jurisdiction when sole authority is vested in the court. With exclusive jurisdiction there is no provision for delegating responsibility to other judicial agencies. Several types of cases fall under the exclusive jurisdiction of the juvenile court. Juveniles who commit minor offenses or engage in behavior that is prohibited only to juveniles are cases that routinely come under the exclusive authority of the juvenile court. In addition, MINS and PINS are routinely handled by the juvenile court (or family court), which prescribes appropriate care. Few states (Texas is an exception) provide for exclusive jurisdiction to the juvenile court for all youngsters within statutory age limits without qualification.[20] Several states specify exclusive jurisdiction for children under the age of majority unless a capital offense is involved (Vermont, Iowa, and Indiana).[21]

In some states exclusive jurisdiction is vested in the criminal courts, regardless of the age of the offender, if the offense is of a particular type. A felony offense, such as the killing of a police officer, or other capital offense, for which the punishment may be execution or a long sentence, is frequently within the exclusive jurisdiction of the criminal courts.

ORIGINAL JURISDICTION

A juvenile court has original jurisdiction in cases in which the court has priority. Here the authority to handle cases may be transferred to another court by waiver. Various states specify original jurisdiction by statute (Alaska, Florida, Hawaii, Missouri, Utah).[22] Where original, but not exclusive, jurisdiction is vested in the juvenile court, the juvenile judge may waive jurisdiction and transfer a case to the criminal court, where the juvenile is tried as an adult. If the youngster is 14, 16, or 18 or older (the age varies from state to state) and the offense is a serious felony if committed by adults, transfer to an adult court may be justified. Some older offenders may not benefit from further handling in a juvenile institution, while the need for protection of the society may suggest adult handling is necessary.[23] The number of such cases is relatively small and should include only the most difficult cases in which juveniles are already committed to criminal careers. No standard lower age limit applies nationally for the handling of juvenile offenders by the criminal courts. The National Council of Juvenile Court Judges proposed setting the lower age limit for criminal court handling at 14 years, but other authorities, such as the National Council on Crime and Delinquency, prefer age 18 for the lower limit.[24]

CONCURRENT JURISDICTION

Concurrent jurisdiction is found where there are no distinct jurisdictional boundaries. Neither the juvenile court nor the criminal court has priority or sole responsibility for a particular case. In most states, the juvenile court and the criminal courts have concurrent or overlapping jurisdiction in cases that involve felonies and older offenders (California, Colorado, Illinois, Michigan).[25] Informal procedures may evolve in these cases to facilitate the acceptance of such cases by one court or the other.

Jurisdictional Standards

In the United States, there are no uniform age limits for juvenile or criminal jurisdiction. As a general rule, a juvenile court has jurisdiction after the age of 7. Before this age, children are handled informally by law enforcement authorities and private social agencies. The line of authority that divides juvenile and criminal court jurisdiction is much less clearly drawn. The power and perceived legitimacy of the criminal courts is such that they frequently become a dominant force in the handling of juvenile offenders.

Juveniles are sometimes tried in the adult criminal courts, and some have been sentenced to terms in adult prisons. This practice is limited, however. Judicial authorities generally concede that much harm may result from sentencing young first offenders to terms in adult prisons. The young offender may learn advanced criminal attitudes and techniques through association with older and more sophisticated criminals. Legal or administrative policies have evolved to deal with such cases. A case may be transferred to the juvenile court for sentensing or disposition, charges may be reduced or dismissed, the case may be continued without judgment during good behavior, or probation may be granted. The severe, punitive treatment of juveniles that may result from adult criminal proceedings may be lessened by the use of these procedures and may reduce the likelihood of long-term harm to the juvenile.

COURT-APPROVED PROGRAMS

Cases that come before the juvenile court are subject to a wide variety of dispositions. The juvenile judge has considerable discretion in handling any case; juvenile court statutes do not specify a range of "sentences" that may be applied in a given case. The determinant sentences (minimum and maximum legal requirements) offered in the criminal statutes do not apply to youths.

Three broad types of dispositions may be used by the juvenile court judge: informal treatment, community-based supervision, or commitment.

Informal Treatment Practices

When an informal disposition is used, no adjudicatory judgment is entered on the juvenile's record. Several different practices come under this category of disposition. Some are very simple, requiring no further court action. The juvenile's case may simply be dismissed. Others require organization and planning, making them more complex. Over half of the cases that come before the juvenile court are disposed of without a formal hearing. Several informal practices are discussed below. Although this discussion does not cover the full range of informal procedures, it does suggest the variety of alternatives available.

PRELIMINARY CONFERENCE

The juvenile judge (or another officer of the court) may request a conference with the juvenile and his or her family. Participation by the parents is entirely voluntary. If it is determined that the child's behavior is a result of resolvable problems in the home situation, the judge will discuss the possible solutions with the parents and the child. Where arrangements can be made to modify or eliminate the elements that are believed to trigger the child's behavior, the judge may dismiss the case without further deliberation or court hearing. The agreements hammered out in the informal meeting are not legally binding on the parents or juvenile involved. In some cases, the court officer may wish to hold the case open until the proposed conditions are met.

CONSENT AGREEMENTS

Some officials believe that adjudication by the juvenile court is a stigmatizing process. Judges who hold this opinion may be reluctant to use the official authority of the court even where the need for treatment is evident. The consent agreement enables the judge to pro-

vide treatment without applying the delinquent label. After consideration of the juvenile's social history and the facts surrounding the
alleged misbehavior, the judge will come to a decision regarding the
treatment that would promote the best interests of the child. The judge
may suggest that the parents or guardian of the child assume responsibility for enrolling the offender in appropriate community programs
or utilize existing facilities. If the parents consent, the judge may continue the case with the promise to dismiss after the program is successfully completed.

There is some suggestion that programs of this type operate
informally in many jurisdictions throughout the country. However,
there is little indication of the precise manner in which consent agreements are arrived at or the success of these programs in changing the
behavior of the youth involved. A Presidential Commission has suggested that the procedures should be made more formal and constitute legally binding agreements between the juvenile and the juvenile
court.[26]

CONDITIONAL RELIEF

A juvenile may appear before a juvenile judge after a period of
detention promising to reform his or her behavior. The judge has the
option of releasing the juvenile without official action. Aware that
he or she has spent a period of time in detention, the judge may dis-
creetly suggest the possible consequences of future juvenile misbehavior. The child is informed that he or she will be allowed to return
home following this appearance but that further misconduct will be
dealt with more severely. Because this disposition is unofficial and is
not entered into the record as a formal disposition, behavior so sanctioned may be used in subsequent proceedings as evidence to support
a finding of delinquency.

Where the juvenile justice system is not fully elaborated with
supportive treatment agencies in the community, this method of
handling may be relatively popular. The practice of using detention as
a punitive measure has been soundly condemned by the President's
Commission.[27]

Community-Based Supervision

A treatment program is an official disposition if it follows a
finding of delinquency. Not all official dispositions are equally formalized or structured; however, each disposition approach uses the authority and supervisory capacity of the juvenile court to achieve a change
in the juvenile's behavior. Most of these involve supervision of the
child in the community setting. The commitment alternative (discussed in Chapter 14) involves removal from the community and is
generally used only as a last resort for older, more serious offenders.
Community-based treatment alternatives are discussed below.

CONDITIONAL OR SUSPENDED SENTENCE

Following a finding of delinquency, the next logical step in the juvenile justice program is the disposition. At this point, the juvenile judge's staff generally provides a social investigation report prepared to provide for the judge information upon which to base a decision that will be in the best interests of the child. Under certain circumstances, the judge may decide that no treatment program is indicated and delay disposition until additional evidence of the child's general behavior patterns is available. Where good behavior ensues, the case may remain open indefinitely.

A judge may, alternatively, specify a disposition but delay its imposition on the juvenile. The child is released to his parents who agree to supervise his behavior with the understanding that the disposition will be vacated or suspended if the child does not misbehave within a specified time period. Of course, if the agreement is not carried out, the youth's formal disposition will be imposed.

Either of these dispositions are informal arrangements which involve continuing supervision by the court. In light of the heavy caseloads that often characterize the system, it is not surprising that these procedures are often downgraded in favor of more standardized methods of disposition that can be more easily monitored by the court.

PROBATION

Disapproval without official supervision may be ineffective in discouraging unacceptable behavior. Where there is little threat of danger to the community as a result of a juvenile's release, probation may be the solution specified in the juvenile court disposition. Under a probation disposition, the delinquent is released into the community under the guidance and supervision of an officer of the court.

The goal of probation is to rehabilitate the juvenile offender. In order to accomplish this goal, the court generally imposes conditions that must be met by the juvenile to show evidence of progress in the program. The child is, in essence, given another chance to establish his or her worth as a normal juvenile. The assumption of probation is that a youth who is given guidance and assistance will make an adjustment to the demands of community life.

Unfortunately, however, the ideal conception does not always coincide with probation in practice. Probation officers are often evaluated in terms of their failure rates. The most glaring failure is an inability to deter serious misbehavior. The primary preoccupation of juvenile probation officers may be the demand that they keep their juvenile charges in line to prevent trouble. Under these circumstances, supervision may be emphasized to the detriment of guidance goals. Probation often becomes more concerned with short term control mechanisms which erect physical barriers to delinquent behavior than with measures to effect rehabilitation of youth.

Commitment

The judge may prescribe treatment in a correctional facility—training school, forestry camp, group home, foster home, mental institution, or diagnostic center. Commitments are often viewed as the most severe of all the alternatives available to the juvenile judge. As a result, most judges approach this alternative with a degree of caution and prefer to use less severe treatment whenever possible.

An older youth who commits relatively serious offenses or who has repeatedly been before the court is more likely to receive the commitment alternative. On the other hand, a younger child appearing for a first offense, with some helpful and interested adult present, will generally be given more lenient treatment. Even though commitment is not a highly favored alternative disposition, a large number of children are placed in correctional facilities each year. Correctional facilities for juveniles will be discussed in greater detail in Chapter 15.

CONSTITUTIONAL PROTECTIONS FOR THE OFFENDER

Because the juvenile court acts on behalf of children, full constitutional rights have not generally been guaranteed to juveniles accused of committing criminal acts. The Supreme Court justified this practice in the *Holmes* decision (1955), stating: "Since juvenile courts are not criminal courts, the constitutional rights granted to persons accused of crime are not applicable to children brought before them."[28] The Supreme Court reiterated the juvenile court philosophy, suggesting that Holmes was not being punished for stealing an auto. The juvenile court's efforts were aimed at saving Holmes from a life of crime. Therefore considerations of constitutional safeguards are invalid when the protection and guidance of juveniles are involved.

Traditionally, courts determine guilt or innocence, providing punishments consistent with the seriousness of the offense when guilt is determined. The juvenile court, however, has the dual role of determining involvement and acting as a social welfare agency to provide care and treatment for juveniles. Constraints exist in this dual role, and many courts have vacillated between the two. The juvenile court, however, is less oriented to determination of involvement than to treatment. As a result, the juvenile court has tended to downgrade due process safeguards implicit in adult criminal proceedings. The court may have abandoned a concern for justice in its quest for treatment. Punishments for juveniles have not been selected to fit the offense. Instead, probation, imprisonment, and parole are assigned to juveniles on the basis of court investigatory reports that evaluate the overall social, psychological, and biographical background of the juvenile. Long terms in training schools are often given to juveniles, while similar offenses bring small fines or are ignored if committed by adults.

Recent Advances

Gerald Francis Gault was adjudicated delinquent in 1964 and sentenced to the state industrial school for the period of his minority.[29] Gault was 15 and was, in effect, given an indeterminant disposition which could result in incarceration for as many as six years. The charge against Gault was "lewd phone calls"—an act prohibited by the Arizona Criminal Code, which specified that anyone who used vulgar, abusive, or obscene language was guilty of a misdemeanor. The penalty for adults was a fine of 5 to 50 dollars or imprisonment for a few months.

When Gault and his friend Ronald Lewis were taken into custody, Gault's parents were working and not at home. No attempt was made to inform the parents that their son had been arrested and taken to a detention home. A petition was filed in juvenile court the next day, but it was not served on the Gault family, who had learned of young Gault's imprisonment from neighbors.

When the hearing was held in the chambers of the juvenile judge, the complaining witness was not present. Gerald Gault did not have a lawyer, no one was sworn in at the hearing, and no court transcript or recording of the hearing was made. Gault was questioned by the juvenile judge and may have admitted to making the call and some of the lewd remarks. Gault was returned to the detention home while the judge considered appropriate actions. The Gault family was notified of further hearings by a letter from the probation officer on plain (nonletterhead) stationery. At the new hearing, a "referral report" was presented but was not provided to Gerald or his family. Gerald Gault was committed to the state training school.

On May 15, 1967, the Supreme Court considered the Gault case. Justice Abe Fortas, in writing the majority opinion, said:

> Neither the fourteenth amendment nor the Bill of Rights is for adults only. Under our constitution, the condition of being a boy does not justify a kangaroo court.

The Gault decision represented a major shift in legal opinion regarding the rights of juveniles accused of criminal offenses. Among the rights to be extended to juveniles were (1) the right to receive notice of the charges against them, (2) the right to be represented by counsel, (3) the right to face witnesses and accusers while cross-examining them, (4) the right to remain silent and refuse to answer questions that might result in self-incrimination, and (5) the right to a transcript of all proceedings.

In the *Winship* decision (1970) the Supreme Court ruled that delinquency must be proven beyond a reasonable doubt.[30] In *McKeiver v. Pennsylvania* (1971), the Supreme Court ruled that juveniles accused of delinquent acts may be eligible for jury trials.[31]

The traditional treatment function of the juvenile court was not completely deposed by these rulings. However, the trend suggests that the primary function of the court should be the assessment of guilt or innocence, with greater emphasis being placed on the due process provisions of the United States Constitution. Partially in response to the *Gault* decision, new juvenile court statutes or revisions of existing acts have been passed in many states.[32] These statutes have incorporated features suggested by the Standard Juvenile Court Act[33] and the Model Rules for Juvenile Courts.[34]

Other due process issues have also received the attention of the courts. The *Miranda* rules provide the extension of the right to counsel to suspects in a criminal case. These rights have been implemented for juveniles only in cases in which the juvenile has been charged with a criminal act. Even in this situation, rights may be waived with parental consent.[35] Other rights that may eventually be extended to juveniles include a speedy trial and protection from double jeopardy.[36]

The Road Ahead

Some experts suggest that cases such as truancy, incorrigibility, runaways, and curfew violations should not be brought to the juvenile court.[37] Behavior that does not constitute criminal action if committed by an adult is not well-enough defined to fit under rules of procedure evolving in the juvenile court. Juveniles who display noncriminal but undesirable behavior might be more effectively handled as PINS or MINS. These youngsters could then be diverted to traditional social service agencies.

The juvenile court has changed in recent years, but it may be a long time before all juveniles coming before the juvenile court enjoy the rights guaranteed adult offenders. Despite recent court ruling and changes in the juvenile codes, juvenile courts frequently retain informal procedures that deny due process. Of course, when the right to appeal is absent, as it is in juvenile cases, judicial review and reversals of rulings or dispositions are virtually impossible. The right to appeal is essential if juveniles are to be granted full constitutional rights. Appeal provides a way to bring defiant judges and inappropriate procedures in line with recent statutes and court rulings.

Juvenile courts exercise considerable power over juveniles. Included in this power is the authority to deny basic rights and privileges to youths. The juvenile court may, for example, consider evidence that would not be admissible in a criminal court. These powers have sometimes been used in a highhanded and injudicious manner in the court. The justification for this vast power may be found in the philosophy of the court. *Parens patriae, in loco parentis,* "treatment," and child welfare doctrines have been used to strengthen the authority of the state over children and youths. Because the court was meant to determine the best method of individualized training and rehabilitation for troubled children, wide latitude was given the officers of the court. In the interest of treatment and rehabilitation, justice and equity was, and is, often forgotten.[38]

THE JUVENILE COURT JUDGE

Given the immense power and discretion of his or her office, the court judge needs to be extraordinarily well qualified to deal with children and legal matters. The record suggests that improvement needs to be made in this area.

Demographic Characteristics

McCune and Skoler, in a profile of judges drawn in 1965, reported that 96 percent of the juvenile court judges in the United States were males, with a median age of 53.[39] Most of the judges were married (93 percent), with under 1 percent either divorced or separated. This report suggests that juvenile judges are more likely to be married and have a stable marriage than are adults in the general population. Juvenile court judges were reported to have large families. They were also more likely to be recruited from middle-class, Protestant backgrounds.

Training

Seventy percent of the juvenile judges had completed at least two years of college, the normal requirement for entrance to law school when the judges were completing undergraduate training. Forty-nine percent did not have an undergraduate degree, and 19 percent had had no college education. Seventy-one percent had a law degree, but 24 percent had received no legal education at all. Only 5 percent had received additional legal education beyond the basic law degree, but 8 percent had undertaken graduate work in education, business administration, political science, economics, social work, or medicine.[40]

Recruitment and Commitment

The majority of juvenile court judges are elected to their offices. The rest are appointed to office by public officials or citizens committees. It is apparent that politics is an important feature of their life styles. Political popularity, however, is no guarantee that a judge will have the expertise needed to deal with the problems of children that come before him or her.

Juvenile matters constitute only a minor part of the workload of most juvenile judges. Only 26 percent of the juvenile judges in the McCune and Skoler study devoted half of their time or more to juvenile justice matters. On the other hand, 72 percent spent one-fourth or less of their time on the juvenile court, while about 5 percent classified themselves as full-time juvenile court judges.[41] In addition to delinquency, dependency, and neglect cases, most juvenile judges handle related matters such as custody, guardianship, contributing-to-delinquency charges, termination of parental rights, traffic violations, non-support, adoption, and paternity cases. The juvenile court judge, in many jurisdictions, must handle public relations matters while interpreting the actions of the court to the community. He or she must also administer the services of the court and coordinate court services with a variety of community service agencies. The philosophy and specialized nature of the court demands specialized training and care. Instead, the juvenile court has often become a part of the existing judicial structure without sufficient recognition of the specialized and often demanding nature of its task.[42]

WRITTEN STANDARDS

The National Council on Crime and Delinquency, in cooperation with the National Council of Juvenile Court Judges, listed personal qualifications for a juvenile court judge.[43] A juvenile judge should (1) be an experienced and successful lawyer; (2) be able to benefit from the knowledge and skill of people trained in the behavioral sciences; (3) be understanding, sympathetic, and dedicated to helping others; (4) be hard working and able to work long hours; (5) act as a leader in the community to develop facilities for juveniles and families; (6) work with all individuals and agencies that want to help juveniles; and (7) have humility. To ensure that these qualifications are instituted, it may be important to adopt new procedures for the selection and recruitment of judges for the juvenile court. In addition, juvenile judges must be relieved of some of their duties in order to devote more time and energy to the specialized treatment of juvenile cases.

Juvenile Court Staff

The judge is the center of any court, but in the larger urban areas the work of the judge may be supplemented by numerous specialized personnel. Some of the more common categories of juvenile court staffs are described below.

REFEREE

The referee is sometimes called a commissioner or master. In many states the law provides that a juvenile judge may appoint a referee to assist him by hearing cases and recommending dispositions. The referee is not required to have legal training, and some judges use social workers as referees to handle simple cases. A woman, for example, may be appointed to deal with cases involving females.

PROBATION STAFF

The probation staff is used to complete social evaluations and reports for each case. In addition, they are expected to design probation plans and supervise juveniles placed in their care to assure that rehabilitation programs are completed. Further discussion of probation

is found in Chapter 14, but it should be stressed that effective probation depends to a large measure on the quality and the quantity of the
staff available to the court.

DETENTION STAFF

The size of the detention staff depends on the size of the detention facility. The staff may run from a husband and wife in a small
facility to a staff of a hundred or more in a large urban detention home.
A diverse group of workers may be associated with the detention
facility. Cooks, secretaries, maintenance personnel, social workers,
teachers, and clinical psychologists may be used as support staff for the
head of the detention facility.

OTHER COURT PERSONNEL

A court clerk is often used to keep legal records. This officer of
the court has the responsibility of placing cases on the docket, prepar-
ing calendars, and keeping confidential records. The court reporter
makes a stenographic record, or transcript, of court proceedings and
furnishes copies to those who are legally entitled to them. A bailiff or
court officer is often present in a juvenile court. The bailiff has responsibility for keeping order in the court. He may also be responsible
for keeping unauthorized persons from entering and escort juveniles
into and out of the courtroom for the hearing. He may also be given
charge of the juvenile after the hearing before transfer to a training
school. In addition, he may serve subpoenas and notices in some
courts.

COMMUNITY SERVICE AGENCIES AND PERSONNEL

Each community usually has a variety of agencies and personnel
services which are available to the court. In large cities, juvenile courts
have hired psychiatrists, psychologists, nurses, and doctors to aid the
court in the disposition of cases. In addition, youth service bureaus,
welfare agencies, YMCAs, YWCAs, boys clubs, and other agencies or
individuals may be enlisted or coordinated by the juvenile judge in
efforts to prevent delinquency and rehabilitate offenders.

The Judge as Policy Maker

Juvenile court judges generally have both judicial and administrative responsibilities. They not only determine questions of fact and law
but are also responsible for seeing that their decisions are carried out.
Thus the judge has the primary authority to formulate policy, set
service standards for juveniles, and oversee public relations. In many
ways the judge sets the operational philosophy of a court and determines its direction. His court may be run on a criminal model, which
seeks to punish juveniles, or a corrective model, which seeks to rehabilitate them. If the judge is interested primarily in rehabilitation,

he will make extensive use of community service agencies. Furthermore, if the model is to be effective, the judge must do more than just use the services—he must help ensure that they are adequate to meet the needs of the youngsters who will use them. To obtain and maintain adequate social service agencies and personnel, the judge must interpret the needs of the court to the community and ensure that the community is aware of the services available to children.[44]

The juvenile judge may not administer court services directly. Instead, a probation officer or other official may be appointed as chief administrator. In courts where the probation department is a part of the structure of the court, a probation officer is often used; but this procedure does not relieve the judge of his ultimate responsibility for policy formulation and administration.

THE JUVENILE COURT IN ACTION

The function of the juvenile court is to investigate all cases that fall under its jurisdiction and provide equitable plans to protect the welfare of juveniles under its care. This function is carried out through the processes that distinguish the juvenile court from the criminal court.

Intake and Classification

The juvenile court machinery is put into operation when a complaint is filed against a juvenile. The petition can originate from many sources. A school official, parent, neighbor, or any other "responsible" adult may initiate a petition calling for juvenile court action. The probation department attached to the court usually operates an intake department to screen incoming cases. Probation department intake personnel review each case to establish the facts surrounding it and generate a social history report for the use of the court. Most juveniles have at this point already been through a police screening process, because most complaints are channeled through the police department. The juvenile may already be in a detention facility, in a jail, or on informal supervision by the police or the probation department.

After review of the case, the intake department may make an informal disposition. The youngster may be released to his or her parents, placed on informal supervision with a probation officer from the department, or referred to a community agency. Some probation departments accept the premise that the interests of the juvenile are better served if he or she is handled in an informal manner without official contact with the juvenile court. It is believed that formal contact results in stigmatization and further delinquency. Informal handling also prevents the development of extensive records on a juvenile which may find their way to prospective employers or the military even though they are supposed to be secret and confidential.

The intake unit of the probation department may determine,

however, that further action is necessary. A formal petition can be initiated by the department. The petition states the facts or circumstances surrounding the case. Once a formal petition is filed, the case must be presented for a preliminary court hearing. In the initial hearing, the juvenile court judge must decide whether the facts warrant further court action. At this point, the case may be dismissed unconditionally or dismissed with a suggestion for voluntary action, or an adjudicatory hearing may be sought.

Adjudication Hearing

The youth and witnesses are questioned about the alleged offense, the facts, and the circumstances surrounding the case. If the evidence is not sufficient, the case can be dismissed at this hearing. However, a juvenile may be adjudicated delinquent at this time and officially labeled a delinquent. In addition, a finding of neglect, dependency, in need of supervision, and so on may be entered in the record at this hearing. The date for the disposition hearing is set.

The time between adjudication and disposition hearings will be used to prepare a detailed social history or court report on the juvenile, which can be used by the judge in determining alternative courses of action. The social history or court report investigates family relationships, home supervision, and school and community behavior problems. In addition, the circumstances surrounding current problems, any previous record, attitudes, and other factors may be considered.[45] Parents, school officials, ministers, and anyone who knows the juvenile can be questioned to provide relevant information.

Disposition Hearing

After consulting the prepared social report, the judge may question the parents, the youngster, and the probation officer to elaborate on the material found in the report. The juvenile judge will then announce the disposition of the case. A variety of alternatives are available to the judge. For example, the case may be dismissed or the juvenile may be released to his parents, placed on probation, committed to a training school or other juvenile institution, or placed in a foster home.

If the youngster is found to be neglected or dependent, he may be made a ward of the court so that provision for medical, psychiatric, or other services can be made. The court has the power to terminate parental rights, and this power may be used in cases of severe neglect (or in adoption cases). Decisions involving the removal of a child from his or her natural parents and the termination of parental rights are generally used only as a last resort. The primary consideration for a juvenile court judge in choosing a course of action is the best interests of the youngster weighed against the needs of the community.

The responsibility of the court is not terminated with the disposition decision. Officers of the court are responsible for seeing that the disposition decision is carried out. A juvenile may be required to report to an officer of the court at regular intervals. Any action, except dismissal, results in continued court supervision. These functions, however, are transferred to officials other than the judge until the case merits review. Probation and institutionalization are discussed in Chapters 14 and 15.

RELATIONSHIP TO OTHER COURTS

The juvenile court is not the only judicial agency that deals with problem youths. Other courts have been established to cover a broad range of children's and family problems. In some areas, the juvenile court's jurisdiction is being narrowed, and many cases are being referred to courts that deal with the entire family.

Youth and Family Courts

Youth and family courts are often similar in many ways to the juvenile court, but a wider variety of cases coming from different age groups may be legally handled in these courts. Youth courts, for example, extend the methods and philosophy of the juvenile court to broader age ranges. Some justification for courts of this type may exist in states where juvenile court jurisdiction ends at age 16 or 17, but the youth court often extends its jurisdiction to include youths up to age 21. Youth courts, where they exist, are often part of a criminal court, but they offer a last chance for rehabilitation and reform before the adult criminal court assumes jurisdiction over the young adult. Youth courts are rare in the United States, but the Youth Court of Chicago and similar courts in Philadelphia and New York serve as examples.[46]

A family court goes beyond the traditional cases handled by juvenile courts—delinquency, dependency, and neglect. Cases involving a youngster or any member of his or her family can be handled. The family, not just the youngster, is the focus of attention in court action. The Standard Family Court Act and the National Advisory Commission on Criminal Justice Standards recommended that a family court should have jurisdiction similar to that of the juvenile court, but that it also should include jurisdiction over some cases in which adults are involved.[47] Thus the family court may hear the traditional juvenile cases—delinquency, dependency, neglect, adoptions, guardianship determination, custody, termination of parental rights, commitment of mentally ill youngsters, consent for youthful marriage, and so on. The family court may also hear cases involving adults for offenses against children, child support, paternity, divorce, separation, and alimony. Felony offenses or offenses for which jury trials are either required or permitted will be transferred to a criminal court.

THE JUVENILE COURT IN PERSPECTIVE

Since the first juvenile court was established in 1899, the court's philosophy has enjoyed considerable support from experts and laymen alike. Acting as *parens patriae*, protector, and guardian for children, the court has developed a language and procedures to serve the needs of the wayward child and prevent stigmatization. Unfortunately, the court has in many cases served its philosophy only superficially. Many critics claim that the juvenile court hides behind a disguise of protective father to subvert the juvenile's constitutional rights.

The court has not always lived up to its promise. Lack of public concern and inadequate funding have produced a bare skeleton from which justice cannot always be served. Judges are often undertrained or too busy with other duties to give juvenile offenders the individual attention they need and have been promised by the court philosophy. Jurisdictional confusion and vague juvenile delinquency laws add to the problems encountered by the juvenile judge and his youthful clients.

The future of the juvenile court is uncertain. The recent trend has been toward change that will bring the procedures of the juvenile court in line with the procedures of the criminal court. Resistance to such change is strong in many influential quarters.

NOTES

[1] Frederick B. Sussman and Frederic S. Baum, *Law of Juvenile Delinquency* (Dobbs Ferry, N.Y.: Oceana, 1968), pp. 5–6.

[2] Joseph M. Hawes, *Children in Urban Society: Juvenile Delinquency in Nineteenth Century America* (New York: Oxford University Press, 1971), p. 280.

[3] Some authorities believe that early state courts held equity jurisdiction only over children with property. However, in 1849 an Illinois court ruled that equity jurisdiction extended to the "person of all minors," not just their property. Thus, the court obtained jurisdiction over juveniles *and* property of juveniles.

[4] For a discussion of the differing views regarding the historical basis of the present-day juvenile court, see President's Commission on Law Enforcement and Administration of Justice, *Task Force Report: Juvenile Delinquency and Youth Crime* (Washington, D.C.: Government Printing Office, 1967), p. 2.

[5] *Task Force Report, op. cit.,* p. 3.

[6] Sussman and Baum, *op. cit.,* p. 15.

[7] *Ibid.,* p. 16.

[8] *Ibid.,* p. 15.

[9] National Council on Crime and Delinquency, *Model Rules for Juvenile Courts* (New York, 1969), pp. 2–3.

[10] Evaline Belden, *Courts in the United States Hearing Children's Cases* (Department of Labor, Children's Bureau) (Washington, D.C., 1920).

[11] *Task Force Report, op. cit.,* pp. 3–4.

[12] See C. S. Lewis, "The Humanitarian Theory of Punishment," in *Crime and Justice: The Criminal in Confinement,* ed. Leon Radzinowicz and Marvin Wolfgang (New York: Basic Books, 1971), pp. 43–48.

[13] Paul Tappan, "Treatment Without Trial," *Social Forces* 24 (March 1946): 306–311.

[14] *Task Force Report, op. cit.*, pp. 19–21.

[15] Don C. Gibbons, *Delinquent Behavior*, 2d ed. (Englewood Cliffs, N.J.: Prentice-Hall, 1976), p. 266.

[16] Edwin M. Lemert, *Social Action and Legal Change* (Chicago: Aldine, 1970).

[17] David Duffee and Larry Siegel, "The Organization Man: Legal Counsel in the Juvenile Court," *Criminal Law Bulletin* 7 (July–August 1971): 544–553.

[18] Second United Nations Congress on the Prevention of Crime and Treatment of Offenders, cited in Charles V. Morris, "Worldwide Concern with Crime," *Federal Probation* 24 (December 1960): 21–30.

[19] The *Gault* decision can be found in *Task Force Report, op. cit.*, pp. 57–76.

[20] Sussman and Baum, *op. cit.*, p. 85.

[21] *Ibid.*

[22] *Ibid.*

[23] Miriam Schwartz Alers, "Transfer of Jurisdiction to Criminal Court," *Crime and Delinquency* 19 (October 1973): 519–527.

[24] National Council on Crime and Delinquency, *Standard Juvenile Court Act*, 6th ed. (New York, 1959), p. 33.

[25] Sussman and Baum, *op. cit.*

[26] *Task Force Report, op. cit.*, p. 21.

[27] *Ibid.*, p. 17.

[28] For a discussion of this case, see Paul W. Tappan, *Crime, Justice and Correction* (New York: McGraw-Hill, 1960), pp. 390–392, and Martin R. Haskell and Lewis Yablonsky, *Crime and Delinquency*, 2d ed. (Skokie, Ill.: Rand McNally, 1974), pp. 395–396.

[29] The *Gault* case and its decision can be found in *Task Force Report, op. cit.*

[30] *In re Winship.*

[31] *McKeiver v. Pennsylvania.*

[32] Jeffery E. Glen, "Developments in Juvenile and Family Court Law," *Crime and Delinquency* 16 (April 1970): 198–208.

[33] *Standard Juvenile Court Act, op. cit.*

[34] *Model Rules for Juvenile Courts, op. cit.*

[35] Glen, *op. cit.*

[36] *Ibid.*

[37] Leonard Edwards, "The Rights of Children," *Federal Probation* 37 (June 1973): 34–41.

[38] *Kent v. United States*, 383 U.S. 541 (1966); Alan Neigher, "The Gault Decision: Due Process and the Juvenile Courts," *Federal Probation* 31 (December 1967): 8–18; Paul Lerman, "Beyond Gault: Injustices and the Child," in *Delinquency and Social Policy*, ed. Paul Lerman (New York: Praeger, 1970).

[39] Shirley McCune and Daniel L. Skoler, "Juvenile Court Judges in the United States," *Crime and Delinquency* 11 (April 1965): 121–131.

[40] *Ibid.*

[41] *Ibid.*

[42] *Ibid.*

[43] National Council on Crime and Delinquency, *Guides for Juvenile Court Judges* (New York, 1957), p. 127.

[44] *Ibid.*, p. 15.

[45] *Ibid.*, pp. 49–56.

[46] John Otto Reinemann, "The Expansion of the Juvenile Court Idea," *Federal Probation* 13 (September 1949): 34–40; Frederick J. Ludwig, *Youth and*

the Law: Handbook on Laws Affecting Youth (Mineola, N.Y.: Foundation Press, 1955).

[47] National Council on Crime and Delinquency, Standard Family Court Act (New York, 1959); National Advisory Commission on Criminal Justice Standards and Goals, Corrections (Washington, D.C.: Government Printing Office, 1973).

CHAPTER 14
Community-based corrections

For centuries children were subjected to the same punitive measures that were used to correct adult offenders. The form of punishment varied over time, but imprisonment, mutilation, and death have been the all-time favorites. As the concept of responsibility began to play an important role in the determination of law and justice, there was considerable concern about the severity of the treatment of children. Lacking guidelines to distinguish between adults and children, many early criminal courts simply refused to apply the law to very young children. The family and the broader community were given responsibility for retraining these youths.

Over time, ideas about justice and correction have evolved to deal specifically with children. Juveniles are separated from adults throughout all stages of the process of justice. Methods of detection and pre-judicial handling of children differ from those used for adults. Juveniles come under the jurisdiction of their own special court, and corrections programs have been adapted especially for children.

Admittedly, the corrections programs designed for juveniles roughly parallel that of the adult system. Some involve the segregation of offenders in special institutions, away from law-abiding citizens; others provide treatment within the community setting. However, there are distinct differences between the juvenile and adult programs, particularly in the community-based facilities. A wider range of alternatives is available to officials dealing with juveniles, treatment procedures are more flexible, and a great deal less formality is required.

PRE-JUDICIAL TREATMENT PROGRAMS

It is generally assumed that correction follows judicial proceedings. The traditional conception of justice holds that an individual is innocent until proven guilty. After guilt has been determined in a court of law, the offender is subject to the sanctions imposed or treatment prescribed by the judge of the court. The ideal conception, however, does not hold up in practice. Alleged offenders, both adults and juveniles, are often handled without benefit of trial. This deviation from the ideal may be more advantageous to the adult, however.

Court officials often deal with offenders who need some type of treatment or supervision but may not benefit by formal disposition in court. When criminal prosecutors are faced with this problem, they usually lack alternatives other than charging, dismissing, or reducing the charge. The President's Commission on Law Enforcement and Administration of Justice states: "In most localities programs and agencies that can provide such treatment and supervision are scarce or altogether lacking, and in many places where they exist there are no regular procedures for the court, prosecutors and defense counsel to take advantage of them."[1] The commission also indicated that "informal and discretionary pre-judicial dispositions already are a formally recognized part of the process to a far greater extent in the juvenile than in the criminal justice system."[2] Police may require juveniles to make modifications in their behavior patterns or may place them under the supervision of various community agencies. Probation officers and judges may also refer juveniles to community agencies, place them in detention facilities, or place them under the informal supervision of probation personnel, all without benefit of a court hearing. A majority of all juvenile cases are handled informally; many of them involve submission to various treatment programs.

Although informal handling and disposition are undertaken with the "voluntary" consent of the juvenile and his guardians, the practice is not unlike plea bargaining in the criminal justice system. The choice available to the juvenile is not one of treatment or release, but rather a matter of choosing between the unofficial treatment program specified or taking his chances in court.

Unofficial programs vary widely from one community to another. The resources of the school, medical organizations, mental health clinics, social welfare agencies, and other community organizations may be mobilized to handle troublesome youths. Because it exists outside of and beyond the guidance and control of standardized, articulated policies and legal restraints, the informal system is largely invisible and unknown in its detailed operations.[3] Uniform policies are rarely shared by police, probation officers, and juvenile judges. Therefore informal disposition is generally utilized on an ad hoc basis, making it subject to charges of discrimination and inequitable application.

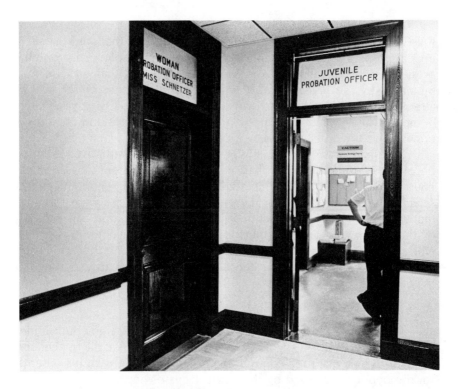

POSTADJUDICATORY PROGRAMS

Youngsters who are adjudicated delinquent are not automatically routed to juvenile correctional institutions. If the social investigation indicates that the child has physical or emotional problems, the judge may order treatment to correct them. The juvenile's parents or guardian are required to report the child's progress to the court or court-related agencies. Adjudicated children have taken advantage of the services of hearing clinics, medical facilities, psychiatric clinics, and remedial education programs.

Because juvenile correctional institutions are viewed with disfavor, the juvenile judge may be amenable to the suggestions of parents for disposition alternatives. When the child's background or behavior suggests the need for supervision and discipline, private military or boarding schools may provide a nonstigmatizing solution. If this alternative is elected by the parents and the judge, the child's disposition may be suspended for the duration of enrollment or indefinitely.

When the home environment is believed to be a major factor in producing the child's delinquent behavior, he or she may become a ward of the state. Children from undesirable homes are sometimes placed in foster homes. A child will remain with foster parents until conditions are much improved at home or until he reaches the age of majority. Foster parents generally prefer dealing with younger children; therefore few older youths are placed.

Most of the postadjudicatory programs mentioned above are not fully developed in many communities. Each requires that some qualifying criterion be met. Treatment of medical and psychological problems presupposes the availability of community facilities that may be manipulated by the juvenile court judge. The use of the private school alternative, on the other hand, rests on the parent's ability to pay. Foster homes are always in short supply for young delinquents and are almost nonexistent for older youths.

Fortunately, there are a few postadjudicatory alternatives that can be, and are, used widely. Probation is the most frequently used offical court disposition. It has the dual advantages of being economical and retaining the child in the local community without much of the stigmatization of juvenile correctional institutions. Probation can be used by the rich or poor under sophisticated or simple juvenile justice networks. Other programs which serve as additional alternatives are based on the probation philosophy. These are for the most part experimental in nature.

Probation

Probation is the conditional release of an adjudicated youth under the formal supervision of an officer of the court. A child placed on probation remains in the community, usually residing with his parents, for the period prescribed by the court. If his or her behavior becomes unacceptable during the probationary period, the child may be remanded to the court for an alternative disposition. While on probation, a youngster is expected to abide by the rules set up for him in the probation plan and to visit his probation officer at regular intervals.

In theory, probation is available to any juvenile who might benefit from guidance in a free environment and who would not constitute a danger to the security of the local community. A number of criteria for selecting potential successes have evolved through probation practice. The availability of alternative programs and space in institutions, however, sometimes assumes priority in disposition decisions. The guidance ideal of probation is all too frequently limited to theory. In practice, probation offices are understaffed and unable to undertake more than a superficial monitoring function.

QUALIFICATION FOR PROBATION

First offenders, very young juveniles, and minor offenders are more likely to be placed on probation than repeat offenders or those who commit serious offenses. A middle-class youth accompanied to court by an interested, helpful adult is also a good candidate for probation. Juveniles who appear in court regularly, those who have experienced failure in previous probation programs or while on suspension, or those who exhibit deterioration in behavior are frequently institutionalized.

Probation is a popular disposition. However, its use is selective. Ralph Emerson reported that the offender's demeanor is very important.[4] Judges, for example, may not understand the motives, fears, or behavior patterns of lower-class youngsters, because juvenile judges are predominantly drawn from the middle class. Some forms of behavior, dress patterns, demeanor, and so on may be quite acceptable within the lower class or within certain ethnic groups; but to the juvenile judge, these same attributes may be viewed as symptomatic of delinquent behavior. Long hair, sloppy clothing, and a beard may signify a particular life style, but for the judge they may mean that the individual engages in delinquent conduct. Commitment to a youth authority or juvenile correctional institution is more likely in these situations.

Judges and probation officers prefer to deal with lower-middle-class youngsters because they are more easily controlled than other juveniles. Lower-class youths may rebel against the court, the probation officers, and the restrictions placed on them. These youths are often perceived as uncontrollable, violent, and challenging to the authority of the judge and the probation system. On the other hand, upper-middle-class and upper-class youths have the characteristics that make assignment to probationary supervision unlikely: an intact family and adult friends and contacts are easily produced. Possibly because of their backgrounds, these youngsters are often viewed as disrespectful, aggressive, and uncontrollable by a probation staff recruited from the lower middle class. Youngsters from the lower middle class are ideal candidates for probation because they often exhibit the characteristics perceived as desirable by probation staffs. They appear controllable, and they respect the power of probation officers, the police, and parents. They are not violent and they do not accept the "free and easy" style of the upper classes.

The judge is also guided by a presentence investigation report.[5] Ideally, the report contains information regarding the facts surrounding the offense, the offender's attitude toward his behavior, previous juvenile misconduct, family background, neighborhood, close associates, educational background, work history, alcohol use, drug use, and medical history. The report also contains the probation officer's assessment of whether or not the youth is "probationable," what caused his behavior, his strengths and weaknesses, and his needs if probation is granted.[6]

David Fogel divided the presentence court report into two parts— a description of the offense and a social analysis.[7] The interrelationship between the two parts was analyzed using ten cases committed to a training school after repeated court appearances. Fogel reported that the recommendations of the probation officer were evident in the reports. The officer would select an outcome and widen or narrow the social report and biography depending on the career or offense of the juvenile. If the officer recommended a less severe outcome (probation),

TABLE 14.1 UPPER AGE LIMITS OF
JUVENILE COURT JURISDICTION IN 51 STATES,[a] 1973

BIRTHDAY TO WHICH JURISDICTION EXTENDS	NUMBER OF STATES	PERCENTAGE
Sixteenth	6	12
Seventeenth	12	23
Eighteenth	33	65
Total	51	100

Source: Data derived from Law Enforcement Assistance Administration, *Children in Custody: A Report on the Juvenile Detention and Correctional Facility Census of 1971* (Washington, D.C.: Government Printing Office, 1974), p. 1.

[a] The fifty-first state refers to the District of Columbia. Only Texas, Oklahoma, and Illinois had different ages for males and females, but the distinctions were not functional as they were declared unconstitutional by state courts.

the report "dramatizes the complexity of the child's biography." On the other hand, if a severe outcome was intended by the officer, a narrow biography was presented.[8] In reports following first offenses, youths were rarely held responsible for their actions, but Fogel reports that the youth's volition becomes more important with each court appearance and each offense. Statements such as "the child failed to rehabilitate," "he did not profit from the experience," and "he knew the court orders but failed to be guided by them" were often used.[9] Thus after several court appearances, the youth is increasingly blamed for his failure to be rehabilitated.

The age limit for eligibility for juvenile probation is set by state statute. A limit of 18 was endorsed by the United States Children's Bureau, the Standard Juvenile Court Act,[10] and the President's Commission on Law Enforcement and Administration of Justice.[11] Lower age limits often depend on state law and judicial practice. Table 14.1 gives a breakdown of these limits (the fifty-first state refers to the District of Columbia). Inspection of this table suggests that by 1973 most states had chosen 18 as the upper limit, with some opting for a lower age limit. Different age limits for males and females were once common but have now been declared unconstitutional.

After receiving the preprobation report, the judge will decide how to dispose of the case within the age guidelines set by state statute. The juvenile judge is not compelled to follow recommendations from probation officers, social caseworkers, or clinics. Parents, juveniles, and others may appeal to the judge for different courses of action, or the judge may decide that some other course of action will work better for a particular offender.

THE PROBATION PLAN

Probation usually begins with a plan agreed to by both the judge and the probation officer assigned to the youth. The plan is based on information from a social investigation prepared by the probation officer after interviews with the youth, the parents, and community resource agencies. Probation has often been regarded as a lenient sentence whereby the juvenile remains in the community; thus the court's power to impose conditions on a probationer and his or her family has rarely been challenged.

The plan may stipulate that the youth attend school regularly, obey parents, attend church, obey curfew, and avoid friends and acquaintances who might have a bad influence. In addition, the judge might require that long hair be cut, beards shaved off, counseling or psychiatric treatment be accepted, charitable contributions be given, and so on. He may also counsel the youth regarding choice of jobs and specify how any money earned is to be spent.[12] Some of the conditions may be helpful to bring about positive change in the youth. Others may have no effect or even create hostility. Some conditions imposed as evidence of progress and successful probation may be impossible to accomplish. The requirement that a youth maintain a high grade average, for example, cannot always be met. Orders of restitution may be beyond the earning capacity of the youth. Several authorities have advised that financial restitution for damages or fines should be imposed on the juvenile only if they are part of a broader treatment program.[13]

If the youth is expected to pay for damages or injury, the amount should be small enough so he or she can earn the money without seeking help from the parents or placing a burden on them. In some vandalism cases or personal injury cases, the amount of money involved might be so large that the juvenile cannot be expected to repay the cost without suffering serious difficulties while attending school. If money payments are viewed by the youth as a way to cancel bad behavior, they should not be used. Thus fines and payments for restitution may prevent or limit efforts to rehabilitate the offender in situations in which the youth cannot reasonably be expected to pay. When it will help to impress the person with the consequences of his or her actions, the use of a fine or restitution may reasonably be considered. Of course, in personal injury cases or vandalism, the laws in various states differ regarding whether the parents can be held responsible for the actions of their children. The question of who will pay for property damage or hospital bills can become serious, especially if the injured party is not able to pay the costs. Some states have laws that allow victims compensation regardless of whether the acts were committed by juveniles or adults. Of course, judges differ regarding the advisability of imposing fines or requiring youths to pay for damages to property or compensate victims.

The probation plan necessarily includes regular, periodic visits with the probation officer appointed by the court. The juvenile may be required to visit the probation office, or the probation officer may call on the youth in his home setting. Usually the probation plan involves both types of visitation. Because they have wide latitude in handling their charges, probation officers may be a deciding factor in the outcome of the juvenile's case.

THE PROBATION OFFICER

The probation officer has the responsibility for the success or failure of probation. Several different methods may be used to assign a particular probation officer to a given case. Frequently an officer is assigned all probationers within a certain territorial area. Other methods, however, provide more of an opportunity for effective use of probation officers. One method involves the assignment of offenders to a probation officer according to age, sex, or religion of the offender. Another method is based on the type of offense or the needs of the offender. Some probation officers have more experience and are better able to deal with serious offenders. Others may be specially trained to provide particular forms of therapy. Still others may find that the care of young first offenders is their specialty.

The officer is responsible for interpreting and implementing the probation plan. If the youth has been instructed to seek counseling, the probation officer facilitates contact with the appropriate community service agencies and checks to see if the youth actually attends the counseling sessions. The officer sees the youth occasionally in the home, in the office, or at some other meeting place. The officer may meet with the parents or consult with school officials and other interested community agency officials.

The probation officer spends little time in actual contact with youngsters on probation, particularly if he or she has a large caseload. The mandatory supervisory interview with a youngster might last only a few minutes, during which time a few questions are asked, and a warning or lecture could be given to the probationer. The youngsters placed in foster homes or in a group home, for example, require little time. A recidivist, a youth needing medical or other special care, new cases, or cases involving serious offenders often require more time than is available to the overworked probation officer.[14] Time for intensive counseling may be lost as the officer travels to do the investigative work needed to develop a court report and probationary plan for new cases. In addition, the officer may need to transport juveniles to the court, clinics, foster homes, or the training school and return runaways. Furthermore, the officer may have to wait outside the court for an hour or two while waiting for one of his cases to be called. Probation officers must be in court if one of their cases is called, but they may know only the day of the case and have only a vague idea of what hour the case will be called before the court.[15]

Close contact with a youth is often difficult to maintain with heavy caseloads and other limits on the officer's time. If an officer wanted to interview all of his cases in a week, he might find it difficult to set up meetings with each one. Only a few might actually show up for the interview, and if each interview lasted only a few minutes, several hours would be necessary. Of course, some of the youngsters will be late, and some interviews will be interrupted for phone calls and other duties, resulting in little privacy. As a result, interviews by the probation officer tend to become routine and infrequent. Quick questions about home, school, friends, and recreational activities are common.[16] Probation officers are expected to make unannounced visits to a youngster's home, but they may find that few people are home during these visits unless they visit in the evening hours. A considerable amount of the probation officer's time may be spent on unproductive travel.

Probation officers, even if they are well qualified and dedicated, may find that they are constrained by limitations on their time and energy. A heavy caseload, a wide variety of duties, travel, waiting for cases to be called, and other factors all reduce the time needed for casework, serious counseling, and supervision.

Probation officers often use lecturing or preaching as a way of interacting with and controlling delinquents and avoiding trouble.[17] Initial interviews with the delinquent and the interviews that follow "trouble" routinely employ this type of moral exhortation. The lecture provides a means of reinforcing the officer's control over the youth. The preaching implies, however, that the behavior in question is completely within the juvenile's power to control. The influence of family, friends, and others is often ignored as juveniles are blamed by officers for their failure to follow the rules of their probation. The implied threat of serious consequences for continued misconduct is usually stressed in these interviews (see Case 14.1).

Partially as a result of lack of time, the probation officers are not able to exercise direct control over the youngsters. Instead, the responsibility for control is shifted to the school, the family, or a church.[18] The influence of the basic control mechanisms in society is reaffirmed. These practices, however, rest on the assumption that delinquency results from the loss of supervisory control from the school, family, or church. Thus if the supervisory control can be reestablished, delinquent behavior should cease. Adults in various institutions become secondary supervisors. Surveillance efforts by the probation officer often mean reliance on reports of these adult secondary supervisors, and the officer may assume that all is well until a negative report from family, school, church, or other adults involved with the youth is received. When the probation officer confronts the juvenile with these reports, the officer may appear all-knowing and all-powerful. Many probation officers attempt to cultivate this image to deter the youth from future misbehavior.[19] The youth may see all adults as potential informants and believe that he or she is constantly being watched and checked on by the probation officer and other people.

CASE 14.1

HERE COMES THE P. O.

About midnight on a warm summer evening, the probation officer caught a glimpse of a familiar figure walking along the street several yards in front of him. He called her name, and when she turned around the following conversation ensued:

P.O.: What is a fifteen year old girl like you doing walking the streets this time of night?

Girl: Taking this here book back to Judy. I got it from her last week.

P.O.: At midnight? You're supposed to be at home in bed!

Girl: I didn't do nothin.

P.O.: Out on the streets at this time of night all you can do is get into trouble.

Girl: I didn't do nothin!

P.O.: You get in trouble and you can go to [a juvenile correctional institution for females]. Its no picnic up there either. How would your mom like that? That's what they do to girls who don't know how to behave. If I catch you out at this time of night again, I'll write you up and you'll be off the streets for good! Now go on and get home. Don't let me catch you out here like this again.

Probation may have little lasting effect on the lives and activities of a delinquent youth. Cicourel suggests that under probation too little attention is directed toward changing the delinquent.[20]

Neither the probation officer nor the community and its agents is able or willing to commit the resources necessary for change. Instead, the delinquent is handled in a bureaucratic and routine fashion, leaving probation without its potential for directed rehabilitation. Formal authority and lectures are often not enough to bring lasting change in behavior. A personalized trust relationship is essential to prevent trouble, but even if the officer tries to break the formal authoritative ties with the youth, these attempts may be received with distrust and suspicion.

Probation relies on the enforcement of rules. The probation officer applies the rules specified by the court in the probation plan and threatens sanctions for misconduct. Some juveniles, of course, seem to require little attention, and they may be seen infrequently by the probation officer after the court hearing. More troublesome juveniles receive active and strict rule enforcement and control action. Controlling the behavior of the juvenile is an essential first step to rehabilitation. The probation officer may increase his involvement in the case of a delinquent youth if more control appears warranted. The probation officer has the authority to impose some additional restrictions on the youth and may "surrender" an individual if probation is violated.[21] Surrender may bring commitment to a training school or placement in a detention home until the court can act. The threat of incarceration is one of the primary control weapons.[22]

Surveillance by the probation officer, if properly carried out, may have a therapeutic value for the juvenile. It can be a way to help youths become aware that they must take responsibility for their behavior. Furthermore, it can be a device to individualize the treatment of the offender, provide support, and illustrate that adults are interested and willing to help the offender avoid future troublesome behavior. The probation officer must be in touch with the school, the parents, and others who might be interested in the juvenile. The officer should be informed about whether the probation plan is being carried out, whether the family is fulfilling its responsibility, and whether the juvenile adequately responds to efforts to help him or her adjust.[23] Surveillance, however, should be used in conjunction with service and counseling for an effective approach to juvenile probation.[24] Service involves mustering the available resources in the community to serve and meet the needs of the individual juvenile offender. The probation officer must find out what problems confront the youth and the family and bring the resources of the community to help alleviate the problems.

Counseling is an important aspect of the probation officer's task. It is perhaps the most important, because it allows the others to be performed more effectively. The youth and the family may be helped through counseling to understand as well as to face problems connected with the youth's delinquent behavior. They may also learn how to prevent future problems.[25]

In addition to surveillance, service, and counseling, probation departments provide the central tasks involved in intake or original screening of youths referred to the juvenile court. The court is provided with the social history and biographical and diagnostic information. In addition, auxiliary duties often include operating or providing mental health clinics, foster home programs, forestry camps, group homes and other residential or nonresidential treatment facilities. Some probation departments vigorously engage in community planning and community organization efforts on behalf of children and youth. Others even operate delinquency-prevention services for endangered youth.[26]

PROBATION USE

By the mid 1960s, the juvenile system had grown to the point where it touched the lives of a large number of young people each year. In 1972, about 141,000 dependency and neglect cases and about

332 COMMUNITY-BASED CORRECTIONS

1,112,500 delinquency cases were handled by the juvenile courts.[27] Most of the delinquency cases referred to the court were handled non-judicially (59 percent) without the filing of a formal petition.[28] The proportion of cases handled nonjudicially was higher in urban areas (56 percent) and semiurban areas (67 percent) than in rural areas (44 percent).[29] The differences were probably due to the availability of probation staffs in larger urban centers.[30] The probation departments now divert youngsters from the court with informal probation or through other means, and this factor may help account for a slight drop in the number of cases handled officially by the juvenile court between 1964 and 1972.[31] According to rough estimates from the Children's Bureau, 11 percent of all children, and 18 percent of all males, will be referred to the juvenile court during adolescence.[32] Probation will be used for most of the official cases. The annual national cost in 1965 was $74 million.[33]

Probation is authorized by statute in all 50 states. The periods of probation supervision range from three months to three years, with the median period under supervision 13 months.[34] In 31 states, all counties have a probation staff; nevertheless, only 74 percent of all counties in the United States have probation staffs. In some of these counties, there may be only a token probation service provided for the juveniles. In the states where counties lack probation staffs, some limited services are typically available. Volunteer probation officers, child welfare offices, or a combination of sheriff, welfare, and other agency staffs are often used to provide probation service for juvenile offenders. No probation service at all is provided in at least 165 counties.[35] In the United States the larger and more heavily populated urban areas typically provide probation staffs, but in the smaller, more rural areas the coverage may not be adequate if it exists at all.

Some state agencies that are assigned the responsibility for providing probation services are not adequately prepared for the task. Personnel who are oriented and trained to treat problem youths are essential if adequate probation supervision is to be provided. Sheriffs or police officers should not be expected to become expert in both law enforcement as well as the special problems associated with the diagnosis and treatment of problem youths. The use of full-time paid specialists who are oriented specifically to the problems of youths would seem to be basic for providing adequate probation supervision and treatment.

ORGANIZATIONAL STRUCTURE

Juvenile probation is usually bureaucratically organized into either a centralized state system, a county or city system, or a combination of the two with bigger and more prosperous urban jurisdictions operating their own departments, with the state providing service in other areas. The centralized state plan is preferred by many because it offers the advantages of (1) uniformity of standards and practice; (2) research, statistical, and budgetary control; (3) recruitment of a qualified and highly trained staff; (4) flexible and centralized staff assignment, and (5) coordinated relationships with other correctional programs.[36]

County or city systems may be in a better position to respond to local conditions, but state-wide efforts to set standards and recruit and train the staffs are essential if an adequate program is to be maintained. The county or city systems are usually organized in one of two ways. In the prevalent practice, the juvenile court administers the probation services. In the other, an administrative agency, established as a separate department of local government, may be the administrator. Juvenile courts administer juvenile probation in 32 states, but state agencies (either correctional or public welfare agencies) administer the programs in 12 states. Other state agencies or a combination of agencies administer probation in seven states.[37] Regardless of who administers juvenile probation, a citizen's advisory panel is often helpful in interpreting probation problems to the public and participating in policy-making decisions.

In 45 states, at least some probation departments are city or county departments, but in 13 states, the state government sets some staffing and practice standards. In 19 out of 45 states, the state provides some funds to help with local services, such as personnel or operating costs, but complete data is not available to determine the extent to which the local agency depends on the state for operating funds.[38]

PROBATION SUCCESS

It is not unusual to find reports of at least 70 percent success rates for juvenile probation. But can we call a program successful just because youngsters stay out of trouble with the police for one year after getting out of the program? Should we measure success by community adjustment criteria? Should those youngsters who fail to successfully complete their probation plan be included in measuring whether probation is successful? Probation success has been measured in a variety of ways, because there is little agreement on the answers to these questions.

Scarpitti and Stephenson provided good evidence on the success of probation by following 1210 delinquent boys for four years.[39] The delinquents had been assigned to four programs, which included institutional placement (training school), placement in a residential group home, nonresidential group counseling, and probationary supervision. Success rates for completing programs of probation, group nonresidential counseling, and residential groups were similar and ranged from 72 to 77 percent. Probation appears more successful when lack of recidivism is used as the criterion for success. Fifteen percent of the probationary-status boys reappeared before the juvenile court, compared with 48 percent for nonresidential counseling, 41 percent for the residential group home, and 55 percent for the training school. Thus it might be concluded that probation is the most successful program for preventing subsequent offenses and future trouble with law enforcement agencies.

Remember, however, that probation is more likely to be given to first offenders, to younger offenders, and to those whose offenses were less serious. These are often youngsters with less antisocial attitudes and behavior patterns. The lower rate of failure for probation may be due to the fact that the successful probationers were less delinquency oriented, and probation had little to do with their success. Scarpitti and Stephenson, however, statistically controlled for some of these factors and found that the probationers were more successful than were youngsters assigned to other programs.

Other studies have not provided such optimistic evidence for the effectiveness of juvenile probation. After a careful review of research on probation effectiveness, Sparks concluded that probation was at least as likely to prevent recidivism as an institutional stay. Furthermore, the individual offender's attitude was the factor most determinative of success. Probation successes are frequently accomplished without significant assistance by probation caseworkers.[40]

Experimental Programs

Variations on traditional probation practices have been used in some areas. For example, in 1956 Emprey and some associates started the Provo Experiment for repeat offenders from 15 to 17 years of age.[41] Peer group pressures were used as a means of social control among juveniles. Both conforming and constructive behavior was developed and supported by the peer group. Each member of the group was expected to attend school and complete assigned work tasks, but any failures were referred to the group for attention and sanction. Research based on the Provo Experiment and later the Silverlake Experiment[42] suggests that the programs may achieve a 73 to 84 percent success rate respectively (i.e., juveniles who leave the group are not arrested for at least one year). These programs, however, did not exhibit superior success rates when compared with control groups receiving similar dispositions.[43] A 73 percent success rate is not unusual for youngsters assigned to probationary status, but Emprey noted that the Provo probationers over a period of time experienced increased success (from 55 percent to 77 percent). The Silverlake Experiment would probably have been more successful if delinquents had been classified according to the type of offense committed and the individuals assigned to more appropriate treatment groups.[44]

Robert Geertsma reported using group therapy with parents and delinquent youths on probation. The delinquent youths met in one group, and parents met in a separate group. Both parents were expected to attend, but Geertsma reported that typically only one met

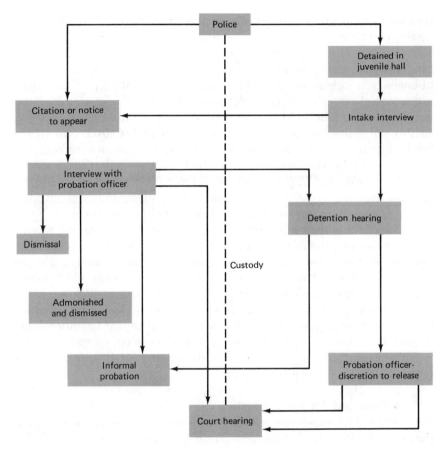

Figure 14.1 Decisions in the Handling of Juveniles

Source: Janet T. Carey, Joel Goldfarb, Michael J. Rowe, and Joseph D. Lohman, *The Handling of Juveniles from Offense to Disposition* (Washington, D.C.: Government Printing Office, 1967), p. 26.

with the group. The boys selected for the experiment were not severely disturbed or chronic or serious offenders. In the group therapy sessions, both parents and youths were encouraged to express themselves freely. The goal of the program was to gradually achieve a better understanding of problems and possible solutions which involved both parents and their children in problem-solving activities.[45]

MOVING THROUGH THE SYSTEM

Janet Carey and her associates illustrated some of the decisions in the handling of juveniles by probation departments.[46] Most referrals are initiated by the police, who may detain youngsters in a juvenile hall or a detention house. In addition, the police may issue a citation or notice to appear. At this point, as illustrated in Figure 14.1, the probationary department, in its intake capacity, will enter into the case.

Interviews with probation officers may lead to dismissal of the case, or the youngster may receive a lecture before the case is dismissed. Some youngsters are placed on informal probation with a probation officer, which may divert the youngster from the more serious consequences of a formal, and possibly stigmatizing, contact with the juvenile court. There should be a detention hearing to determine if the youngster should be held or released pending a formal court hearing. At this point the probation officer may exercise his discretion to release, detain, or place on informal probation. On the other hand, the decisions of probation officers may result in a formal court hearing.

Thus probation departments are intimately involved in the intake process by which youths are brought into contact with the juvenile court. During the intake phase, many juveniles are diverted from formal contact with the juvenile justice system. Consideration should be given to using the available community resources and social service agencies to help youths in trouble. Despite laws and judicial rules to the contrary, contact with the court may result in records which eventually get into the hands of potential employers. Contact with the court may limit life chances and seriously affect a child's chance for rehabilitation or for staying out of trouble. Serious and repeat offenders may require incarceration to protect society or themselves from harm, but whenever possible, the youths are diverted from official or formal contact with the juvenile justice system.

A Proposed Alternative System

Figure 14.2 illustrates an alternative juvenile justice system proposed by the President's Commission on Law Enforcement and Administration of Justice.[47] Youngsters can be referred by parents, school officials, or the police, but the youngster may go to Youth Services Bureau, discussed more completely in Chapter 17, provides preventive and helping services as an alternative to juvenile court referral. A juvenile may receive help and leave the system or may eventually be referred to the juvenile court. More serious offenders detected by the police may be referred directly to the juvenile judge. When he receives a case, the judge has a number of options: referral to Youth Services, a conditional sentence, a consent decree, probation, institutionalization (such as a training school), holding the case open, or the youngster may leave the juvenile justice system through dismissal.

This plan does not carry the force of law and merely serves as a guide to planning. Efforts to control delinquency operate on three levels. The first is preventing delinquency on the societal level, and this involves all youths. The second level includes the juvenile justice system. Some youngsters engage in muggings, holdups, assaults, and other less threatening but dangerous acts. Protection of society may sometimes require detection of the act, custody, adjudication, and sanctioning of an individual's behavior. These measures, if they are to

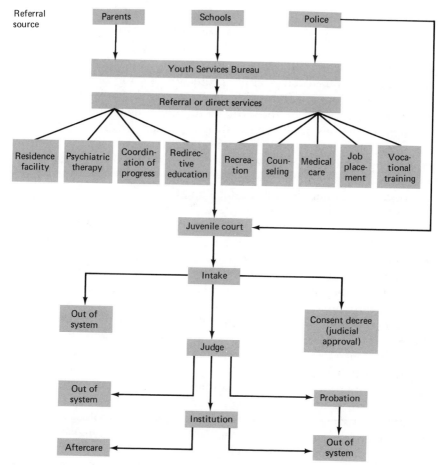

Figure 14.2 Proposed Juvenile Justice System

Source: President's Commission on Law Enforcement and Administration of Justice, *The Challenge of Crime in a Free Society* (Washington, D.C.: Government Printing Office, 1967), p. 89.

accomplish anything, require an effective juvenile justice system. The third involves a response to juveniles who have special needs or problems but may or may not have committed delinquent acts. Some juveniles may be alienated, become behavior problems in school, or engage in other forms of disruptive behavior; the youngster may need help. Youth Services Bureaus have been established in some areas to provide services without stigmatizing them or separating them from parents, peers, or the community.

COMMUNITY-BASED CORRECTIONS
IN PERSPECTIVE

A number of alternatives have been developed to divert juveniles from juvenile institutions. Some of these involve informal, semiofficial measures; others are based upon treating youths more formally in their community setting. The most often-used official plan is probation.

Youths on probation live in the community where their offenses may have been committed, but society does little physically to restrain their actions and receives little protection from possible criminal actions. Probation is a form of leniency which deemphasizes punishment. Supervision from the probation officer helps protect society through restrictions on the youth, such as prohibitions against drinking, gambling, late hours, and association with former friends. Ideally, counseling should be provided by a probation officer or through contact with other community agencies so that rehabilitation and adjustment to the community will be facilitated.

Of course, it is cheaper to place the offender on probation than to send him or her to an institution, and maybe less harmful to the individual. On the other hand, the individual may remain in the community and face the same constellation of forces that led to delinquent behavior in the first place. As a result of official handling, the youth receives the label of "delinquent" and may suffer severe consequences, despite efforts to keep the records secret. Delinquent youths may find that some friends refuse, or may not be allowed, to associate with them. Others may regard them as "big shots" because of their delinquent behavior or their brush with the law. The youth may develop a reputation that is difficult to counteract. In fact, it may be easier to react as others expect and to continue or reengage in delinquent activity than to adjust to the community and engage in responsible behavior, especially with the probation officer, school officials, and family members watching closely. Still, most probationers complete their period of supervision successfully, and most of them are apparently able to avoid further contact with the juvenile or criminal justice system.

Current practices have been examined and found less than satisfactory. As a result, new systems have been proposed and experiments conducted to find a more equitable system. Thus far, the alternatives have not been significantly more successful. Further experimentation and evaluative research is needed.

NOTES

[1] President's Commission on Law Enforcement and Administration of Justice, *The Challenge of Crime in a Free Society* (Washington, D.C.: Government Printing Office, 1967), p. 133.

[2] *Ibid.*, p. 82.

[3] *Ibid.*

[4] Robert M. Emerson, *Judging Delinquents: Context and Process in the Juvenile Court* (Chicago: Aldine, 1969), pp. 219–245.

[5] Edwin Sutherland and Donald R. Cressey, *Criminology*, 6th ed. (Philadelphia: Lippincott, 1960), pp. 427–428.

[6] Walter Reckless, *The Crime Problem*, 2d ed. (New York, Meredith Publishing Co., 1955), p. 511.

[7] David Fogel, "The Fate of the Rehabilitative Ideal in California Youth Authority Dispositions," *Crime and Delinquency* 154 (October 1969): 479–498.

[8] *Ibid.*, p. 479.

[9] *Ibid.*, p. 493.

[10] National Council on Crime and Delinquency, *Standards Juvenile Court Act*, 6th ed. (New York, 1959).

[11] President's Commission on Law Enforcement and Administration of Justice, "Juvenile Probation," *Crime and Delinquency* 13 (January 1966): 39–70.

[12] Carl H. Inlay and Charles R. Glasheen, "See What Condition Your Conditions Are In," *Federal Probation* 35 (June 1971): 3–11.

[13] National Council on Crime and Delinquency, *Guides for Juvenile Court Judges on News Media Relations* (New York, 1957), pp. 80–82; Joseph L. Thimm, "The Juvenile Court and Restitution," *Crime and Delinquency* 6 (1960): 279–286.

[14] Gertrude Hengerer, "Organizing Probation Services," in *Reappraising Crime Treatment, 1953 Yearbook* (New York: National Probation and Parole Association, 1954), pp. 45–59.

[15] Alfred J. Kahn, *A Court for Children: A Study of New York's Children's Court* (New York: Columbia University Press, 1953), p. 7.

[16] *Ibid.*

[17] Aaron V. Cicourel, *The Social Organization of Juvenile Justice* (New York: Wiley, 1968); David Matza, *Delinquency and Drift* (New York: Wiley, 1964), pp. 145 ff.; Emerson, *op. cit.*, pp. 222–235.

[18] Emerson, *op. cit.*, pp. 224–225.

[19] *Ibid.*, p. 227.

[20] Cicourel, *op. cit.*, p. 223.

[21] *Ibid.*

[22] *Ibid.*

[23] "Juvenile Probation," *op. cit.*

[24] *Ibid.*, p. 46.

[25] *Ibid.*

[26] Janet T. Carey, Joel Goldfarb, Michael Rowe, and Joseph D. Lohman, *The Handling of Juveniles from Offense to Disposition* (Department of Health, Education, and Welfare) (Washington, D.C.: Government Printing Office, 1967).

[27] Department of Health, Education, and Welfare, Office of Youth Development, *Juvenile Court Statistics, 1973* (Washington, D.C.: Government Printing Office, 1974), pp. 11, 14.

[28] *Ibid.*, p. 8.

[29] *Ibid.*

[30] Department of Health, Education, and Welfare, Office of Juvenile Delinquency and Youth Development, *Juvenile Court Statistics, 1968* (Washington, D.C.: Government Printing Office, 1970), pp. 2–10.

[31] *Juvenile Court Statistics, 1973, op. cit.*

[32] Department of Health, Education, and Welfare, Children's Bureau, *Juvenile Court Statistics, 1964* (Washington, D.C.: Government Printing Office, 1965).

[33] "Juvenile Probation," *op. cit.*

[34] *Ibid.*, p. 49.

[35] *Ibid.*, p. 50.

[36] Emerson, *op. cit.*, p. 51.

[37] *Ibid.*, pp. 51–52.

[38] *Ibid.*

[39] Frank R. Scarpitti and Richard M. Stephenson, "A Study of Probation Effectiveness," *Journal of Criminal Law, Criminology and Police Science* 59 (September 1968): 361–369.

[40] Richard Sparks, "The Effectiveness of Probation: A Review," in *Crime and Justice: The Criminal in Confinement,* ed. Leon Radzinowicz and Marvin Wolfgang (New York: Basic Books, 1971), pp. 211–218.

[41] Lamar T. Emprey and Jerome Rabow, "The Provo Experiment in Delinquency Rehabilitation," *American Sociological Review* 26 (October 1961): 679–696.

[42] Lamar T. Emprey and Steven G. Lubek, *The Silverlake Experiment* (Chicago: Aldine, 1971).

[43] Lamar T. Emprey, "The Provo Experiment: Research and Findings," in *Combatting Social Problems: Techniques of Intervention,* ed. Harry Gold and Frank R. Scarpitti (New York: Holt, Rinehart and Winston, 1967), pp. 395–404.

[44] Emprey and Lubek, *op. cit.,* p. 274.

[45] Robert H. Geertsma, "Group Therapy with Juvenile Probationers and Their Parents," *Federal Probation* 24 (March 1960): 46–52.

[46] Carey, Goldfarb, Rowe, and Lohman, *op. cit.*

[47] *The Challenge of Crime in a Free Society, op. cit.,* p. 89.

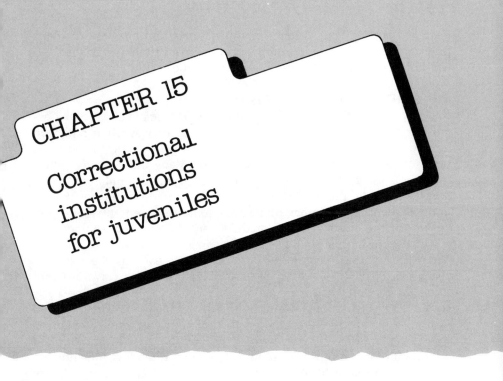

CHAPTER 15
Correctional
institutions
for juveniles

Correctional institutions for juveniles are often known as training or reform schools. When originally developed, juvenile institutions were patterned after adult prisons. Over the years, however, the major characteristic that has set them apart from adult institutions has been their increased emphasis on education and occupational training. Unfortunately, juvenile institutions often fall short of the goals set for them by other agencies of the juvenile justice system. As a result, they are used only as a last resort when all other methods of handling have been exhausted or when the juvenile is too dangerous to remain at large in the community.

Juveniles may be placed in secure residential institutions for a number of reasons. They may be committed to a training school as a result of a juvenile status offense (truancy, curfew violation, or consuming alcohol), an offense for which an adult is liable for prosecution, or a parent's request for help in controlling a child. Commitment may also result from factors unrelated to the delinquent acts of the youth. Children who are neglected, dependent, or in need of supervision have been temporarily housed in these institutions in some jurisdictions until other arrangements can be made for their care.

State-managed training schools, forestry camps, and other residential institutions for juveniles receive adjudicated youngsters referred by the juvenile courts, those awaiting court action, or probation violators. Although some youngsters remain in the institution for only a short time, it is designed for extended care and treatment in a secure, restricted setting. The training school has the responsibility of trying to change the behavior, attitudes, and values of its inmates so that they will not get into trouble after release from the institution.

EARLY JUVENILE CORRECTIONS

Special treatment for child offenders is a relatively recent phenomenon.[1] Although the severity of punishment was often mitigated by virtue of their age, children for centuries were liable to the same types of punishment meted out to adults. Many of the early public treatments for crime involved corporal punishment. Mutilation, whipping, and public humiliation were used for a wide variety of crimes. Imprisonment for criminal offenses is a more recent phenomenon. Reform of the criminal codes gradually substituted imprisonment for corporal punishment in all but capital crimes.[2]

Houses of correction were established as early as the sixteenth century in England; however, the use of such facilities was not widespread until the end of the eighteenth century.[3] Most of the early correctional institutions were multipurpose facilities. They housed males and females, children and adults, and petty and serious offenders. Apart from a few widely scattered experiments, most institutions did not develop programs for separating the various offenders. One notable exception, the Council of Amsterdam (1597), created a separate house of correction for girls and women, emphasizing work as a disciplinary measure. The Hospice of San Michele was founded by Pope Clement XI in 1703 to discipline unruly boys under age 20.

The Ghent experiment (1773) is considered a significant step in the development of juvenile corrections. The correctional facility in Ghent, Belgium, received a wide variety of offenders, but unlike other houses of correction, there was an attempt to classify the prisoners on the basis of sex, age, and offense. A portion of the institution was set aside for juveniles. Under the children's program, juveniles were encouraged to work hard, learn a trade, and obey their masters.[4]

The first institutions specifically designed to separate youthful offenders from adult criminals were established in Europe and the United States during the nineteenth century. Children found wandering the streets, living in gutters or alleys by their wits and without adult supervision, were a matter of great concern to early reformers. Some of the youths were orphans, deserted by parents, or runaways from other parts of the country.

The New York House of Refuge was opened in 1825 under the auspices of the Society for the Reformation of Juvenile Delinquents. The house represented the earliest American attempt to provide separate correctional facilities for child offenders. An empty arsenal was used to house and provide care and education for vagrants and minor offenders picked up by the police. These young people had formerly been sent to adult correctional facilities for short periods or ignored.

A program of training was included in the regime for the inmates. The house received public acclaim and private support. The state eventually assumed financial responsibility for the facility. Similar facilities were soon established in several major cities on the East Coast.

The earliest juvenile institutions were little more than workhouses, as were the adult houses of correction. Large, congregate facilities were used to house children of all sorts. Neglected or orphaned youngsters shared facilities with those accused of committing criminal offenses. Strict discipline, hard work, and moral exhortation characterized the correctional programs. The harsh, punitive measures used in these miniature prisons soon made them a target for reform. Experimental plans used in Europe inspired their evolution to a new form. Cottage-type training schools were first established in Lancaster, Massachusetts (1854), and Lancaster, Ohio (1858). The new system spread rapidly, and the cottage plan was to become the dominant organizational arrangement for handling juvenile offenders. Along with the trend toward small, group-based facilities came an increased emphasis on rehabilitation, occupational training, and education. Therapeutic services were introduced in the 1930s and given a permanent place in the institutions by the late 1960s.

PHILOSOPHY OF JUVENILE CORRECTIONS

The earliest public treatment facilities for juveniles were called reform schools. Programs to accomplish reform placed primary emphasis on discipline and obedience to authority. Corporal punishment was used liberally to discourage deviation from the rules. Education and vocational training were a part of the stated goals of these institutions. However, in practice the treatment goals were given a back seat to the custodial function. In the houses of refuge and the reform schools, a major portion of the children's time was spent in work activities rather than in school. Furthermore, work assignments were based upon the needs of contracting agencies rather than concern for the vocational training of the juveniles involved. Moral teachings offered throughout a daily schedule emphasized conforming behavior and following the "right" path. The old treatment philosophy and the methods used to implement it were destined to fail. Escapes were frequent and recidivism rates were high under this system.

The abolition of the contract system and the development of group-oriented residential centers on the cottage plan was accompanied by a shift in the dominant operating philosophy of the juvenile institutions. In the absence of contract work, programs were instituted to provide skills and vocational training to youths. Also, time spent in educational pursuits was increased. The cottage plan meant more individualized treatment and an increased opportunity for interaction. New conceptions of treatment which emphasized guidance and retraining the individual grew out of the failures of the old programs.

Unfortunately, lack of financial support has been a persistent problem for juvenile corrections. A lack of funds has often subverted the goals of the new philosophy. Vocational training has not been effectively provided in many reform or training schools. Urban youngsters are frequently sent to rural environments to learn farming skills. Training may involve the learning of low-demand skills or prepare the individual for only the lowest-paying jobs.

A Working Philosophy

If a treatment program is to produce lasting change in behavior, it must reach the delinquent and the reasons for his or her behavior. Appeals or exhortations to good or right conduct are not enough. Superficial conformity amounts to training in deception. Most training school inmates can distinguish between "playing it cool" and those who are really doing good. In order to produce genuine behavior change, the juvenile must be compelled honestly to examine his behavior and face the reasons for it. He should not be allowed to just get by. Reform or retraining cannot be accomplished until the juvenile begins to believe that conforming behavior is the best course of action.[5]

The use of positive inducements to bring about new, conforming attitudes and thereby acceptable behavior is an idea increasingly advocated by specialists in juvenile corrections. It is suggested that the use of negative sanctions or punishment focuses the juvenile's attention on the institution and away from his or her own behavior. Disciplined juveniles are likely to see corrections personnel as adversaries and refuse to cooperate in their own treatment programs. A hostile attitude toward authorities and a belief in the unjustness of the system may only strengthen delinquent resolve.

Modern treatment philosophy often conflicts with societal demands. Communities demand protection from dangerous and serious offenders, and its institutions have the obligation to meet this requirement. Ideally, the correctional institution should strike a delicate balance between concern for the safety of the community and the welfare of offenders. In practice, security measures often take precedence. Administrators often believe they are evaluated on the basis of the number of escapes that occur under their management. As a result, tough management procedures and security systems are devised and justified as appropriate measures to protect the institution. The youngster is expected to conform to rigid standards which serve the institution and the administrative staff.[6]

The President's Commission suggested that the effectiveness of training schools is impaired by its use as a multipurpose facility.[7] The training school is sometimes used as a temporary holding facility for juveniles awaiting court action. It may also be used as temporary housing for youths in anticipation of foster home placement. The use of a correctional facility to handle retarded youths and other problem children places an added burden on staff and results in overcrowding. Juveniles are frequently returned to the community not because they have been successfully treated but because practical considerations of space, staff, or finances indicate release.

The failure of modern juvenile corrections to meet the treatment goals incorporated in the philosophy of juvenile corrections has been pointed out by numerous authorities. Much of the criticism involves a restatement and elaboration of goals. A Children's Bureau report, for example, states:

> The prime function of a training school is to re-educate and train the child to become a responsible well-adjusted citizen. . . . Training schools must be essentially treatment institutions with an integrated professional service, wherein the disciplines of education, casework, group work, psychology, psychiatry, medicine, nursing, vocational rehabilitation, religion, all play an important role. Through such an integrated treatment program the child is expected to learn self-discipline, to accept more responsibilities, and act and react in a more socially acceptable manner.[8]

In practice, juvenile corrections have a long way to go in meeting these far-reaching goals. Public support must be increased considerably if the programs are to become highly developed.

Most correctional facilities for juveniles provide some academic and vocational education for their inmates. Forestry camps, ranches, and farms for juveniles are somewhat more likely to offer only academic education than training schools, halfway houses, or group homes. Almost all correctional facilities also offer individual or group counseling; about 60 percent offer counseling with both the juvenile and his or her family. Job placement programs have not been as well received in juvenile correctional institutions. The Law Enforcement Assistance Administration reported their acceptance in 1971 in only 46 percent of the training schools, 37 percent of the halfway houses and group homes, and 16 percent of the ranches, forestry camps, and farms.[9] Primarily the programs of correctional institutions include vocational and academic education supplemented by some individual and group counseling.

Another aspect of the correctional program for juveniles involves recreational activities and facilities. Recreation facilities are usually provided for the inmates of correctional institutions. Most offer radio, movies, or television. Training schools and farm-oriented facilities offer libraries, while halfway houses and group homes are more likely to use community facilities. Gymnasiums or athletic fields are provided in over 95 percent of the training schools and farm-oriented institutions. Many of the halfway houses and group homes either use community facilities or do not offer this type of recreation.[10]

CORRECTIONAL FACILITIES IN USE

Only a small proportion of children in trouble are eventually placed in a juvenile correctional facility. Many authorities have argued that the institutionalization of youths is an unworkable, ineffective treatment strategy. The general consensus is that juvenile correctional institutions probably do more harm than good. As a result of such unfavorable attitudes, many juveniles are placed on probation or diverted from the juvenile justice system. Juveniles are institutionalized as a last-resort measure to protect the interests of community safety or to provide a setting in which the juvenile can be protected from himself.[11]

The Target Population

In 1971 there were 85,000 youngsters housed in a variety of juvenile residential correction facilities. Most were placed in the high-security environments of training schools; however, some were assigned to semisecure facilities such as halfway houses or group homes. The majority of the inmates were males. Females were more likely than males to be sent to maximum-security facilities. Ninety percent of all institutionalized females were placed in training schools, compared with 77 percent of the institutionalized males. Males (2.9 percent) and females (3.4 percent) were about equally likely to be placed in minimum-security halfway houses or group homes. While boys were more often assigned to medium-security facilities, this is probably a function of the types of medium-security institutions available. Ranches, forestry camps, and farms are generally considered male facilities. Only 6 percent of the inmates of these facilities were girls. Table 15.1 provides a summary view of the dispersion of youths in juvenile correctional institutions in 1971.[12]

TABLE 15.1 ADMISSIONS TO JUVENILE CORRECTIONAL FACILITIES BY TYPE OF INSTITUTION, SEX, AND TYPE OF FACILITY

| | ADMISSIONS | | | COMMITTED BY COURT | | | | RETURNED FROM AFTERCARE OR PAROLE | | TRANSFERRED IN | | OTHER | |
| | | | | FIRST COMMITMENTS | | RECOMMITMENTS | | | | | | | |
	TOTAL	MALE	FE-MALE	MALE	FE-MALE	MALE	FE-MALE	MALE	FE-MALE	MALE	FE-MALE	MALE	FE-MALE
Training schools													
Number	67,558	52,960	14,598	31,453	9,413	4,706	416	9,821	2,735	4,118	989	2,862	1,045
Percentage	100	78	22	47	14	7	1	14	4	6	2	4	2
Ranches, forestry camps, and farms													
Number	14,956	14,062	894	9,222	701	1,336	68	898	57	2,191	68	415	0
Percentage	100	94	6	62	5	9	a	6	a	15	a	3	0
Halfway houses and group homes													
Number	2,566	2,007	559	785	296	33	6	150	45	562	74	477	138
Percentage	100	78	22	31	12	1	a	6	2	22	3	9	5
All correctional facilities													
Number	85,080	69,029	16,051	41,460	10,410	6,075	490	10,869	2,837	6,871	1,131	3,754	1,183
Percentage	100	81	19	49	12	7	1	13	3	8	1	4	1

a 0.5 percent or less. Percentages might not add up to 100 because of rounding off.
Source: Law Enforcement Assistance Administration, *Sourcebook of Criminal Justice Statistics, 1974* (Washington, D.C.: Government Printing Office, 1975), tab. 6.3, p. 418.

TABLE 15.2 NUMBER OF JUVENILE FACILITIES AND
NUMBER OF CHILDREN HELD, JUNE 30, 1971 AND JUNE 30, 1973

TYPE OF FACILITY	1971		1973	
	NUMBER OF FACILITIES	NUMBER OF CHILDREN HELD	NUMBER OF FACILITIES	NUMBER OF CHILDREN HELD
Detention centers	303	11,748	319	10,782
Shelters	18	363	19	190
Reception and diagnostic centers	17	2,486	17	1,734
Training schools	192	35,931	187	26,427
Ranches, forestry camps, and farms	114	5,666	103	4,959
Halfway houses and group homes	78	1,045	149	1,602
Total all facilities	722	57,239	794	45,694

Source: Law Enforcement Assistance Administration, *Children in Custody: Advance Report on the Juvenile Detention and Correctional Facility Census of 1972–73* (Washington, D.C.: Government Printing Office, 1975), pp. 8–9, and *Children in Custody: A Report on the Juvenile Detention and Correctional Facility Census of 1971* (Washington, D.C.: Government Printing Office, 1974), p. 1.

Most of the admissions to juvenile institutions are referred by the juvenile court as a result of a first commitment; however, juveniles may be admitted for other reasons. In 1971, 61 percent were admitted as first commitments from the juvenile court; 8 percent of the admissions were second commitments. Aftercare failures accounted for 16 percent of the population. Transfers and those referred for other reasons made up 14 percent of the admissions.[13]

The number of children held in public detention and correctional institutions has *decreased* significantly since 1971. The population on June 30, 1971, was 54,729; on June 30, 1973, it was 45,694.[14] Female commitments decreased more rapidly than male commitments. During this same period, the number of public detention and correctional facilities for juveniles *increased* from 722 to 794.[15]

A comparison of the distribution of types of facilities in use in 1971 and 1973 provides some insight into the changes that have occurred in the treatment philosophy (see Table 15.2). It appears that small-group care in minimum-security facilities is the trend in juvenile corrections. The actual number of minimum-security facilities (halfway houses and group homes) has nearly doubled. These facilities were used by 4 percent of all children in custody in 1973; in 1971 they were used by less than 2 percent of these youths. Maximum-security institutions (training schools) have fallen into increasing disfavor. Although they have decreased only slightly in number, training schools have had a significant decrease in clientele. In 1971 these facilities were handling 63 percent of the children in custody; in 1973 they sheltered only 57 percent of these youths.

Social Organization of Juvenile Facilities

The social organization of the juvenile training school is similar to that of adult prisons, even though the physical plant is usually quite different. The training school frequently gives the outward appearance of an old, dilapidated boarding school. Groups of a dozen or more live in small cottages or dormitories on a "campus" which features structures such as classrooms, farm buildings, shops, and an administration building. However, the "student" is not free to leave the grounds for holidays or long weekends. The social life of the resident is restricted to activities that take place within and between these structures.

Training schools usually have a superintendent as the chief administrative officer. Traditionally the superintendent came to the institution as a beneficiary of the political spoils system of the state. An ex-sheriff or other retired politico is often appointed to the post in institutions for males. As a result, many of the superintendents have not generally brought impressive credentials, adequate skills, expert knowledge of training and rehabilitation techniques, or organizational management expertise to the institutions. Although the recent trend has emphasized professionalization of the position, many superintendents are still appointed by the old system.

The rest of the training school staff can be divided into three major groups. The first includes the kitchen personnel, clerks, maintenance personnel, and similar workers involved in maintaining the facilities. The second group is made up of teachers, supervisors, social workers, and others in charge of juvenile retraining and rehabilitation. The third group includes cottage parents or supervisors. It is this third group that has responsibility for the young inmate during the day when the inmate is not taking part in formal programs and at night. The cottage workers have closer and more sustained contact with the juvenile than any other group within the institution. The opportunity to develop warm, positive relationships with the juveniles in their charge is limited, however, by the cottage supervisor's responsibility to enforce institutional rules and guard against escape or disturbance. These workers, by virtue of their sustained contact, are in the best position to assess the effects of the institutional program on the young offenders.[16]

Louis Harris and Associates reported that in 1968 most personnel in juvenile institutions were male, with a median age of 41.5. About 79 percent were white, while 21 percent were listed as black. Both blacks and women were more likely to find employment in juvenile institutions than in adult institutions.[17] When polled about the goals of the juvenile correctional institution, a large majority (75 percent) of the correctional workers chose correction as the primary goal; 15 percent chose protection of society as the major goal. Only 5 percent responded that punishment or societal change was a major goal.[18]

In the past, training schools have offered minimal treatment programs (limited formal education, vocational training, and some job-related experience). Individual or group therapy was infrequent. The major concern of the institution centered around the prevention of escape and major disruptions. Escapes create problems for the institution because the community tends to react negatively. Frequent escapes may lead to harsh vocal criticism, even though most escapees are quickly recaptured without incident. Few escapes, however, lead to major disruption in the community. Running away, or "rambles," from the institution are nevertheless perceived as serious acts which must be prevented, and the offender is usually punished by loss of privileges or by other techniques.

Juvenile correctional institutions face severe structural problems. Uncooperative individuals must be controlled or restrained, but a lack of adequately trained staff often precludes the use of positive, effective measures. Corporal punishment has occasionally been used to keep the juveniles in line in the absence of other techniques. Aside from institutional and societal disapproval, there are other reasons why such practices should be abandoned. First, they are ineffective; second, they create safety hazards for institutional personnel. A cottage supervisor who uses physical attack as a disciplinary measure is in danger of reprisals from the inmates. Some innovative correctional personnel have experimented with nonpunitive measures. Nevertheless, most institutions still rely on limitation of privileges and special living quarters arrangements for rule violators.

THE PEER SUBCULTURE

A peer-centered subculture develops in most correctional centers and is passed on to each new set of recruits as they enter and become socialized into the institution. Aside from interaction with cottage supervisors, teachers, and other staff, the resident's contact with straight individuals is severely limited. The inmates, however, constantly interact among themselves. Through intensive contact, a common system of values, attitudes, and norms is developed. Older, bigger, and more mature inmates often become a powerful force in the closed youthful community. With the tacit approval of institutional staff, inmate leaders may coerce younger and less sophisticated youth into acceptable forms of behavior. In return, the leader may be allowed to victimize his fellow inmates undisturbed.

New arrivals are introduced into a preexisting culture by outsiders (the juvenile court judge or institutional staff). As an unknown quantity, they are a potential threat to existing arrangements and understandings. Thus the group must test new members to discover their strengths and weaknesses and properly assign their positions in the structure. Weaklings and informers, who may be destructive of the system, must be identified so they can be controlled. Physical force may be used, or the new residents may be tricked into violating institutional rules, to assess their ability to handle themselves and their attitude toward the juvenile subculture.[19]

Studies of the social structure in boys' juvenile institutions suggest that the system that develops is fairly standard. Breed found five distinct levels of authority in his study.[20] The structure is not unlike that found among organized juveniles in the community. In fact, membership in a clique and position in the power structure of the institution may be related to prior gang membership on the outside. (Case 15.1 illustrates this connection.) One or more leaders can be identified at the top of the hierarchy. A leader is able to manipulate the group to support him, and he uses the power of the majority to enforce his authority. He may be a good fighter, but qualities such as sensitivity to the group, personality, good verbal ability, and daring often seem to be more important.

On the second level of the structure are the lieutenants, tough boys, or con artists. This group usually operates directly under the auspices of the leader (or leaders) and will be the most influential group in the cottage or the institution. This group implements the policy of the leader, and from its ranks a new leader will emerge when the old leader leaves the institution. They are often the biggest, strongest, toughest, and most verbal of the inmates. A third level of the power structure is composed of straights or conformists. These individuals try to remain quietly in the background. While not acting tough, they often cooperate with the leaders to stay out of trouble in the institution. The fourth group includes the "mess-ups," who are constantly in trouble. Childish behavior, fighting, and arguing are frequent within this group. "Finks," stool pigeons, or tale bearers are also found in this group. They are not trusted or liked by the others. The "kissy," who tries to ingratiate himself with staff members, has low status even in this group. Generally the "mess-ups" as a group are disliked because their behavior is inappropriate when measured by the standards of the inmate subculture. In addition, their behavior sometimes leads to punishment of the entire inmate population. The lowest level of the hierarchy is reserved for punks, scapegoats, drug freaks, and newcomers. They are, because of their position, exploited by individuals from all other levels. New inmates may move out of this position rather rapidly, but mental defectives, some homosexuals, cowards, and those with severe personality disorders remain at the lowest level indefinitely.

Mobility from one level to another is possible, but it is usually determined by the leaders. An individual must prove his ability by

CASE 15.1

THE BIG REUNION

One inmate described his reception and acceptance into a juvenile correctional institution as a reunion with close friends and associates. Being accepted as a member and leader was a great source of prestige. Some kids derive more personal satisfaction playing the game in the institution than trying to make it in the straight world of the street. Listen to this account:

> When I got to Warwick [a juvenile correctional institution in New York], it was like coming home, a great reunion! I had only been home for about four months, and most of the cats I'd left at Warwick were still there, so there was a place for me. . . . I still had my rep at Warwick. Before I left the second time, I was running B-1 cottage; I had become the "main man" . . . I knew how to operate up there. I had an extortion game going, but it was a thing that the cats went along with because I didn't allow anybody to bully anybody and that sort of thing. Since I didn't get many visitors from home, I made other guys pay protection fees to me when they received visits or packages from home. I just ran the place, and I kept it quiet. I didn't have to bully anybody. . . . My reputation for hurting cats was indisputable. I could run any cottage that I'd been in with an iron hand.

Source: Claude Brown, <u>Manchild in the Promised Land</u> (New York: New American Library [Signet], 1965), pp. 154-156.

fighting, by cooperating with the leaders, by previous institutional experience, and by learning the correct patterns of behavior.[21] Other prized personal characteristics that could lead to mobility include group loyalty, fighting ability, generosity, verbal skill, and familiarity with the underworld.[22]

Interaction with peers may be an important part of the maturing and socializing process for any individual; juveniles improve their ability to develop friendships and get along with others while they are in the institution. On the other hand, not all peer interactions in the institution are healthy or helpful for the juvenile. The negative aspects of the peer subculture are obvious. The patronage system and victimization of other inmates is difficult to justify. Victimization involves practices in which weaker inmates are used by the elite to get even for some real or imagined offense or to get scarce goods such as toys, candy, or drugs.[23]

Howard Polsky examined the inmate structure of a boys' cottage in a private correctional facility and found a diamond-shaped power structure in which most boys held a middle position and few held either high or low positions. The system persisted over time, even when the inmates entered and left the institution. For short periods after leaders left, competition or conflict was present as the remaining lieutenants sought to fill the power vacuum. Significantly, Polsky observed that the inmate system was aided and supported by the staff of the institution.[24] The failure of staff to intervene served to legitimize the peer power structure among the inmates.

There appears to be considerable agreement on the composition of the inmate structure. Staff and inmates identify nearly the same hierarchy when asked to rank individuals. When an inmate engaged in disruptive behavior, the staff frequently interpreted the behavior as indicating psychological maladjustment rather than behavior resulting from the inmate social structure. Authorities do not always undermine the inmate social structure; instead, they may react to it by differentially rewarding individuals who hold high status in the peer social structure. Furthermore, Fisher reported that both inmates and supervisors victimize some individuals.[25]

STAFF-INMATE RELATIONSHIPS

The inmate code stresses the necessity of developing and maintaining social distance between the staff and the inmates. Inmates develop a united front against the staff, and they often resent the efforts of some inmates to bridge the gap or initiate close contacts with institutional personnel. As a result, the treatment staff faces severe obstacles in trying to help inmates. Sometimes viewed as "stoolies" by the inmates, clinical personnel are often "jived," "conned," or manipulated to suit the needs or whims of inmates. Because the treatment staff may have the power to influence work assignments, length of stay, and other features of inmate life in the institution, the juveniles often attempt to create favorable impressions through superficial conformity rather than open resistance and defiance.

STAFF CONFLICTS

Organizational problems result when rehabilitation rather than custodial handling is introduced as a major institutional goal. Jenkins suggests that a major change in institutional goals must be accompanied by a change in staff if it is to be fully effective. Unless the staff is favorable to the treatment goal, the diagnostic and treatment recommendations made by specialized staff may be ignored or subverted by custodial-oriented staff.[26]

George Weber and Lloyd Ohlin suggest that conflict may result from a redefinition of the roles of key staff members when new treatment goals are introduced. One problem centers on the difficulties of the cottage parents or supervisors. Treatment goals are often perceived as an attempt to undermine or reduce the authority and prestige of the cottage supervisor. Not only are the workers expected to run a cottage program, but they are expected to contribute to therapy. On the other hand, the cottage worker is seldom given clear instruction on how to meet these demands. As a result, they often face role conflict and status ambiguity. They may know little about what they are to do or what their position is in the hierarchy of the institution.[27] Weber and Zald note an additional problem that may arise when rehabilitation is introduced into custodial institutions. Cooperation among staff members is often replaced by conflicts between treatment and custodial workers. Inmates often recognize the conflicts and manage to manipulate them for their own benefit.[28]

Street, Vinter, and Perrow compared the organizational structures of six juvenile training schools which varied in size, type of program offered, and source of support. Generally the researchers found that size and source of support influenced the social structure of the school. State-supported schools were under more pressure from the public than were the private schools. Treatment-oriented schools reported more conflicts among staff. Conflicts were heightened when staff members from different parts of the total school program engaged in communication and joint decision making. They also reported that the most effective and conflict-free institutions were those characterized by high degrees of staff consensus on goals and where the treatment program was adequately staffed and funded.[29]

WHO GOES TO TRAINING SCHOOLS?

Youths are committed to juvenile correctional institutions for a variety of reasons. The popular idea that only unmanageable and dangerous offenders are committed to juvenile institutions is certainly not an accurate one. The Law Enforcement Assistance Administration reported that in 1972–1973 less than 50 percent of all institutionalized males, and approximately 10 percent of all institutionalized females, were placed after commission of felony offenses.[30] Although males are about equally likely to be committed for felonies as for misdemeanors, females are much more likely to be placed in institutions for status offenses. Sexual permissiveness, running away, and ungovernability were common reasons for female commitments. The distribution of types of offenses represented in juvenile institutions in 1971 is shown in Figure 15.1.

There are indications that the institutional population may be changing. In recent years, more and more females are being apprehended for offenses traditionally associated with the male delinquent.[31] Offenses that require physical skill or aggressiveness are no longer in

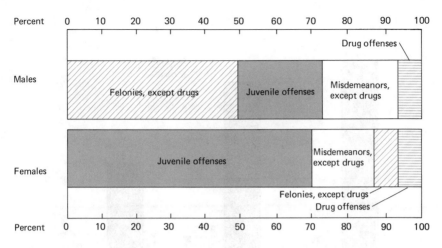

Figure 15.1 Percentage Distribution by Sex and Offense

Source: Law Enforcement Assistance Administration, *Children in Custody: Report of the Juvenile Detention and Correctional Facility Census of 1971* (Washington, D.C.: Government Printing Office, 1974).

the exclusive domain of the male subculture. Although females have been more likely to receive unofficial handling in the past, their new freedom and willingness to venture into traditionally male activities may result in more formal handling in the future.

Although adjudicated delinquents make up the major proportion of the total institutional population, other juveniles may be placed in the facilities for varying periods of time. Figure 15.2 reports the proportion of youths who have been adjudicated. The fact that offense data is unavailable in some jurisdictions may reflect some of the local practices of handling troublesome youths. Juveniles in some states can be committed under the labels of PINS, CHINS, incorrigible, unruly, or unmanageable and not for a specific statute offense. If the individual sent to a correctional facility falls into one of these classifications, an offense may not be specified. Thus the correctional facility is not able to provide offense data for all its inmates.[32] Some parents still seek the juvenile court's aid in controlling a troublesome youth, and the individual may be sent to a correctional facility under the label of incorrigible or "in need of supervision."[33]

The training school and other correctional facilities are used for a variety of purposes. The facilities are sometimes used in place of a detention home to house juveniles who are being held prior to a court hearing. In fact, 6,397 juveniles were held in these facilities pending court action in 1973, and in the same year another 528 dependent and neglected children were held in correctional facilities. Some youngsters, including 460 held in 1973, are held in the correctional institutions while waiting to be transferred to some other jurisdiction.[34]

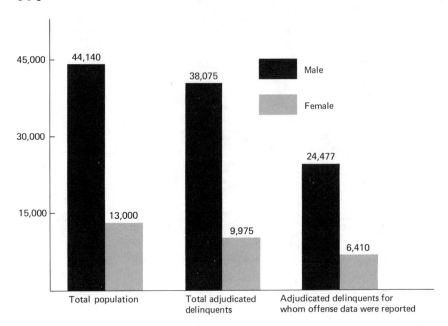

Figure 15.2 Total Population of Juvenile Facilities, Total Adjudicated Delinquents Held, and Number of Adjudicated Delinquents for Whom Offense Data Were Reported, by Sex

Source: Law Enforcement Assistance Administration, *Children in Custody: Report of the Juvenile Detention and Correctional Facility Census of 1971* (Washington, D.C.: Government Printing Office, 1974).

The effects of housing these diverse groups of youngsters in the same facilities as individuals who have been adjudicated delinquent as a result of a felony or because of repeated delinquent acts is not well understood. The effects, however, are probably not beneficial. Detention homes for those awaiting court action or transfer to other institutions should be provided. In addition, the dependent and neglected should be placed in foster homes or group homes to escape the effects of training school placement.

THE COST OF CORRECTION

Juvenile correction facilities are expected to accomplish a change of behavior in the juveniles under their charge. Considerable financial assistance has been provided by local and state authorities for this purpose. The Law Enforcement Assistance Administration has compiled information regarding the expenditures of public funds.[35] Much of this information for 1971 is presented in summary form in Table 15.3. There does not appear to be a wide range of expenditures from one type of institution to another. The average per capita expenditure was $6,760 in 1971. By 1973, the per capita operating expenditure had risen to $9,582.[36] This represents a rapid increase in total expenditures over

TABLE 15.3 AVERAGE DAILY POPULATION,
TOTAL OPERATING EXPENDITURES,
AND PER CAPITA OPERATING EXPENDITURES
OF JUVENILE INSTITUTIONS BY TYPE OF FACILITY, 1971

TYPE OF FACILITY	AVERAGE DAILY POPULATION DURING FISCAL YEAR 1971	TOTAL OPERATING EXPENDITURES (THOUSANDS OF DOLLARS)	PER CAPITA OPERATING EXPENDITURES
Training schools	36,640	248,234	6,775
Ranches, forestry camps, and farms	5,544	37,238	6,717
Halfway houses and group homes	1,003	6,494	6,475
Total correctional facilities	43,187	291,966	6,760

Source: Law Enforcement Assistance Administration, *Children in Custody: A Report on the Juvenile Detention and Correctional Facility Census of 1971* (Washington, D.C.: Government Printing Office, 1974), p. 19.

a short period of time, but it was during a period of runaway inflation in most economic areas. Therefore the increase in expenditures does not necessarily represent improvement in correctional facility operations. While the cost per child may appear to be high when compared to the average expenditure for raising a child in the community, it must be remembered that these children have special problems which resulted in community failures. Expert guidance and treatment are needed to bring these children into the mainstream of society so that they may eventually achieve a successful reintegration into the community.

Juvenile institutions have not always been successful. Some of the juveniles commit further delinquencies or crimes after their return to the community. No doubt, additional funds may be required to upgrade existing institutions, implement new innovative programs, and hire additional trained personnel. However, it is also apparent that juvenile institutions do not always use available funds in the most efficient ways. Most institutions would benefit from a review of the effectiveness of programs offered and from reassigning priorities.

EFFECTIVENESS OF INSTITUTIONAL PROGRAMS

The evidence regarding the effectiveness of institutional programs is conflicting. Simpson reports that juveniles frequently believe the institutional experience is effective.[37] Institutionalized youngsters report greater support for ambition, rationality, responsibility, and consideration of others on release than at the time of their admission. These changed attitudes were used to support the conclusion that institutionalization has a slightly favorable impact on delinquent youths.

Objective measures of effectiveness have been difficult to construct. Juveniles might be considered successful if they are not returned to a correctional institution, regardless of whether they adjust to the community. On the other hand, they might be considered successful only if they adopt conventional life styles and do not exhibit any indication of social maladjustment. One solution is to use several measures of program success. Some training schools may be adept at helping juveniles avoid future contact with the police, but they may have little, or even a negative, effect on their social adjustment. Others may be effective in the opposite way. Research programs to evaluate the effects of institutionalization are needed.[38]

The best evidence suggests that about half of all juveniles from training schools are later incarcerated in a jail, adult prison, or another training school. Some institutions, however, are more successful than others. H. Asley Weeks reported that the Highlands Center in New Jersey had a 63 percent success rate for completing the program and avoiding imprisonment for at least eight months after release. Weeks found a 47 percent success rate for Annandale, a state reformatory, using the same success criteria.[39] Gibbons and Prince found a 63 percent success rate in Borstal (Great Britain). Their criterion for success was adoption of noncriminal careers.[40] But Alan Little, using a different criterion of success—subsequent reconviction during the five years after release—found only a 44 percent success rate for Borstal.[41]

These studies do not consider the different types of inmates assigned to institutions. If this factor is considered, an interesting finding is noted. Martinson found little support for the idea that correctional facilities with rehabilitation programs will turn out more successful individuals than custodial institutions. He concluded that rehabilitation programs had little effect on recidivism.[42] Martinson did not consider the effects of social and psychological factors that exist outside the institution. These are not under the control of training schools. It is possible that factors exist in the family and community that may prevent successful rehabilitation despite the best efforts of the training school and that the training school cannot change.

JUVENILES IN ADULT INSTITUTIONS

In 1970—the last year in which commitments to state prisons were reported by age—at least 15,665 individuals under age 20 were sent to state prisons or reformatories. This figure represented about 9 percent of all prison and reformatory commitments. Robbery, burglary, and larceny are frequent offenses for members of this group, who are usually older adolescents. Fewer than 2000 of the juvenile prisoners in these institutions were under age 16. State adult correctional institutions, however, housed 53 children under age 5! Most of these were infants of female inmates.[43]

The 1975 *Sourcebook of Criminal Justice Statistics* reports that 79 youngsters aged 17 and under were housed in federal correctional institutions in 1970. Another 705 prisoners aged 18 and 19 were lodged in the same year. Most of the youngsters of age 17 and under were admitted under the Federal Juvenile Delinquency Act.[44]

Other youths are held in local jails and workhouses operated by cities or counties. Persons awaiting trial or serving short sentences may be kept in these institutions. The *Sourcebook* reports that 60 children under 5 years old and 76 between the ages of 5 and 9 years were held in these institutions. In addition, about 619 youngsters between the ages of 10 and 14 and 19,015 between 15 and 19 years of age were being held in these institutions in 1970.[45]

JUVENILE CORRECTIONS IN PERSPECTIVE

Few juvenile correctional facilities offer effective therapeutic programs in a warm, friendly setting. Any secure facility that handles large numbers of youths has some limitations when compared with treatment in the community setting. However, some youths are not successfully handled in the community and require the more intensive supervision provided by a restricted residential institution.

The average length of stay in a juvenile institution varies according to the type of institution. In training schools nine months is the norm, while other facilities, such as halfway houses, forestry camps, and farms have an average stay of seven months. Generally the facilities are segregated by sex, with institutions for males outnumbering those for females. Most juvenile facilities provide multifaceted treatment programs. Nearly all offer vocational and academic training programs. A large proportion also offer group or individual counseling and recreation programs. The existence of these facilities and programs, however, has not been accepted as evidence that the institutions are doing an adequate job in the correction of juveniles.[46]

The future of juvenile institutions is not clear. Correctional officials, judges, criminologists, sociologists, and others are dissatisfied with the concept of training schools. The rate of institutionalization has dropped even as the juvenile arrest rate has continued to increase. Although some facilities are still overcrowded, others are operating at less than 70 percent of full capacity.[47] Much of the decline is the result of the juvenile judge's reluctance to place juveniles in training schools unless their acts are serious or repeated. Diversion to foster homes, YMCAs, or shelters is common, and independent placements and other means have been found to avoid sending juveniles to training schools. Of course, this means that the training schools are probably receiving the youngsters who are the most difficult to rehabilitate or treat. The return to a custodial institution with the segregation of these young offenders from society may be a needed step, but seriously disturbed and delinquent youngsters require the best rehabilitative programs that can be devised. Complete pessimism over treatment in training schools or other institutions, however, is probably not warranted. Treatment can and does bring changes for some people. In addition, the techniques available for treatment are continuing to change and improve. In the future, the success rate for treatment programs may improve if resources are channeled in this direction.

NOTES

[1] Chapter 1 provides a more in-depth discussion of juvenile corrections.

[2] Harry Elmer Barnes and Negley K. Teeters, *New Horizons in Criminology*, 3d ed. (Englewood Cliffs, N.J.: Prentice-Hall, 1959), p. 290.

[3] *Ibid.*

[4] Stephen Schafer and Richard K. Knudten, *Juvenile Delinquency: An Introduction* (New York: Random House, 1970), p. 321.

[5] President's Commission on Law Enforcement and Administration of Justice, *Task Force Report: Juvenile Delinquency and Youth Crime* (Washington, D.C.: Government Printing Office, 1967), pp. 141–145.

[6] *Ibid.*

[7] *Ibid.*

[8] Department of Health, Education, and Welfare, Children's Bureau, *Institutions Serving Delinquent Children* (Washington, D.C.: Government Printing Office, 1957).

[9] Law Enforcement Assistance Administration, *Children in Custody: A Report of the Juvenile Detention and Correctional Facility Census of 1971* (Washington, D.C.: Government Printing Office, 1974).

[10] *Ibid.*

[11] *Ibid.*, p. 6.

[12] Data on the sex composition of juvenile inmate populations are not yet available beyond 1971. Due to the change in format, Law Enforcement Assistance Administration statistics are not always strictly comparable from 1971 to 1973.

[13] *Children in Custody, op. cit.*

[14] Law Enforcement Assistance Administration, *Children in Custody: Advance Report on the Juvenile Detention and Correctional Facility Census of 1972–73* (Washington, D.C.: Governing Printing Office, 1975), p. 1.

[15] *Ibid.*

[16] See Sethard Fisher, "Social Organization in a Correctional Residence," *Pacific Sociological Review* 9 (fall 1961): 87–93; Howard Polsky, "Changing Delinquent Subcultures: A Social-Psychological Approach," *Social Work* 10 (October 1959): 3–15; Howard Polsky, *Cottage Six* (New York: Russell Sage Foundation, 1962).

[17] Louis Harris and Associates, *Corrections 1968: A Climate for Change* (Joint Commission on Correctional Manpower and Training, Washington, D.C., 1968).

[18] *Ibid.*

[19] Allen Breed, "Inmate Subcultures," *California Youth Authority Quarterly* 16 (spring 1953): 6–7.

[20] *Ibid.*

[21] *Ibid.*

[22] Claude Brown, *Manchild in the Promised Land* (New York: Macmillan, 1965).

[23] Breed, *op. cit.*

[24] Polsky, "Changing Delinquent Subcultures," *op. cit.*, and Polsky, *Cottage Six, op. cit.*

[25] Fisher, *op. cit.*

[26] Allen Jenkins, "Treatment in an Institution," *American Journal of Orthopsychiatry* 11 (January 1941): 85–91.

[27] George Weber, "Emotional and Defensive Reactions of Cottage Parents," in *The Prison*, ed. Donald R. Cressey (New York: Holt, Rinehart and Winston, 1961), pp. 189–228; Lloyd Ohlin, Robert B. Coates, and Alden D. Miller, "Radical Correctional Reform: A Case Study of the Massachusetts Youth Correctional System," *Harvard Educational Review* 44 (February 1974): 74–111.

[28] Weber, *op. cit.*; Meyer Zald, "Power Balance and Staff Conflict in a Correctional Institution," *Administrative Science Quarterly* 7 (June 1962): 22–49.

[29] David Street, Robert D. Vinter, and Charles Perrow, *Organization for Treatment* (New York: Free Press, 1966).

[30] *Children in Custody* (1971), *op. cit.*

[31] *Ibid.*, p. 7.

[32] *Ibid.*

[33] *Ibid.*

[34] *Children in Custody* (1972–73), *op. cit.*, p. 12.

[35] *Children in Custody* (1971), *op. cit.*, p. 19.

[36] *Children in Custody* (1972–73), *op. cit.*, p. 1.

[37] Jon E. Simpson et al., "Institutionalization as Perceived by the Juvenile Offender," *Sociology and Social Research* 48 (October 1963): 13–23.

[38] Paul Lerman, "Evolutive Studies of Institutions for Juveniles," *Social Work* 13 (July 1968): 55–64.

[39] H. Ashley Weeks, *Youthful Offenders at Highfields* (Ann Arbor: University of Michigan Press, 1958), p. 42.

[40] Terence Gibbons and J. Prince, *The Results of Borstal Training*, Sociological Review Monograph, no. 9 (1965), pp. 230–239.

[41] Alan Little, "Penal Theory, Reform and Borstal Practice," *British Journal of Criminology* 3 (January 1963): 257–275.

[42] Robert Martinson, "What Works? Questions and Answers About Prison Reform," *Public Interest* 35 (spring 1974): 25–33.

[43] Law Enforcement Assistance Administration, *Sourcebook of Criminal Justice Statistics, 1974* (Washington, D.C.: Government Printing Office, 1975), p. 461.

[44] *Ibid.*

[45] *Ibid.*

[46] *Children in Custody, 1972–1973, op. cit.*

[47] *Ibid.*

CHAPTER 16

Release and reception of delinquents

A delinquent boy or girl may spend time under supervision after release from an institution. The purpose of continued supervision is to provide guidance and assist the juvenile in making a successful adjustment upon reentering the community. The delinquent is usually released into the same community from which he or she came; therefore the family and the community that receives him will probably not be radically different from the one he left. The delinquent youth often must return to the same school with old gang members. The physical, social, cultural, and other aspects of the community in which he became delinquent will be unchanged. However, the returned juvenile may find that teachers and other people in the community react differently toward him as a result of his delinquent label. Without support, the juvenile may not be able to withstand the pressures to return to old behavior patterns. Further trouble with police and readmission to a juvenile institution is a frequent outcome.

The National Council on Crime and Delinquency defines juvenile aftercare as "the release of a child from an institution at a time when he can benefit from release and from life in the community under the supervision of a counselor."[1] *Juvenile aftercare* is a term used to make a clear distinction between juvenile programs and the adult system of parole. Unfortunately, this term has not been accepted in all areas, and some juveniles are still "paroled." If the behavior of a child is such that it warrants confinement in an institution, a complex set of correctional services may be set in motion to help the individual when he or she leaves the institution.

Institutionalization may do different things to different individuals. For some, adjustment to community life is facilitated by a relatively short confinement in a training school. For others, increased sophistication in delinquent activities and more antisocial behavior may be the result. Others may become dependent on training school personnel and require help to break their ties with the school. Aftercare provides an additional opportunity to achieve the objective of correction or rehabilitation. Thus aftercare is frequently regarded as an integral part of the correctional program.

EARLY JUVENILE AFTERCARE PROGRAMS

Informal aftercare programs have long been a feature of the juvenile justice system. Even the early houses of refuge provided release from the institution under supervision. The earliest juvenile institution, the New York House of Refuge, indentured a small percentage of the released inmates, but many more were released without provision for supervision. When the New York Juvenile Asylum was chartered in 1851, it was given authority to keep children in custody until they had "shown sufficient improvement" and to indenture them to responsible families. When this practice was challenged in 1872, the New York Supreme Court found the practice of apprenticeship to be beneficial and necessary.[2] Under the apprenticeship and indenture systems, the child was expected to work, obey the master, and learn job skills. The total responsibility for the juvenile's food, clothing, shelter, and training rested with the family contracting his or her services. Final release was granted either after a specified period of time or when the contracting family decided the youth had earned his or her freedom.

A variation on these programs involved foster home placement. Responsible citizens could volunteer to take in wayward children and provide guidance. This type of aftercare persisted until parole came into widespread use for adults, after which time aftercare programs tailored to the needs of youths began to evolve.

USE OF AFTERCARE

In 1971—the most recent year for which statistics are available—over 85,000 juveniles were released from correctional institutions designed for youths. Table 16.1 indicates the percentage of releases by type of institution. Many of these youths were placed in aftercare or parole programs. Table 16.2, which provides a summary of releases from juvenile institutions, indicates that 71 percent of all releases involved provision of aftercare services. Only 8 percent of the discharges involved unconditional release.

An aftercare program uses a wide variety of resources both within and outside of the institution. Implementation of an aftercare program

usually takes place in the community from which the child was adjudicated and uses community resources to aid the juvenile's reentry. The process should contribute to the juvenile's chances of successful readjustment and help him or her avoid future misconduct. It has taken the United States a long time to develop aftercare services for juvenile offenders, and some states have not yet developed sound programs. Only since 1950 has aftercare been given the scrutiny and attention necessary to begin developing effective programs. As a result of this late start, aftercare is probably the least developed and most inadequate aspect of the juvenile justice system.

Organization of Aftercare

There is no standard pattern of administrative authority for aftercare programs and services. State departments, cities, counties, private agencies, or public welfare departments may take responsibility for developing, organizing, or managing aftercare services. The National Council on Crime and Delinquency surveyed state aftercare programs in 1965 and found that state welfare departments and correctional agencies predominate.[3] The organizational arrangements for the administration of aftercare in the 50 states and the District of Columbia are shown in Table 16.3. The various patterns of administration developed for a number of reasons. For example, there may have been no state agency that could supervise juveniles at the local level and some other organization, such as a social welfare agency, performed this task. In other states, jurisdiction was given to local officials, because it was believed that at this level the juveniles would receive more effective, individualized care.

TABLE 16.1 DISCHARGES FROM JUVENILE CORRECTIONAL FACILITIES BY TYPE OF DISCHARGE, SEX, AND TYPE OF FACILITY, 1971

	TOTAL DISCHARGES			DISCHARGED WITHOUT SUPERVISION		PLACED IN AFTERCARE/ PAROLE		TRANSFERRED OUT		OTHER	
	TOTAL	MALE	FEMALE	MALE	FEMALE	MALE	FEMALE	MALE	FEMALE	MALE	FEMALE
Training schools											
Number	68,749	54,164	14,585	4,269	1,695	37,825	10,164	6,415	1,258	5,655	1,468
Percentage	100	79	21	6	2	55	15	9	2	8	2
Ranches, forestry camps, and farms											
Number	14,141	13,343	798	558	37	9,994	614	1,684	73	1,107	74
Percentage	100	94	6	4	a	71	4	12	1	8	1
Halfway houses and group homes											
Number	2,219	1,702	517	123	52	1,174	375	272	26	133	64
Percentage	100	77	23	6	2	53	17	12	1	8	1
Total all correctional facilities											
Number	85,109	69,209	15,900	4,950	1,784	48,993	11,152	8,371	1,357	6,895	1,606
Percentage	100	81	19	6	2	58	13	10	2	8	2

[a] 0.5 percent or less. Percentages might not add up to 100 because of rounding off.
Source: Law Enforcement Assistance Administration, Department of Justice, Sourcebook of Criminal Justice Statistics, 1974 (Washington, D.C.: Government Printing Office, 1975), p. 10.

TABLE 16.2. NUMBER AND PERCENTAGE OF DISCHARGES FROM
JUVENILE CORRECTIONS INSTITUTIONS BY TYPE OF DISCHARGES AND SEX

	TOTAL DIS- CHARGES	DIS- CHARGED WITHOUT SUPER- VISION	PLACED IN AFTERCARE PAROLE	TRANS- FERRED OUT	OTHER
Male					
Number	69,209	4,950	48,993	8,371	6,895
Percentage	100	7	71	12	10
Female					
Number	15,900	1,784	11,152	1,357	1,606
Percentage	100	11	70	9	10
Total male and female					
Number	85,109	6,734	60,145	9,728	8,501
Percentage	100	8	71	11	10

Source: Law Enforcement Assistance Administration, *Sourcebook of Criminal Justice Statistics, 1974* (Washington, D.C.: Government Printing Office), p. 423.

Legal and jurisdictional disputes are often found in aftercare programs. In some states the problem is complicated because the committing judge is, under law, required to be involved in the decision to release a juvenile for an aftercare program. The judge rarely has sufficient information on the youth's behavior at the training school or in the home community. The training school staff member who has worked with the juvenile may find that his or her recommendations are turned down by the judge, who doesn't fully understand the case.

Aftercare programs are highly centralized in some states. A single

TABLE 16.3 ORGANIZATIONAL ARRANGEMENT
FOR ADMINISTRATION OF AFTERCARE
IN THE 50 STATES AND THE DISTRICT OF COLUMBIA

TYPE OF STRUCTURE	NUMBER OF STATES
State Department of Public Welfare	13
State Youth Correction Agency	12
State Department of Correction	10
Institution Board	6
State Training School Board	4
State Department of Health	1
Other	5
Total	51

Source: President's Commission on Law Enforcement and Administration of Justice, "Juvenile Aftercare in the United States," *Crime and Delinquency* 13 (January 1967): 97–112.

office may be located at the state capital to supervise all aftercare enrollees. Courtesy supervision is provided by local welfare agencies or voluntary personnel. Where aftercare organizations have not been fully developed, supervision may be provided only in crisis situations. Other states have more comprehensive organizational structures. Regional and local offices are provided to maintain strict supervision requirements. The provisions made for aftercare services vary considerably from state to state.

Admission to Aftercare Programs

Juveniles remain in correctional institutions for varying lengths of time. Although many experts recommend the use of indefinite sentencing for juveniles, several states have adopted minimum or maximum requirements. Where formal minimum terms are established, they range from less than a year to 18 months. Only three states have statutory minimum requirements; however, informal standards are often established by institution superintendents or classification committees.[4] The suggested standard for a maximum term is three years.[5]

The authority to release juveniles into the community may rest with a variety of persons, organizations or agencies. A youth authority, a training school board, the department of corrections, the department of public welfare, a parole board, a board of control, or an institutional board may be involved in the decision. In most cases, these organizations have members appointed by the governor and may have a full-time paid staff. Most of the boards, however, have volunteer staffs. Volunteers are often not trained for their duties. The general national trend has been for the training school, forestry camp, or halfway house to make release recommendations to a centralized state agency that has the authority to authorize release from the correctional facility.

A key question is when to release the individual so that he or she may benefit from a supervised life in the community. In some institutions the child is expected to remain for a specified period of time, and release is conditional upon progress toward rehabilitation (measured by the inmate's acquisition of merit points). In other institutions personal adjustment is taken as a measure of rehabilitation and release potential. These methods, of course, do not assure rehabilitation or successful reintegration of the juvenile into the community. Correctional institution personnel involved in satisfactory treatment programs, however, should be in a better position than personnel of other agencies to determine when a juvenile is ready to be released back into the community.

TEMPORARY RELEASE

Because many juveniles face adjustment problems following release from the institution, some schools have developed trial or temporary release techniques. Furlough or other prerelease programs can be used to allow the youth to return to the community for short periods of time. If the youth is caught engaging in unapproved behavior, he or she can be returned to the institution with little or no formal action. The juvenile may be given another chance to demonstrate his or her ability to adjust to the community at a later date. Furloughs allow the juvenile to maintain some contact with normal community and family life.

In addition, some training schools have developed other techniques to keep the youngster in touch with life outside the institution. Supervised work in the community, periodic home visitation, and recreational visits to the community are often used. These techniques allow the youth to observe the community and to avoid becoming so accustomed to institutional life that he or she forgets about life in the community. Contact with members of the community gives the youth an idea of what is expected behavior and provides practice in work and living in a setting in which there are few institutional restrictions.

Period of Aftercare Supervision

Supervised release has different meanings in various jurisdictions, and therefore different stipulations or conditions apply for final release (termination of supervision). In some areas, specific time requirements are placed on aftercare, and the juvenile receives final release after the time period expires unless new delinquencies are noted. Other jurisdictions condition final release on evidence of rehabilitation. The juvenile is placed in the community for a specified period of time during which he is expected to exhibit particular behaviors specified by the aftercare officer. If the conditions are met, final release is granted.

The length of stay in aftercare supervision varies, but the average supervision period appears to be about one year following release. The President's Commission reported that there is a tendency to keep females under supervision longer than males.[6] The reason may be that in American society females are often believed to require protection for a longer period of time than males. In addition, the female offender is kept in the institution longer than the male. The female delinquent is perceived to require more intense and prolonged services than the delinquent male. These beliefs and assumptions, however, are questionable, and the future trend will probably tend toward equalization in length of confinement, services, and supervision for male and female offenders.

TYPES OF AFTERCARE PROGRAMS

Aftercare may involve the use of vastly different approaches to supervision. The most common aftercare program involves occasional visits by the juvenile to his or her aftercare officer. In other programs, residential shelters may be provided, or the youth may be given the benefit of various community service agencies. Data on the precise number of each of the various types of programs are not available. However, each type will be described briefly.

Office Supervision Programs

Most aftercare programs are based upon interview counseling by aftercare staff. Aftercare officers are expected to have close contact with the newly returned juvenile and be available to offer counsel and guidance when decisions must be made. They are also expected to keep themselves constantly apprised of the juvenile's activities and associations. By compiling information in these areas, aftercare personnel may be able to forecast possible difficulties and steer their charges in a more positive direction. Unfortunately, the aftercare ideal is often not achieved in practice. Training, caseload size, and geographic problems reduce the effectiveness of this type of program.[7]

STAFF QUALIFICATIONS

Aftercare standards suggest that supervision of juveniles is a form of social work and that the aftercare officer should be a trained social worker. Professional staff are needed to handle the difficult task of reintegrating the youth into the community. Attempts to professionalize staffing and program operations, however, have often been thwarted by power struggles in state and local politics. Many aftercare workers have less than a college education, and in-service training programs or educational leaves are too often inadequate to provide essential skills. The salaries for aftercare staff are not large enough to draw highly trained individuals. Caseloads in excess of 50 may also discourage the potential aftercare personnel applicant. In general, it appears that aftercare personnel are undertrained, underpaid, and overworked. Such a state is not likely to create a situation in which the juvenile returnee may best be served.

PRACTICAL CONSIDERATIONS

Geography often complicates the operation of state-wide aftercare agencies. In some states, a small supervisory staff must travel vast distances to visit a youthful offender. As a result, contacts between the supervisor and the juvenile are often crisis oriented. Juveniles from rural areas or small towns may never see a counselor. Individuals from urban areas are more likely to receive active supervision. In many areas, supervision may consist only of a written report completed by the juvenile and mailed each month to the state office. Spotty and irregular implementation is often the norm in the traditional program.

The Halfway House

The halfway house bridges the gap between life in the correctional institution and life in the community by providing a residential center where juveniles can adjust to their surroundings. An attempt is usually made to select names that do not use the term *halfway*. Residents of halfway houses are not "halfway" rehabilitated, and the names chosen for the houses attempt to correct this misconception, which is generally held by local residents. Halfway house residents are ready to enter the life of the community, but they need support, guidance, and additional training to make their first contact with the community successful.

THE PROGRAM

A complete program is often planned for the residents. They stay in the house except for periods of time spent in school, at work, on recreational excursions, or for other approved activities. The juveniles are still under the control of the staff of the home, and individual attention is considered important. The halfway house usually houses only 10 to 25 people.[8] While a wide variety of juveniles are accepted by most halfway houses, the house is especially useful for youths who do not have a home to return to after a stay in the training school.[9]

The time spent in the house is usually short, because it is viewed as a final preparation for full release. It is not meant to be a full-time juvenile residence hall. After release, continued supervision may be needed for some individuals, but other juveniles are ready for final release from the authority of the juvenile court (they may be old enough to be considered adults).

COMMUNITY REACTION

The success of a halfway house program often rests upon its acceptance by residents of the local community and their willingness to provide support. Before a halfway house can be established, preliminary work within the community is necessary.[10] Community or neighborhood opposition has at times precluded establishment of some houses and forced other halfway houses to close. In the absence of a preliminary public relations program, residents have often been afraid that the presence of such a house will have negative effects on the neighborhood and its children.

THE FUTURE OF THE HALFWAY HOUSE

The halfway house concept is new, but it is often considered a promising means of contributing to the success of juveniles released from correctional institutions and is increasingly being used.[11] Use of halfway house-type facilities is still very limited, but significant advances are now being made. Most of those currently in operation are privately financed and operated. Although a few state-supported halfway houses have been established, they are the exception rather than the norm.

Diversified Aftercare

Juveniles require a variety of services after they are released from a correctional institution and return to the community. Foster homes and group homes have been welcomed as supportive agencies to help the youth in adjusting to the local community. In addition, the use of group treatment programs, family-centered services, youth employment programs, job training, and other programs may stimulate the released youth's adjustment. Most communities have a variety of service organizations, welfare agencies, and other services that may be enlisted in the effort to help the youth adjust and make a productive contribution to the life of the community.

The fully developed and diversified aftercare program is far from the norm in most communities. Such a plan is often no more than an idea in the minds of liberal corrections experts. The resources needed to implement a comprehensive help program for returnees already exist in many local communities. However, cooperation, coordination, and planning are still needed to bring all of the necessary elements together. Implementation of the Youth Services Bureaus proposed by a presidential commission might be a first step in this direction.[12]

RELEASE AND FAILURE

Not all juveniles who are released into the community will make a successful adjustment. Many of the youths who enter training schools or other juvenile correctional institutions have already failed on aftercare, probation, parole, or in previous experiences with the training school. Some individuals are returned two or more times in a single year for violations. About 20 to 30 percent of released juveniles will return to the institution within one year. When juveniles who are returned during the second year and those treated as adults and sent to adult correctional facilities are considered, the failure rate appears to be quite high.

Failure Rates

Table 16.4 illustrates the failure rates after two years for youthful federal offenders in 1970. Notice that the failure rate increased with the number of disciplinary infractions engaged in while held in the correctional institution. The individual who poses a disciplinary problem within the institution is likely to fail upon release into the community. The known failure rate for individuals with three or more disciplinary infractions while in the institution was about 53 percent, compared with a 30 percent failure rate for persons with no disciplinary infractions. In addition, the failure rate for individuals who received aftercare or parole supervision upon release from the correctional institution was lower than the rate for those whose sentence had expired and those under mandatory release. There was a 50 percent failure rate for mandatorily released individuals and a 37 percent

TABLE 16.4 SUCCESS AND FAILURE RATES OF
FEDERAL OFFENDERS RELEASED IN 1970 AFTER TWO YEARS

	TOTAL		ESTIMATED SUCCESS RATE	KNOWN SUCCESS RATE	KNOWN FAILURE RATE	DISPOSITION UNKNOWN
	NUMBER	PERCENTAGE	PERCENTAGE	PERCENTAGE	PERCENTAGE	PERCENTAGE
PRISON DISCIPLINARY INFRACTIONS						
Number of offenders	309	100	61.6	60.5	37.2	2.3
None	181	58.6	68.3	66.9	30.4	2.8
One	63	20.4	54.8	54.0	44.4	1.6
Two	35	11.3	52.9	51.4	45.7	2.9
Three or more	30	9.7	46.7	46.7	53.3	0.0
TYPE OF RELEASE						
Number of offenders	309	100	61.7	60.5	37.3	2.3
Parole	268	86.7	62.7	62.3	36.9	0.7
Mandatory release	4	1.3	50.0	50.0	50.0	0.0
Expiration	37	12.0	55.4	48.6	37.8	11.5

Source: "Statistical Report, Fiscal Years 1971–1972," in *Sourcebook of Criminal Justice Statistics* (Law Enforcement Assistance Administration) (Washington, D.C.: Government Printing Office, 1975), p. 439.

failure rate for youthful parolees from federal correctional institutions.[13] The failure rates are probably similar for juveniles released from state correctional institutions.

CAUSES OF FAILURE

Failure should not be blamed completely on the institutions. The juvenile justice system usually comes in contact with a youth only after years of socialization in the family and the community. The available correctional programs cannot be expected to erase the cumulative effects of this experience in only a few months. The programs and institutions can do little to change the family, community, or interpersonal relationships that helped create problems for the juvenile. Failure rates provide an indication of the seriousness of the problem and the difficulties faced by institutions as rehabilitation is attempted.

Many delinquent youths do not become adult criminals, but many face problems of adjustment as they become adults. Some institutionalized youths develop adult drinking problems and other psychological difficulties, but the chief problem is probably the persistence of juvenile misconduct and behavior patterns into adult life. For example, juveniles who become court cases are more likely to become divorced as adults. This finding suggests that at least some of the basic problems of juveniles may plague them even in adult life.[14]

JUVENILE AFTERCARE IN PERSPECTIVE

The harsh reality is that the nation has not fully come to grips with the problem of juvenile aftercare. Many juveniles leave institutions each year with the hope of developing meaningful and productive lives in the community. The response by the national government and the states has often shown little imagination and considerable neglect. Many of the juveniles who need a sound aftercare program receive only minimal assistance during a critical period in their lives. Some delinquent youths cannot or should not return to their homes; for these individuals a more complete restructuring of their lives is needed. This may be especially true for neglected or dependent females who have engaged in some type of sexual delinquency. Imaginative aftercare programs that provide alternatives and avoid the return of youths to delinquency-producing situations must be developed. Included in a comprehensive program should be foster homes, shelter homes, halfway houses, and the use of community agencies.

The trend in juvenile aftercare appears to emphasize the development of state-operated aftercare programs which remove aftercare decisions and planning from the authority of training school officials. A complete organizational separation of the probation, corrections, and aftercare functions of the juvenile system is becoming a reality. There are some indications that fragmentation of the system will result in a further decline of the effectiveness of rehabilitation efforts for juveniles. Aftercare will probably suffer from this development more than the other programs. It is the least-developed and most-ignored element of the system.

The financial cost of aftercare is small in comparison with the cost of state-operated juvenile institutions. Unfortunately, this may reflect the inadequacy of the programs and not the economy of aftercare. Programs are understaffed and supervisors poorly paid. In some cases, supervisors are located in the state capital or in a training school a considerable distance from the youth's home community. Thus the effectiveness of the program is reduced. Aftercare programs are relatively cheap, but they may reflect a false economy. It may cost more to make a program effective in preventing recidivism and facilitating the youth's adaptation on reentry into the home community.

NOTES

[1] President's Commission on Law Enforcement and Administration of Justice, "Juvenile Aftercare in the United States," *Crime and Delinquency* 13 (January 1967): 97–112.

[2] Joseph M. Hawes, *Children in Urban Society* (New York: Oxford University Press, 1971), p. 133.

[3] *Ibid.*

[4] Law Enforcement Assistance Administration, *Sourcebook of Criminal Justice Statistics, 1974* (Washington, D.C.: Government Printing Office, 1975), p. 103.

[5] *Juvenile Aftercare in the United States, op. cit.,* p. 103.

[6] *Ibid.*

[7] *Ibid.,* pp. 106–109.

[8] See Francis McNeil, "A Detailed Description of a Halfway House Program for Delinquents," *Crime and Delinquency* 13 (1967): 538–544.

[9] Kenneth Carpenter, "Halfway Houses for Delinquent Youth," in *Children* (Department of Health, Education, and Welfare) (Washington, D.C.: Government Printing Office, 1963), p. 224.

[10] Department of Health, Education, and Welfare, Children's Bureau, "Halfway House Programs for Delinquent Youth" (Washington, D.C.: Government Printing Office, 1965).

[11] Robert C. Trojanowicz, *Juvenile Delinquency* (Englewood Cliffs, N.J.: Prentice-Hall, 1973), p. 269.

[12] President's Commission on Law Enforcement and Administration of Justice, *Task Force Report: Juvenile Delinquency and Youth Crime* (Washington, D.C.: Government Printing Office, 1967), p. 20.

[13] Patricia O'Neal and Lee Robins, "Childhood Patterns Predictive of Adult Schizophrenia," *American Journal of Psychiatry* 115 (1959): 385–391.

[14] Lee Robins and Patricia O'Neal, "The Marital History of Former Problem Children," *Social Problems* 5 (1958): 347–358.

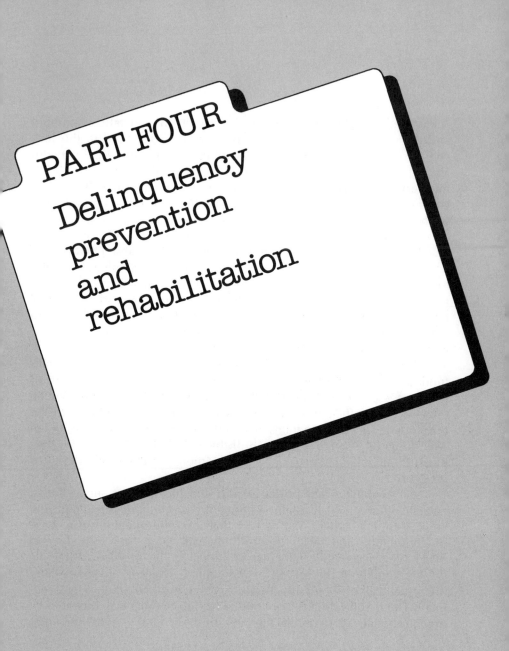

PART FOUR

Delinquency
prevention
and
rehabilitation

A knowledge of the nature of delinquency, its theoretical background, and the structure of the juvenile justice system discussed in the preceding sections provides an understanding of past and present concern about juvenile delinquency. Part Four looks into the future by examining current trends in strategies for the treatment, prevention, and control of juvenile delinquency and assessing their impact on the lives of the juveniles these programs touch.

The social policy implications of current theory and research are covered in Chapter 17. The link between theory and practice has sometimes been weak, but modern programs are beginning more and more to rely on delinquency theory and evaluative research. Communication among theorists, researchers, and program administrators has not yet developed fully. Efforts to close the communications gap will contribute significantly to the development of effective prevention and rehabilitation programs in the future.

Chapter 18 emphasizes the need for broadly based and well-funded research programs in juvenile delinquency. Verified theories of the causes of juvenile delinquency will provide a base from which effective and efficient prevention and treatment programs can be developed. Current programs may not stand under the scrutiny of well-designed evaluative research. If this is found to be the case, they must be altered or replaced by newer, more systematically designed programs.

An examination of present needs and past failures suggests that current programs of juvenile delinquency prevention, treatment, and control are inadequate. We believe that the reintroduction of a sense of community and civic responsibility will go a long way toward developing acceptable, effective solutions to the problem. After all, the community is the setting of delinquent behavior. Juveniles carry on virtually all of their daily activities in the local community environment. The mobilization of community resources (financial, human, and organizational) is an essential element for the reduction of delinquency.

CHAPTER 17
Social policy
and
delinquency prevention

Prevention of juvenile delinquency is a much sought-after goal. A number of programs have been instituted to this end. Many of the existing programs and approaches to prevention, however, make assumptions about human behavior that are not firmly grounded in research or theories of causation. And there is some evidence that suggests that many treatment programs or strategies are not effective or do not do what they are purported to do. Some are even considered harmful. Although rigorous research evaluation is of critical importance, such efforts have been conspicuously absent in most prevention and treatment programs. How do we know whether a program is successful unless an evaluative research program is initiated? The answer is that we don't. Evaluation is essential when judgments must be made about the effectiveness of alternative methods of delinquency prevention, control, and treatment. Critical evaluation would offer a base from which expensive but ineffective, or even harmful, programs could be eliminated in favor of more promising prevention or rehabilitative programs.

There are no "proven methods for reducing the incidence of serious delinquent acts through preventive or rehabilitative procedures."[1] The knowledge gained by social scientists has not generally been translated into effective programs. There has been instead a division of labor in which the theorists and researchers have steered clear of the policy implications of their work, while the policy makers rely on common-sense approaches that have little connection to theory. Furthermore, critical evaluative research is seldom applied to ongoing programs.

DIVERSITY OF PREVENTION PROGRAMS

Most early prevention programs were local, urban, or community-based efforts established by citizen's committees or private organizations interested in the prevention and control of juvenile delinquency. More recent efforts have seen the involvement of official city or state agencies and national organizations. Unfortunately, many of these programs have been scattered and uncoordinated. Although public welfare agencies, schools, churches, housing authorities, recreation departments, private social work agencies, and health agencies frequently become involved in delinquency prevention, control, and treatment, all of these organizations tend to operate their programs independently of each other in many cities throughout the country.[2] Each organization sets its own goals, based upon its personnel's understanding of the causes of delinquency. Often these goals overlap or conflict with those of other organizations. The failure to communicate and coordinate programs within the community has resulted in a profusion of diverse, but inadequate, programs.[3]

Focus of Prevention

Many prevention programs focus on the individual. An attempt is made to change the attitudes, beliefs, or values that lead the individual to conclude that delinquency is acceptable social behavior. Alternatively, there may be the assumption that delinquency is merely a symptom of underlying emotional problems; the juvenile who engages in delinquent activities is merely asking for help to solve inner conflicts or problems. When either of these assumptions guides prevention programs, a clinical approach is deemed appropriate. Individual psychological pathology can only be eliminated by intensive counseling of troubled youths. The elimination of emotional problems should in turn reduce the incidence of juvenile delinquency. Most of the early delinquency programs took this direction.

Other prevention programs focus on the environment. The assumption that individuals are influenced by their physical and social surroundings has been adopted by some organizations. When this assumption guides prevention programs, agencies attempt to enrich the environments of juveniles. Social scientists at the University of Chicago were early supporters of this approach and offered the rationale for the development of community intervention programs in areas characterized by high delinquency rates.[4] Treatment and prevention programs that seek to change the environment emphasize informal street and neighborhood programs rather than treatment clinics.[5]

Goals of Prevention Programs

Several classification schemes have been used to distinguish between the goals of prevention programs. Trojanowicz distinguishes

between primary and secondary prevention.[6] In primary prevention, attempts are made to inhibit or prevent delinquent acts before they occur. Youths identified as potential delinquents are involved in adult-sponsored programs that emphasize socially approved behavior. Youth centers, boys clubs, and other facilities for youths are often used to divert the attentions of youths out of the street and into more easily controlled situations. Secondary prevention, on the other hand, involves the treatment of youths who have already experienced delinquency. The primary goal of secondary prevention is to avert continued delinquency. These programs frequently deal with children who have had contact with the juvenile justice system as a result of minor infractions. An attempt is made to reach and treat the child before his or her activity leads to serious violations of law and formal, stigmatizing involvement with the juvenile justice system.

Prevention Techniques

Whatever the focus of prevention programs, several different social action techniques may be used to accomplish prevention goals. Lejins identifies three major methods of prevention: punitive, corrective, or mechanical measures.[7] Punitive prevention programs involve the education of youths in the consequences of delinquent behavior. It is based on the assumption that individuals will alter their behavior if punishment is threatened. The stern hand of discipline is used to guide the behavior of youths who are in danger of pursuing a delinquent course of action. Corrective prevention involves the alteration of factors that are believed to cause delinquency. This prevention method attempts to eliminate delinquent motivation by restructuring the potential delinquent's physical, social, or psychological environment. Mechanical prevention refers to the practice of putting physical barriers or obstacles in the way of the juvenile so that delinquent activity is very difficult to accomplish. The underlying assumption of this technique suggests that if temptations are removed, children will not consider delinquent behavior. The movement to secure the ignition systems of automobiles is an example of this type of technique. Warning systems serve as a reminder to drivers to take their keys when leaving their cars and make auto theft more difficult for youths.

The Prevention Program

It is apparent that *prevention* has a great variety of meanings. There is little agreement on what the goal of prevention programs should be or their proper focus. The methods used to accomplish stated goals may vary considerably. No single definition of *prevention* or *prevention program* exists. It is often difficult to distinguish between prevention and other types of programs. There is, for example, no clear distinction between prevention and rehabilitation. These concepts may overlap considerably.

While a standard conception of the focus, goals, and techniques of prevention programs is unlikely to be developed in the immediate future, it is possible that we might come to an intuitive understanding of the problems of prevention by examining current programs.

FEDERAL PREVENTION PROGRAMS

The federal effort to prevent and control juvenile delinquency was initiated with the passage of the Juvenile Delinquency and Youth Offenses Control Act of 1961.[8] Since that time, the federal government has increasingly become involved in enriching and supplementing state and local prevention and control programs. The programs discussed here do not represent a comprehensive list of all government efforts to reduce the incidence of delinquency, but they do tend to illustrate the wide range of prevention efforts supported by the United States government. Many of the programs are relatively new and have not been thoroughly evaluated. As a result, we often know little about their effectiveness in reaching stated delinquency prevention goals.

Law Enforcement Assistance Administration

The Law Enforcement Assistance Administration (LEAA) was organized under the Department of Justice after the passage of the Omnibus Crime Control and Safe Streets Act. The LEAA has provided grants to states and cities to plan and equip for improved law enforcement and to encourage research on methods for prevention and control of crime and delinquency. Because states are given the responsibility for establishing priorities, programs vary from state to state, but the primary areas of concern have been the enrichment and expansion of police, court, and correction programs. A few new and innovative programs for delinquency prevention have been developed in some cities. For example, programs designed to prevent gang violence, rioting, and participation in civil disorders were initiated in Philadelphia. Educational programs, job placement, and counseling are offered in San Antonio, Texas.[9] Most of the money under LEAA's program has gone into adult rather than juvenile programs.

Office of Economic Opportunity

The Office of Economic Opportunity provided funds for a number of programs designed to prevent or reduce the incidence of juvenile delinquency. Recreation and drug rehabilitation programs managed by local community action agencies were emphasized.[10] Areas with high rates of delinquency were given high priority for funding. These programs were designed to allow youths to become involved in other than destructive or delinquent behavior and thus prevent delinquency. The Office of Economic Opportunity has been disbanded, and the delinquency prevention programs have either been discontinued or transferred to other departments.

Department of Health, Education, and Welfare

The Department of Health, Education, and Welfare has a wide range of programs designed to prevent delinquency. The agency provides funding and guidance for educational research, training programs, and mental health facilities. The program most directly involved in delinquency prevention—Upward Bound—is designed to produce changes in skill and motivation to promote educational success for children in low-income families. The program has included summer study, cultural enhancement programs, tutoring, and other educational aids.[11] Participating schools are given special financial support through the Office of Education, which administers the program. The program is designed to prevent delinquency by providing alternative avenues of success.

Department of Housing and Urban Development

The Department of Housing and Urban Development administers a number of prevention programs under the Model Cities program established by the Demonstration Cities and Metropolitan Development Act of 1966. The Model Cities programs focus primarily on deteriorated urban areas characterized by high crime and delinquency rates. Projects that have benefited youths include the construction of modern juvenile aftercare centers, recreation centers, youth councils, and teen centers. Special aid programs have provided scholarships for disadvantaged youths, youth placement centers, service centers for unwed mothers, legal services for youths, college prep programs, medical career projects, police aid programs, and drug prevention activities. Several programs have also been developed in cooperation with the Upward Bound and Big Brother programs administered by other agencies.[12] The Model Cities program works for delinquency prevention by attacking social problems that are believed to encourage the development of delinquent attitudes.

Department of Agriculture

The extension division of the Department of Agriculture has for many years provided programs for juveniles, the most notable being the 4-H program for rural youths. Although not established primarily as a prevention program, it has provided adult-sponsored and adult-supervised activity for millions of rural youths. In recent years its services have been extended to youths in urban areas. VISTA and 4-H programs in cities such as Providence, Hartford, and Wilmington have been used by community leaders to establish youth centers and provide solutions to youth-related problems in a city environment. Extension agents frequently work through community organizations, such as schools, churches, public housing authorities, clubs, and correctional institutions for youths, to develop delinquency prevention programs.

Department of Labor

The Labor Manpower Administration became involved in delinquency prevention through the Neighborhood Youth Corps program authorized in 1964 by the Economic Opportunity Act. The in-school program operates through high schools to provide part-time jobs, job training, and work experience for juveniles who need financial aid to remain in school. A summer work program is also offered to provide work experience and income to enable low-income juveniles to return to school in the fall rather than becoming dropouts. A third out-of-school program offers job training, job placement, and supportive services to dropouts and other unemployed or underemployed low-income individuals.[13] The Manpower Administration reported that by 1969, more than 620,000 juveniles from disadvantaged areas of American cities were enrolled in the Neighborhood Youth Corps.[14]

A closely related program, the Job Corps, was designed to remove urban youths from their high-delinquency settings. Young adults, age 16 to 21, are lodged in residential centers after enrolling in government-sponsored job-training programs. Conservation centers and national parks and forests are used to train youths for fire fighting and building campgrounds and trails. The urban centers train youths in cooking, auto repair, small appliance and machine repair, and other skill areas. A number of controls are used to assure completion of training. For example, enrollees are not permitted to leave the center without special passes. Job Corps trainees are not guaranteed a job upon completion of training, but the government does provide job placement assistance.[15] Both the Job Corps and the Neighborhood Youth Corps programs are based on the assumption that employed people are less likely to engage in juvenile delinquency than the hard-core unemployed.

Scope of Federal Programs

Most of the delinquency prevention programs offered by the federal government are relatively new and therefore have not been subjected to systematic evaluation to determine whether their accomplishments have exceeded their costs. An examination of the programs presented, however, suggests the focus, goals, and techniques used in government efforts. Federal prevention programs do not attempt to identify specific delinquency-prone youths for special attention. They focus instead on the environmental factors believed to promote crime and delinquency. Several environmental factors, such as poverty, lack of educational opportunity, cultural deprivation, and deteriorated physical surroundings, have been singled out for special attention. The primary goals stated and implied by action programs include the elimination or reduction of the effects of poor environmental conditions and the creation of alternative legitimate opportunity structures for disadvantaged youths. The techniques used to reach delinquency prevention goals have generally been oriented to corrective prevention methods. However, mechanical prevention has been utilized in some programs, such as the Job Corps, where enrollees are required to remain in the center. Unfortunately, some of these programs have been discontinued without the benefit of evaluative research to determine their effectiveness.

COMMUNITY-BASED PROGRAMS

A program is a community prevention program if resources of the local area are mobilized to prevent or treat delinquency. It is not essential that the community assume sole support of the effort. Many community programs are funded in part by the state or federal government or private sources. Only a few of the many types of locally operated delinquency prevention programs are discussed here.

Specialized Area Programs

Some local communities have developed special programs tailored to their needs. Standard programs developed for use nationwide are often unsuitable for particular areas. For example, programs operated successfully in urban core areas may have little relevance for rural communities. Resources for the implementation of prevention programs may be more limited in some areas than in others. As a result of these problems and others, several communities have initiated their own specialized programs. Two such programs are examined here.

SOUTH CENTRAL YOUTH PROJECT

The South Central Youth Project was established in Minneapolis by the Community Welfare Council of Hennepin County and directed by a planning committee with representatives from both public and private agencies. The primary goal of the project was to locate individuals in the early stages of delinquency and concentrate local resources to achieve prevention. This goal was to be achieved not through the development of new agencies but by the efficient use of programs already established in the community. In order to achieve this goal, communication was initiated among local agencies to promote the coordination of diverse efforts. The program had far-reaching effects. Efforts to identify delinquency-prone youths involved working with low-income families, many of whom had been unable to use community resources. Prevention activities included providing information on available community agencies and how to use them.[16]

THE HARYOU ACT

The Harlem Youth Opportunities, Unlimited, Community Associated Teams was developed in New York City's Harlem, where the large majority—over 250,000—of residents are black. The program was designed to increase the opportunities for juveniles in Harlem and encourage acceptable behavior. Difficulties were encountered as conflicts within the program developed. The expectations of rapid change exceeded the capacity of the organization to produce results fast enough to satisfy residents, participants, and organizational personnel. The multifaceted problems in Harlem coupled with intraagency conflicts prevented effective action.

Standard Programs

Other programs have reached a large number of communities. The standard programs generally involve activities to integrate juveniles into local community institutions or organizations. Favorable attitudes toward major institutions are seen as a basis for developing youths into useful, active citizens in the community. A sample of programs of this nature is presented below. Many communities do not offer the full range of programs or else provide some services on an ad hoc basis only. Other communities have regularized and institutionalized these services.

RECREATION AND SUPERVISED ACTIVITY

As a prevention program for juveniles, this type of program is certainly not new. Outdoor playgrounds, athletic fields, summer camps, Boy Scouts, Girl Scouts, Campfire Girls, and 4-H programs are all at least partially based on the belief that idleness may leave the youngster time to get into trouble. The youngster has to be kept busy and off the streets to learn the value of organization and productive labor. Although there is little evidence to suggest that the absence of supervised activity and recreation leads to delinquency, many city recreation programs have been developed and expanded for this purpose. Nondelinquents, however, appear to have more favorable attitudes toward supervised play and are more likely to use the facilities than are delinquent or delinquency-prone youths.

POLICE AND SCHOOL LIAISON PROGRAMS

A number of police and school liaison programs have been adopted throughout the United States to reduce hostility toward the police and encourage communication between police and juveniles. A police officer plays a triple role—as a counselor, law enforcer, and resource person to the schools. The officer is expected to encourage a better understanding of the police, listen and talk to students, and provide practical information. The primary purpose of the program is to provide better and more positive attitudes toward police officers and police work. The liaison program serves as a base for building the police department's community relations program and is believed to decrease the incidence of delinquency by building respect for law.

Reaction to programs of this type has often been positive. Negative comments generally center on the possibility of police using young people as informers and the desire to keep weapons of all types off school property. Some persons believe that the police use the program to question juveniles freely, thereby violating their rights. A further objection centers on the question of whether it is appropriate for police to be in the schools at all, because the presence of police represents a recognition of the failure of the schools and the parents (the primary socializing institutions in American society) to guide and control the behavior of youths. If an offense is committed in school, should the school and the parents become involved or should it come to the attention of the police? Some people feel that the liaison program is only the first step toward wider participation by the police in the schools and the education of children.

Weirman's study of a police liaison program suggests that negative attitudes toward police exist even in junior high schools. The liaison program under study was deemed relatively effective because attitudes did not get more negative with the presence of a liaison officer. In a control group, attitudes became more negative where there was no liaison program.[17] In other words, the liaison officer's absence resulted in an increase of negative attitudes. The program's value may be measured in terms of its ability to forestall deterioration of relations between youths and police. The basic underlying assumption of the program is that positive attitudes toward police will result in a decrease of delinquent activity and promote cooperation with the police.

EDUCATIONAL PROGRAMS

In addition to the police liaison program, other educational programs have been established to teach juveniles about the problems and consequences of various types of behavior (e.g., drug abuse and personality problems). Americans often assume that the solution to any problem lies in the dissemination of factual information. The result has been a proliferation of seminars and counseling programs designed to promote the reasoned rejection of undesirable behavior. Drug clinics have been established in elementary and secondary schools as well as in some colleges. Doctors, lawyers, pharmacists, ministers, and others provide assistance, while funding may come from a wide variety of sources.

Some schools have adopted programs to provide job training to youths unlikely to continue their education beyond high school. Some school systems have converted part of their high school facilities to vocational training use. This may mean an entire campus is devoted to technical education with other campuses providing college preparatory programs. Des Moines provides an example of such a program. In other systems, courses in vocational skills are provided alongside general preparatory courses.

Schools have also experimented with personality improvement programs for juveniles who have proved disruptive in the classroom. The program used in Flint, Michigan, is probably one of the most stringent. When school officials believe a youngster is excessively disruptive, they may petition the probate court to enroll the child in the Personality Improvement Program for a period of 12 weeks. If the child is so ordered, he or she is placed in the county children's facility for a six-week behavior modification program. During the second six-week period, he or she is gradually reintegrated into the school program under the guidance and supervision of Personality Improvement staff.

Effectiveness of Local Programs

Local programs exhibit a wide variety of goals, techniques, and focuses. They may focus on particular troublesome youths or on the environmental setting. Some attempt to provide primary prevention, while others seek to establish secondary prevention. The methods used to accomplish goals range from coercive prevention (i.e., the Flint program) to corrective prevention techniques. The amount of time, effort, and funds spent on the diverse programs would suggest that at least some of these programs should be effective. Unfortunately, most of these programs have not been systematically evaluated. Research to evaluate the success of each project should be designed into the program to determine whether or not the goal or mission is being reached. Evaluation research can identify the areas of success as well as the areas of failure so that change to improve effectiveness can be more readily implemented. Furthermore, evaluation research provides the evidence of success often required by officials in order to receive continued government funding. In the absence of research and evaluation, it is advisable to be skeptical about the success of a program even if the personnel are motivated, enthusiastic, and idealistic. A program designed to prevent delinquency should be able to demonstrate some success in achieving its goal or it should be abandoned in favor of other, more effective proposals.

SELECTION OF DELINQUENCY-PRONE YOUTHS

If children who are likely to become delinquent could be identified before they got into trouble or came in contact with the juvenile justice system, delinquency prevention efforts would be greatly simplified. Prevention programs have, to the present time, taken a shotgun approach to the problem of delinquency. Because there has been no systematic way of identifying problem youths, the programs have been aimed at the general population of youths, both conforming and deviating. In the interest of efficiency, a program that sorts out delinquency-prone youths would appear to have positive value. These juveniles would be selected out and energies concentrated on their problems. Early detection is an important factor in the eventual treatment and rehabilitation outcomes for youths.

Programs designed to identify delinquency-prone youths also have negative aspects. The major objection centers around the ethics of intervention into the lives of individuals who have not yet violated societal laws. The traditional view is that the individual has the right to privacy and self-determination unless or until he or she interferes with the rights of others. Identification, stigmatization, and intervention would represent a shift from current standards of justice and would be difficult to justify. Authorities point to the limited effectiveness of individual or group therapy used on delinquency-prone youths[18] and suggest that such treatment may even have harmful effects.[19]

Prediction Efforts

There is some question as to whether attempts to identify delinquency-prone youths can be effective. If the benefits envisioned by proponents of these programs are to be secured, identification must take place among 6-, 7-, or 8-year-olds. However, the personalities of these children are not fully developed, and inaccuracies are likely to occur. Inaccurate prediction reduces the effectiveness of any prevention program. If "normal" youngsters as well as potential delinquents are included in the program, much of the therapy and other treatment efforts will be wasted. The normal youngster doesn't need therapy, and it may have little positive effect on him or her. On the other hand, being identified as a potential delinquent and receiving special attention in a treatment program may have a negative impact on the youth. The youngster may be labeled early in life as a potential or actual troublemaker and delinquent. The label and the prevention program with all its good intentions may produce the delinquent behavior that it seeks to prevent.

Many of the instruments used to predict delinquency among youths have not been subjected to critical research evaluation. The Glueck Social Prediction Table, one of three scales developed by Sheldon Glueck and Eleanor Glueck to detect delinquency-prone youths, has been subjected to a great amount of research analysis.[20] The scale was designed to measure five types of family relationships, including discipline by the father, supervision by the mother, affection of the father, affection of the mother, and cohesiveness of the family unit.[21] If all of the relationships were unfavorable, a youngster was judged to be predelinquent. If, on the other hand, the relationships were favorable, nondelinquency was predicted. Some youngsters were not placed in either category. The large number of children placed in a middle or questionable category appears to decrease the value of the scale.

In 1952 the Glueck Social Prediction Table was first used with boys in the public schools of New York City; a continuous analysis of the results have followed each year.[22] Jackson Toby and others have criticized the Gluecks and their claims for a high degree of accuracy for the scale. Toby points out that the instrument is inaccurate because it depends heavily on family relationships. Some youngsters may have normal family relationships but become delinquent because of peer influences.[23] In addition, factors other than family and peer influence may produce delinquency. For example, a change in family relationships, gang membership, movement to new neighborhoods, school pressures, and numerous other factors may be involved in delinquency.

One problem with the Glueck Social Prediction Table was that it identified as predelinquent many boys who had no father. One revision of the scale drops all reference to the father and uses only three items to predict delinquency—cohesiveness of the family, supervision by the mother, and affection of the mother.[24]

Persuading parents that their children should participate in a delinquency prevention program because of their identification as predelinquent is a major problem. Parents do not readily accept predictions based on the Glueck scale. The scale is inaccurate about 3 times in 20, and the parents may feel that it is wrong in the case of their child. In addition, the parents may feel that placement of their child in a delinquency prevention program may stigmatize the child unnecessarily.[25]

Even if the Glueck Social Prediction Table proved to be reliable and extremely accurate, or even if some other prediction device were developed, this would not remove all the objections to their use.

Prevention programs based on the need to identify delinquency-prone youths may represent an unwarranted intrusion into the family. The delinquency-prone youth has not broken the law and might not be engaging in troublesome behavior in school, at home, or in the community. How can we justify separating such individuals from their peers for special, and possibly stigmatizing, treatment as potential juvenile delinquents or criminals? Aside from the moral, ethical, and constitutional questions that are raised by such programs, the social effects on the youngster may be devastating despite the good intentions of the Gluecks and others. Just because we may be able to predict delinquency does not mean that we must do so. Programs aimed at correcting or rehabilitating delinquents who are known to have commited illegal acts may have a much firmer base.

PEOPLE-CHANGING PROGRAMS

It is often difficult to convince funding agencies that broad prevention programs, which deal with the total population of juveniles, are effective and efficient. The taxpayers and their representatives want concrete results. Programs that concentrate on specific people, changing them radically, find greater favor among laymen and public officials alike. As a result, a great deal of emphasis has been placed on secondary prevention programs, in which juveniles who have committed minor offenses are the focus. Resources are concentrated on these children to prevent their becoming career delinquents and criminals.

The modern emphasis on individual improvement has been a topic of much discussion. It has been said that we live in a period in which changing people has become a profession and a "moral injunction."[26] Martinson elaborates this point, saying, "Some are oriented through doctrine, selective recruitment, idealistic graduate education and other means towards useful endeavors to change man. In a nation which has, in addition, suffered the ravages of prohibition and the 'Carrie Nation' syndrone, this may be an especially powerful force."[27]

Professions vary in the degree to which they have become dissatisfied with humanity and the degree to which they want to change youths. However, all assume that nondelinquent behavior is the normal condition. These "people changers" are more likely to be found in sociology than in engineering, in social work rather than in art, and in psychiatry rather than in meteorology. The people-changing ideology and professions are growing in areas where people to be helped are found. The most helpless, difficult individuals, who deviate from the white Anglo-Saxon Protestant ideal, are generally the targets of people-changing efforts. There are few who are willing to accept the fact that instead of helping, changing, or offering the delinquent therapy, we might sometimes be more successful if we did nothing.[28]

The Change Setting

Efforts to implement people-changing programs may be adapted to a variety of environmental settings. They may involve the voluntary participation of the individuals to be changed or result from official or semiofficial action on the part of community organizations. When the change process is initiated by official community agencies, there is not always a clear line drawn between prevention and rehabilitation.

INFORMAL SUPERVISION

Troublesome youths are often identified by individuals who hold positions of responsibility in the community. School personnel, religious leaders, local merchants, parents, and others frequently come in contact with youths in uncertain circumstances or engaged in disapproved behavior. Many of these individuals are reluctant to bring the youth to the attention of authorities. On the other hand, they may believe that the behavior is too serious to be ignored. Under such circumstances, they may warn the youth about his or her behavior and indicate that it will not be forgotten. Further discussion may reveal that the adult intends to keep an eye on the youth for evidence of further disapproved behavior. The knowledge that someone is watching along with the threat of disclosure, it is believed, may be sufficient to bring about a change in behavior.

Youths who come in contact with police for minor infractions may also be the subjects of informal supervision. The police can make special efforts to check up on the minor offender for evidence of commitment to delinquency. Police may also make deals with juvenile offenders and their parents. Freedom from official action may be secured in some instances by voluntary commitment to a public or private program that has people-changing goals.

PROBATION

Formal supervision in the community has been used as both a secondary prevention device and a rehabilitative technique. Probation may be formal or informal. Some juveniles enter the probation program after adjudication by the juvenile court; others come under the supervision of a probation department without court action. Those in this latter category are often accepted on a informal trial basis. If they stay out of trouble for a period of time, their court cases may be dismissed. Probation programs differ from state to state, but the probation officer often uses techniques associated with vocational and personal guidance counseling. It is difficult to handle adequately the large caseloads (often over 75), which results in little time for individual attention, except possibly for those few individuals felt to be in greatest need.[29] A few pilot programs have been initiated to bring volunteers and community resources to concentrate rehabilitative services on the probationers, but the programs generally have not been adequately evaluated.

Sarpitti and Stephenson investigated the effectiveness of probation as a treatment program. They compared 16- and 17-year-old boys on probation with boys assigned to group treatment programs of various types, as well as with boys assigned to the state training school. They noted that probationary boys came from more stable backgrounds, were better educated, had shorter delinquent careers with fewer offenses, and were less delinquent or represented easier cases than the boys assigned to other correctional programs and therefore probably did not need extensive treatment.[30] Scarpitti and Stephenson found that most probationers successfully completed their probation program, but successful completion did not lead to psychological or attitude change. The successful graduates had fewer problems to begin with than the other, less successful groups. Boys assigned to probation do much better than those assigned to other programs. The failures were essentially eliminated from the program by being returned to the court and assigned to other treatment programs. The authors concluded that probation is an effective treatment and secondary prevention program for certain types of boys but cautioned that not all boys can benefit from probation.[31] The extension of its use must be carefully watched, and those assigned to probation must be carefully chosen for maximum benefit from the program.

JUVENILE INSTITUTIONS

Reformatories or training schools for juveniles were originally designed to parallel the programs in adult prisons. They have, however, emphasized occupational training programs to a greater extent.[32] One purpose of juvenile correctional institutions has been to provide juveniles with education and training so that their energies may be directed to productive activity. Still others have adopted the goal of treatment; professionals from numerous disciplines play a role in altering the attitudes of the juvenile so that his or her behavior becomes more socially acceptable. Secondary prevention goals are probably not well served by incarceration of youths. Many of these institutions do not have adequate staffs, resources, or facilities to produce real change in the juvenile. The people-changing ideal has often been replaced in practice with custodial norms, which emphasize control over the youth until time for release. The youth returns to the community no better and probably far worse than when he or she entered the institution. The stigma associated with being sent to a reformatory may reduce the chances of obtaining an adequate adjustment to the community, and when coupled with the youth's experiences in the training school, further delinquent behavior or even adult crime may be the expected result.

PUBLIC AND PRIVATE TREATMENT PROGRAMS

Some relatively new community-based treatment programs have been initiated in recent years to deflect or divert the juvenile from formal contact with the juvenile justice system. The programs emphasize people-changing techniques to reduce or eliminate delinquent behavior without removing the offender from the community. The family treatment program represents one such program designed to treat juvenile delinquents on a group basis through the use of detention facilities and volunteers (such as members of VISTA). The youngsters are housed in a detention home to participate in intensive group activities but return home on weekends. Group treatment techniques are used to change behavior and get the youngsters to better understand their behaviors.[33]

In the Provo Experiment, which began in 1956 in Utah, professionals and laymen were organized as the Citizen's Advisory Council to the juvenile court. Habitual offenders were assigned to the program if they were boys between the ages of 15 and 17. The program was only able to take 20 boys at one time.[34] The youths were allowed to remain in their homes but were required by the court to spend some time during the day at a center for a period specified by the juvenile court. Treatment consisted of creating a group situation in which behavioral change was possible. Community adjustment was emphasized in a second phase of the program. Efforts to support the boys' new behavior patterns were supplemented with periodic meetings of the group. The program continued in this manner for a period of months to reinforce behavior modifications that may have occurred as a result of intensive group participation in the first phase. Peer pressure was used to encourage, change, and reinforce behavior. The recidivism rate for the boys in the group was lower than that for a comparable group placed in training schools.[35]

TREATMENT METHODS

Prevention and control programs use various methods to treat the delinquent or predelinquent juvenile. Each of these is usually related to one or another of the theories of delinquency causation discussed in Part Two. Treatment methods attempt to change the factors that are believed to cause delinquency. For example, if psychological factors are believed to be causal, then psychoanalytical approaches might be used to treat delinquent individuals. Several people-changing treatment techniques will be discussed in this section. Punishment, which some believe to be useful in preventing recurral of delinquency, will not be treated.

Treatment methods are usually classified as involving either an individual (treatment of the offender as an individual) or group (treatment within a framework or system that includes peers) approach. There are, however, some approaches that represent mixtures of group and individual treatment methods. Psychologists, psychiatrists, and social workers are more likely to use the individual approach to treatment, while sociologists and others usually prefer group methods. The methods used by a professional will usually reflect his or her background and training. The variety of mixed procedures is such that not all sociologists prefer group methods, nor do all psychologists prefer individual methods.[36]

Individual Treatment Methods
PSYCHOTHERAPY

Psychotherapy emphasizes the treatment of emotional and personality problems believed to cause delinquent behavior.[37] The psychotherapist attempts to achieve personality, attitude, and value change so that behavior alteration is possible. A basic part of psychotherapy is transference. Juveniles direct their feelings about significant people (usually a parent) in their past to the therapist, thereby enabling the therapist to understand better the emotions and attitudes of their patients. Aichhorn reported that experiences in transference suggest that delinquent boys have almost constant fights with parents. Such a situation may lead to hate, retarded emotional development, and impulsiveness which is expressed in delinquent behavior. Aichhorn used transference and a friendly, accepting atmosphere without punishment to encourage acceptable behavior.[38] Friedlander and Long and Kamada reported that transference is important and effective.[39] Juveniles react to the therapist by expecting him or her to act like a parent. They soon learn, in an accepting atmosphere, that not all adults act like their parents. This revelation results in a changed attitude toward adults, institutions, and behavior. Szurek emphasized that the juvenile who had been denied a "home" should be provided one in the therapeutic situation.[40] Love, justice, frankness, firmness, and a well-adjusted person (the therapist) with which to identify is considered essential for the maladjusted youth.

Holmes also stressed the need for directness, firmness, and fairness in reacting to devious, manipulative behavior by the delinquent. The therapist does not punish but rather interprets the meaning of the behavior and provides alternative behavior patterns for the juvenile. The juvenile is expected to take responsibility for his or her own behavior even though he or she may be detained in some type of correctional facility.[41]

CASEWORK

The caseworker deals directly with individuals in trouble to locate the source of their problems so that adequate help can be provided.[42] Casework is related to, but not the same as, psychotherapy, even though some professionals find it difficult to separate the two.[43] The caseworker relies on face-to-face interaction with individual delinquents to build a relationship within which problem-solving activities may be encouraged. A social history, developed by the caseworker, summarizes the client's social and environmental background and serves as a basis for building an individualized plan of action to aid the client. Counseling or other treatment programs may be prescribed on the basis of this report. Trojanowicz reported that casework has not been very successful when used with juvenile delinquents. The caseworker is frequently met by critical, aggressive, and hostile parents as well as juveniles, especially when developing the social history.[44]

REALITY THERAPY

Reality therapy is another technique developed to treat individual delinquents. A basic assumption underlying this approach is that each juvenile has a set of basic needs. If the person has been able to fulfill these needs, he or she acts responsibly. Irresponsible or delinquent behavior results from blockage of need fulfillment. The goal of reality therapy is to encourage need fulfillment and thereby responsible behavior. William Glasser, the developer of this method, suggests that the method should be used by all members of the justice system.[45] Excuses, a bad background, extenuating circumstances, neuroses, or unloving parents do not relieve the juvenile of responsibility for his or her behavior. Therefore extensive social histories, psychological testing, and other records are not necessary. The past cannot be altered, so present behavior is all that is important. The only records needed are short notes specifying evidence of increased responsibility to encourage the juvenile to modify present behavior rather than reflect on past problems.[46]

Glasser suggests that juveniles do not commit delinquent acts because they are unhappy. Therefore, attempts to make them happy will fail to reduce delinquent behavior. Delinquents are unhappy because their acts generate negative evaluations from others. They need to feel good about themselves and have peers and significant others evaluate them positively. Reality therapy, then, is oriented toward obtaining responsible behavior leading to positive evaluation by others that will eventually be reflected in the delinquent's own self-concept. The therapist assumes that if he or she treats the juvenile as a responsible person, the juvenile will act responsibly. A reality therapist is expected to be warm, honest, confident, supporting, and nonrejecting in his or her approach while stressing the consequences of law-violating behavior. The question "why" is never asked.

Glasser has provided some evidence that the reality therapy method works, even though some experts have criticized it as being based on an oversimplified view of human behavior. The method can become a hostile and punitive technique if used by an incompetent therapist.[47]

VOCATIONAL GUIDANCE AND COUNSELING

Vocational guidance and counseling is a treatment method that does not rely on attempts to understand or diagnose personality adjustment. The goal is to help the juvenile by providing information on job choices, types of jobs available, and qualifications and training needed for success in the job market. A counselor may use aptitude and interest tests to help the juvenile choose a career that will be satisfying and productive. The goal of the vocational counselor is to train and retrain youths so that they become responsible, productive members of society rather than juvenile delinquents.

Programs such as the Neighborhood Youth Corps and the New Careers Program have emphasized help to youths through vocational guidance and counseling. These programs offer vocational training, work experience, education, and counseling. The programs, when used with delinquent youths, rely on the assumption that delinquency can be prevented and individuals rehabilitated by providing legitimate avenues for success in the community.[48]

BEHAVIOR MODIFICATION

Behavior modification is based on the assumption that delinquency is a type of learned behavior. In order to change individual behavior and reduce or eliminate delinquent behavior, new responses must be learned to replace old ones. Behavior is learned by adjusting rewards and punishments that act as reinforcements. The therapist is expected to reward nondelinquent behavior (positive reinforcement) and provide punishment for delinquent or nonresponsible behavior (negative reinforcement) so that the individual learns new and positive responses. In order to use behavior modification effectively, the therapist must be able to identify the factors that are reinforcers for an individual. He or she must also be able to identify behaviors that can be learned or unlearned.[49] The therapist begins with the immediate behavioral aspects of the client and uses valued materials (reinforcers such as money, food, and praise) to change behavior. Behavior modification has been used with some success by Schwitzgebel and in the National Training School Project.[50]

CRISIS INTERVENTION

Crisis intervention is an individual delinquency rehabilitation technique used to deal with juveniles who are acting out their problems. According to Villeponteaux, the technique is based on the belief that people in crisis situations are psychologically overburdened and vulnerable to additional problems. When the crisis is resolved, other problems are averted at the same time. Villeponteaux compares crisis intervention to first aid provided at the time of an accident.[51] It is used in a threatening situation to help the juvenile understand his or her behavior and strive for adjustment. One problem that limits the effectiveness of crisis intervention is that delinquent youths, especially chronic delinquents, may not experience guilt or anxiety about their behavior. Therefore it is difficult to get them involved in the behavioral change process. On the other hand, for individuals who do experience anxiety or guilt, crisis intervention can be used to produce change. Like initial first aid after an accident, though, the technique may only be a band-aid that is used to patch up people and send them on their way without providing a cure.[52]

Group Treatment Methods
GUIDED GROUP INTERACTION
Guided group interaction is a rehabilitative technique similar to group therapy and group psychotherapy in that group processes are used to help delinquents solve problems. The technique is based on the assumption that individuals benefit from free discussion within a like-minded group of peers. Individuals with similar backgrounds and experiences are brought together under conditions that encourage the free exchange of ideas. The participants are made aware that they are expected to take responsibility for the actions of all members of the group. The group has considerable power and is able to sanction members who do not cooperate.[53] The leader of the group directs group processes within a democratic group framework, allowing the participants to vent their hostility, aggression, and other feelings but strives to develop the group along positive productive lines.

MILIEU THERAPY
Milieu therapy is a group-oriented rehabilitation technique aimed at producing a satisfactory environment which will aid change, growth, and adjustment in delinquent youths. If the environment of a delinquent is such that it contributes to delinquency-related problems, a change in environment might be indicated. A controlled setting such as a halfway house or other institution may encourage a change in behavior.[54] The milieu is constructed to produce behavior alteration; the environmental change is in itself therapy. A broad treatment orientation is used in milieu therapy; the total environment is emphasized as a treatment tool. The technique is difficult to use outside a controlled setting. Other, more specialized group and individual people-changing techniques may be used within the altered environment to help eliminate delinquent behavior.[55]

GROUP PSYCHOTHERAPY
Group psychotherapy is a group technique in which the group is used as a tool to provide more extensive insight and personality change in the individual participants. The primary difference between group psychotherapy and other group techniques that are often confused

with it is the high degree of personality change, involvement, and intensity sought. Trojanowicz reported that it is often difficult to form close, intense groups among delinquent youths because of the diverse nature of their delinquent activities. This problem can be overcome, however, if adequate selection procedures are used for the group.[56] Hersko reported that delinquents are generally self-centered, and intense group involvement is therefore difficult.[57] Shulman stated that as a result of these and other problems, traditional psychotherapy has to be modified for effective treatment of delinquents by stressing the benefits of participation that each individual will receive from the group.[58]

FAMILY THERAPY

A variant of group psychotherapy is family therapy. The entire family is involved in the treatment process. All members of the group are treated on the same basis. The goal is to provide parents with insights into their influence on their child's behavior. Children are also apprised of their effect on the family unit. Family psychotherapy has not been extensively evaluated in regard to its effectiveness in delinquency rehabilitation.[59]

Mixed Treatment Programs
SOCIAL GROUP WORK

Social group work is similar to other group methods described in this chapter; however, the emphasis is on helping the individual within a group setting. The group is used to help the individual learn to function in groups and be satisfied with group relationships. The technique is similar to social casework, but group work stresses group accomplishments and is more complex because of the number of people involved in the group networks.[60] The social group workers are expected to understand and sympathize with individual problems but remain alert to possible group input for individual solutions. Pierce claims that individual members experiment with new behavior patterns which are accepted or rejected by other group members.[61] A variant of this method is used in natural settings. Group workers deal with gangs, street corner groups, and other small groups using natural group processes to obtain responsible behavior. Group workers often experience difficulty gaining trust and acceptance in natural groups. The problem is amplified when gang members believe the group worker is an informer for the police or is in the area for some other purpose. If the worker can convince the group that he or she is trustworthy and valuable, benefits will result from participation, and some behavioral change may result.

INDIVIDUAL AND GROUP COUNSELING

Counseling is used by either groups or individuals; the major goal is education and support. The counselor usually attempts to get juveniles to understand and solve their immediate problems without fundamental personality or behavior modifications. Group counseling programs are sometimes found in juvenile institutions, where a group setting is used to encourage discussion of the personal problems of participants.[62] Group counseling is also used in conjunction with more individualized treatment and/or rehabilitation programs.[63] Role playing, skits, games, and similar techniques may be used in the group to establish a comfortable, uninhibited atmosphere within which a youngster can come to a better understanding of his or her behavior and problems.[64]

Comparison of Treatment Methods

Treatment methods can be viewed in terms of a continuum which suggests scope and intensity of focus. Vocational, individual, and group counseling are somewhat broad approaches to juvenile problems. They require few diagnosis procedures or personality and behavior changes for success. Casework and psychotherapy are at the other end of the continuum. They require extensive personality and behavioral reorientation and treatment procedures but do not deal with other aspects of the individual's life. Behavior modification would probably be classified between the two extremes. A juvenile may receive more than one type of assistance, either concurrently or at different points in time as need suggests.[65]

There are additional treatment procedures that could replace or supplement the ones described in this chapter. Some religious, secular, and fraternal agencies operate programs designed to modify the attitudes, values, and behaviors of juveniles. YMCA/YWCA programs, Big Brother, and some church-oriented programs have experienced some success with juveniles. They are frequently used to supplement other types of treatment or rehabilitative programs. Furthermore, stimulants (such as amphetamines and Ritilin) have been used with juveniles with minimal brain damage or hyperactivity to calm or modify their behavior. This treatment alternative has been shown to be quite successful if used in conjunction with some of the rehabilitative programs described earlier. Tranquilizers are also used for some youngsters. Stimulants and tranquilizers are medical treatment techniques which should be carefully supervised when used to supplement other people-changing techniques. If drugs calm the individual or modify behavior so that conventional treatment methods can be used, they can be a great aid in reducing delinquent behavior.

PREVENTION POLICY IN PERSPECTIVE

There is little evidence to suggest that doing something is better than choosing to do nothing. Authorities may not be certain that they are doing what is best for the community or the juvenile when they choose one course of action over another. Any intervention into the life of a juvenile that has the potential to help also has the potential to harm, regardless of how well intentioned the motives. Many treatment and rehabilitation programs described in this chapter lack strong and consistent evidence regarding their effectiveness in changing behavior. There are often more reasons in support of nonintervention than intervention. Family and individual problems may be severe, but the power of contemporary treatment techniques for producing harm should not be underestimated.

The increased use of professional treatment personnel in the juvenile justice system and in prevention and control agencies may lead to a tendency to define more and more people as needing some type of treatment. Judges, police personnel, and various treatment-oriented professionals, as they become more sophisticated or use more sophisticated techniques, tend to see more problems, more people needing help, and more reasons to intervene in the lives of individuals. Perhaps intervention should only be considered when it is known that programs are effective or when the behavior of the person is such that the protection of the individual and the community is necessary.[66]

A comprehensive approach to delinquency prevention, treatment, and control requires overall community planning and coordination. Zweig and Morris emphasize that planning for treatment requires a theory of causation.[67] A treatment program will be oriented and shaped by the planners' conception of juvenile delinquency causation. The social sciences offer a variety of conceptual models specifying causal factors. It is significant that the federal government requires comprehensive criminal justice planning based upon specified conceptions of crime in order to receive certain types of federal funding.[68] If planning is ever to be more than a formality or a game played to obtain federal funding, it must be based on conceptual models backed with adequate empirical evidence.

In the past, delinquency control was considered a private matter. The family and the church were expected to deal with the misbehavior of children. In recent years delinquency control has become more and more complicated and increasingly involves more professional occupational groups seeking to change the delinquent. Delinquency control has become more difficult possibly because (1) delinquency rates have increased, (2) public attention is focused on the problems of youths, and (3) the growth of the population and large cities suggests even greater increases in delinquency.[69] As a result, the police and other occupational groups have assumed a more important role in delinquency prevention, rehabilitation, and control, while the church and the family have become less important.

Because delinquency prevention, rehabilitation, and control have become more complex, there is an urgent need for evaluative procedures. The development of effective policies will require adequate information to use as a base for decision making and sound planning.

National, state, and local planning agencies increasingly depend on accurate statistics and research studies on delinquency. There is a shortage of accurate and detailed information in many areas. Extensive programs of evaluation research are needed to assess the effects of prevention and rehabilitation programs on delinquency rates and recidivism and to examine cost and other criteria of program effectiveness. Research is also needed on the question of how successful results are achieved. It is not enough to know that a program is successful; we need to know how it was done so that it can be repeated in new locations with equal success. In addition, research is needed to test, verify, and build theories related to delinquency causation. A verified theory of causation would have important implications for prevention, rehabilitation, and control by suggesting appropriate modes of intervention. The present situation suggests that "the actual consequences accruing to people being treated differ very little from the consequences accruing to people being punished."[70]

NOTES

[1] Stanton Wheeler and Leonard Cottrell, Jr., *Juvenile Delinquency: Its Prevention and Control* (New York: Russell Sage Foundation, 1966), p. 3.

[2] Department of Health, Education, and Welfare, Children's Bureau, *Juvenile Delinquency Prevention in the United States* (Washington, D.C.: Government Printing Office, 1965), p. 2.

[3] *Ibid.*, p. 17.

[4] James F. Short, Jr., "Juvenile Delinquency: The Sociocultural Context," in *Review of Child Development Research*, vol. 2, ed. Lois Hoffman and Martin Hoffman (New York: Russell Sage Foundation, 1966).

[5] Wheeler and Cottrell, *op. cit.*

[6] Robert C. Trojanowicz, *Juvenile Delinquency: Concepts and Control* (Englewood Cliffs, N.J.: Prentice-Hall, 1973), pp. 188–189. Much of the information in this section relies heavily on this book.

[7] Peter Lejins, "The Field of Prevention," in *Delinquency Prevention: Theory and Practice*, ed. William Amos and Charles Welford (Englewood Cliffs, N.J.: Prentice-Hall, 1967), p. 3.

[8] Wheeler and Cottrell, *op. cit.*

[9] Department of Health, Education, and Welfare, Social Rehabilitation Service, *Annual Report of Federal Activity in Juvenile Delinquency, Youth Development and Related Fields* (Washington, D.C.: Government Printing Office, 1971), pp. 89–90.

[10] *Ibid.*, p. 111.

[11] *Ibid.*, p. 79.

[12] *Ibid.*, p. 83.

[13] *Ibid.*, p. 109.

[14] Department of Health, Education, and Welfare, Manpower Administration, *The Neighborhood Youth Corps: Hope and Help for Youth* (Washington, D.C.: Government Printing Office, 1969), p. 6.

[15] Martin R. Haskell and Lewis Yablonsky, *Crime and Delinquency* (Skokie, Ill.: Rand McNally, 1970), pp. 444–445.

[16] Gisele Konopka, "South Central Youth Project: A Delinquency Control Program, 1955–1957," *Annals of the American Academy of Political and Social Science* 322 (1959): 30–37.

[17] Charles L. Weirman, "A Critical Analysis of Police-School Liaison Program to Implement Attitudinal Change in Junior High Students" (masters thesis, Michigan State University) as cited in Trojanowicz, op. cit.

[18] Ruth Shonle Cavan and Theodore N. Ferdinand, Juvenile Delinquency, 3d ed. (Philadelphia: Lippincott, 1975), p. 294.

[19] Allen E. Bergin, "When Shrinks Hurt: Psychotherapy Can Be Dangerous," Psychology Today, November 1975, p. 96.

[20] Sheldon Glueck and Eleanor Glueck, Unraveling Juvenile Delinquency (Cambridge, Mass.: Harvard University Press, 1950).

[21] Sheldon Glueck and Eleanor T. Glueck, "Early Detection of Future Delinquents," Journal of Criminal Law, Criminology and Police Science 47 (1956): 175.

[22] Maude M. Craig, "Application of the Glueck Social Prediction Table on an Ethnic Basis," Crime and Delinquency 11 (1965): 175–185; Eleanor T. Glueck, "Efforts to Identify Delinquents," Federal Probation 24 (June 1960): 49–56.

[23] Jackson Toby, "An Evaluation of Early Identification and Intensive Treatment Programs for Predelinquents," Social Problems 13 (fall 1965): 160–175.

[24] Maude M. Craig and Selma Glick, "Ten Years Experience with the Glueck Prediction Table," Crime and Delinquency 9 (July 1963).

[25] Cavan and Ferdinand, op. cit., p. 297.

[26] Robert Martinson, "The Age of Treatment," in Criminal Justice in America, ed. Richard Quinney (Boston: Little, Brown, 1974), p. 324.

[27] Ibid.

[28] Ibid.

[29] Haskell and Yablonsky, op. cit., p. 432.

[30] Frank Scarpitti and Richard M. Stephenson, "A Study of Probation Effectiveness," Journal of Criminal Law, Criminology and Police Science, September 1968, pp. 361–369.

[31] Ibid.

[32] Haskell and Yablonsky, op. cit., p. 419.

[33] Department of Health, Education and Welfare, Social Rehabilitation Service, National Strategy to Prevent Delinquency (Washington, D.C.: Government Printing Office, 1972), p. 4.

[34] Lamar T. Emprey and Jerome Rabow, "The Provo Experiment in Delinquency Rehabilitation," American Sociological Review 26 (October 1961): 679–695.

[35] President's Commission on Law Enforcement and Administration of Justice, Task Force Report: Juvenile Delinquency and Youth Crime (Washington, D.C.: Government Printing Office, 1967), p. 39.

[36] Trojanowicz, op. cit.

[37] Lawrence C. Kolb, Noyes' Modern Clinical Psychiatry (Philadelphia: Saunders, 1968).

[38] August Aichhorn, Wayward Youth (New York: Viking Press, 1963).

[39] Kate Friedlander, The Psycho-analytical Approach to Juvenile Delinquency (London: Routledge and Kegan Paul, 1947), p. 243; Anna Marie Long and Samuel I. Kamada, "Psychiatric Treatment of Adolescent Girls," California Youth Authority Quarterly, summer 1964, pp. 23–24.

[40] S. A. Szurek, The Antisocial Child (Palo Alto, Calif.: Behavior Books, 1969), pp. 80–81.

[41] Donald Holmes, The Adolescent in Psychotherapy (Boston: Little, Brown, 1964), p. 262.

[42] Paul Tappan, Juvenile Delinquency (New York: McGraw-Hill, 1949), p. 362.

[43] *Ibid.;* Elizabeth Ferguson, *Social Work* (Philadelphia: Lippincott, 1963).

[44] Trojanowicz, *op. cit.,* p. 237.

[45] William Glasser, "Reality Therapy: A Realistic Approach to Young Offenders," in *Readings in Delinquency and Treatment,* ed. Robert Schasre and Jo Wallach (Los Angeles: University of California, Youth Studies Center, 1965).

[46] *Ibid.*

[47] *Ibid.*

[48] See Trojanowicz, *op. cit.*

[49] Ronald Thorp and Ralph Wetzel, *Behavior Modification in the Natural Environment* (New York: Academic Press, 1969); Saleem A. Shah, "Treatment of Offenders: Some Behavioral Concepts, Principles and Approaches," *Federal Probation* 23 (September 1959): 29.

[50] Ralph Schwitzgebel, *Streetcorner Research* (Cambridge, Mass.: Harvard University Press, 1965); Shah, *op. cit.*

[51] Lorenz Villeponteaux, "Crisis Intervention in a Day School for Delinquents," *Crime and Delinquency* 16 (July 1970): 318–319.

[52] *Ibid.*

[53] Emprey and Rabow, *op. cit.*

[54] S. R. Slavson, *Reclaiming the Delinquent* (New York: Free Press, 1965).

[55] Trojanowicz, *op. cit.*

[56] *Ibid.,* p. 258.

[57] Marvin Hasko, "Group Psychotherapy with Delinquent Adolescent Girls," *American Journal of Orthopsychiatry* 32 (January 1962): 170–171.

[58] Irving Schulman, "Modifications in Group Psychotherapy with Antisocial Adolescents," *International Journal of Group Psychotherapy* 7 (1957): 310.

[59] Trojanowicz, *op. cit.*

[60] *Ibid.,* p. 255.

[61] F. J. Pierce, "Social Group Work in a Women's Prison," *Federal Probation* 27 (December 1963): 37–38.

[62] Rosemary C. Sarri and Robert D. Vinter, "Group Treatment Strategies in Juvenile Correctional Programs," *Crime and Delinquency* 11 (October 1965): 330.

[63] E. Preston Sharp, "Group Counseling in a Short Term Institution," *Federal Probation* 23 (September 1959): 8.

[64] George Gazda, *Basic Approaches to Group Psychotherapy and Group Counseling* (Springfield, Ill.: Thomas, 1968).

[65] Trojanowicz, *op. cit.*

[66] Wheeler and Cottrell, *op. cit.*

[67] Franklin M. Zweig and Robert Morris, "The Social Planning Design Guide," *Social Work* 2 (April 1966): 13–21.

[68] Daniel L. Skoler, "Comprehensive Criminal Justice Planning," *Crime and Delinquency* 14 (July 1968): 197–206.

[69] Peter G. Garabedian and Don C. Gibbons, *Becoming Delinquent* (Chicago: Aldine, 1970), pp. 285–299.

[70] Paul J. Brantingham and Frederic L. Faust, "A Conceptual Model of Crime Prevention," *Crime and Delinquency* 22 (July 1976): 285.

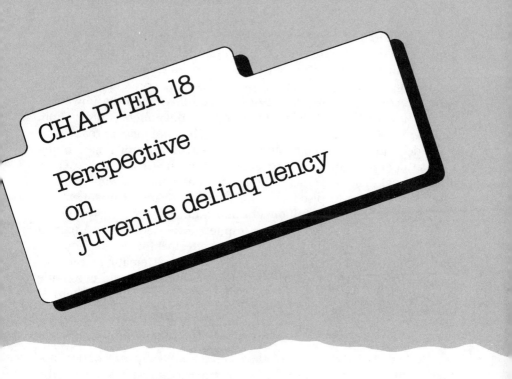

CHAPTER 18
Perspective on juvenile delinquency

Juvenile delinquency is a new and relatively ill-defined field. It has borrowed many theories, prevention programs, and control techniques from criminology, often without adequate consideration of whether they are appropriate for dealing with young people. At the same time, the juvenile justice system has maintained a separate existence with its special proceedings and philosophy for handling juveniles. Yet despite all the resources, theories, research, and special programs, the threefold goal of effective prevention, treatment, and control has not been achieved. New departures may be needed in a variety of areas before delinquency can be prevented, delinquents rehabilitated, and a better understanding of the complex forces that produce juvenile delinquency obtained.

STATE OF THE FIELD
Theory Development

Strange as it may seem to action-oriented people, a well-developed and verified theory is a practical device for effective control, prevention, and treatment of delinquency. Some people believe that a program staffed with trained and well-intentioned people is all that is required. Many people do not see the necessity of using abstract and frequently obscure theories which attempt to describe the causes of juvenile delinquency to provide a foundation for programs. Instead, they would prefer to get on with the job of prevention, treatment, and control.

Little could be more practical for developing a social action program designed to control, prevent, or treat delinquency than a theory with a high degree of research support. An awareness of the causes of juvenile delinquency enables us to focus on correcting or eliminating its sources. In the absence of verified theories or an unwillingness to use them in developing programs, delinquency prevention, treatment, and control is a primitive art. The shotgun approaches of many delinquency programs currently in vogue are not unlike hiring a witch doctor to treat a heart attack victim in a space-age society. It is essential that we research the problem and show a willingness to adopt the findings to discover more effective means of treatment.

Action-oriented practitioners often intuitively develop programs in the absence of verified theory. Despite good intentions and trained staff, these programs often prove no more effective than doing nothing. Furthermore, more often than not, there is little systematic research to evaluate their effectiveness. The following questions should constantly be asked: Is the money being spent on the program being wasted? Is the delinquent being helped? Is delinquency being prevented? If the answers to these questions are no, the programs should either be eliminated or altered.

A few social action programs are theoretically based. Psychoanalytic theory, for example, has been cited as a justification for the use of individual and group therapy in the treatment of delinquents and predelinquents. A basic assumption of psychoanalytic theory is that the individual is ill or maladjusted and should receive treatment. On the other hand, when differential association is cited as the base for program development, the juvenile is removed from contact with peers who have attitudes favorable to the violation of law. An attempt is made to replace delinquent peers with productive and conforming peer groups. Where labeling is used, a different type of program is developed. An attempt is made to keep the juvenile, law-violating or not, from coming into contact with the juvenile justice system.

A well-developed and verified theory of delinquency causation can provide policy implications from which more adequate control, prevention, and treatment policies can be developed. We have reviewed a variety of theories that purport to explain delinquency, and it is evident that the list of potential causes is a long one. Biological, psychological, sociological, and popular conceptions have been explored, and the research support, or the lack of it, has been shown for each. The general conclusion must be that there is no generally applicable theory that adequately explains juvenile delinquency. There is research support for some hypotheses, but no comprehensive theory has been adequately verified. Probably the most well-researched theory, and the one with the greatest research support, is differential association. Another potentially fruitful area for the further development of a delinquency theory may be in the general area of learning theory.

The goal of developing a generally applicable theory may not be realistic for juvenile delinquency at this time. It is, after all, a young, immature discipline. A more realistic and productive avenue may be found in the construction of a number of middle-range theories which are applicable to a limited range of delinquent behaviors. From our perspective, theory development should proceed on a broad front and include a variety of disciplines and perspectives. Furthermore, the theories of most value to juvenile delinquency analysts should provide a broad understanding of both normal and delinquent behavior. Delinquent behavior can probably best be understood as a variant of normal, rather than abnormal, behavior. Delinquent behavior is something that happens in all social classes, races, and ethnic groups and in both sexes. An evenhanded approach is needed to rid the field of the class bias so pointedly described by Thio.[1]

Another area in which theory development might fruitfully progress is the identification and listing of hypotheses for which research support has been provided. These hypotheses need to be reordered and combined or recombined to construct theories that provide a new perspective on delinquency. Don Gibbons has begun the task of listing some verified hypotheses, but a vast amount of work is left undone.[2] In fact, the work has just begun. It is imperative that new theories be developed by experts to cope with the full complexity of the delinquency problem. A long-term theoretical research and development program should be initiated with the goal of explaining how and why American society is plagued by juvenile delinquency. Such a program would involve broadening the framework within which the problem of delinquency is analyzed. It would also involve a willingness to challenge, rather than ignore, traditional theories and approaches.

Verification Research

Theories provide ideas about the phenomena that lead to delinquent behavior, but they remain little more than speculation until research is initiated to test their power to explain or predict behavior. If a theory can be shown to be accurate, practitioners may have more confidence that action programs and policies based on the theory will be effective. Research does far more than perform the rather passive role of checking and verifying theory, however. It may contribute to an understanding of delinquency by discrediting inadequate theories. It can also help clarify the concepts involved in theory. Furthermore, research may suggest the practical implications of a theory for policies promoting delinquency control, prevention, and treatment. Unexpected findings often lead to new theory or a refinement of an existing one. In any event, research is an integral part of the search for, and the development of, a theoretical understanding of juvenile delinquency.

There are a number of areas in which research is badly needed. A review of Part Two should suggest several potential areas for research; there are many neglected areas. A long-term and well-financed commitment to research is essential if society is to understand and develop a capacity to cope with the delinquency problem. In the absence of adequate and reliable information about juvenile delinquency, each organization that deals with the delinquent should allocate a portion of its budget to research. Research provides a problem-solving orientation and suggests policy that is theoretically sound. The research process itself provides the data that are vital to effective planning and administration.

Evaluation Research

Evaluation research is somewhat different from research designed to verify theory. Evaluation research is designed to assess the effectiveness of a control, prevention, or treatment program in accomplishing its goals. The focus is on the program and finding out whether it is doing what it was designed to do. Delinquency control, prevention, and treatment programs cost millions of dollars each year.[3] Unfortunately, many of these costly programs have never been systematically evaluated, and others have been proved ineffective or even harmful. All programs must still be evaluated to determine if they are effective. The delinquency problem is too serious and extensive to waste limited, valuable resources on ineffective or harmful programs.

Evaluation research also provides the data base for informed and intelligent judgment about the relative merits of the various programs currently available. Furthermore, research may indicate which type of treatment is most effective for a particular type of delinquent offender.

When changes are introduced into a program, research provides an opportunity to assess the effect of the change in terms of the goals of the overall program.

Too often, delinquency prevention, treatment, and control programs are haphazardly planned and administered in the absence of sound research programs. Unfortunately, evaluation research is often perceived as threatening by staff members of social action programs. It is frequently suggested that a poor evaluation will mean the end of the program and their jobs. As a result, evaluation research efforts may be frustrated or sabotaged. The perceived threat of evaluative research is not based in experience. When staff members have cooperated with evaluative researchers, the transition to a more effective program has not generally involved a great number of personnel changes. Cooperative staffers may be evaluated as valuable personnel in view of their flexibility.[4]

The evaluative research program may have implications beyond improving the effectiveness of a specific program. Information about the effectiveness of the various aspects of a program may be applied to other agencies. Such information is invaluable in exposing the various pitfalls and traps to be avoided. The effective aspects of a program can confidently be adopted in new programs elsewhere.

SOCIAL CONTROL

The ability of the community to influence the behavior of its members is called social control. In a homogeneous society, there is considerable consensus on what constitutes proper and acceptable behavior. When an individual deviates from the norm, the forces of the community are mobilized in an effort to bring the offender back into line. Community processes, then, provide treatment for behavior problems. In the modern industrialized society, however, a sense of community may be absent.

The Loss of Community

In the simple society, the village and the community were synonymous. Their norms, values, and life styles were the same. All citizens in this sense were interrelated. Over time, however, the village underwent rapid social change. It grew larger and became a city. For the first time heterogeneous groupings were brought together into a single social area. Each of the groups brought with it its own distinct norms, values, and life styles. Differences between the groups were magnified by comparison, and the sense of community interrelatedness broke down. The members of the social area no longer acted in concert as a community to influence the behavior of its members. In this sense, the large modern urban area is said to be disorganized.

Rapid social mobility, urbanization, and social change alter the face of modern societies. The community is no longer a cohesive, integrated unit capable of exercising control over its members. The informal social controls used by small towns and rural societies are not effective in the city. Sheer numbers of people may preclude the effectiveness of informal sanctions. In large cities formal and impersonal relationships have replaced closely knit personal and informal relationships between people. For example, police officers often make their homes in neighborhoods other than those in which they serve. The automobile gives them increased mobility, but it reduces their chances of acquiring an intimate knowledge of members of areas in which they work or live. The police (and the whole justice system) have become separated from the community so that the community's informal and personal relationships become less effective for controlling its members.

The family was at one time the most important agency of social control. However, various organizations have taken over its traditional functions and diminished its control. The automobile and the work place have taken family members out of the home. The government and the schools have assumed education and protection tasks once performed by the family. In the past, the activities of family members revolved around the home, the church, and the school. Intimate, personal, face-to-face relationships developed within this uncomplicated setting. Entrepreneurs knew their customers and workers, and people knew their neighbors. Much of this has changed. The informal networks of social relationship have been disrupted. As a result, the ability of the family and the community to control their members has weakened.

Where a sense of community exists, everyone shares responsibility for the actions of the area's youths. If a child is involved in misconduct, the family is notified and feels pressure to apply corrective measures. Where interpersonal relations are kept at a minimum, on the other hand, informal demands may invite hostility. Formal, authoritative, and impersonal controls have been instituted by large bureaucratic organizations to replace informal controls. These agencies cannot fully and effectively replace the community, however. They cannot exert the intensive, intimate forms of control practiced in the true community.

If a sense of community could be reestablished, social control over juveniles might once again be effective. The task of reestablishing a sense of community, however, is not an easy one. Rapid social change, mobility, urbanization, and other factors have firmly established a trend toward fragmentation of community functions. The schools, the churches, welfare agencies, and many other organizations are oriented to the performance of specialized tasks in relative isolation from other organizations. A reversal of this trend will require cooperation and coordination of these agencies along with a revival of citizen involvement.

Planning and Citizen Participation

Most communities have a maze of agencies directly or indirectly concerned with the problems of juvenile delinquency. The police, the courts, welfare agencies, and many other organizations deal with juvenile delinquents at one time or another. Unfortunately, these organizations generally work in isolation, each tied to its own special program for dealing with troublesome youths. Their programs having been developed in isolation, may conflict or cancel each other out. A campaign by local business owners to press charges against all shoplifters, for example, may run at cross-purposes with a Youth Services Bureau's goal of diversion. An effective prevention, treatment, or control plan must be free of such conflicts. It must necessarily involve the cooperative and coordinated participation of all concerned organizations and individuals.

The task of achieving a unified network of organizations and individuals to combat juvenile delinquency will require intensive and extensive planning. Some funds for this purpose are provided by the federal government through the Juvenile Delinquency Prevention and Control Act of 1969. The act encourages planning at the community level. Funds are also available for research to determine program needs and set up action councils for citizen involvement.

An effective planning process involves several interrelated stages. The first planning stage must involve the locating and cataloguing of all services offered to juveniles in the community. Very often, program administrators may be ignorant of the full range of resources and services offered to juveniles in the community. Before cooperation or coordination can be achieved, the agencies must be aware of each other. A careful study of the diverse resources in the community will indicate the strengths and weaknesses of the existing programs.

Once a comprehensive list is obtained, the second step is achieving cooperation and communication among the various agencies. Any number of community organizations may resist efforts that involve a diversion of resources or loss of control over their spheres of influence. Coordination efforts may be perceived as threatening and unnecessary. Intrusions on the agencies' internal programs or operations are less than welcome. Each organization may have a vested interest in autonomy. The suspicion and distrust of cooperative programs can only be alleviated by the establishment of an extensive communications network in which all organizations have an opportunity to provide input and share accumulated information. Community action councils may be set up to accomplish this goal. Organizational representatives, private citizens, and juveniles should be brought together to assess current programs and make plans for coordinated future efforts. If all these diverse groups will participate voluntarily, a unified, effective community organization can be established and a comprehensive prevention, treatment, and control plan developed.

Local plans should accomplish a number of objectives. The first objective is to establish realistic goals for the community. The goals should be one that the residents can identify with and support. The goals must not conflict with the basic values of the community. It would, for example, be possible to rid the community of its delinquency problem or reduce the problem by restricting the number of youths who may live in the community. However, few citizens would be interested in supporting a program of this nature. Nor would there be widespread support for a program that gave yearly cash awards to children who managed to stay out of trouble. Realistic goals are those that appear attainable and do not conflict with community values.

A second objective of effective planning is a built-in evaluation process. If the plan is to maintain citizen support and interest, there must be visible and clear-cut evidence of plan effectiveness. The absence of simple measures to gauge program effectiveness suggests to citizens that nothing is being done. Both short-term and long-term goals must be established and published to enable the participants to maintain interest and support.

An effective plan must invite and encourage voluntary participation in both program development and implementation. All potential resource providers must be included and encouraged to provide input. When the concerned organization has a vested interest, it is more likely to mobilize its resources to accomplish the agreed-upon goals. Even when all community resources are mobilized, they may fall short of what is necessary to reach the overall goals of the community action organization. Priority decisions may be necessary to meet short-term objectives. Involvement in priority decisions may convince reluctant organizations of their influence in, and importance to, the overall program.

A fourth objective of planning is to provide a structure for the sharing of information gained by verificational and evaluative research. The network developed for program planning may be used to pool and disseminate new knowledge and information gained by the cooperating groups. Constant updating of community action-related information will assure that program resources are not wasted on ineffective and inefficient methods of prevention, treatment, and control.

A fifth, and probably the most important, objective of planning is coordination. Coordination is essential to prevent the duplication of effort and waste of human or monetary resources. When several organizations perform overlapping functions, coordination of efforts may result in greater efficiency and comprehensiveness. Several small programs for juvenile placement are not likely to provide the quality or quantity of solutions that result from the pooling of resources. Cooperation in itself, however, is not sufficient to sustain a community action organization. The perceived failure of a single organization may result in the breakdown of a system that is built upon cooperation alone. Conflict, bickering, and wasted effort is a likely outcome. When each organization assumes responsibility for a particular coordinated function, it has a vested interest in completing its tasks to maintain its standing relative to the other community organizations. Too often, initial interest in a community project wanes after a short time, but the accomplishment of planning goals requires a sustained, long-term interest and motivation to handle the problem of juvenile delinquency.[5] If the organization has a vested interest in maintaining the program, the plan is more likely to be sustained.

COMPLEXITY OF THE PROBLEM
The problem of delinquency is not simple, and its solution is complex and difficult. A well-conceived plan that enlists the aid of citizens (including youths), welfare organizations, the local government, the juvenile justice system, and business groups is essential to the development of an effective approach to delinquency. Many people assume that established theories, trained personnel, and good intentions automatically combine to produce effective action programs. But far more is needed for an effective solution to delinquency. For example, an effective organizational structure is needed to promote coordination and cooperation between competing programs and interests within the community so that the goals of control, prevention, and treatment can be achieved.[6]

The Mobilization of community resources is essential to achieve the goals of planning and produce a common orientation to problem solving.[7] Sharing of ideas, expertise, resources, and common efforts in solving problems should be a common rather than a rare occurrence. Juveniles frequently have problems that demand immediate attention and solution. Their problems are not diminished if the youngsters are shuffled from one agency to another until they get lost in a maze of agencies, rules, regulations, and competing jurisdictions. Effective coordination, where it exists, helps reestablish a sense of community for integrated, comprehensive social control over juvenile offenders.

Coordination
There are many theories and treatment strategies available that may be applied to alleviate the problems of juvenile delinquency. However, they are only abstract concepts until they are put in practice by individuals or organizations. Human and organizational resources must be mobilized for coordinated and cooperative effort. Public and private welfare agencies, businesses, interested citizens, and youths must be brought into planning, implementation, administration, and improvement processes if support is to be obtained and maintained for the program.

Coordination requires that a variety of separate organizations, groups, and individuals agree to a degree of integration and cooperation which has been foreign to them in the past. Laymen are often unaware of the competition, mistrust, and suspicion that exists among just the welfare agencies in a community. If new programs are to be supported, the existing organizations must be able to justify their participation and see the new program as acceptable in terms of their own goals. If some basic agreements are not reached prior to the initiation of a program, conflict, opposition, and even sabotage may be expected.

Communities may organize a resource assistance office to help individuals locate the resources they need from the maze of agencies and programs in the community. Some people could be helped within the existing system if they knew how to locate the help they needed or knew whether a specific program existed to handle their special problems. A technical assistance office could at least direct individuals to the appropriate service agencies. Of course, the assistance specialists would need to know what resources are available in the community and have some idea about how the particular problem could be resolved. In fact, a troubled individual may require the services of more than one agency. The resource specialist could refer individuals or families to the appropriate agencies, check on the assistance provided to prevent duplications, and provide further help if required. The key to the success of such an undertaking is the cooperation of the agencies that provide services.

Before a coordination program can be initiated, relevant community groups must be located. Personnel from the juvenile court, welfare agencies (both public and private), and other interested organizations and interested citizens must be identified and brought together for meetings. The meetings should be designed to develop a spirit of cooperation and not be allowed to degenerate into hostile verbal attacks. Cooperation is essential for coordinated approaches to problem solving within a complex community.

Programs that serve the interests of all groups have a better chance of receiving the support and participation necessary to ensure success. Additional meetings and good communications will be essential after the initiation of a program to insure that a high level of interest, morale, and effectiveness is maintained and conflict, dissension, and apathy minimized. If the different groups develop vested interests in a program providing mutual benefits, a coordinated effort to secure adequate services for juveniles can be achieved at the local level.

NEW DIRECTIONS IN JUVENILE DELINQUENCY

In understanding future trends in the field of juvenile delinquency, a knowledge of where we have been is instructive. A glimpse backward to examine the roads that have been traveled and the mistakes that have been made is essential to steering us away from a repetition of past errors. We have presented historical reviews of the development of juvenile delinquency as a discipline and introduced old and sometimes outdated theories to illustrate the development of the field. Even the chapters concerned with the juvenile justice system treated the history of intervention into the lives of juveniles. Historically, theory and research have been related to the types of control, prevention, and treatment strategies that are used in the field. This relationship will probably be continued and reemphasized. Given the history of juvenile delinquency and its present status, several trends can tentatively be identified.

Diversion

The labeling perspective described in Chapter 9 emphasized the negative effects associated with the official application of the juvenile delinquent label. The label itself is believed to have negative consequences because of what other people in the community believe about the person so labeled. A delinquency label can lead to secondary delinquency, negatively affect self-concepts, lead to problems in getting a job, and so on. We are led to sympathize and understand the delinquent who becomes, in essence, a victim of an evil justice system and well-intentioned but inappropriate efforts to help. The logical policy implications specify diversion from the system. In effect, we are asked to save the unfortunate youngster from contact with the system by either treating him or her informally or doing nothing.[8]

The technique of benign neglect is very old and is frequently used. We noted, for example, that the police admonished and released a large percentage of their cases. In addition, youth services, informal parole, and supervision are a few of the alternatives to formal handling of the juvenile within the juvenile justice system. The federal government has supported numerous projects that divert youngsters from the juvenile justice system, provide alternatives to the official handling of juveniles, and promote the sympathetic understanding of delinquents.

Several advantages of diversion have been cited: (1) a reduction in the number of juvenile delinquents (at least in the number who are officially labeled as delinquent), (2) a possible but unsubstantiated reduction in delinquency among individuals negatively affected by a previously applied delinquent label, (3) a revival of interest and concern for problems of youths, and (4) the development of destigmatizing organizations for youths who need services.[9] Diversion and benign neglect may also have disadvantages: (1) diversion may contribute to a belief that nothing is being done to solve the problem of juvenile delinquency; (2) diversion may contribute to a belief that nothing happens if an illegal act is committed even if the individual is caught; (3) the diversion techniques may contribute to a belief that delinquents are helped and provided with expensive community services and sympathetic understanding while their victims are forgotten or ignored; (4) the new diversionary policies may lead to a belief that sympathy directed toward the delinquent is actually misdirected; (5) a new set of labels and terms, such as "person in need of services" may replace the delinquency label, and these new labels may be even more insidious in their effect because they are informally rather than officially applied; (6) a disrespect for law and the legal system may be reinforced; (7) community efforts to control the behavior of its citizens are short-circuited and replaced by a largely invisible and uncontrollable system; and (8) the new organizations and procedures may contribute to the denial of constitutional and procedural rights to juveniles. Americans decry recent revelations about the Soviet system of mental hospitals for political dissidents, but Americans have been willing to do much the same thing to their juveniles without the procedural rights that are given to adults who may have committed identical illegal acts.

For very young children who commit only minor offenses, diversion and benign neglect may be acceptable alternatives to official handling within the juvenile justice system. On the other hand, it should be recognized that the whole diversionary system that is being created in this country denies juveniles the basic constitutional and procedural rights that are provided routinely to adults. Informal probation, supervision, and treatment may be imposed even in the absence of proof that an offense has been committed. Thus juveniles still get the worst of two worlds. They don't get the legal guarantees routinely granted to adults, and they don't receive the individualized and kindly treatment promised by the juvenile court. Instead, they are pushed into a never-never land and subjected to the whims of an uncontrolled, invisible, and untested diversion system.

When the juvenile is diverted out of the system and hidden from public view, the natural power of the community to control the actions of its members is short-circuited. The norms and values in a community define acceptable behavior, and the community can bring sanctions to bear on an offender to help prevent deviance. The diversion process precludes the involvement of the broader community in social control efforts.

The sympathetic treatment of the offender may provoke justified hostile reaction from the community. By treating offenders as victims, an important aspect of delinquency is ignored. The juvenile offender has not been the passive receiver of arbitrary action. Rather, in most cases he or she has aggressively victimized others. The victim of the juvenile's assault, robbery, or rape receives little sympathy from the courts, police, or other agencies in the community. The rape victim or target of robbery is left to pick up the pieces as best he or she can without organized community assistance. The juvenile offender, on the other hand, finds that vast organizational resources, both financial and human, are concentrated on him or her. The perceived lack of justice in a system of this nature may promote a lack of respect for the system of law and further break down social control mechanisms.

Our prediction is that the trend toward diversion and benign neglect will continue, but a reaction to the situation will eventually ensue. The reaction will probably be one in which the problems of, and sympathy for, the victims of crime will be given more attention. Despite the fact that there are a myriad of organizations for dealing with delinquents and criminals, none exist to deal systematically with victims. Some of these agencies could and should do double duty and provide services for victims as well. The juvenile will increasingly be accorded some of the procedural rights that are provided to adults. If this happens (and we believe it will), it will be increasingly difficult to divert individuals from contact with the juvenile justice system. In the future it may be necessary for the juvenile to receive a court disposition before he is referred to community agencies for help, treatment or other services.

Correctional Facilities for Juveniles

Some evidence suggests that institutional placement of juveniles is harmful. Training schools and similar custodial institutions tend to be schools for crime. They are not the treatment and individualized care facilities they were once believed to be. The youngster who is not committed to delinquent values and attitudes may become a confirmed delinquent as a result of training school experience and associations. Currently a nationwide trend has begun to address this problem. Fewer and fewer youngsters are placed in training schools, and the system is relying more heavily on community-based corrections. There is no reason to expect that this trend will be reversed in the future.

Massachusetts closed all of its juvenile correctional facilities in 1973 and replaced them with alternative programs. The state had discovered that training schools were expensive but ineffective. Over 70 percent of all youths committed to their training schools returned as recidivists. The youngsters continually reappeared in either the juvenile or adult correctional system.[10] An additional reason given for closing the training schools was that they had become custodial and not treatment facilities. So much time was spent in preventing escapes and controlling behavior that there was no time or resources for treatment. A third reason given for the closings was the deteriorated conditions in the facilities. Violence from both staff and inmates, boredom, loneliness, and solitary confinement was common. The school, in effect, did little to prepare the individual for release and reintegration into the community.[11]

Training schools were replaced in Massachusetts by residential and nonresidential treatment programs organized on a regional purchased-care basis.[12] Youngsters are diverted from the juvenile institutions, and an attempt is made to provide services to the individual before problems become serious enough to warrant other types of action. In order to avoid the supposed negative effects of a delinquency label, troublesome youths are known as "children in need of services."[13]

Most juveniles do not need to be removed from the local community to receive effective treatment. In fact, treatment programs are probably more effective if the individual is not locked up in an abnormal, institutional setting. Programs in which the individual spends part of the day in school, at work, or in constructive activities and part of the day in a therapeutic atmosphere seem to be relatively inexpensive but effective. Probation involving small caseloads and intensive supervision can be effective with some youngsters who might have been sent to a training school in the past. One of the major advantages of community-based corrections is that the youngster is not removed from the community. The natural community influences on an individual may be used to develop adequate internal and external controls to prevent future misconduct. The individual in the community can be directed into conforming activities and groups rather than into the delinquent associations found in the training school.

A few youngsters will require removal from the community because they represent a danger either to themselves or to others. Of course, some of these youngsters will be sent to institutions similar to a training school or to a mental hospital. The youngster with severe problems should receive intensive and specialized treatment as close to home as possible to allow home visits and receive visitors. If possible, a close and positive contact with normal community life should be maintained even for these youngsters.

The general trend is away from institutionalization and toward community-based corrections. The trend will probably continue, and more training schools will be closed. In place of these custodial institutions, the community and its agencies and facilities will be used to control and treat juveniles. As this trend continues, the need for comprehensive, coordinated, and effective community-based programs will be reemphasized. Effective, sensitive, and well-trained personnel are a key aspect of such a program.

Personnel

The quality and quantity of the personnel in community-based corrections must be considered if problems are to be solved on a local basis. Adequate services, good facilities, and effective programs depend to a large extent on competent personnel. Specialists in all phases of control, prevention, and treatment will need to be trained and recruited at the local level so they can be put to work in the local community. A major problem centers around the identification of individuals who have the skills and training needed for work with juveniles. There are people in the adult correctional system with the relevant background, training, and skills, but some of these people are more effective in working with adults. It may require a special type of person to work closely with juveniles.

The training of personnel is important, but local communities may not be in a position to deal with it.[14] The National Council on Crime and Delinquency suggests that federal financial support is needed in this vital area.[15] The following types of support are recommended: (1) scholarship programs and stipend support, (2) grants for in-service training programs, (3) grants to develop plans and assess program needs, (4) grants and subsidies to develop a program to set standards for local programs and encourage the attainment of standards, and (5) consulting services to aid planning and implementation of standards so that state and local areas can be encouraged to develop similar programs.[16]

The Juvenile Court

The juvenile court has become a much-maligned institution. Some critics have observed that the court does not provide adequate procedural safeguards for juveniles or individualized handling and treatment as promised in the philosophy of the court. Adding insult to injury, adherents of labeling approaches suggest that contact with the court may do more harm than good and may actually create delinquency. Other people note that juvenile judges are often only part-time personnel who have little interest in service on the juvenile court. Service on the court will not advance their legal career, and it does not provide the opportunity for the demonstration of legal expertise. Many judges therefore avoid serving as juvenile judges, so the youngster may be denied the kindly, sympathetic, and knowledgeable authority figure promised by the early reformers.

The juvenile court is undergoing rapid change. Court decisions such as *Gault* have forced the court to provide some of the procedural and legal safeguards associated with adult status. The process of extending these legal rights to juveniles will probably continue. There may have been undue worry about the stigmatizing impact of the court and too little concern about the denial of legal rights to juveniles in the past. In fact, as legal rights are increasingly extended to juveniles, we might soon discover that the court has a far greater role to play in the handling of juveniles. Many juveniles are referred informally to a variety of treatment programs. If juveniles had the right to judicial review, there might be far fewer informal referrals. The court may be needed to legitimize referrals and ensure that the procedural and constitutional rights of juveniles are not violated. If the court serves no other function, it will be a vital part of any treatment, prevention, or control program.

Many things are done to and for juveniles because they are children. The same flexibility of handling is not provided to adults because of their constitutional guarantees of due process and equal protection. The extension of these rights to juveniles will have a profound impact on the court and on the entire juvenile justice system. The court is not likely to die or wither away, but it may become more like the adult court, at least in procedure. At the same time, recognition that juveniles are immature and have a diminished degree of responsibility must be maintained. Procedural rights should be extended and protected, but the court should make every effort to rehabilitate rather than punish the juvenile offender.

Differential Handling of Juveniles

The decision to process a youngster formally or informally through the juvenile justice system may depend on a number of background factors. Family background, financial status of the parents, racial heritage, sex, neighborhood, and political influence of the father or other relatives have all been used at one time or another to determine disposition. Background is sometimes even more important than the type of offense committed or its seriousness in determining outcomes. Young black males from poor sections of town who come to court without influential parents are more likely to be formally handled and even to be committed to a juvenile correctional facility. Youngsters from affluent white families are more likely to be handled informally and receive more desirable court dispositions, if they are not diverted before reaching the court.[17]

Power and influence help keep some people out of trouble even when a law has been violated. Even though individuals from the middle and upper classes may commit as many delinquent acts as lower-class juveniles, the lower-class youth is more likely to appear in court and receive a less favorable court disposition.[18]

Power and influence should not determine who receives the services of treatment and rehabilitation agencies. An evenhanded approach is essential if respect for the law is to be maintained. Unfortunately, the elimination of discrimination is not a simple matter. It may take time, research, and a commitment of adequate resources to correct the situation. The legal process must be fair and the procedures applied equally to all, regardless of race, sex, or class.

SUMMARY

Effective prevention, treatment and control requires theoretical development and systematic verificational research. Planning for an effective juvenile justice system is needed, but plans for program development must be based on adequate research. Evaluations of ongoing community programs are necessary to discover their strengths and weaknesses. Research can contribute to strengthening some programs, but it may result in the alteration and elimination of others because of ineffective or harmful elements in the program.

The resources of the community should be mobilized to accomplish the threefold goal of prevention, treatment, and control. The trend is toward community-based correction, but if the juvenile is to be handled within the context of the community, it is imperative that organizations, welfare agencies, businesses, and citizens become involved in planning and implementing a cooperative and coordinated community-wide effort to deal effectively with delinquency. Competent personnel must be trained and recruited. Innovative programs must be created, and individuals must be processed through the system in an equal and impartial manner, while retaining full legal rights for all juveniles.

There is no scarcity of tasks in the field of juvenile delinquency. Delinquency is a new and relatively underdeveloped area, and the problems of delinquency are immense. Knowledgeable, committed, sensitive, and innovative people are needed in all phases of the field. Contributions can be made in areas ranging from the construction of theory and verificational research to probation and cottage work practice. Even if you do not enter the field in any of its major aspects, participation as a citizen in developing adequate programs is essential. If one person is encouraged to tackle seriously an aspect of the field, we have done our job.

NOTES

[1] Alex Thio, "Class Bias in the Sociology of Deviance," *American Sociologist* 8 (February 1973): 1–12.

[2] Don Gibbons, *Delinquent Behavior*, 2d ed. (Englewood Cliffs, N.J.: Prentice-Hall, 1976).

[3] Department of Health, Education, and Welfare, Social Rehabilitation Service, *Annual Report of Federal Activities in Juvenile Delinquency, Youth Development and Related Fields* (Washington, D.C.: Government Printing Office, 1971), p. 137.

[4] Robert C. Trojanowicz, *Juvenile Delinquency* (Englewood Cliffs, N.J.: Prentice-Hall, 1973), pp. 306–307.

[5] Department of Health, Education, and Welfare, Social Rehabilitation Service and Law Enforcement Assistance Administration, *Juvenile Delinquency Planning* (Washington, D.C.: Government Printing Office, 1971), pp. 3–13.

[6] Trojanowicz, *op. cit.*, p. 291.

[7] *Ibid.*

[8] See Trojanowicz, *op. cit.*, pp. 294–302, and Christopher Sower et al., *Community Involvement* (New York: Free Press, 1957).

[9] Edwin Schur, *Radical Non-intervention: Rethinking the Delinquency Problem* (Englewood Cliffs, N.J.: Prentice-Hall, 1973).

[10] Yitzhak Bakal, "The Massachusetts Experience," *Delinquency Prevention Reporter* 3 (April 1973): 1–5.

[11] *Ibid.*

[12] *Ibid.*

[13] *Ibid.*, p. 5.

[14] Trojanowicz, *op. cit.*, pp. 310–311.

[15] Stanton Wheeler, Leonard S. Cottrell, and Anne Ramasco, "Juvenile Delinquency: Its Prevention and Control," in *Task Force Report: Juvenile*

Delinquency and Youth Crime, President's Commission on Law Enforcement and Administration of Justice (Washington, D.C.: Government Printing Office, 1967), p. 426.

[16] *Ibid.*

[17] Department of Health, Education, and Welfare, *Delinquency Today: A Guide for Community Action* (Washington, D.C.: Government Printing Office, 1971).

[18] John M. Martin, *Toward a Political Definition of Delinquency* (Youth Development and Delinquency Prevention Administration) (Washington, D.C.: Government Printing Office, 1970), p. 9.

Bibliography

Abbott, Grace. *The Child and the State*. Chicago: University of Chicago Press, 1938.

Abrahamsen, David. *The Psychology of Crime*. New York: Columbia University Press, 1960.

Aichhorn, August. *Delinquency and Child Guidance*. New York: International Universities Press, 1969.

———. *Wayward Youth*, New York: Viking Press, 1963.

Alers, Miriam Schwartz. "Transfer of Jurisdiction to Criminal Court." *Crime and Delinquency* 19 (October 1973): 519–527.

Alexander, Franz and Hugo Staub. *The Criminal, the Judges and the Public*. New York: Free Press, 1956.

Amir, Menachem and Yitzchak Berman. "Chromosomal Deviation and Crime." *Federal Probation* 35 (June 1970): 57–58.

Amos, William and Charles Welford. *Delinquency Prevention: Theory and Practice*. Englewood Cliffs, N.J.: Prentice-Hall, 1967.

Arnold, William R. "Race and Ethnicity Relative to Other Factors in Juvenile Court Dispositions." *American Journal of Sociology* 87 (September 1971): 211–227.

Audry, R. G. *Delinquency and Parental Pathology*. London: Metheun, 1960.

Axelrod, Sidney. "Negro and White Institutionalized Delinquents." *American Journal of Sociology* 57 (May 1952): 569–574.

Bakal, Yitzhak. "The Massachusetts Experience." *Delinquency Prevention Reporter* 3 (April 1973): 1–5.

Baker, Harry J. and Virginia Traphagen. *The Diagnosis and Treatment of Behavior-Problem Children*. New York: Macmillan, 1935.

Banay, Ralph. "Physical Disfigurement as a Factor in Delinquency and Crime." *Federal Probation* 7 (January–February 1943): 20–24.

Bandura, Albert. "What TV Violence Can Do to Your Child." *Look*, October 22, 1963, pp. 46, 48.

Barker, Gordon H. and W. Thomas Adams. "Glue Sniffers." *Sociology and Social Research* 47 (1963): 298–310.

Barnes, Harry Elmer and Negley K. Teeters. *New Horizons in Criminology.* 3d ed. Englewood Cliffs, N.J.: Prentice-Hall, 1959.

Barron, Milton L. *The Juvenile in Delinquent Society.* New York: Knopf, 1956.

Bauer, E. Jackson. "The Trend of Juvenile Offenders in the Netherlands and the United States." *Journal of Criminal Law, Criminology and Police Science* 55 (September 1964): 359–369.

Bealer, Robert C., Fern K. Willits, and Peter R. Maida. "The Myth of a Rebellious Adolescent Subculture: Its Detrimental Effects for Understanding Rural Youth." In *Proceedings of a National Conference on Rural Youth in a Changing Environment,* edited by Lee Burchiral. Washington, D.C.: Government Printing Office, 1965.

Beccaria, Cesare. *An Essay on Crimes and Punishment.* Philadelphia: Philip H. Nicklin, 1819.

Becker, Gary S. "Crime and Punishment: An Economic Approach." *Journal of Political Economy,* March–April 1968, pp. 169–217.

Becker, Howard S. *Outsiders.* New York: Free Press, 1963.

———. "The Professional Dance Musician and His Audience." *American Journal of Sociology* 57 (1951): 136–144.

———. "Whose Side Are We On?" *Social Problems* 14 (1967): 239–247.

Belden, Evaline. *Courts in the United States Hearing Children's Cases* (Department of Labor, Children's Bureau). Washington, D.C., 1920.

Bergin, Allen E. "When Shrinks Hurt: Psychotherapy Can Be Dangerous." *Psychology Today* 9 (November 1975): 96.

Berman, Eric. *Scapegoat.* Ann Arbor, Mich.: University of Michigan Press, 1973.

Berman, Sidney. "Antisocial Character Disorder." In *Readings in Juvenile Delinquency,* edited by Ruth Cavan. Philadelphia: Lippincott, 1964.

Black, Donald J. and Albert Reiss. "Police Control of Juveniles." *American Sociological Review* 35 (February 1970): 63–77.

Blackstone, William. *Commentaries on the Laws of England.* Vol. 4. Oxford: Clarendon Press, 1796.

Blalock, Hubert M. *Social Statistics.* New York: McGraw-Hill, 1972.

———. *Theory Construction.* Englewood Cliffs, N.J.: Prentice-Hall, 1969.

Block, Herbert A. and Authur Niederhoffer. *The Gang: A Study in Adolescent Behavior.* New York: Philosophical Library, 1958.

Bodine, George E. "Factors Related to Police Disposition of Juvenile Offenders." Paper read at American Sociological Association Annual Meeting, Montreal, August 1964.

Bonger, W. A. *Criminology and Economic Conditions.* Boston: Little, Brown, 1916.

Bordua, David J. "Delinquent Subcultures: Sociological Interpretations of Gang Delinquency." *Annals of the American Academy of Political and Social Science* 338 (November 1961): 119–361.

———. "Juvenile Delinquency and Anomie: An Attempt at Replication." *Social Problems* 6 (winter 1958): 230–238.

———. "Recent Trends: Deviant Behavior and Social Control." *Annals of the American Academy of Political and Social Science* 369 (January 1967): 149–163.

———. *Sociological Theories and Their Implications for Juvenile Delinquency.* Juvenile Delinquency, Facts and Facets, no. 2 (Children's Bureau). Washington, D.C.: Government Printing Office, 1960.

———. "Some Comments on Theories of Group Delinquency." *Sociological Inquiry* 32 (spring 1962): 245–260.

Breckenridge, Sophoniska P. and Edith Abbott. *The Delinquent Child and the Home.* New York: Random House, 1912.

Breed, Allen. "Inmate Subcultures." *California Youth Authority Quarterly* 16 (spring 1953): 6–7.

Briar, Scott and Irving Pilliavin. "Delinquency: Situational Inducements and Commitment to Conformity." *Social Problems* 13 (summer 1965): 35–45.

Brown, Claude. *Manchild in the Promised Land.* New York: Macmillan, 1965.

Browning, Charles J. "Differential Impact of Family Disorganization on Adolescents." *Social Problems* 8 (1960): 37–44.

Burgess, Robert L. and Ronald Akers. "A Differential Association-Reinforcement Theory of Criminal Behavior." *Social Problems* 14 (fall 1966): 128–147.

Burt, Cyril. *The Young Delinquent.* London: University of London Press, 1938.

Caldwell, Robert G. *Criminology.* New York: Ronald Press, 1956.

Carey, Janet T., Joel Goldfarb, Michael Rowe, and Joseph D. Lohman. "The Handling of Juveniles from Offense to Disposition" (Department of Health, Education, and Welfare). Washington, D.C.: Government Printing Office, 1967.

Carpenter, Kenneth. "Halfway Houses for Delinquent Youth." In *Children* (Department of Health, Education, and Welfare). Washington, D.C.: Government Printing Office, 1963, pp. 224–229.

Carter, Robert M. *Middle Class Delinquency: An Experiment in Community Control.* Berkeley School of Criminology, University of California Press, 1968.

Casey, M. D., et al. "YY Chromosomes and Antisocial Behavior." *Lancet* 2 (1966).

Cavan, Ruth Shonle. *Juvenile Delinquency.* Philadelphia: Lippincott, 1962.

Cavan, Ruth Shonle and Jordan T. Cavan. *Delinquency and Crime: Cross-cultural Perspectives.* Philadelphia: Lippincott, 1968.

Cavan, Ruth Shonle and Theodore N. Ferdinand. *Juvenile Delinquency.* 3d ed. Philadelphia: Lippincott, 1975.

Chambliss, William J. "The Saints and the Rough Necks." *Society* 11 (December 1973): 24–31.

Charles, Cecil M. "A Comparison of the Intelligence Quotients of Incarcerated Delinquent White and Negro Boys and a Group of Public School Boys." *Journal of Applied Psychology* (August 1936): 499–510.

Chilton, Roland. "Continuity in Delinquency Area Research: A Comparison of Baltimore, Detroit and Indianapolis." *American Sociological Review* 29 (February 1964): 71–83.

————. "Middle Class Delinquency and Specific Offense Analysis." In *Middle Class Juvenile Delinquency*, edited by Edmund W. Vaz. New York: Harper & Row, 1967, pp. 91–100.

Chilton, Roland and Gerald E. Markle. "Family Disruption, Delinquent Conduct and the Effects of Subclassification." *American Sociological Review* 37 (February 1972): 93–99.

Cicourel, Aaron. *The Social Organization of Juvenile Justice.* New York: Wiley, 1968.

Clark, John P. and Eugene Wenninger. "Social Class and Area as Correlates of Illegal Behavior Among Juveniles." *American Sociological Review* 8 (February 1973): 1–12.

Clinard, Marshall. "Criminological Research." In *Sociology Today*, edited by Robert K. Merton, Leonard Broom, and Leonard Cottrell. New York: Basic Books, 1959.

————. *Sociology of Deviant Behavior.* New York: Holt, Rinehart and Winston, 1957.

————. *Sociology of Deviant Behavior.* 2d ed. New York: Holt, Rinehart and Winston, 1963.

————, ed. *Anomie and Deviant Behavior.* New York: Free Press, 1964.

Cloward, Richard A. and Lloyd E. Ohlin. *Delinquency and Opportunity.* New York: Free Press, 1960.

Cohen, Albert K. *Delinquent Boys: The Culture of the Gang.* New York: Free Press, 1955.

Cohen, Albert and James F. Short, Jr. "Research on Delinquent Subcultures." *Journal of Social Issues* 14 (1958): 20–37.

Coleman, James S., et al. *Equality of Educational Opportunity.* Washington, D.C.: Government Printing Office, 1966.

Conger, John Janeway and Wilber C. Miller. *Personality, Social Class and Delinquency.* New York: Wiley, 1966.

Costner, Herbert L. and Hubert M. Blalock, Jr. "Scientific Fundamentalism and Scientific Utility: A Reply to Gibbs." *Social Science Quarterly* 52 (March 1972): 827–844.

Cressey, Donald R. "Application and Verification of the Differential Association Theory." *Journal of Criminal Law, Criminology and Police Science* 43 (May–June 1952): 44.

————. "Changing Criminals: The Application of the Theory of Differential Association." *American Journal of Sociology* 61 (September 1955): 116–120.

————. "The Differential Association Theory and Compulsive Crimes." *Journal Law, Criminology and Police Science* 45 (May–June 1954): 29–40.

————. "The Language of Set Theory and Differential Association." *Journal of Research in Crime and Delinquency* 3 (January 1966): 23.

————. "Organized Crime and Inner-City Youth." *Crime and Delinquency* 16 (April 1970): 129–138.

————. "The Theory of Differential Association: An Introduction." *Social Problems* 8 (summer 1960): 3.

————, ed. *The Prison.* New York: Holt, Rinehart and Winston, 1961.

Cressey, Donald and Rita Volkman. "Differential Association and Rehabilitation of Drug Addicts." *American Journal of Sociology* 69 (September 1963): 129–131.

Craig, Maude M. "Application of the Glueck Social Prediction Table on an Ethnic Basis." *Crime and Delinquency* 11 (1965): 175–185.

Craig, Maude and Selma Glick. "Ten Years Experience with the Glueck Social Prediction Table." *Crime and Delinquency* 9 (July 1963).

Craig, Mender M. and Lila A. Budd. "The Juvenile Offender: Recidivism and Companions." *Crime and Delinquency* 13 (1967): 344–351.

Darwin, Charles. *The Descent of Man.* Englewood Cliffs, N.J.: Prentice-Hall, 1880.

Davis, F. James, Henry Foster, Jr., C. Roy Jeffrey, and E. Eugene Davis. *Society and the Law.* New York: Free Press, 1962.

DeFleur, Melvin L. and Richard Quinney. "A Reformulation of Sutherland's Differential Association Theory and a Strategy for Empirical Verification." *Journal of Research in Crime and Delinquency* 3 (January 1966).

Department of Health, Education, and Welfare. *Delinquency Today: A Guide for Community Action.* Washington, D.C.: Government Printing Office, 1971.

————. *LSD: Some Questions and Answers,* Public Health Service Publication, no. 1828. Washington, D.C.: Government Printing Office, 1970.

————. *Marihuana: Some Questions and Answers,* Public Health Service Publication, no. 1829. Washington, D.C.: Government Printing Office, 1970.

————. *Stimulants: Some Questions and Answers,* Public Health Service

Publication, no. 2097. Washington, D.C.: Government Printing Office, 1970.

———. Children's Bureau. *Halfway House Programs for Delinquent Youth.* Washington, D.C.: Government Printing Office, 1965.

———. Children's Bureau. *Institutions Serving Delinquent Children.* Washington, D.C.: Government Printing Office, 1957.

———. Children's Bureau. *Juvenile Court Statistics, 1964.* Washington, D.C.: Government Printing Office, 1965.

———. Children's Bureau. *Juvenile Court Statistics, 1970.* Washington, D.C.: Government Printing Office, 1971.

———. Children's Bureau. *Juvenile Delinquency Prevention in the United States.* Washington, D.C.: Government Printing Office, 1966.

———. Children's Bureau and International Association of Chiefs of Police. *Police Services for Juveniles.* Washington, D.C.: Government Printing Office, 1954.

———. Manpower Administration. *The Neighborhood Youth Corps: Hope and Help for Youth.* Washington, D.C.: Government Printing Office, 1969.

———. Office of Youth Development. *Juvenile Court Statistics, 1968.* Washington, D.C.: Government Printing Office, 1970.

———. Office of Youth Development. *Juvenile Court Statistics, 1973.* Washington, D.C.: Government Printing Office, 1974.

———. Social Rehabilitation Service. *Annual Report of Federal Activities in Juvenile Delinquency, Youth Development and Related Fields.* Washington, D.C.: Government Printing Office, 1971.

———. Social Rehabilitation Service. *National Strategy to Prevent Delinquency.* Washington, D.C.: Government Printing Office, 1972.

———. Social Rehabilitation Service and Law Enforcement Assistance Administration. *Juvenile Delinquency Planning.* Washington, D.C.: Government Printing Office, 1971.

Dinitz, Simon, Barbara Kay, and Walter Reckless. "Group Gradients in Delinquency Potential and Achievement Scores of Sixth Graders." *American Journal of Orthopsychiatry* 28 (July 1958): 598–605.

Dinitz, Simon, Frank Scarpitti, and Walter Reckless. "Delinquency Vulnerability: A Cross Group and Longitudinal Analysis." *American Sociological Review* 27 (August 1962): 515–517.

Dubin, Robert. *Theory Building.* New York: Free Press, 1969.

Duffee, David and Larry Siegal. "The Organization Man: Legal Counsel." *Juvenile Court Criminal Law Bulletin* 7 (July–August 1971): 44–53.

Dugdale, Richard L. *The Jukes: A Study in Crime, Pauperism, Disease and Heredity.* New York: Putnam, 1910.

Durkheim, Emile. *The Division of Labor in Society.* New York: Free Press, 1933.

———. *The Rules of Sociological Method.* New York: Free Press, 1938.

———. *Suicide.* Translated by John A. Spaulding and George Simpson. New York: Free Press, 1951.

Duxbury, Elaine. *Youth Service Bureaus in California.* Sacramento: Department of the Youth Authority, 1971.

Eaton, Joseph W. and Kenneth Polk. *Measuring Delinquency.* Pittsburgh: University of Pittsburgh Press, 1961.

Edwards, Leonard. "The Rights of Children." *Federal Probation* 37 (June 1973): 34–41.

Elliott, Delbert S. "Delinquency, School Attendance and Drop Outs." *Social Problems* (Winter 1966): 307–314.

Emerson, Robert M. *Judging Delinquents: Context and Process in the Juvenile Court.* Chicago: Aldine, 1969.

Emprey, Lamar. "Delinquency Theory and Recent Research." *Journal of Research in Crime and Delinquency* 4 (January 1967): 28–42.

Emprey, Lamar T. and Maynard L. Erickson. *Hidden Delinquency: Evidence on Old Issues.* Provo, Utah: Brigham Young University, 1965.

———. "Hidden Delinquency and Social Status." *Social Forces* 44 (June 1966): 546–554.

Emprey, Lamar T. and Steven G. Lubek. *The Silverlake Experiment.* Chicago: Aldine, 1971.

Emprey, Lamar T. and Jerome Rabow. "The Provo Experiment in Delinquency Rehabilitation." *American Sociological Review* 26 (October 1961): 679–696.

England, Ralph, Jr. "A Theory of Middle Class Juvenile Delinquency." *Journal of Criminal Law, Criminology and Police Science* 50 (April 1960): 539–540.

Erickson, Kai T. "Notes on the Sociology of Deviance." *Social Problems* 10 (1962): 307–314.

———. *Wayward Puritans.* New York: Wiley, 1966.

Erickson, Maynard L. and Lamar Emprey. "Class Position, Peers and Delinquency." *Sociology and Social Research* 49 (April 1965): 268–282.

Fannin, Leon F. and Marshall B. Clinard. "Differences in the Conception of Self as a Male Among Lower and Middle Class Delinquents." *Social Problems* 13 (fall 1965): 205–214.

Federal Bureau of Investigation. *Uniform Crime Reports, 1971.* Washington, D.C.: Government Printing Office, 1972.

———. *Uniform Crime Reports, 1972.* Washington, D.C.: Government Printing Office, 1973.

———. *Uniform Crime Reports, 1973.* Washington, D.C.: Government Printing Office, 1974.

———. *Uniform Crime Reports, 1975.* Washington, D.C.: Government Printing Office, 1976.

Ferdinand, Theodore N. *Typologies of Delinquency.* New York: Random House, 1966.

Ferdinand, Theodore N. and Elmer C. Luchterhand. "Intercity Youth, the Police, the Juvenile Court, and Justice." *Social Problems* 17 (spring 1970): 510–526.

Ferguson, Elizabeth. *Social Work.* Philadelphia: Lippincott, 1963.

Ferrera, Gina L. Introduction to *Lombroso's Criminal Law*, by Cesare Lombroso. New York: Putnam, 1911, pp. xiv–xvi.

Ferri, Enrico. *Criminal Sociology.* Translated by J. I. Kelley and John Lisle. Boston: Little, Brown, 1917.

Filstead, W. J., ed. *An Introduction to Deviance. Chicago:* Markham, 1972.

Fisher, Sethard. "Social Organization in a Correctional Residence." *Pacific Sociological Review* 4 (fall 1961): 87–93.

Fleischer, Belton M. *The Economics of Delinquency.* New York: Quadrangle, 1968.

Fogel, David. "The Fate of the Rehabilitation Ideal in California Youth Authority Dispositions." *Crime and Delinquency* 15 (October 1969): 479–498.

Fort, Joel. "Major Drugs and Their Effects." *Playboy*, September 1972, pp. 143–145.

Fox, Lionel. *The English Prison and Borstal Systems.* London: Routledge and Kegan Paul, 1952.

Fox, Richard, "The XYY Offender: A Modern Myth." *Journal of Criminal Law, Criminology and Police Science* 62 (March 1971): 61.

Friedlander, Kate. *The Psycho-analytical Approach to Juvenile Delinquency.* London: Routledge and Kegan Paul, 1947.

Galle, O. "Population Density and Pathology: What Are the Relations of Man?" *Science* 176 (April 1972): 23–30.

Galton, Francis. *Hereditary Genius.* London, 1892.

———. *Inquiries into Faculty and Its Development.* London, 1883.

Garabedian, Peter G. and Don Gibbons. *Becoming Delinquent.* Chicago: Aldine, 1970.

Garfinkel, Harold. "Conditions of Successful Degradition Ceremonies." *American Journal of Sociology* 61 (1956): 420–424.

Garofalo, Raffaelo. *Criminology.* Boston: Brown and Co., 1914.

Gazda, George. *Approaches to Group Psychotherapy and Group Counseling.* Springfield, Ill.: Thomas, 1968.

Geertsma, Robert H. "Group Therapy with Juvenile Probationers and Their Parents." *Federal Probation* 24 (March 1960): 46–52.

Geis, Gilbert. "Statistics Concerning Race and Crime." *Crime and Delinquency* 11 (April): 142–150, 1965.

Giallombardo, Rose. *Delinquency Rehabilitation in Juvenile Delinquency: A Book of Readings.* New York: Wiley, 1966.

Gibbons, Don C. *Changing the Lawbreaker.* Englewood Cliffs, N.J.: Prentice-Hall, 1965.

———. *Delinquent Behavior.* Englewood Cliffs, N.J.: Prentice-Hall, 1970.

———. *Delinquent Behavior.* 2d ed. Englewood Cliffs, N.J.: Prentice-Hall, 1976.

———. *Society, Crime and Criminal Careers.* 2d ed. Englewood Cliffs, N.J.: Prentice-Hall, 1973.

———. "Types as Role Careers." In *Faces of Delinquency,* edited by John P. Reed and Faud Baali. Englewood Cliffs, N.J.: Prentice-Hall, 1972, p. 156–182.

Gibbons, T. C. N. and R. H. Ahrenfeldt. *Cultural Factors in Delinquency.* Philadelphia: Lippincott, 1966.

Gibbons, Terence and J. Prince. *The Results of Borstal Training.* Sociological Review Monograph, no. 9 (1965).

Gibbs, Jack. "Causation and Theory Construction." *Social Science Quarterly* 52 (March 1972): 815–826.

———. *Sociological Theory Construction.* New York: Dryden Press, 1972.

Glaser, Daniel. "Criminality Theories and Behavioral Images." *American Journal of Sociology* 61 (March 1956): 440.

———. "Differential Association and Criminological Prediction." *Social Problems* 8 (summer 1960): 6–14.

Glasser, William. "Reality Therapy: A Realistic Approach to Young Offenders." In *Readings in Delinquency and Treatment.* ed. Robert Schasre and Jo Wallach. Los Angeles: University of California, Youth Studies Center, 1965.

Glen, Jeffery E. "Developments in Juvenile and Family Court Law." *Crime and Delinquency* 16 (April 1970): 198–208.

Glueck, Eleanor T. "Efforts to Identify Delinquents." *Federal Probation* 24 (June 1960): 49–56.

———. "Varieties of Delinquent Types." In *Faces of Delinquency,* edited by John P. Reed and Faud Baali. Englewood Cliffs, N.J.: Prentice-Hall, 1972.

———. *Delinquents in the Making.* New York: Harper & Row, 1952, pp. 118–129.

———. *Family Environment and Delinquency.* Boston: Houghton Mifflin, 1962.

————. *Delinquents and Nondelinquents in Perspective.* Cambridge, Mass.: Harvard University Press, 1968.

————. *Unraveling Juvenile Delinquency.* Cambridge, Mass.: Harvard University Press, 1957.

————. *Physique and Delinquency.* New York: Harper & Row, 1956.

————. "Early Detection of Future Delinquents." *Journal of Criminal Law, Criminology and Police Science* 47 (1956): 175.

Goddard, Henry H. *Feeblemindedness: Its Causes and Consequences.* New York: Macmillan, 1923.

————. *Human Efficiency and Levels of Intelligence.* Princeton, N.J.: Princeton University Press, 1920.

————. *The Kallikak Family: A Study on the Heredity of Feeblemindedness.* New York: Macmillan, 1919.

Gold, Harry and Frank R. Scarpitti, eds. *Combatting Social Problems: Techniques of Intervention.* New York: Holt, Rinehart and Winston, 1967.

Goldman, Nathan. *The Differential Selection of Juvenile Offenders for Court Appearance.* New York: National Council on Crime and Delinquency, 1963.

Gordon, David M. "Capitalism, Class and Crime in America." *Crime and Delinquency* 19 (April 1973): 163–186.

Gordon, I. J. *Human Development: Birth to Adolescence.* New York: Harper & Row, 1962.

Gordon, Robert A. "Social Level Disability and Gang Interaction." *American Journal of Sociology* 73 (July 1957): 42–62.

Griffin, Brenda S. "Approaches to the Sociology of Sociology." *Sociological Inquiry* (forthcoming).

Griffin, Brenda S. and Charles T. Griffin. "Drug Use and Differential Association." *International Journal of Addictions* (1978, forthcoming).

————. "Marihuana Use Among Students and Peers." *Drug Forum* 6 (1978, forthcoming).

Grupp, Stanley. *The Marihuana Muddle.* Lexington, Mass.: Heath, 1973.

————. "Observations on Experienced and Exclusive Marihuana Smokers." *Journal of Drug Issues* 2 (1972): 32–36.

————. "Work Release and the Misdemeanant." *Federal Probation* 29 (June 1965): 6–12.

Grupp, Stanley and Warren Lucas. "The Marihuana Muddle as Reflected in California Arrest Statistics and Dispositions." *Law and Society Review* 5 (November 1970): 251–269.

Hann, Robert G. "Crime and the Cost of Crime: An Economic Approach." *Journal of Research in Crime and Delinquency* (January 1972): 12–30.

Harris, Louis and Associates. *Corrections, 1968: A Climate for Change.* Joint Commission on Correctional Manpower and Training, Washington, D.C., 1968.

Hartjen, Clayton A. *Crime and Criminalization.* New York: Praeger, 1974.

Hartung, Frank. "A Vocabulary of Motives for Law Violations." In *Delinquency, Crime and Social Process,* edited by Donald R. Cressey and D. Ward, New York: Harper & Row, 1969, pp. 458–459.

Hasko, Marvin. "Group Psychotherapy with Delinquent Adolescent Girls." *American Journal of Orthopsychiatry* 32 (January 1962): 170–171.

Hathaway, Starke and Elio D. Monachesi, eds. *Analyzing and Predicting Juvenile Delinquency with the Minnesota Multiphasic Personality Inventory.* Minneapolis: University of Minnesota Press, 1953.

Hawes, Joseph M. *Children in Urban Society: Juvenile Delinquency in Nineteenth Century America.* New York: Oxford University Press, 1971.

Haskell, Martin R. "Toward a Reference-Group Theory of Juvenile Delinquency." *Social Problems* 8 (winter 1960): 220–230.

Haskell, Martin R. and Lewis Yablonsky. *Crime and Delinquency.* Skokie, Ill.: Rand McNally, 1971.

———. *Crime and Delinquency.* 2d ed. Skokie, Ill.: Rand McNally, 1974.

———. *Juvenile Delinquency.* Skokie, Ill.: Rand McNally, 1974.

Healy, William and Augusta Bronner. *Delinquents and Criminals.* New York: Macmillan, 1926.

———. *The Individual Delinquent.* Boston: Little, Brown, 1915.

———. *New Light on Delinquency and Its Treatment.* New Haven, Conn.: Yale University Press, 1936.

———. *Treatment and What Happened Afterward.* Boston: Judge Baker Guidance Center, 1939.

Hengerer, Gertrude. "Organizing Probation Services." In *Reappraising Crime Treatment, 1953 Yearbook.* New York: National Probation and Parole Association, 1954, pp. 45–59.

Hindelang, Michael J. "Causes of Delinquency: A Partial Replication and Extension." *Social Problems* 20 (spring 1973): 471–487.

Hirschi, Travis. *Causes of Delinquency.* Berkeley: University of California Press, 1969.

Hirschi, Travis and Hanan C. Selvin. "False Criteria of Causality in Delinquency Research." *Social Problems* 13 (winter 1966): 254–268.

Hoffman, Lois and Martin Hoffman, eds. *Review of Child Development Research.* Vol. 2. New York: Russell Sage Foundation, 1966.

Holmes, Donald. *The Adolescent in Psychotherapy.* Boston: Little, Brown, 1964.

Hooton, Ernest A. *Crime and Man.* Cambridge, Mass.: Harvard University Press, 1939.

Illinois Department of Corrections, Juvenile Division. *Semi-annual Statistical Summary, 1974.* Prepared by Garland A. Kingery, Judie Egelhoff, and Rick Nehoff. Springfield, 1974.

Inlay, Carl H. and Charles R. Glasheen. "See What Condition Your Conditions Are In." *Federal Probation* 35 (June 1971): 3–11.

Jackson, Toby. "Affluence and Adolescent Crime." In *Task Force Report: Juvenile Delinquency and Youth Crime,* compiled by President's Commission on Law Enforcement and Administration of Justice. Washington, D.C.: Government Printing Office, 1967.

Jackson, Toby. "The Prospects for Reducing Delinquency Rates in Industrial Society." *Federal Probation* 27 (December 1963).

Jacobs, Patricia, M. Brunton, M. Melville, and W. F. McClemont. "Aggressive Behavior, Mental Subnormality and the XYY Male." *Nature* 208 (1965): 1351.

James, Howard. *Children in Trouble.* New York: McKay, 1969.

Jansyn, Leon. "Solidarity and Delinquency in a Street Corner Group." *American Sociological Review* 31 (October 1966): 600–614.

Jarwik, Lissy, Victor Klodin, and Stephen Matsuyama. "Human Aggression and the Extra Y Chromosome." *American Psychologist* 28 (August 1973).

Jeffrey, Clarence. "Criminal Behavior and Learning Theory." *Journal of Criminal Law, Criminology and Police Science* 61 (September 1965): 294–300.

Jenkins, Allen. "Treatment in an Institution." *American Journal of Orthopsychiatry* 11 (January 1941): 85–91.

Jenkins, R. L. and L. Hewitt. "Types of Personality Structure Encountered in Child Guidance Clinics." *American Journal of Orthopsychiatry* 14 (1944).

Jesness, Carl F. *The Jesness Inventory: Development and Validation.* Report no. 29. Sacramento: California Youth Authority, 1962.

Johnson, Elmer H. *Crime, Correction and Society.* 3d ed. Homewood, Ill.: Dorsey Press, 1968.

Jones, Ernest. *Sex in Psychoanalysis.* New York: Basic Books, 1950.

Jones, Stacy V. "The Cougars: Life with a Brooklyn Gang." *Harpers* (November 1954): 35–43.

Kahn, Alfred J. *A Court for Children: A Study of the New York Children's Court.* New York: Columbia University Press, 1953.

Katkin, Daniel, Drew Hyman, and John Kramer. *Juvenile Delinquency and the Juvenile Justice System.* North Scituate, Mass.: Duxbury Press, 1976.

Keiser, R. Lincoln. *The Vice Lords.* New York: Holt, Rinehart and Winston, 1969.

Kitouse, John I. "Deviance, Deviant Behavior and Deviants." In *An Introduction to Deviance,* edited by W. J. Filstead. Chicago: Markham, 1972, pp. 233–243.

————. Societal Reaction to Deviant Behavior: Problems of Theory and Method. *Social Problems* 9 (1962): 247–256.

Kitouse, John I. and David Dietrick. "Delinquent Boys: A Critique." *American Sociological Review* 24 (April 1959): 208–215.

Klein, Malcolm W., ed. *Juvenile Gang in Context: Theory, Research and Action.* Englewood Cliffs, N.J.: Prentice-Hall, 1967.

Kobrin, Solomon. "The Conflict of Values in a Delinquency Area." *American Sociological Review* 16 (October 1951): 653–661.

Kolb, Lawrence C. *Noyes' Modern Clinical Psychiatry.* Philadelphia: Saunders, 1968.

Konopka, Gisele. "South Central Youth Project: A Delinquency Control Program, 1955–1957." *Annals of the American Academy of Political and Social Science* 322 (1959): 30–37.

Konopka, Gisela. *The Adolescent Girl in Conflict.* Englewood Cliffs, N.J.: Prentice-Hall, 1966.

Koutrelakos, James. "Perceived Parental Values and Demographic Variables As Related to Maladjustment." *Perceptual and Motor Skills* 32 (1971): 151–158.

Kvaraceus, William C. *Juvenile Delinquency and the Schools.* New York: Harcourt Brace Jovanovich, 1945.

Kvaraceus, William C. and William E. Ulrich. "Delinquent Behavior: Principles and Practices." Washington, D.C.: National Education Association, 1959.

Lander, Bernard. *Toward an Understanding of Juvenile Delinquency.* New York: Columbia University Press, 1954.

Lander, William M. "An Economic Analysis of the Courts." *Journal of Law and Economics* (April 1971): 61–108.

Lange, David, Robert K. Baker, and Sandra J. Ball. "Mass Media and Violence." Washington, D.C.: Government Printing Office, 1969.

Law Enforcement Assistance Administration. *Children in Custody: A Report on the Juvenile Detention and Correctional Facility Census of 1971.* Washington, D.C.: Government Printing Office, 1974.

————. *Children in Custody: Advance Report on the Juvenile Detention and Correctional Facility Census of 1972–73.* Washington, D.C.: Government Printing Office, 1975.

————. *Crimes and Victims: A Report on the Dayton-San Jose Pilot Survey of Victimization.* Washington, D.C.: Government Printing Office, 1974.

————. *Criminal Victimization in Five Major Cities.* Washington, D.C.: Government Printing Office, 1975.

————. *Criminal Victimization in Thirteen American Cities.* Washington, D.C.: Government Printing Office, 1975.

————. *National Jail Census.* Washington, D.C.: Government Printing Office, 1971.

————. *Sourcebook of Criminal Justice Statistics, 1974.* Washington, D.C.: Government Printing Office, 1975.

Leader, Arthur L. "A Differential Reinforcement Theory of Criminality." *Sociology and Social Research* 26 (September–October 1941): 45.

Lejins, Peter. "The Field of Prevention." In *Delinquency Prevention: Theory and Practice,* edited by William Amos and Charles Welford. Englewood Cliffs, N.J.: Prentice-Hall, 1967.

Lemert, Edwin M. *Human Deviance, Social Problems and Social Control.* Englewood Cliffs, N.J.: Prentice-Hall, 1967.

————. *Instead of the Court.* Rockville, Md.: National Institute of Mental Health, 1971.

————. *Social Action and Legal Change: Revolution in the Juvenile Court.* Chicago: Aldine, 1970.

————. *Social Pathology.* New York: McGraw-Hill, 1951.

Lerman, Paul. "Evaluative Studies of Institutions for Juveniles." *Social Work* 13 (July 1968): 55–64.

Lerman, Paul, ed. *Delinquency and Social Policy.* New York: Praeger, 1970.

Levin, Mark M. and Rosemary C. Sarri. *Juvenile Delinquency: A Comparative Analysis of Legal Codes in the United States.* Ann Arbor, Mich.: National Assessment of Juvenile Corrections, 1974.

Lewin, Kurt. *Field Theory in Social Science.* New York: Harper & Row, 1951.

Lewis, C. S. "The Humanitarian Theory of Punishment." In *Crime and Justice: The Criminal in Confinement,* edited by Leon Radzinowicz and Marvin Wolfgang. New York: Basic Books, 1971, pp. 43–48.

Little, Alan. "Penal Theory, Reform and Borstal Practice." *British Journal of Criminology* 3 (January 1963): 257–275.

Long, Anne Marie and Samuel I. Kamada. "Psychiatric Treatment of Adolescent Girls." *California Youth Authority Quarterly,* summer 1964, pp. 23–24.

Loth, David. *Crime in the Suburbs.* New York: Morrow, 1967.

Ludwig, Frederick J. *Youth and the Law: Handbook on Law Affecting Youth.* Mineola, N.Y.: Foundation Press, 1955.

Maestro, Marcello. *Voltaire and Beccaria as Reformers of Criminal Law.* New York: Columbia University Press, 1942.

Mannheim, Hermann, ed. *Pioneers in Criminology.* London: Routledge and Kegan Paul, 1960.

Mannkoff, Milton. "Societal Reaction and Career Deviance: A Critical Analysis." *Sociological Quarterly* 12 (1971): 204–218.

Martin, John M. *Toward a Political Definition of Delinquency* (Youth Development and Delinquency Prevention Administration). Washington, D.C.: Government Printing Office, 1970.

Martinson, Robert. "What Works? Questions and Answers About Prison Reform." *Public Interest* 35 (spring 1974): 25–33.

Marx, Karl and Friedrich Engels. *Das Kapital.* New York: Random House, 1906.

Matza, David. *Delinquency and Drift.* New York: Wiley, 1964.

Mayhew, Henry. *London Labor and the London Poor.* London: Routledge and Kegan Paul, 1951.

McCord, Joan, William McCord, and Emily Thurber. "Some Effects of Paternal Absence on Male Children." *Journal of Abnormal and Social Psychology* 64 (May 1962): 361–369.

McCord, William, Joan McCord, and Irving Zola. *Origins of Crime.* New York: Columbia University Press, 1959.

McCune, Shirley and Daniel L. Skoler. "Juvenile Court Judges in the United States." *Crime and Delinquency* 11 (April 1965): 121–131.

McEachern, A. W. and Riva Bauzer. "Factors Related to Disposition in Juvenile Police Contacts." In *Juvenile Gangs in Context,* edited by Malcolm M. Klein. Englewood Cliffs, N.J.: Prentice-Hall, pp. 148–160.

McKay, Henry. "Differential Association and Crime Prevention: Problems of Utilization." *Social Problems* 8 (summer 1960): 25–37.

———. "Criminal Careers of Male Delinquents in Chicago," in *Task Force Report: Juvenile Delinquency and Youth Crime* (President's Commission on Law Enforcement and the Administration of Justice). Washington, D.C.: Government Printing Office, 1967.

McNeil, Francis. "A Detailed Description of a Halfway House Program for Delinquents." *Crime and Delinquency* 13 (1967): 538–544.

Mennel, Robert M. "Origins of the Juvenile Court: Changing Perspectives on the Legal Rights of Juvenile Delinquents." *Crime and Delinquency* 18 (January 1972): 68–78.

———. *Thorns and Thistles: Juvenile Delinquents in the United States, 1825–1940.* Hanover, N.H.: University Press of New England, 1973.

Merrill, Maude A. *Problems of Child Delinquency.* Boston: Houghton Mifflin, 1947.

Merton, Robert K. *Social Theory and Social Structure.* New York: Free Press, 1957.

———. *Social Theory and Social Structure,* 2nd Edition. New York: Free Press, 1968.

Merton, Robert K. and M. F. Ashley-Montague. "Crime and the Anthropologist." *American Anthropologist* 42 (July–September 1940): 384–408.

Merton, Robert K., Leonard Broom, and Leonard Cottrell, eds. *Sociology Today.* New York: Basic Books, 1959.

"Methadone and Heroin Addiction: Rehabilitation Without a Cure." *Science,* May 8, 1970.

Miller, Walter B. "Lower Class Culture as a Generating Milieu of Gang Delinquency." *Journal of Social Issues* 14 (1958): 5–19.

Miller, Walter B., Mildred Geetz, and Henry Cutter. "Aggression in a Boys Street Corner Group." *Psychiatry* 24 (November 1961): 283–398.

Monahan, Thomas P. "Family Status and the Delinquent Child." *Social Forces* 35 (March 1957): 250–258.

Morris, Charles V. "Worldwide Concern with Crime." *Federal Probation* 24 (December 1960): 21–30.

Morris, Terence. *The Criminal Area.* London: Routledge and Kegan Paul, 1958.

Mueller, John H., Karl F. Schuessler, and Herbert L. Costner. *Statistical Reasoning in Sociology.* 2d ed. Boston: Houghton Mifflin, 1970.

Mullins, Nicholas C. *The Art of Theory: Construction and Use.* New York: Harper & Row, 1971.

Murchusion, Carl. "American White Criminal Intelligence." *Journal of Criminal Law* 15 (August 1924): 254–257.

National Advisory Commission on Criminal Justice Standards and Goals. *Corrections.* Washington, D.C.: Government Printing Office, 1973.

National Commission on Marihuana and Drug Abuse. *Marihuana: A Signal of Misunderstanding.* Technical papers of the First Report of the National Commission, appendix, vol. 2, 1972.

National Council on Crime and Delinquency. "Correction in the United States." *Crime and Delinquency* 13 (1967): 1–38.

————. *Directory of Juvenile Detention Centers in the United States.* New York, 1968.

————. *Guides for Juvenile Court Judges on News Media Relations.* New York, 1957.

————. *Model Rules for Juvenile Courts.* New York, 1969.

————. *Standard Family Court Act.* New York, 1959.

————. *Standard Juvenile Court Act.* 6th ed. New York, 1959.

————. *Standards and Guides for the Detention of Children and Youth.* 2d ed. New York, 1961.

National Probation and Parole Association. *Guides for Juvenile Court Judges.* New York, 1957.

————. *Detention Practice: Significant Developments in the Detention of Children and Youth.* New York, 1967. (Reprinted by National Council on Crime and Delinquency.)

Neigher, Alan. "The Gault Decision: Due Process and Juvenile Courts." *Federal Probation* 31 (December 1967): 8–18.

Nettler, Gwen. *Explaining Crime.* New York: McGraw-Hill, 1974.

Newman, Horatio H. *Multiple Human Births: Twins, Triplets, Quadruplets and Quintuplets.* New York: Doubleday, 1940.

Nye, F. Ivan. *Family Relationships and Delinquent Behavior.* New York: Wiley, 1958.

Nye, F. Ivan, James F. Short, Jr., and Virgil J. Olsen. "Socioeconomic Status and Delinquent Behavior." *American Journal of Sociology* 63 (January 1958): 381–389.

Ohlin, Lloyd, Robert B. Coates, and Alden D. Miller. "Radical Correctional Reform: A Case Study of the Massachusetts Youth Correctional System." *Harvard Educational Review* 44 (February 1974): 74–111.

O'Neal, Patricia and Lee Robins. "Childhood Patterns Predictive of Adult Schizophrenia." *American Journal of Psychiatry* 144 (1959): 385–391.

Orcutt, James D. "Self-concept and Insulation Against Delinquency: Some Critical Notes." *Sociological Quarterly* 2 (summer 1970): 381–390.

Palmore, Erdman B. and Phillip E. Hammond. "Interacting Factors in Juvenile Delinquency." *American Sociological Review* 29 (December 1964): 848–854.

Park, Robert E., Ernest W. Burgess, and Robert D. McKenzie. *The City.* Chicago: University of Chicago Press, 1925.

Parker, T. and R. Allerton. *The Courage of His Convictions.* London: Hutchinson, 1962.

Peterson, Donald R. and Wesley C. Becker. "Family Interaction and Delinquency." In *Juvenile Delinquency*, edited by Herbert C. Quay. New York: Van Nostrand, 1965.

Pierce, F. J. "Social Group Work in a Women's Prison." *Federal Probation* 27 (December 1963): 37–38.

Pickett, Robert S. *House of Refuge: Origins of Juvenile Reform in New York State.* Syracuse, N.Y.: Syracuse University Press, 1969.

Piliavin, Irving and Scott Briar. "Police Encounters with Juveniles." *American Journal of Sociology* 70 (September 1964): 206–214.

Platt, Anthony M. *The Child Savers: The Invention of Delinquency.* Chicago: University of Chicago Press, 1969.

Polk, Kenneth. "Delinquency Prevention and the Youth Services Bureau." *Criminal Law Bulletin* 7 (July–August 1971): 490–511.

————. "Juvenile Delinquency and Social Areas." *Social Problems* 5 (winter 1957): 214–217.

————. "Urban Social Areas and Delinquency." *Social Problems* 14 (winter 1967).

Polk, Kenneth and Walter Schafer, eds. *Schools and Delinquency.* Englewood Cliffs, N.J.: Prentice-Hall, 1972.

Polsky, Howard. "Changing Delinquent Subcultures: A Social-Psychological Approach." *Social Work* 10 (October 1959): 3–15.

――――. *Cottage Six.* New York: Russell Sage Foundation, 1962.

Polsky, Ned. *Hustlers, Beats and Others.* Chicago: Aldine, 1967.

President's Commission on Law Enforcement and Administration of Justice. *The Challenge of Crime in a Free Society.* Washington, D.C.: Government Printing Office, 1967.

――――. "Juvenile Aftercare in the United States." *Crime and Delinquency* 13 (January 1967): 97–112.

――――. "Juvenile Probation." *Crime and Delinquency* 13 (January 1966): 39–70.

――――. *Task Force Report: Juvenile Delinquency and Youth Crime.* Washington, D.C.: Government Printing Office, 1967.

Price, W. H., and P. P. Whatmore. "Behaviour Disorders and Pattern of Crime Among XYY Males Identified at a Maximum Security Hospital." *British Medical Journal* 1 (1967).

Public Health Service. Surgeon General's Scientific Advisory Committee on Television and Social Behavior. *Television and Social Behavior.* 5 vols. Washington, D.C.: Government Printing Office, 1972.

――――. *Television and Growing Up: The Impact of Televised Violence.* Washington, D.C.: Government Printing Office, 1972.

Quay, Herbert C., ed. *Juvenile Delinquency.* New York: Van Nostrand, 1965.

Quinney, Richard. *Criminal Justice in America.* Boston: Little, Brown, 1974.

――――. *The Social Reality of Crime.* Boston: Little, Brown, 1970.

Reckless, Walter. *The Crime Problem.* 2d ed. New York: Meredith Publishing Co., 1955.

――――. *The Crime Problem.* 4th ed. Englewood Cliffs, N.J.: Prentice-Hall, 1967.

Reckless, Walter and Simon Dinitz. "Pioneering with Self-concept as a Vulnerability Factor in Delinquency." *Journal of Criminal Law, Criminology and Police Science* 58 (December 1967): 515–523.

Reckless, Walter, Simon Dinitz, and Barbara Kay. "The Self-component in Potential Delinquency and Potential Non-delinquency." *American Sociological Review* 22 (October 1957): 566–570.

Reckless, Walter, Simon Dinitz, and Ellen Murray. "The 'Good Boy' in a High Delinquency Area." *Journal of Criminal Law, Criminology and Police Science* 48 (May–June 1957): 18–25.

Reckless, Walter, Simon Dinitz, and Ellen Murray. "Self-concept as an Insulator Against Delinquency." *American Sociological Review* 21 (December 1956): 744–756.

Reed, John P. and Fuad Baali. *Faces of Delinquency.* Englewood Cliffs, N.J.: Prentice-Hall, 1972.

Reinemann, John Otto. "The Expansion of the Juvenile Court Idea." *Federal Probation* 13 (September 1949): 34–40.

Reinich, Paul Samuel. *English Common Law in the Early American Colonies.* University of Wisconsin Bulletin, no. 31. Madison, 1899, p. 8.

Reiss, Albert J., Jr. "Delinquency as the Failure of Personal Control." *American Sociological Review* 16 (1951): 196–207.

Reiss, Albert J., Jr., and Albert Lewis Rhodes. "The Distribution of Delinquency in the Social Class Structure." *American Sociological Review* 26 (October 1961): 732.

――――. "An Empirical Test of Differential Association Theory." *Journal of Research in Crime and Delinquency* 1 (January 1964): 5–18.

Riggs, John E., William Underwood, and Marguerite Q. Warren. *Interpersonal*

Maturity Level Classification: Juvenile. C.T.P. Research Report, no. 4. Sacramento: California Youth Authority, 1964, pp. 1–12.

Riley, Matilda White. *Sociological Research.* New York: Harcourt Brace Jovanovich, 1963.

Rivera, Ramone and James F. Short, Jr. "Occupational Goals." In *Juvenile Gang in Context,* edited by Malcolm W. Klein. Englewood Cliffs, N.J.: Prentice-Hall, 1967, pp. 57–69.

Roberts, John L. "Factors Associated with Truancy." *Personnel and Guidance Journal* 34 (1956): 431–436.

Robins, Lee and Patricia O'Neal. "The Marital History of Former Problem Children." *Social Problems* 5 (1958): 347–358.

Rodman, Hyman and Paul Grams. "Juvenile Delinquency and the Family: A Review and Discussion." In *Task Force Report: Juvenile Delinquency and Youth Crime* (President's Commission on Law Enforcement and Administration of Justice). Washington, D.C.: Government Printing Office, 1967.

Rosen, Lawrence. "Policemen." In *Through Different Eyes,* edited by P. Rose, S. Rothman, and W. Wilson. New York: Oxford University Press, 1973.

Rosenberg, Bernard, Israel Gerver, and F. Williams. *Mass Society in Crisis.* New York: Macmillan, 1964.

Rothstein, Edward. "Attributes Related to High School Status." *Social Problems* 10 (summer 1962): 75–83.

Roucek, Joseph, ed. *Juvenile Delinquency.* New York: Philosophical Library, 1958.

Rubin, Sol. "The Legal Character of Juvenile Delinquency." *Annals of the American Academy of Political and Social Science,* January 1949.

Sagarin, Edward. *Deviants and Deviance.* New York: Praeger, 1975.

Salisbury, Harrison E. *Reaching the Fighting Gang.* New York: Youth Board, 1960.

———. *The Shook-up Generation.* Greenwich, Conn.: Fawcett Publications, 1958.

Sanders, Wiley B. *Juvenile Offenders for a Thousand Years.* Chapel Hill: University of North Carolina Press, 1970.

Sarri, Rosemary C. and Robert D. Vinter. "Group Treatment Strategies in Juvenile Correctional Programs." *Crime and Delinquency* 11 (October 1965): 330.

Scarpitti, Frank R. and Richard M. Stephenson. "Juvenile Court Dispositions: Factors in the Decision-making Process." *Crime and Delinquency* 17 (April 1971): 142–151.

———. "A Study of Probation Effectiveness." *Journal of Criminal Law, Criminology and Police Science* 59 (September 1968): 361–369.

Scarpitti, Frank R., Ellen Murray, Simon Dinitz, and Walter Reckless. "The 'Good Boy' in a High Delinquency Area: 4 Years Later." *American Sociological Review* 27 (August 1962): 555–558.

Schafer, Stephen. *Theories in Criminology.* New York: Random House, 1969.

Schafer, Stephen and Richard D. Knudten. *Juvenile Delinquency.* New York: Random House, 1970.

Schafer, Walter E. and Kenneth Polk. "Delinquency and the School." In *Task Force Report: Juvenile Delinquency and Youth Crime* (President's Commission on Law Enforcement and Administration of Justice). Washington, D.C.: Government Printing Office, 1967, p. 230.

Schasre, Robert and Jo Wallach. *Readings in Delinquency and Treatment.* Los Angeles: University of Southern California, Youth Studies Center, 1965.

Schmitt, Raymond L. *The Reference Other Orientation: An Extension of the*

Reference Group Concept. Carbondale, Ill.: Southern Illinois University Press, 1972.

Schmitt, Raymond L. and Stanley E. Grupp. "Marihuana as a Social Object." In *The Marihuana Muddle*, edited by Stanley Grupp. Lexington, Mass.: Heath, 1973, pp. 11–31.

Schuessler, Karl. "Components of Variation in City Crime Rates." *Social Problems* 9 (spring 1962): 314–323.

Schuessler, Karl and Donald R. Cressey. "Personality Characteristics of Criminals." *American Journal of Sociology* 60 (March 1950): 476–484.

Schultz, J. Lawrence. "The Cycle of Juvenile Court History." *Crime and Delinquency* 19 (October 1973): 457–476.

Schur, Edwin. *Crime Without Victims.* Englewood Cliffs, N.J.: Prentice-Hall, 1965.

———. *Labeling Deviant Behavior.* New York: Harper & Row, 1971.

———. *Radical Non-intervention: Rethinking the Delinquency Problem.* Englewood Cliffs, N.J.: Prentice-Hall, 1973.

Schwartz, Michael and Sandra Tangri. "A Note on Self-concept as an Insulator Against Delinquency." *American Sociological Review* 30 (December 1965): 922–926.

Schwitzgebel, Ralph. *Streetcorner Research.* Cambridge, Mass.: Harvard University Press, 1965.

Sellin, Thorsten. "Common Sense and the Death Penalty." *Prison Journal* 12 (October 1932): 12.

———. "Culture, Conflict and Crime." Social Science Research Council Bulletin, no. 41 (1938).

———. "The Lombrosian Myth in Criminology." *American Journal of Sociology* 42 (May 1937): 898–899.

Sellin, Thorsten and Marvin E. Wolfgang. *The Measurement of Delinquency.* New York: Wiley, 1964.

Selltiz, Claire, Marie Jahoda, Morton Deutsch, and Stuart W. Cook. *Research Methods in Social Relations.* New York: Holt, Rinehart and Winston, 1959.

Shah, Saleem A. "Treatment of Offenders: Some Behavioral Concepts, Principles and Approaches." *Federal Probation* 23 (September 1959).

Sharp, E. Preston. "Group Counseling in a Short Term Institution." *Federal Probation* 23 (September 1959): 8.

Shaw, Clifford R. and Henry McKay. *Juvenile Delinquency and Urban Areas.* Chicago: University of Chicago Press, 1942.

———. *Report on the Causes of Crime,* vol. 2, no. 13 (National Commission on Law Observance and Enforcement). Washington, D.C.: Government Printing Office, 1931, p. 387.

Shaw, Clifford, Frederick M. Zorbaugh, Henry McKay, and Leonard Cottrell. "The Juvenile Delinquent." In *Illinois Crime Survey*, compiled by Illinois Association of Criminal Justice. Springfield, 1929.

Sheils, Merrill, Elaine Sciolino, and Mary Lord. "A Nation of Dunces?" *Newsweek*, November 10, 1975, p. 84.

Sheldon, William H. *Varieties of Delinquent Youth.* New York: Harper & Row, 1949.

———. *Varieties of Temperament.* New York: Harper & Row, 1942.

Sheldon, William H., Emil M. Hartl, and Eugene McDermott. *Varieties of Delinquent Youth.* New York: Harper & Row, 1949.

Sheldon, William H., S. S. Stevens, and W. B. Tucker. *Varieties of Human Physique.* New York: Harper & Row, 1940.

Short, James F., Jr. "Differential Association and Delinquency." *Social Problems* 4 (January 1957): 233–239.

————. "Differential Association as a Hypothesis: Problems of Empirical Testing." *Social Problems* 8 (summer 1960): 14–25.

————. "Differential Association with Delinquent Friends and Delinquent Behavior." *Pacific Sociological Review* 1 (spring 1958): 20–25.

————. "Gang Delinquency and Anomie." In *Anomie and Deviant Behavior*, edited by Marshall B. Clinard. New York: Free Press, 1964, pp. 98–127.

————. "Juvenile Delinquency: The Sociocultural Context." In *Review of Child Development Research*. Vol. 2. New York: Russell Sage Foundation, 1966.

————. "Youth Gangs and Society." *Sociological Quarterly* 15 (winter 1974): 3–19.

Short, James F., ed. *Gang Delinquency and Delinquent Subcultures*. New York: Harper & Row, 1968.

Short, James F., Jr., and Fred L. Strodtbeck. *Group Process and Gang Delinquency*. Chicago: University of Chicago Press, 1965.

Short, James F., Jr., Roy A. Tennyson, and Kenneth I. Howard. "Behavior Dimensions of Gang Delinquency." *American Sociological Review* 28 (June 1963).

Schulman, Harry M. *Juvenile Delinquency in American Society*. New York: Harper & Row, 1961.

————. *A Study of Problem Boys and Their Brothers*. Albany: State Crime Commission, 1929.

Shulman, Irving. "Modifications in Group Psychotherapy with Antisocial Adolescents." *International Journal of Group Psychotherapy* 7 (1957): 310.

Simon, Julian L. *Basic Research Methods in Social Science*. New York: Random House, 1969.

Simpson, George. *Emile Durkheim: Selections from His Work*. New York: Crowell, 1963.

Simpson, Jon E., Simon Dinitz, Barbara Kay, and Walter Reckless. "Delinquency Potential of Pre-adolescents in a High Delinquency Area." *British Journal of Delinquency* 10 (January 1960): 211–215.

Simpson, Jon E., et al. "Institutionalization as Perceived by the Juvenile Offender." *Sociology and Social Research* 48 (October 1963): 13–23.

Sjoberg, Gideon, ed. *Ethics, Politics and Social Research*. Cambridge, Mass.: Schenkman Publishing, 1967.

Sjoberg, Gideon and Roger Nett. *A Methodology for Social Research*. New York: Harper & Row, 1968.

Skoler, Daniel. "Comprehensive Criminal Justice Planning." *Crime and Delinquency* 14 (July 1968): 197–206.

Slavson, S. R. *Reclaiming the Delinquent*. New York: Free Press, 1965.

Slocum, Walter and Carol L. Stone. "Family Interaction and Delinquency." In *Juvenile Delinquency*, edited by Herbert C. Quay. New York: Van Nostrand, 1965.

Snedecor, George W. and William G. Cochran. *Statistical Methods*. 6th ed. Ames: Iowa State University Press, 1967.

Sower, Christopher, et al. *Community Involvement*. New York: Free Press, 1957.

Sparks, Richard. "The Effectiveness of Probation: A Review." In *Crime and Justice: The Criminal in Confinement*, edited by L. Radzinowicz and M. Wolfgang. New York: Basic Books, 1971, pp. 211–218.

Spergel, Irving. "Male Young Adult Criminality, Deviant Values and Differential Opportunities in Two Lower Class Negro Neighborhoods." *Social Problems* 10 (winter 1963): 237–250.

————. *Racketville, Slumtown and Haulberg*. Chicago: University of Chicago Press, 1964.

Stanley, Fred J. "Middle Class Delinquency as a Social Problem." *Sociology and Social Research* 51 (January 1967): 185–198.

Starkey, Marion L. *The Devil in Massachusetts.* New York: Knopf, 1949.

Sterne, Richard S. *Delinquent Conduct and Broken Homes.* New Haven, Conn.: College and University Press, 1964.

Stigler, George J. "The Optimum Enforcement of Laws." *Journal of Political Economy* (May–June 1970): 526–536.

Stinchcombe, Arthur L. *Constructing Social Theories.* New York: Harcourt Brace Jovanovich, 1968.

Street, David, Robert D. Vinter, and Charles Perrow. *Organization for Treatment.* New York: Free Press, 1966.

Stulliken, Edward. "Chicago's Special School for Social Adjustment." *Federal Probation* 20 (March 1956): 31–36.

———. "Misconceptions About Juvenile Delinquency." *Journal of Criminal Law, Criminology and Police Science* 46 (1966).

Sullivan, Dennis C. and Larry J. Siegal. "How Police Use Information to Make Decisions: An Application of Decision Games." *Crime and Delinquency* 18 (July 1972): 253–261.

Sullivan, Richard F. "The Economics of Crime: An Introduction to the Literature." *Crime and Delinquency* 19 (April 1973): 138–144.

Sussman, Frederick B. and Frederic S. Baum. *Law of Juvenile Delinquency.* Dobbs Ferry, N.Y.: Oceana, 1968.

Sutherland, Edwin. *Principles of Criminology.* 3d ed. Philadelphia: Lippincott, 1939.

———. *Principles of Criminology.* 4th ed. Philadelphia: Lippincott, 1947.

———. "Rejoinder." *Sociology and Social Research* 26 (September–October 1941): 50–52.

———. *White Collar Crimes.* New York: Dryden Press, 1949.

Sutherland, Edwin and Donald R. Cressey. *Criminology.* 6th ed. Philadelphia: Lippincott, 1960.

———. *Criminology.* 8th ed. Philadelphia: Lippincott, 1970.

———. *Criminology.* 7th ed. Philadelphia: Lippincott, 1966.

Swanson, Guy. "The Disturbances of Children in Urban Areas." *American Sociological Review* 14 (October 1949): 676–678.

Sykes, Gresham M. and David Matza. "Techniques of Neutralization: A Theory of Delinquency." *American Sociological Review* 22 (1957): 664–670.

Szurek, S. A. *The Antisocial Child.* Palo Alto, Calif.: Behavior Books, 1969.

Taft, Donald. *Criminology.* 3d ed. New York: Macmillan, 1956.

Taft, Donald and Ralph England, Jr. *Criminology.* 4th ed. New York: Macmillan, 1964.

Tangri, Sandra S. and Michael Schwartz. "Delinquency Research and the Self-concept Variable." *Journal of Criminal Law, Criminology and Police Science* 55 (1967).

Tannenbaum, Frank. *Crime and the Community.* Boston: Ginn and Co., 1938.

———. *Crime and the Community.* New York: McGraw-Hill, 1951.

Tappan, Paul W. *Comparative Survey of Juvenile Delinquency, Part I: North America,* New York: United Nations, 1958.

———. *Crime, Justice and Correction.* New York: McGraw-Hill, 1960.

———. *Juvenile Delinquency.* New York: McGraw-Hill, 1949.

Tarde, Gabriel. *The Laws of Imitation.* New York: Holt, Rinehart and Winston, 1903.

———. *On Communication and Social Influence.* Chicago: University of Chicago Press, 1969.

———. *Penal Philosophy.* Boston: Little, Brown, 1912.

Terry, Robert M. "Discrimination in the Handling of Juvenile Offenders by

Social Control Agencies." *Journal of Research in Crime and Delinquency* 14 (July 1967): 218–231.

Thimm, Joseph L. "The Juvenile Court and Restitution." *Crime and Delinquency* 6 (1960): 279–286.

Thio, Alex. "Class Bias in the Sociology of Deviance." *The American Sociologist* 8 (February 1973): 1–12.

Thorp, Ronald and Ralph Wetzel. *Behavior Modification in the Natural Environment.* New York: Academic Press, 1969.

Thrasher, Frederic M. *The Gang.* Chicago: University of Chicago Press, 1927.

———. *The Gang. Abr. ed.* Chicago: University of Chicago Press, 1963.

———. "Gangs." *Encyclopedia of the Social Sciences* 6 (1968): 564–565.

Toby, Jackson. "Affluence and Adolescent Crime." In *Task Force Report: Juvenile Delinquency and Youth Crime* (President's Commission on Law Enforcement and Administration of Justice). Washington, D.C.: Government Printing Office, 1967.

———. "An Evaluation of Early Identification and Intensive Treatment Programs for Predeliquents." *Social Problems* 13 (fall 1965): 160–175.

———. "The Prospects for Reducing Delinquency Rates in Industrial Society." *Federal Probation* 27 (December 1963).

Trasler, Gordon. *The Explanation of Criminality.* London: Routledge and Kegan Paul, 1962.

Trojanowicz, Robert C. *Juvenile Delinquency: Concepts and Control.* Englewood Cliffs, N.J.: Prentice-Hall, 1973.

United Nations, Bureau of Social Affairs, Department of Economic and Social Affairs. *The Prevention of Juvenile Delinquency in Selected European Countries.* New York: Columbia University Press, 1955.

United Nations, Division of Social Welfare, Department of Social Affairs. *Comparative Survey on Juvenile Delinquency: Asia and the Far East.* New York: Columbia University Press, 1953.

United Nations, International Labor Organization, Third United Nations Congress on the Prevention of Crime and the Treatment of Offenders. *The Role of Vocational Guidance, Training, Employment Opportunity and Work in Youth Adjustment and the Prevention of Juvenile Delinquency.* New York, 1965.

———. *Special Preventive and Treatment Measures for Young Adults.* New York, 1965.

Vaz, Edmund. *Middle Class Juvenile Delinquency.* New York: Harper & Row, 1967.

Villeponteaux, Lorenz. "Crisis Intervention in a Day School for Delinquents." *Crime and Delinquency* 16 (July 1970): 318–319.

Vold, George. *Theoretical Criminology.* New York: Oxford University Press, 1958.

Voss, Harwin. "Differential Association and Reported Delinquent Behavior: A Replication." *Social Problems* 12 (summer 1964): 78–85.

Wade, Andrew L. "Social Processes in the Act of Vandalism." In *Criminal Behavior Systems,* edited by M. Clinard and R. Quinney. New York: Holt, Rinehart and Winston, 1967, p. 181.

Waldo, Gordon P. and Simon Dinitz. "Personality Attributes of the Criminal: An Analysis of Research Studies, 1950–1965." *Journal of Research in Crime and Delinquency* 4 (July 1967): 185–202.

Wallace, E. W. "Physical Defects and Juvenile Delinquency." *New York State Journal of Medicine* 40 (November 1940): 1586–1590.

Weirman, Charles I. "A Critical Analysis of Police-School Liaison Program to Implement Attitudinal Change in Junior High School Students: Masters thesis, Michigan State University.

Wheeler, Stanton and Leonard Cottrell, Jr. *Juvenile Delinquency: Its Prevention and Control*. New York: Russell Sage Foundation, 1966.

Wheeler, Stanton, Leonard S. Cottrell, and Anne Romasco. "Juvenile Delinquency: Its Prevention and Control." In *Task Force Report: Juvenile Delinquency and Youth Crime* (President's Commission on Law Enforcement and Administration of Justice). Washington, D.C.: Government Printing Office, 1967.

White, Morton and Lucia White. *The Intellectual Versus the City*. Cambridge, Mass.: Harvard University Press, 1962.

Whyte, William F. *Street Corner Society*. Chicago: University of Chicago Press, 1955.

Wiers, Paul. *Economic Factors in Michigan Delinquency*. New York: Columbia University Press, 1944.

Wilensky, Harold L. and Charles N. Lebeaux. *Industrial Society and Social Welfare*. New York: Russell Sage Foundation, 1958.

Willie, Charles V. "The Relative Contribution of Family Status and Economic Status to Juvenile Delinquency." *Social Problems* 14 (winter 1967): 326–335.

Wines, E. C. *The State of Prisons and Child-saving Institutions in the Civilized World*. Montclair, N.J.: Patterson Smith, 1968.

Wolfgang, Marvin. "The Culture of Youth." In *Task Force Report: Juvenile Delinquency and Youth Crime* (President's Commission on Law Enforcement and Administration of Justice). Washington, D.C.: Government Printing Office, 1967.

Wood, Arthur Lewis. "Ideal and Empirical Typologies for Research in Deviance and Control." *Sociology and Social Research* 53 (January 1969): 227–241. Also in *Faces of Delinquency*, edited by John P. Reed and Fuad Baali. Englewood Cliffs, N.J.: Prentice-Hall, 1972.

Yablonski, Lewis. *The Tunnel Back: Synanon*. New York: Macmillan, 1965.

————. *The Violent Gang*. Baltimore: Penguin Books, 1966.

Zald, Mayer. "Power Balance and Staff Conflict in a Correctional Institution." *Administrative Science Quarterly* 7 (June 1962): 22–49.

Zetterberg, Hans. *On Theory and Verification in Sociology*. Totowa, N.J.: Bedminister Press, 1965.

Zweig, Franklin M. and Robert Morris. "The Social Planning Design Guide." *Social Work* 2 (April 1966): 13–21.

77 78 79 80 7 6 5 4 3 2 1